VIZ Media Edition

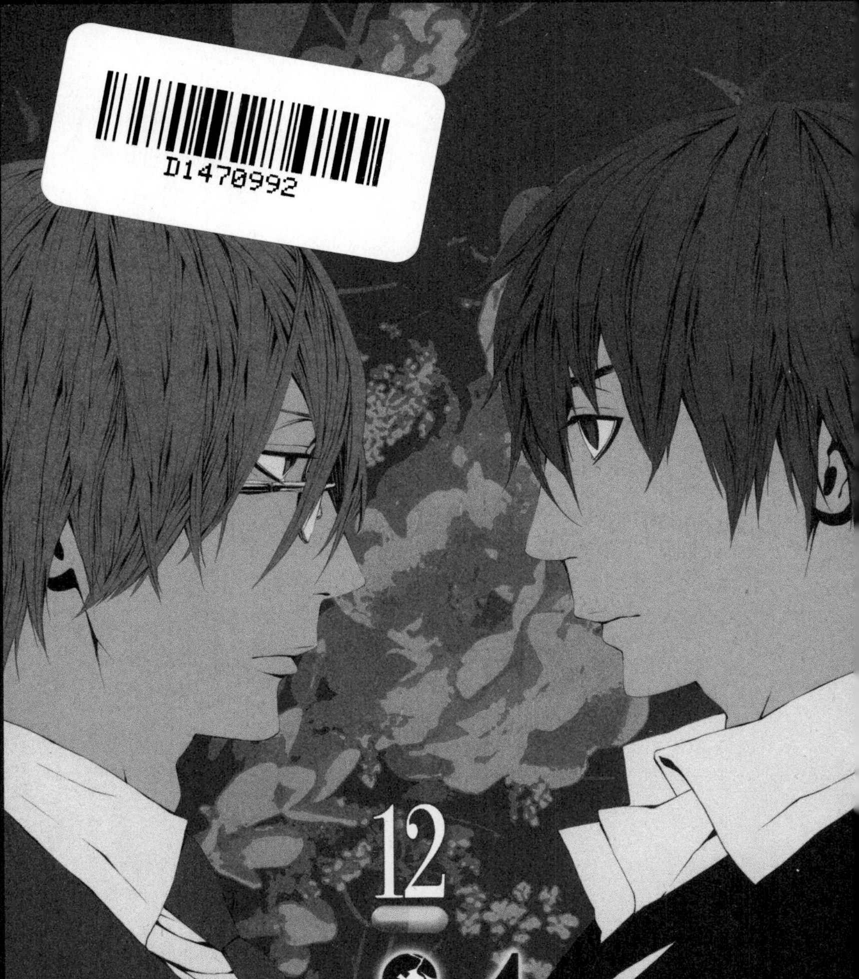

12

switch

naked ape : Saki Otoh & Nakamura Tomom

switch

12

CONTENTS

Switch Characte

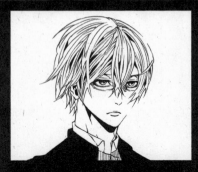

Hal Kurabayashi

A very knowledgeable and resourceful NCD agent. As a boy, he lost his mother in a traffic accident, and his father's whereabouts are unknown. He had an episode of amnesia in the past.

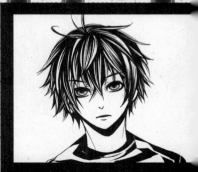

Kai Eto

Rookie NCD Investigator. Kai is normally a gentle soul, but whenever he receives a large psychological shock, he becomes violent as another personality emerges. He lost his memory 16 years ag

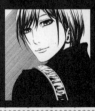

Yoshiaki Saiga

An agent with the police force, Saiga was Narita's mentor. He hates career agents.

COULD YOU PLEASE...
...STOP CALLING ME "BABY AKI"?
(16 Years Ago)

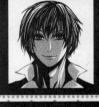

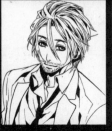

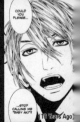

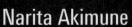

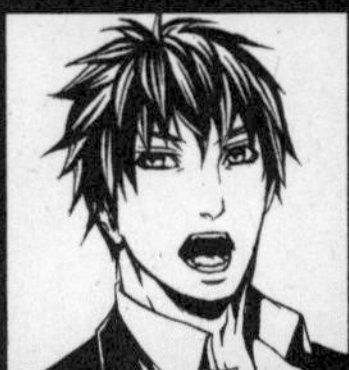

Narita Akimune

A detective attached to the Special Anti-Organized Crime Unit, the "Gangbusters." When he was a rookie, 16 years ago, he was recruited to join the unit.

Ren Kosaka

An agent with the Kanto District Narcotics Control Office (former name). A narc who knew Saiga and Narita 16 years ago.

Keigo Kajiyama

Section Chief of Section 1 of the Greater Kanto Public Welfare Ministry Narcotics Control Division. An energetic leader who has worked with Hiki since they both were young.

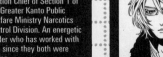

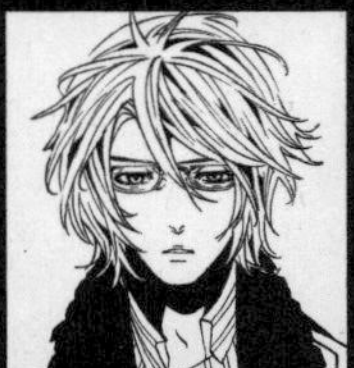

Masataka Hik

Chief of the Greater Kanto Public Welfare Ministry Narcotics Control Division. Possessing amazing situatio awareness and analytical ability, he commands a deep trust from his agents.

Switch

The Story Through The Previous Volume

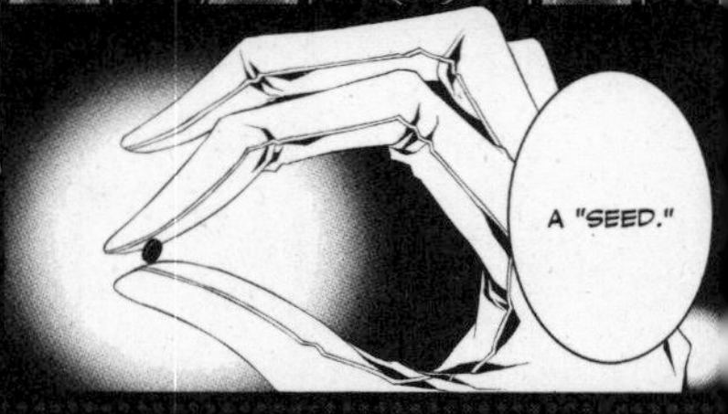
A "SEED."

In the course of a Special Anti-Organized Crime Unit investigation into the new drug "seed," dealers of the drug start turning up dead.

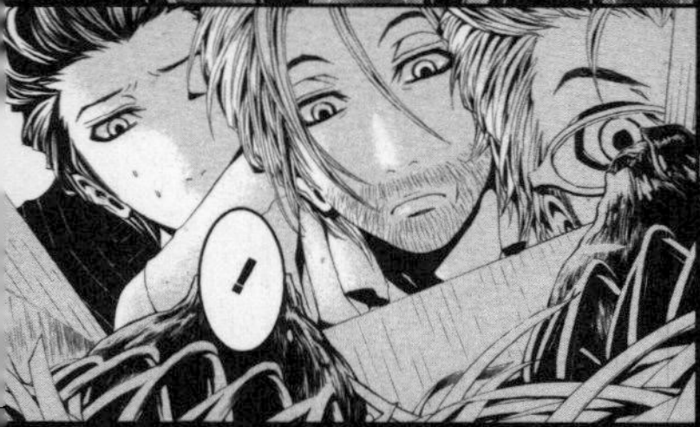
!

ne day, a mysterious package addressed to larita turns up at the Anti-Organized Crime nit. Inside are several pomegranates.

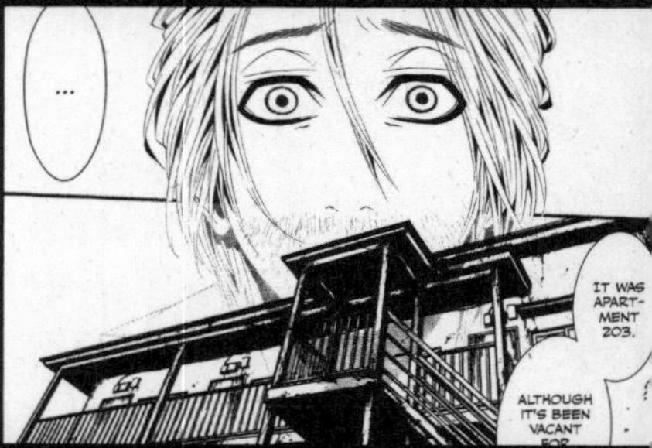
...
IT WAS APARTMENT 203.
ALTHOUGH IT'S BEEN VACANT

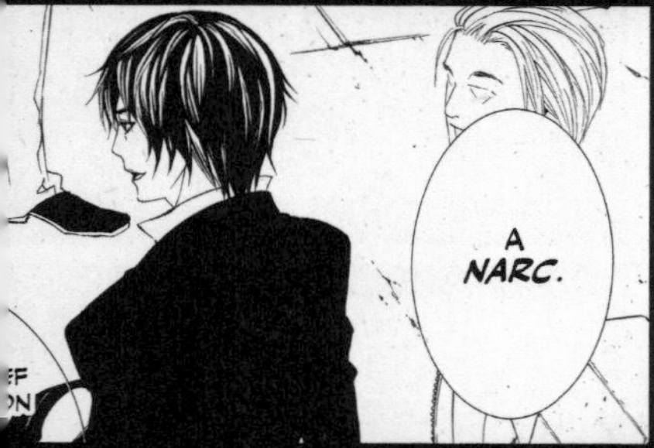
A NARC.

arita tracks the package sender's location to an apartment—the same apartment he went o on his first bust with his former mentor, Saiga, and first met the narcotics officer Ren osaka.

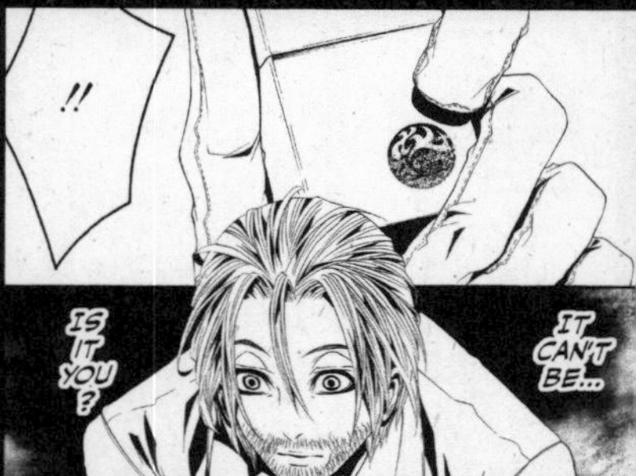
!!
IT CAN'T BE...
IS IT YOU?

Narita finds a lighter with a particular symbol on it at the fateful apartment. Seeing the lighter brings back a rush

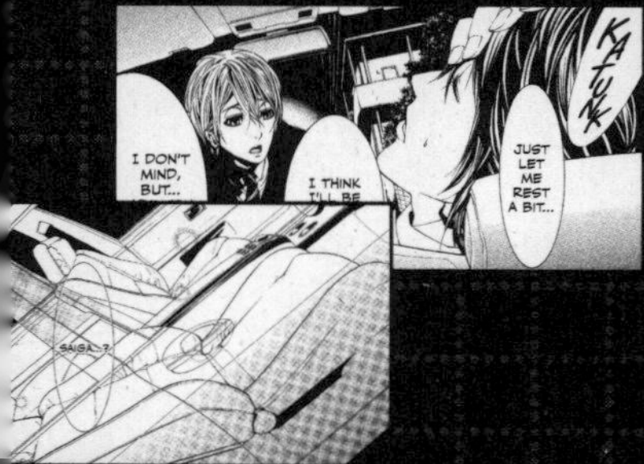
KATUNK
JUST LET ME REST A BIT...
I THINK
I DON'T MIND, BUT...
SAIGA...?

ixteen years ago, during Narita's field aining, his mentor Saiga, feeling nwell, sent him to get a drink. When arita returned to the car with the juice,

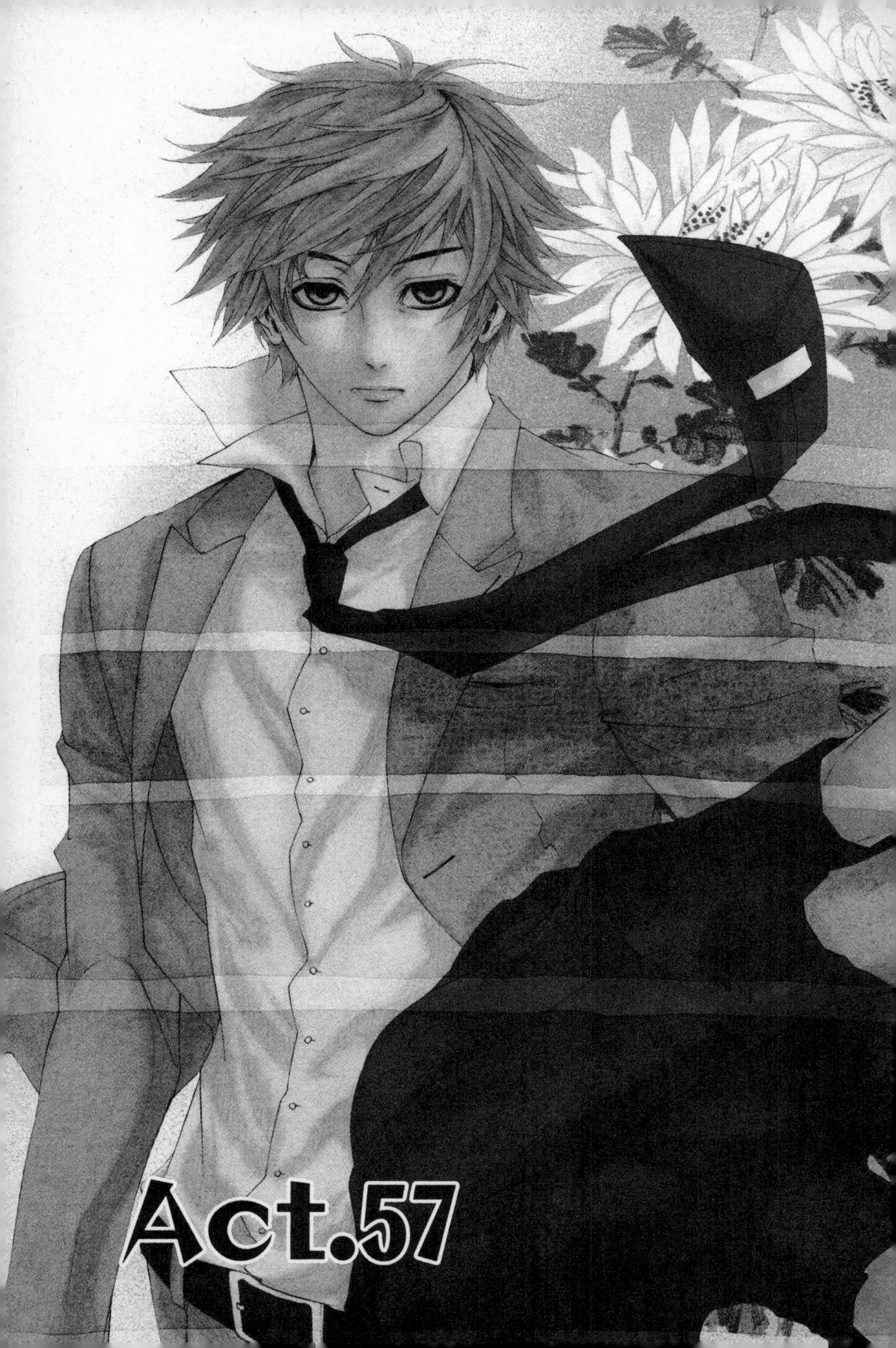
Act.57

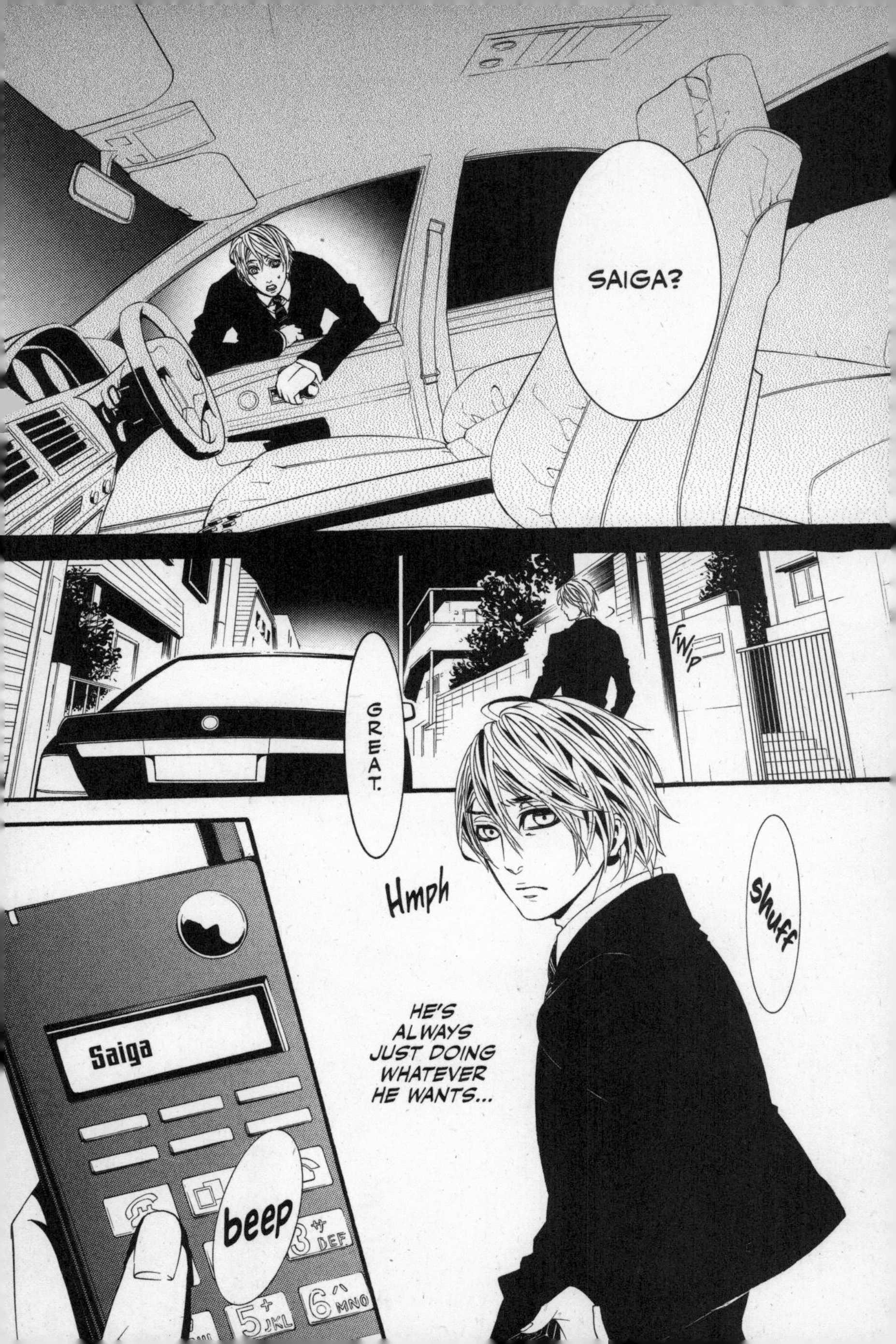
SAIGA?
FWIP
GREAT.
shuff
Hmph
HE'S ALWAYS JUST DOING WHATEVER HE WANTS...
Saiga
beep

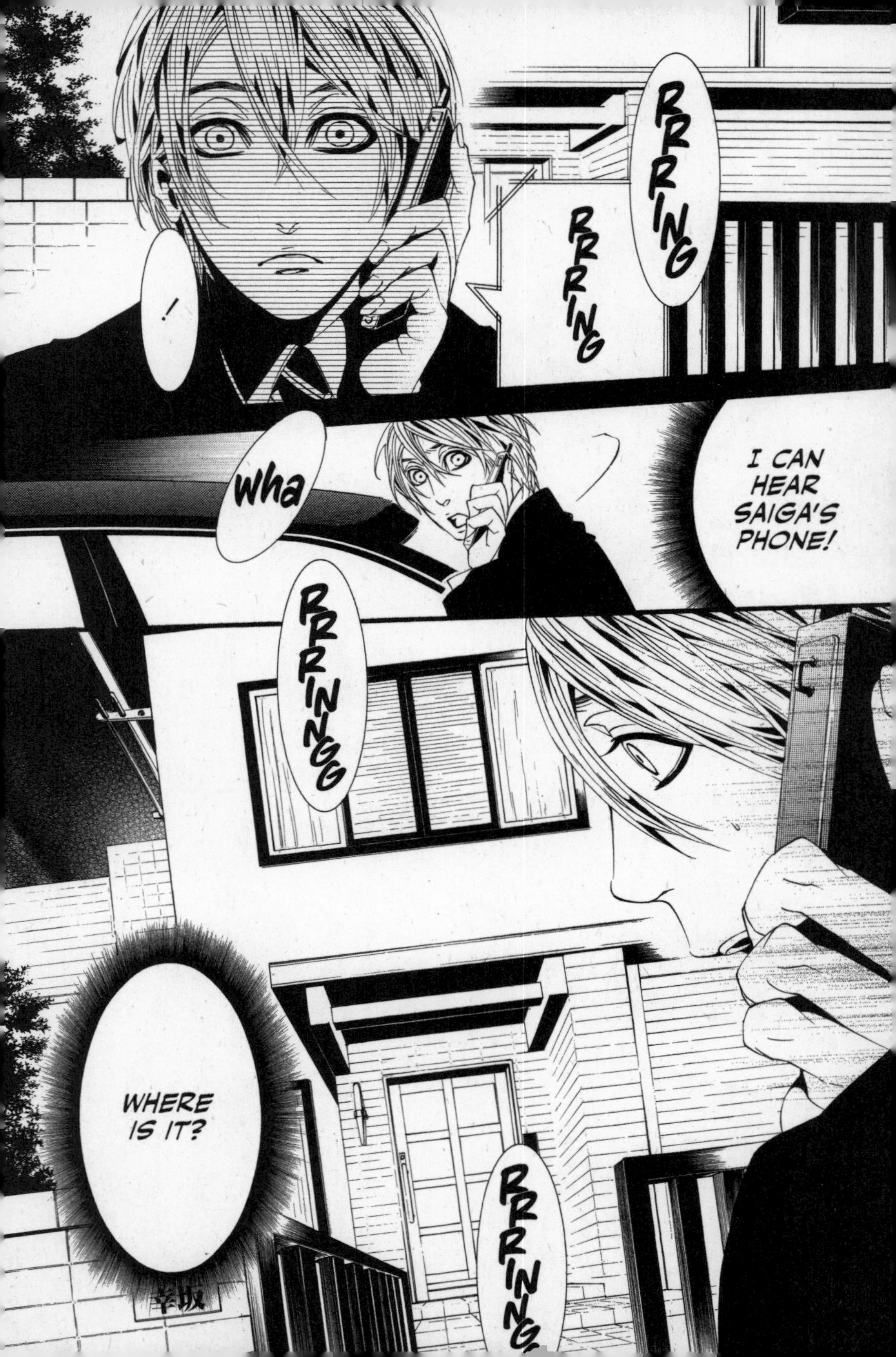
RRRING
RRRING
!
I CAN HEAR SAIGA'S PHONE!
wha
RRRINNGG
RRRING
WHERE IS IT?
幸坂

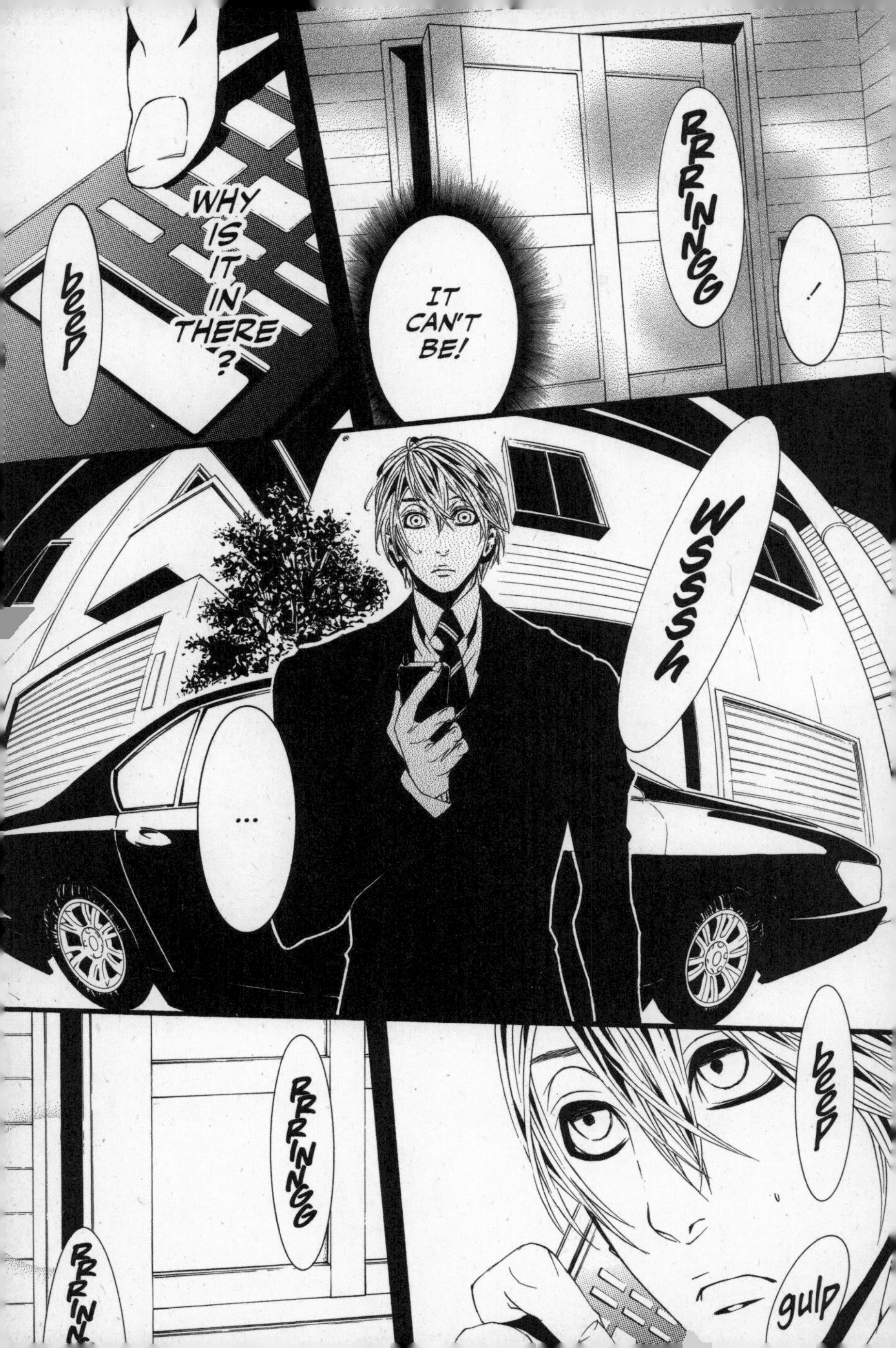
!
RRRINNGG
IT CAN'T BE!
WHY IS IT IN THERE?
beep
WSSSSH
...
beep
gulp
RRRINNGG
RRRINN

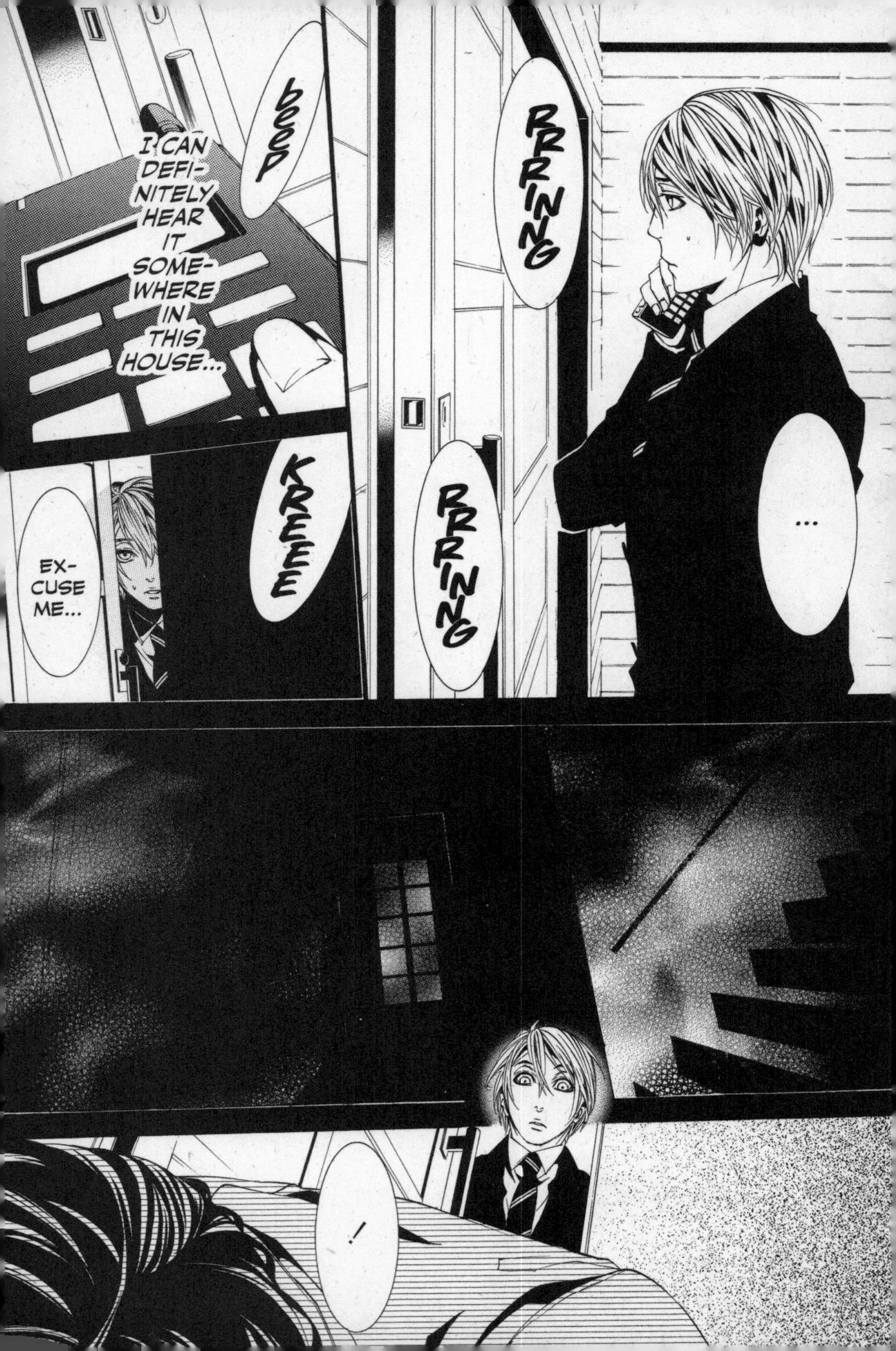
...
RRRING
RRRING
beep
I CAN DEFINITELY HEAR IT SOMEWHERE IN THIS HOUSE...
KREEEE
EXCUSE ME...
!

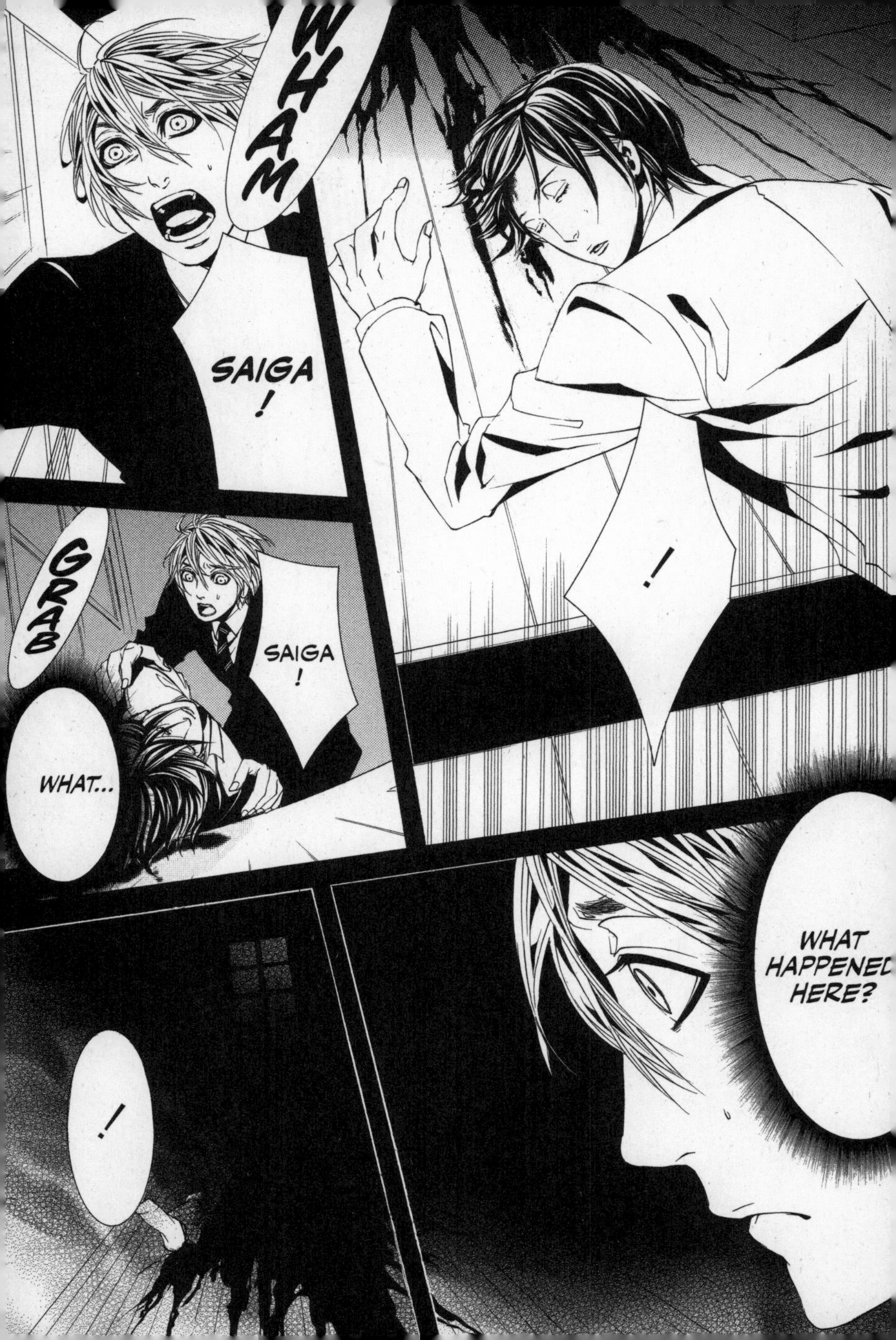
!
WHAM
SAIGA!
GRAB
SAIGA!
WHAT...
WHAT HAPPENED HERE?
!

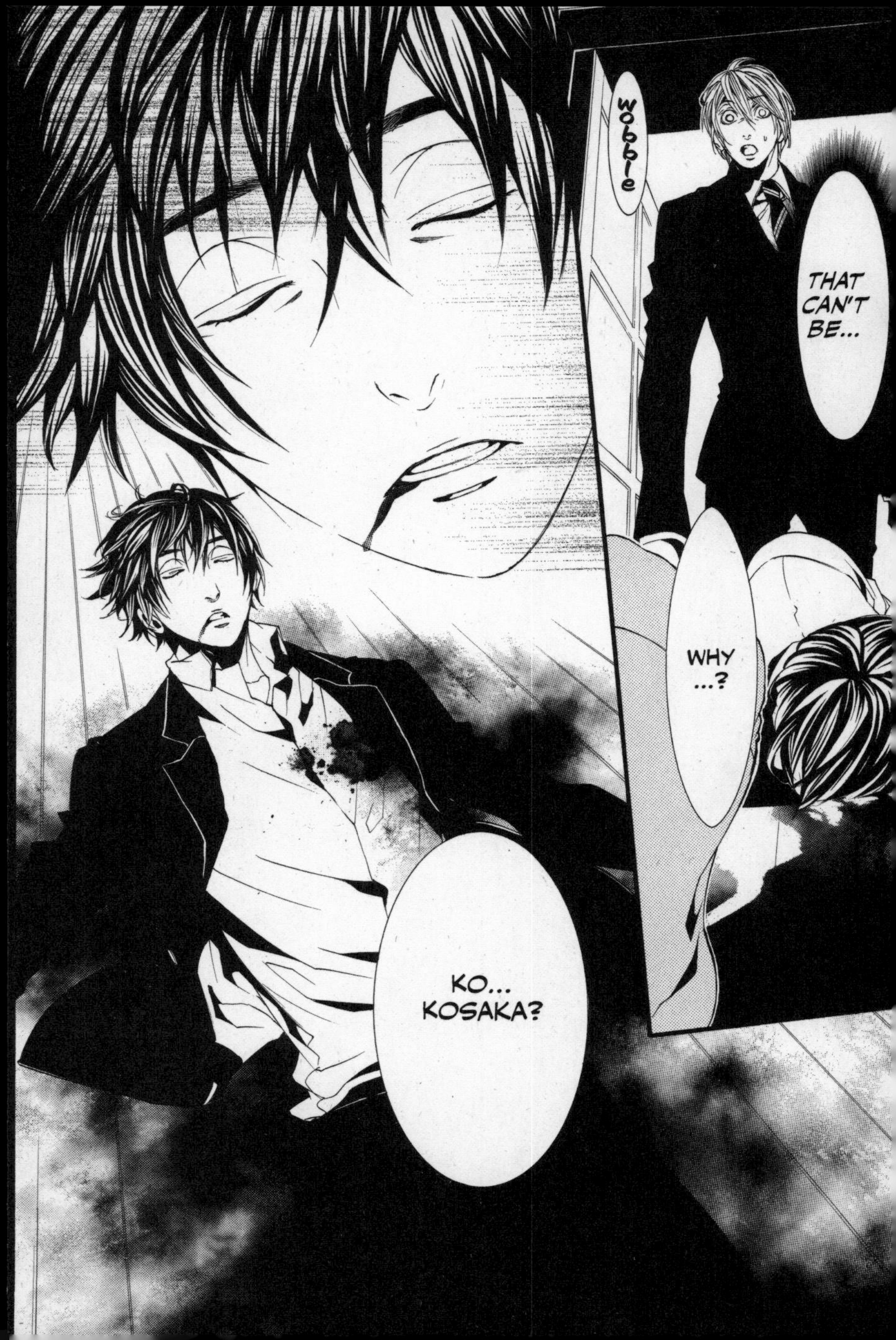
THAT CAN'T BE...
wobble
WHY ...?
KO... KOSAKA?

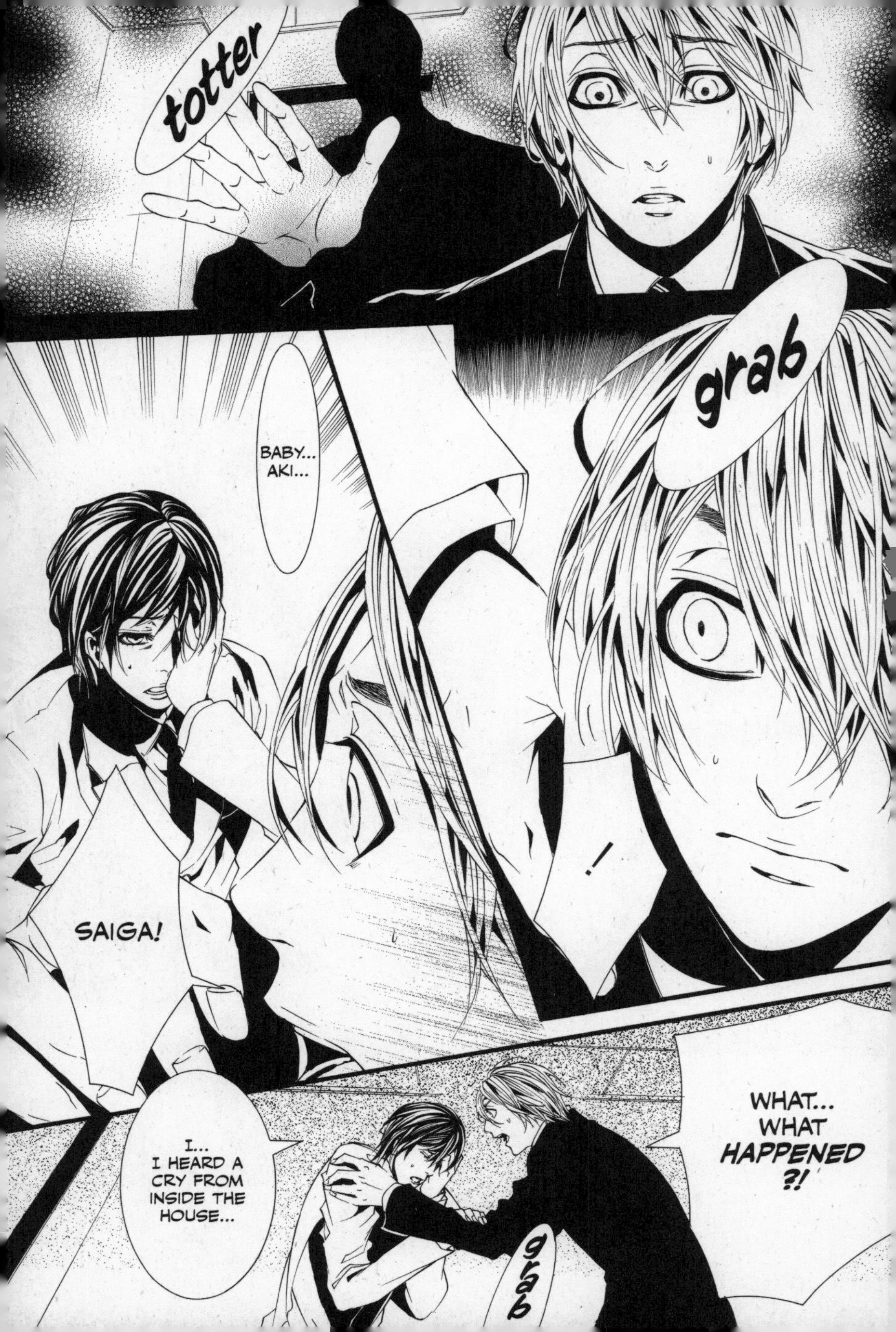
totter
grab
!
BABY... AKI...
SAIGA!
WHAT... WHAT HAPPENED ?!
grab
I... I HEARD A CRY FROM INSIDE THE HOUSE...

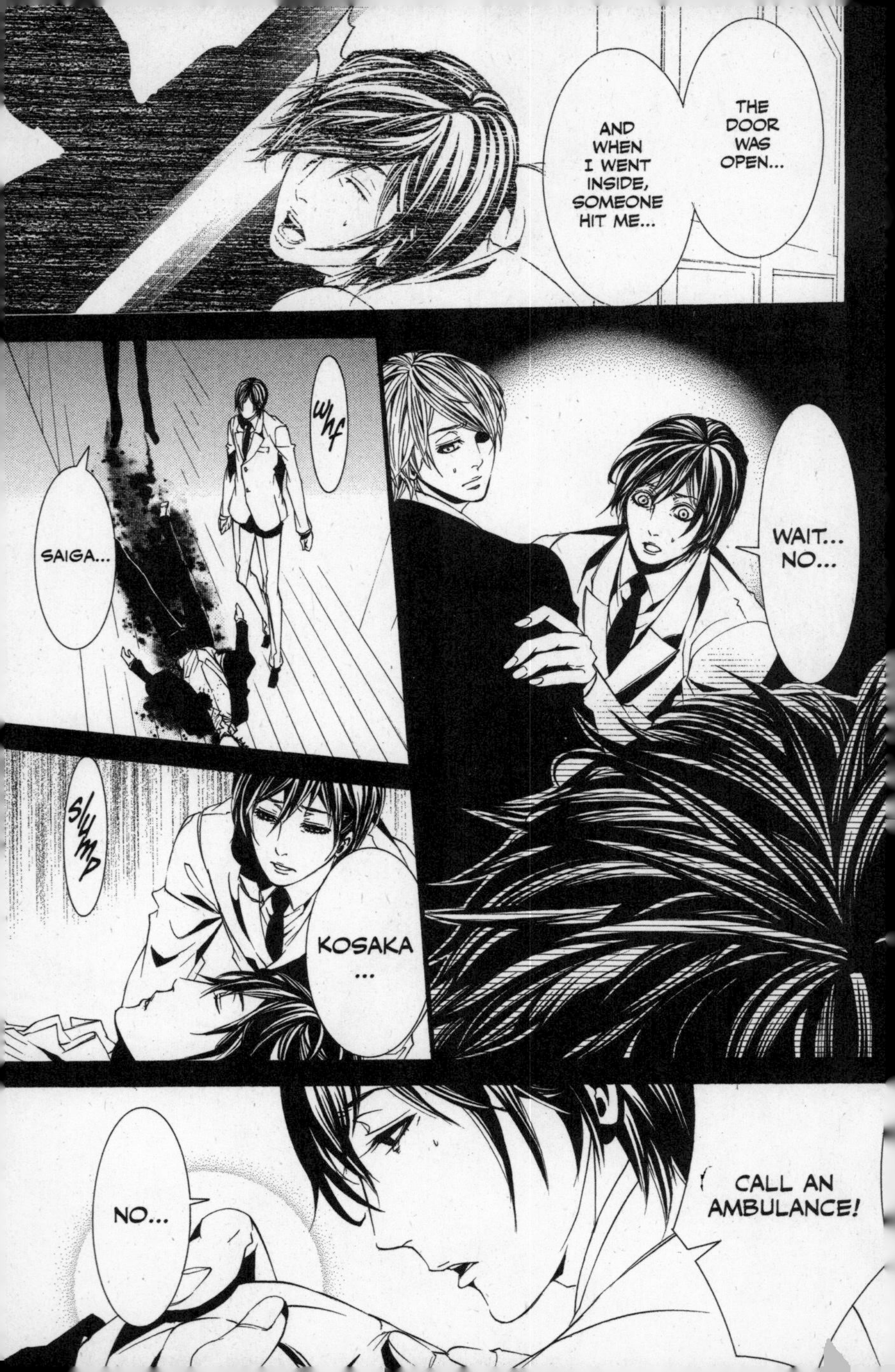
THE DOOR WAS OPEN...
AND WHEN I WENT INSIDE, SOMEONE HIT ME...
WAIT... NO...
whf
SAIGA...
slump
KOSAKA ...
CALL AN AMBULANCE!
NO...

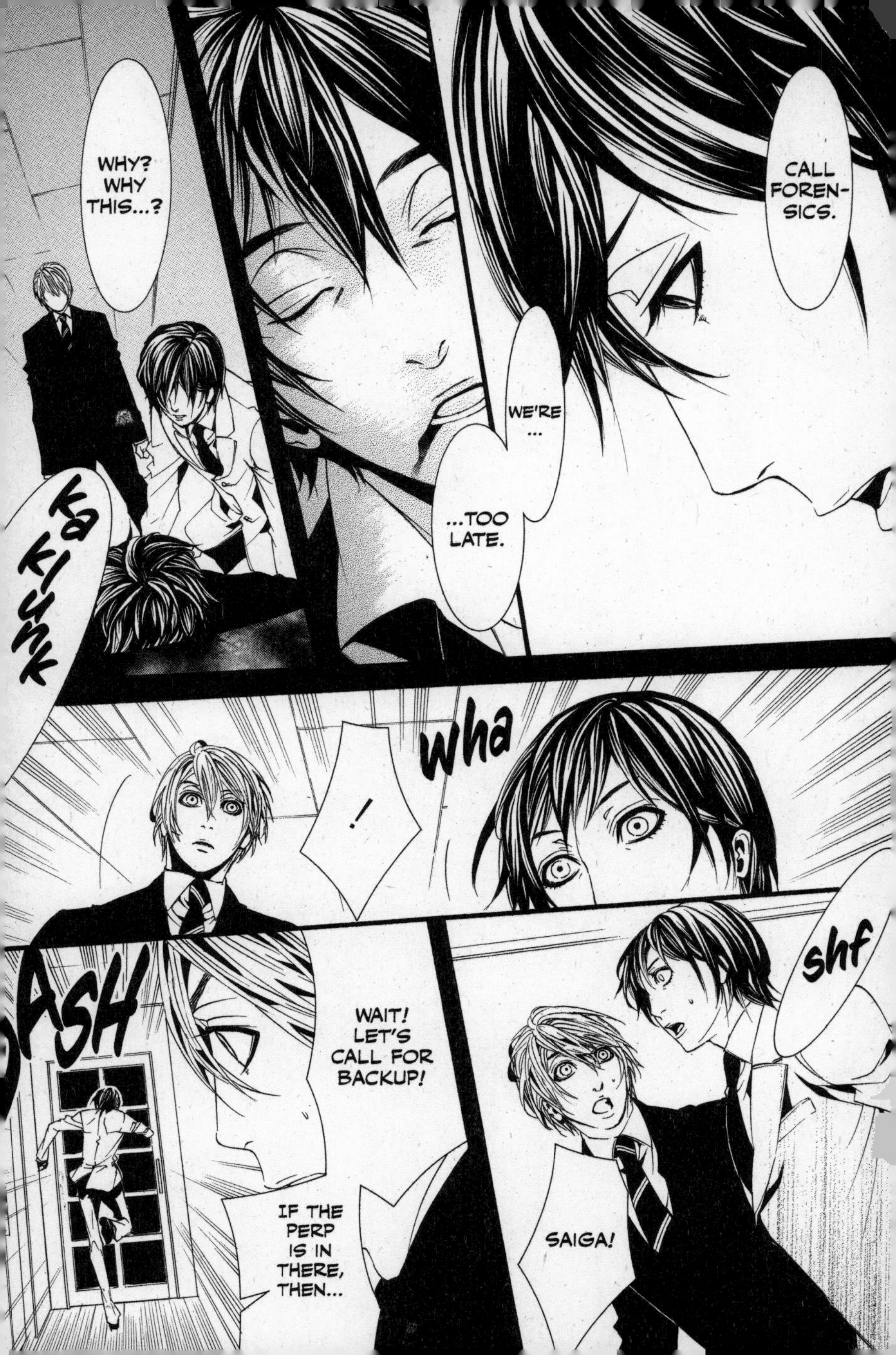
CALL FORENSICS.
WE'RE ...
...TOO LATE.
WHY? WHY THIS...?
ka klunk
wha
!
shf
SAIGA!
ASH
WAIT! LET'S CALL FOR BACKUP!
IF THE PERP IS IN THERE, THEN...

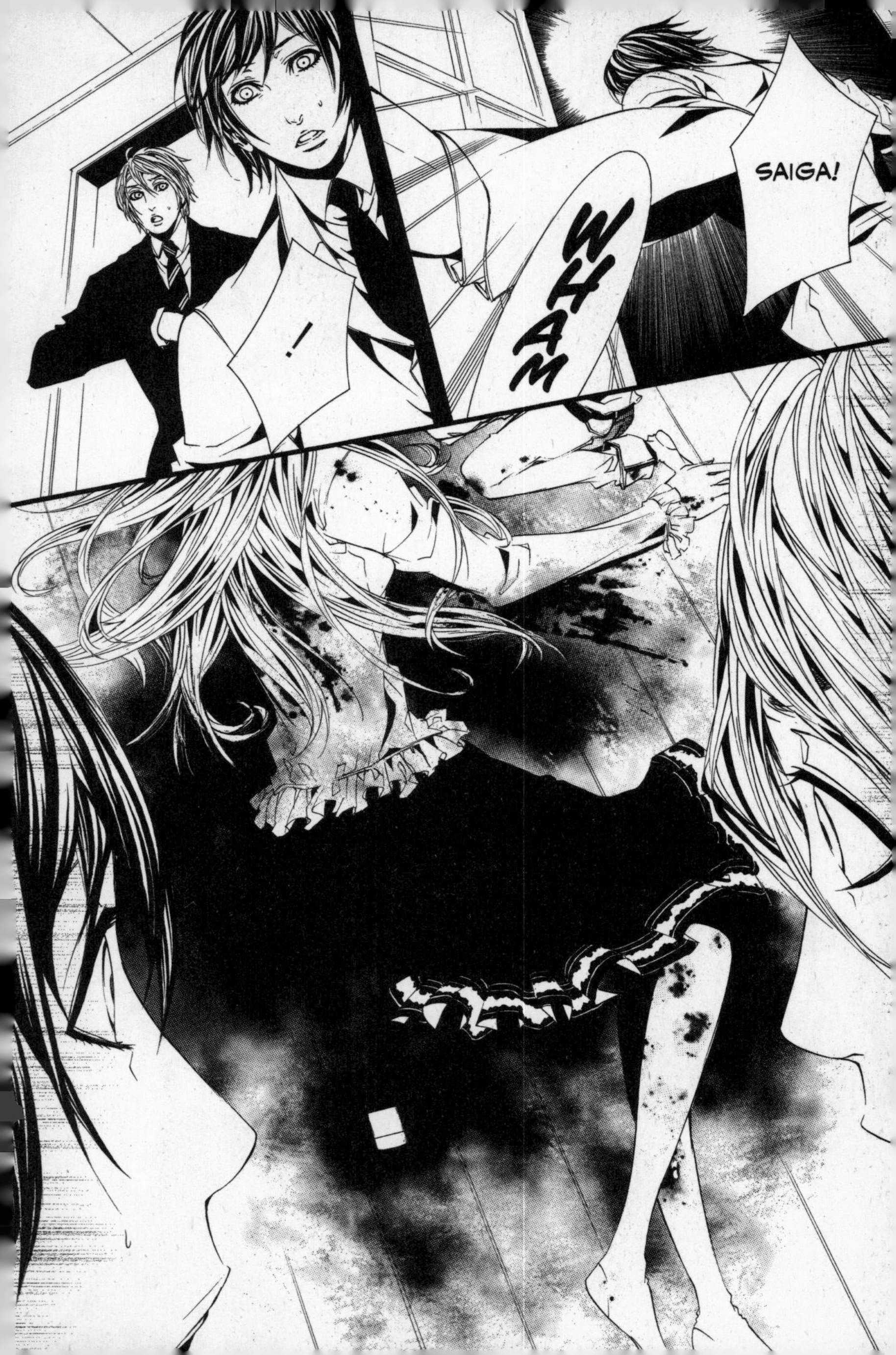
SAIGA!
WHAM
!

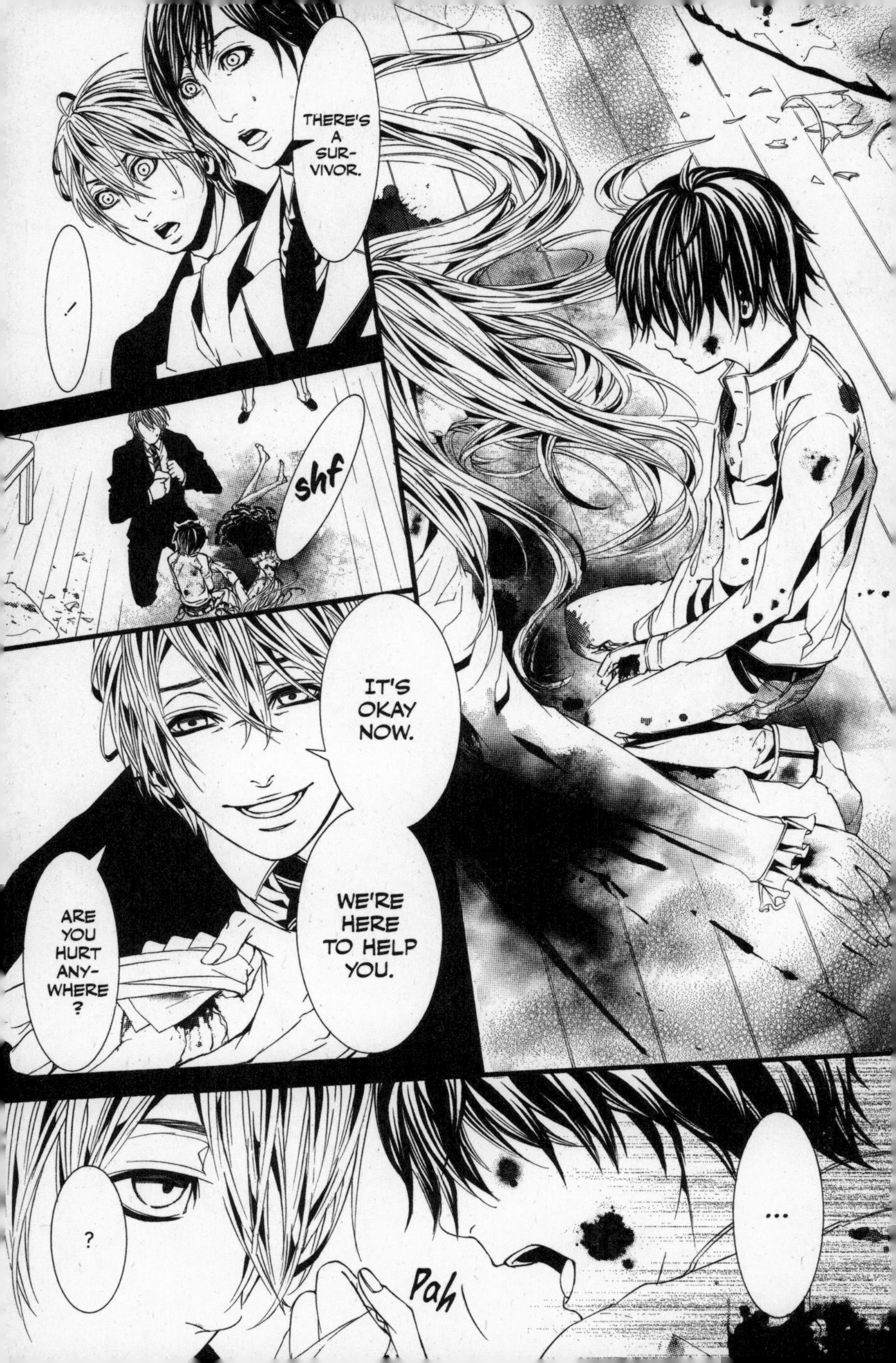

THERE'S A SUR-VIVOR.
!
shf
IT'S OKAY NOW.
WE'RE HERE TO HELP YOU.
ARE YOU HURT ANY-WHERE?
...
Pah
?

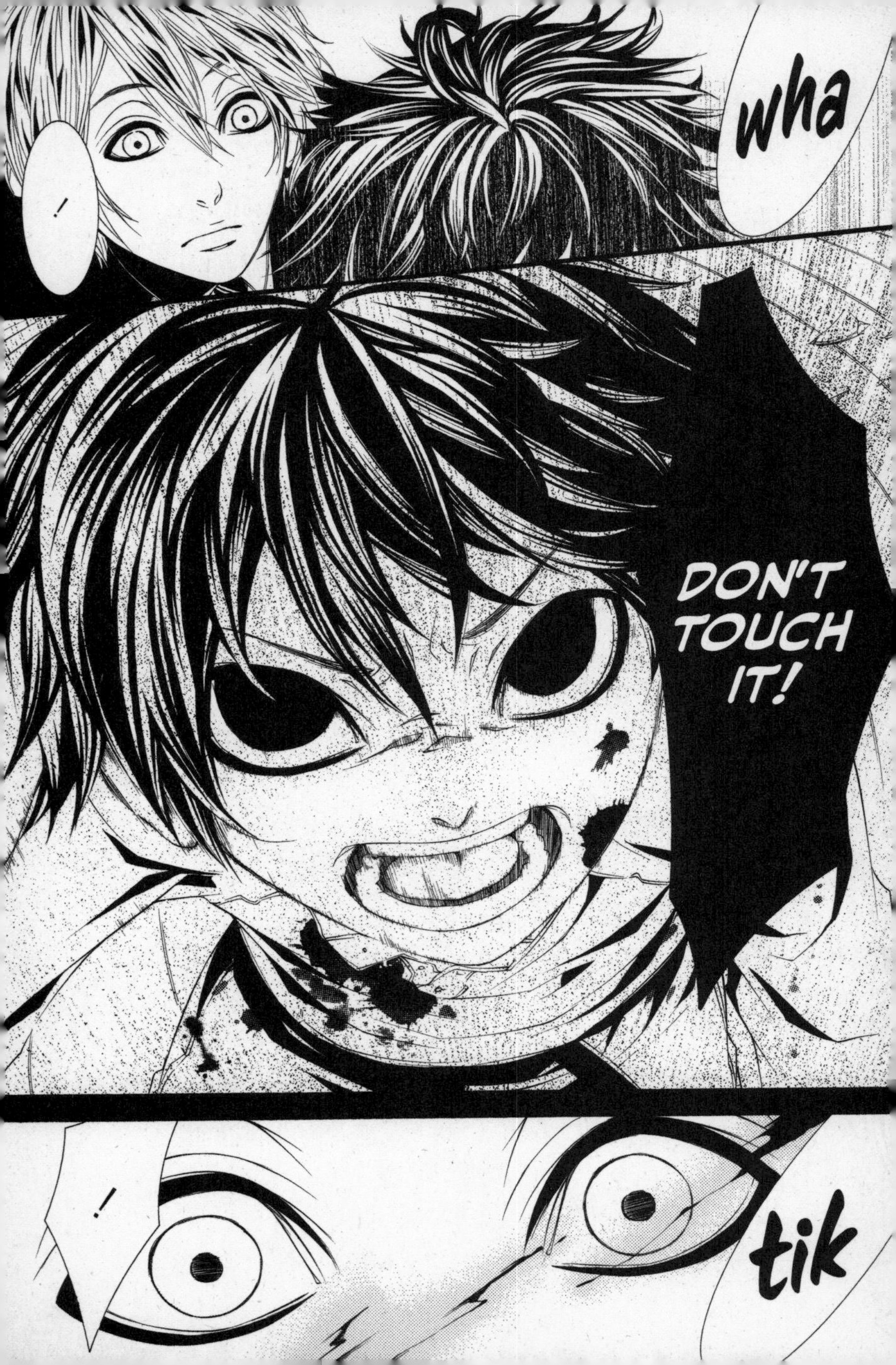
wha
!
DON'T TOUCH IT!
tik
!

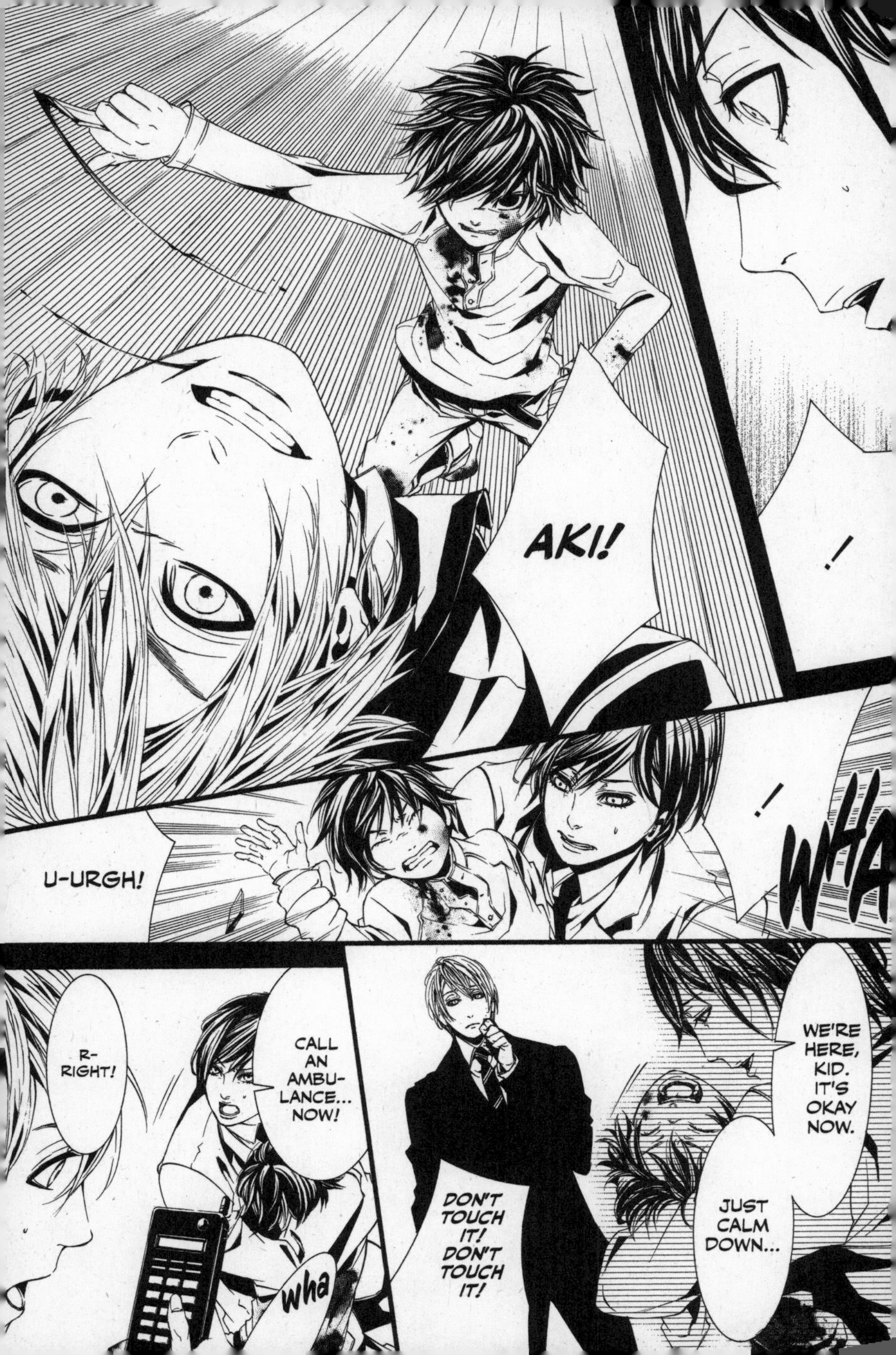
!
AKI!
!
WHA
U-URGH!
WE'RE HERE, KID. IT'S OKAY NOW.
JUST CALM DOWN...
DON'T TOUCH IT! DON'T TOUCH IT!
CALL AN AMBULANCE... NOW!
R-RIGHT!
wha

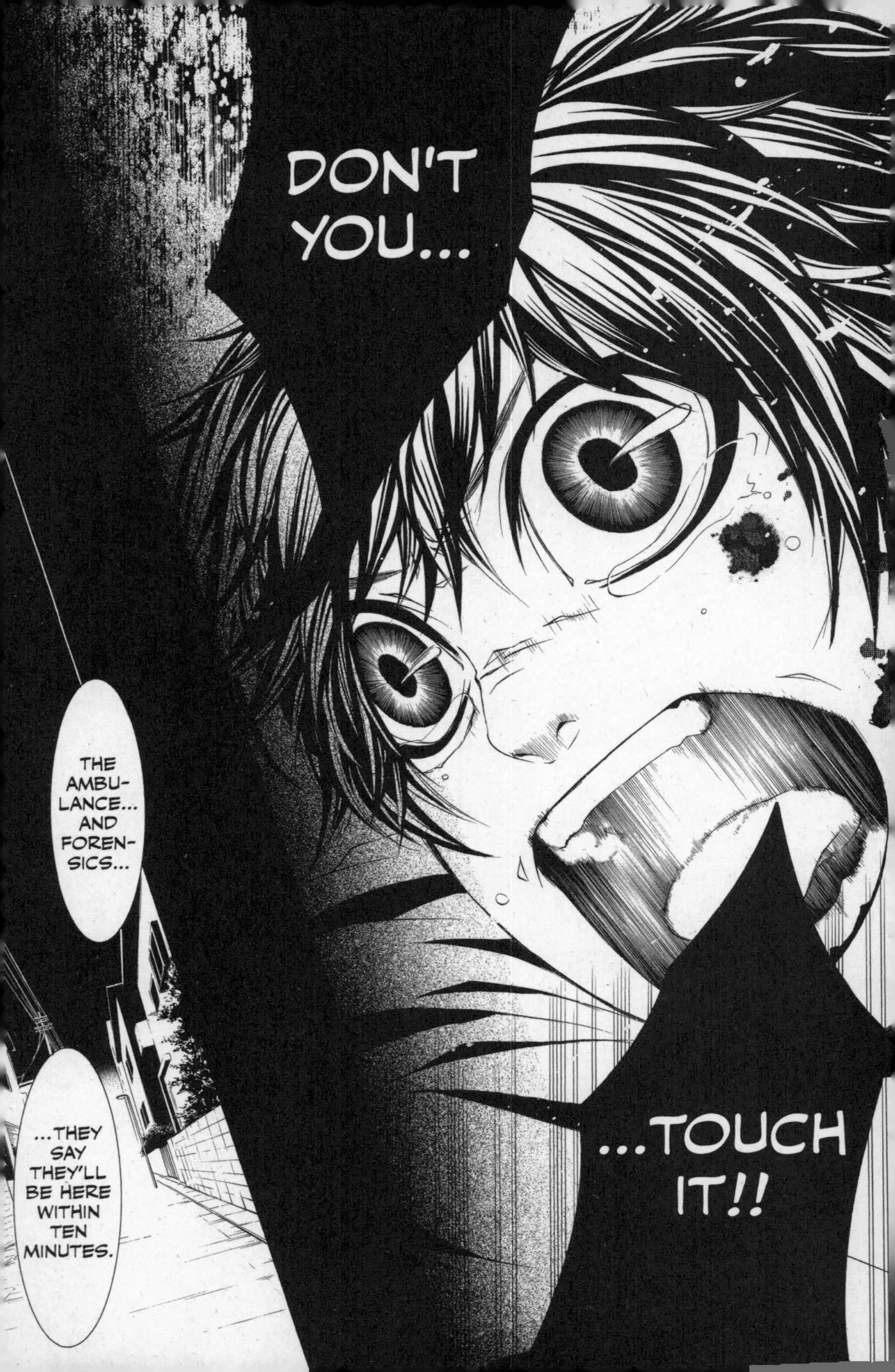
DON'T YOU...
...TOUCH IT!!
THE AMBU-LANCE... AND FOREN-SICS...
...THEY SAY THEY'LL BE HERE WITHIN TEN MINUTES.

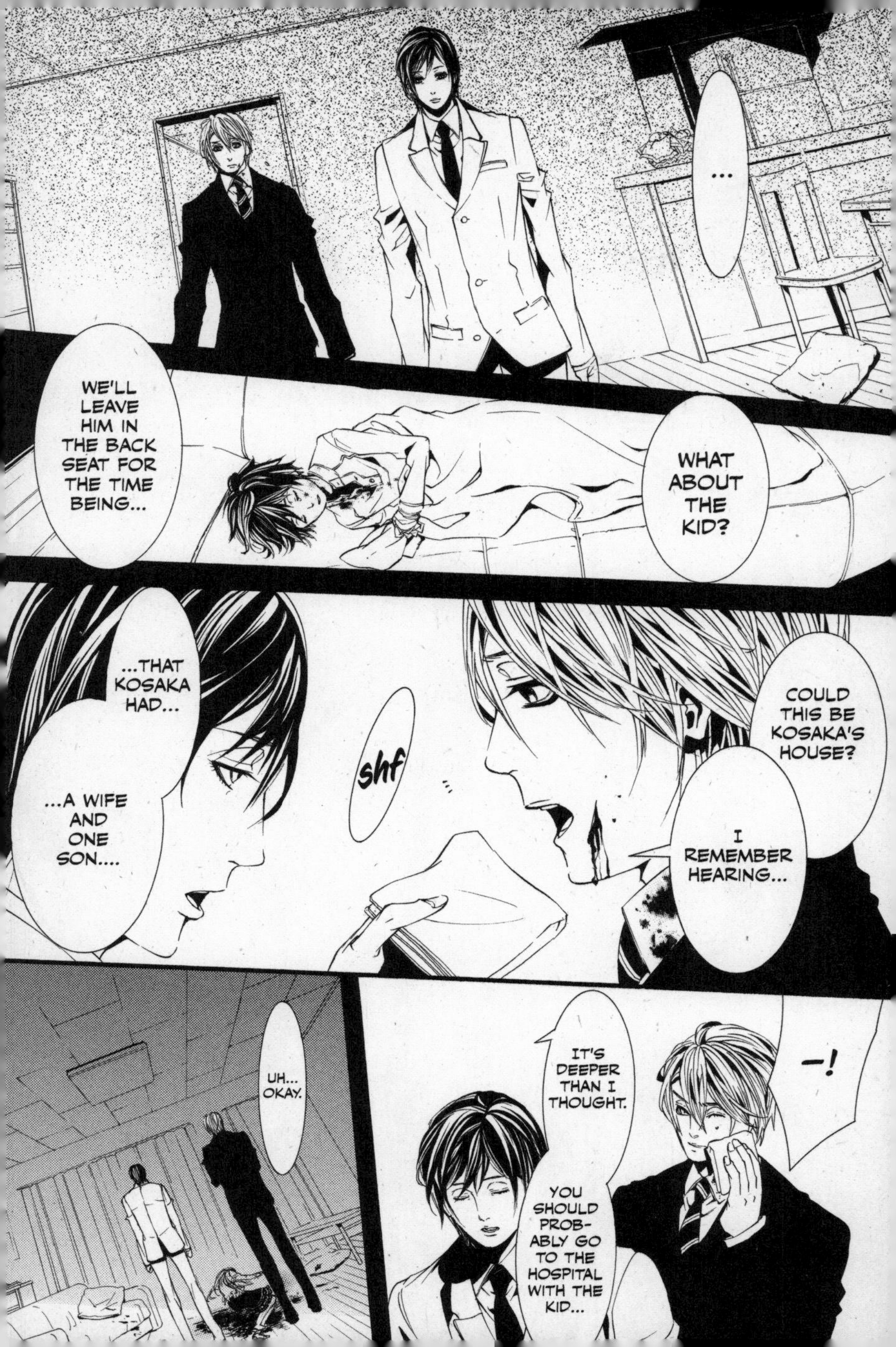
...
WHAT ABOUT THE KID?
WE'LL LEAVE HIM IN THE BACK SEAT FOR THE TIME BEING...
COULD THIS BE KOSAKA'S HOUSE?
I REMEMBER HEARING...
shf
...THAT KOSAKA HAD...
...A WIFE AND ONE SON....
—!
IT'S DEEPER THAN I THOUGHT.
YOU SHOULD PROB-ABLY GO TO THE HOSPITAL WITH THE KID...
UH... OKAY.

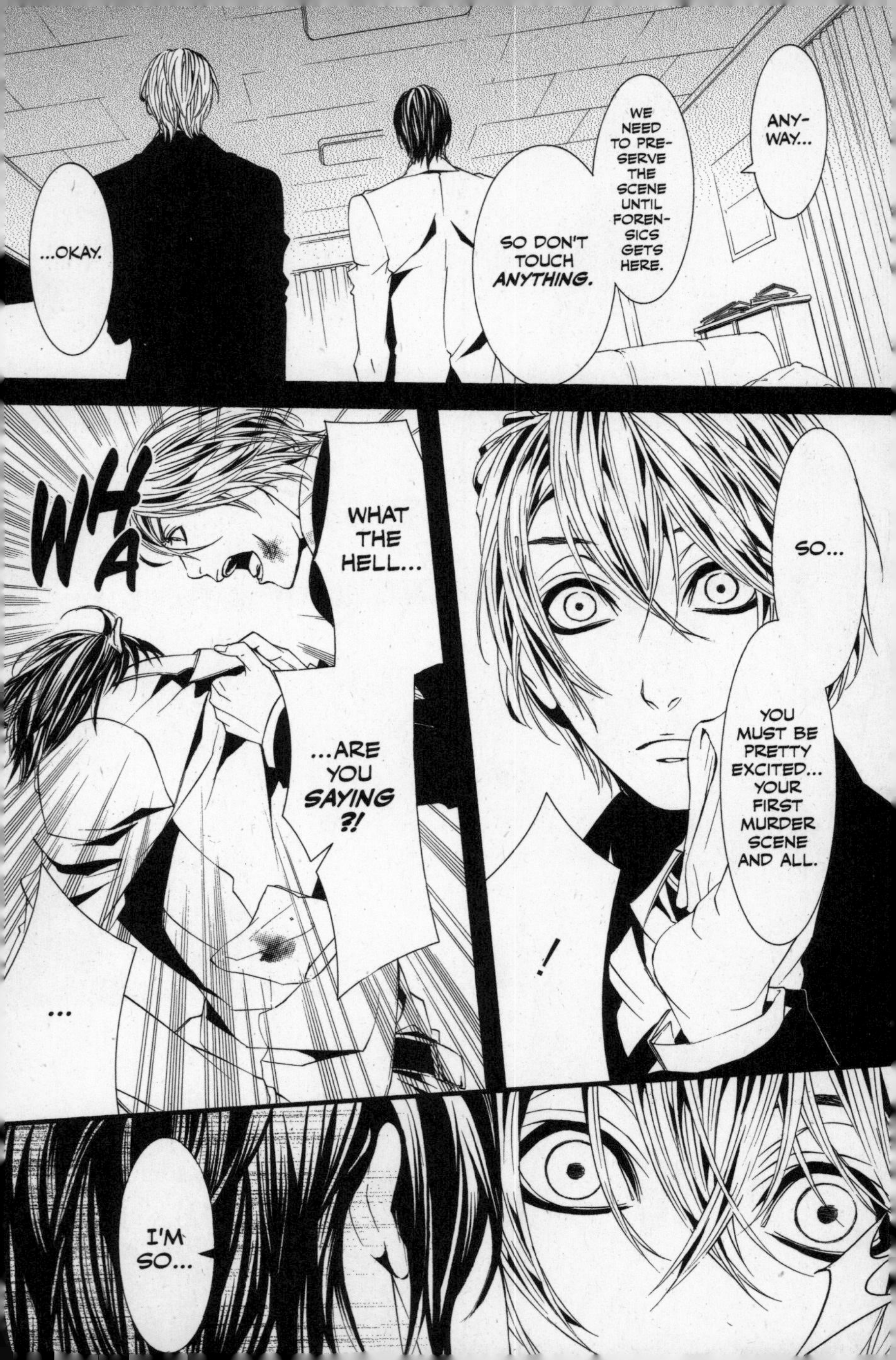
ANY-WAY...
WE NEED TO PRE-SERVE THE SCENE UNTIL FOREN-SICS GETS HERE.
SO DON'T TOUCH *ANYTHING.*
...OKAY.
SO...
YOU MUST BE PRETTY EXCITED... YOUR FIRST MURDER SCENE AND ALL.
!
WHA
WHAT THE HELL...
...ARE YOU *SAYING* ?!
...
I'M SO...

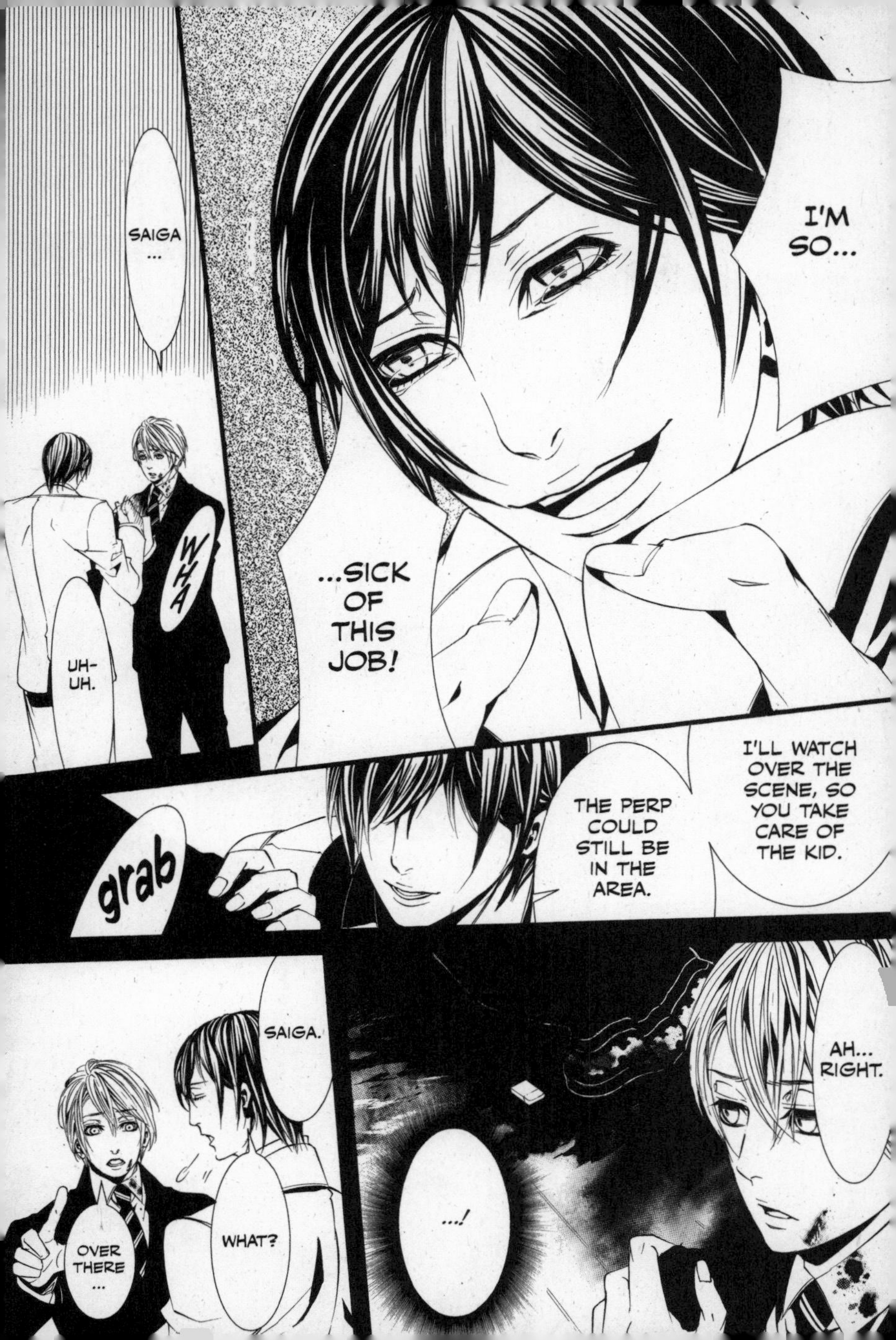
I'M SO...
...SICK OF THIS JOB!
SAIGA ...
WHA
UH-UH.
I'LL WATCH OVER THE SCENE, SO YOU TAKE CARE OF THE KID.
THE PERP COULD STILL BE IN THE AREA.
grab
AH... RIGHT.
...!
SAIGA.
WHAT?
OVER THERE ...

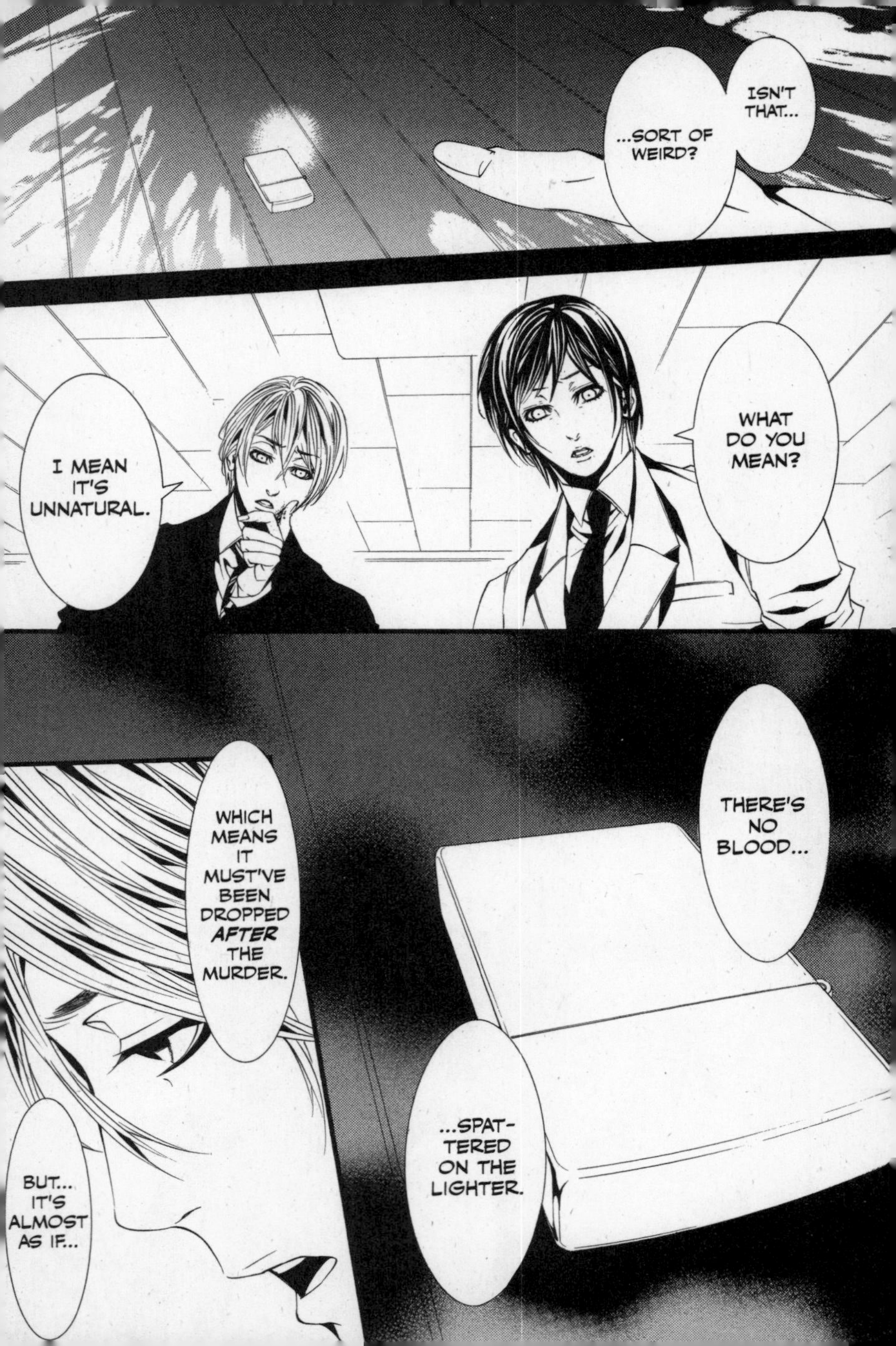
ISN'T THAT...
...SORT OF WEIRD?
WHAT DO YOU MEAN?
I MEAN IT'S UNNATURAL.
THERE'S NO BLOOD...
...SPATTERED ON THE LIGHTER.
WHICH MEANS IT MUST'VE BEEN DROPPED *AFTER* THE MURDER.
BUT... IT'S ALMOST AS IF...

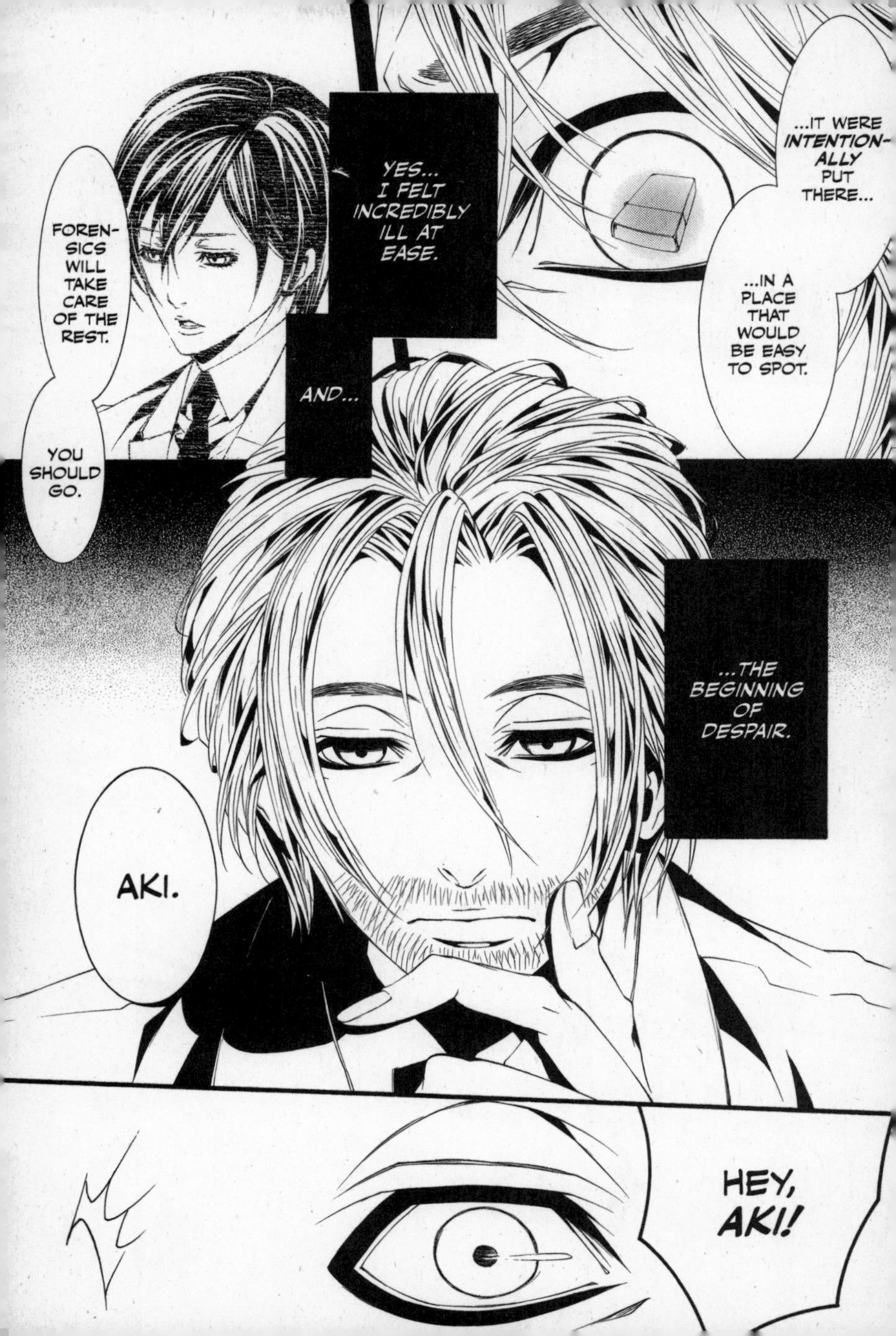
...IT WERE *INTENTIONALLY* PUT THERE...
...IN A PLACE THAT WOULD BE EASY TO SPOT.
YES... I FELT INCREDIBLY ILL AT EASE.
FORENSICS WILL TAKE CARE OF THE REST.
YOU SHOULD GO.
AND...
...THE BEGINNING OF DESPAIR.
AKI.
HEY, AKI!

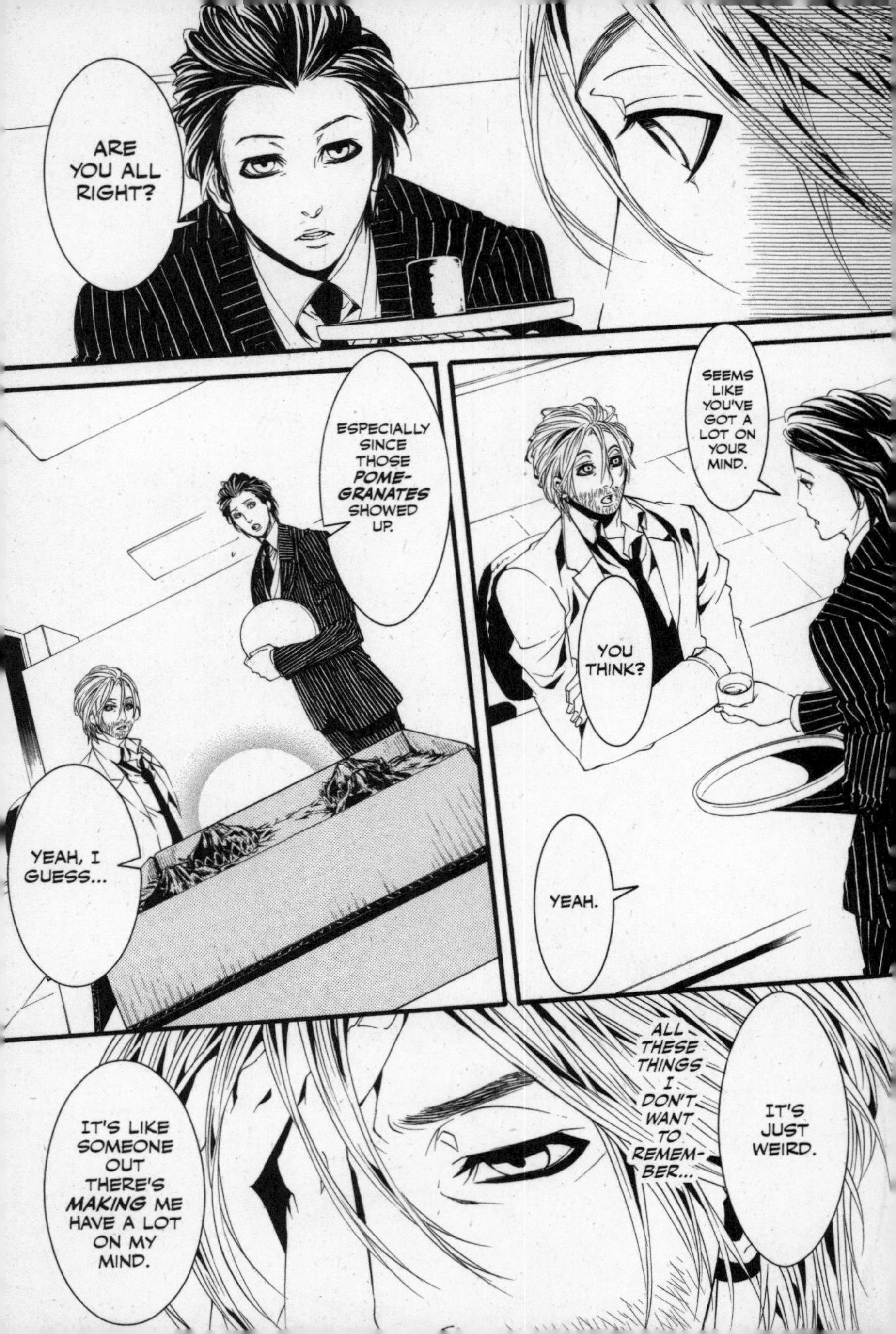
ARE YOU ALL RIGHT?
SEEMS LIKE YOU'VE GOT A LOT ON YOUR MIND.
YOU THINK?
YEAH.
ESPECIALLY SINCE THOSE *POMEGRANATES* SHOWED UP.
YEAH, I GUESS...
IT'S JUST WEIRD.
ALL THESE THINGS I DON'T WANT TO REMEMBER...
IT'S LIKE SOMEONE OUT THERE'S *MAKING* ME HAVE A LOT ON MY MIND.

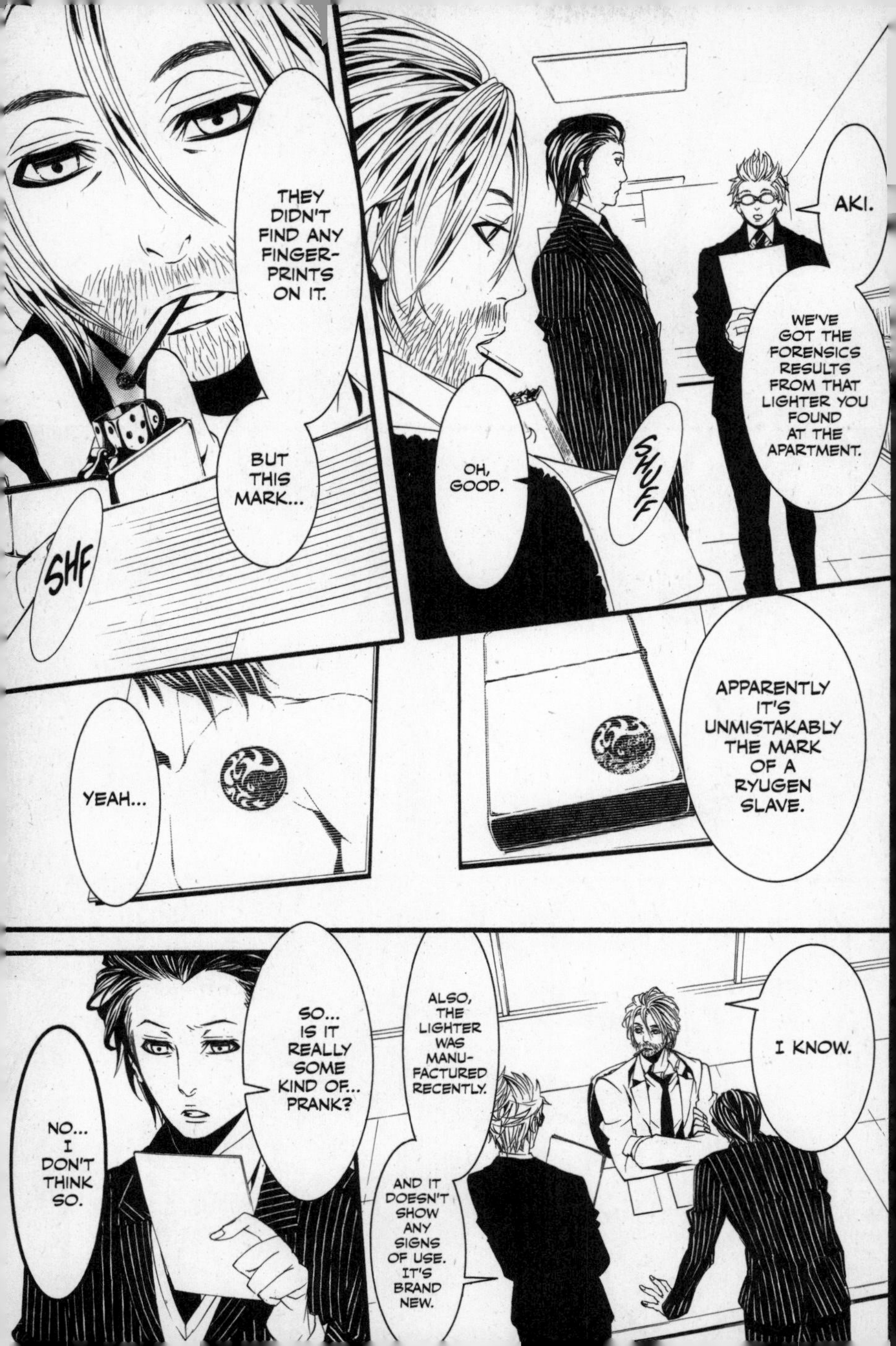
AKI.
WE'VE GOT THE FORENSICS RESULTS FROM THAT LIGHTER YOU FOUND AT THE APARTMENT.
SHUFF
OH, GOOD.
THEY DIDN'T FIND ANY FINGER-PRINTS ON IT.
BUT THIS MARK...
SHF
APPARENTLY IT'S UNMISTAKABLY THE MARK OF A RYUGEN SLAVE.
YEAH...
I KNOW.
ALSO, THE LIGHTER WAS MANU-FACTURED RECENTLY.
AND IT DOESN'T SHOW ANY SIGNS OF USE. IT'S BRAND NEW.
SO... IS IT REALLY SOME KIND OF... PRANK?
NO... I DON'T THINK SO.

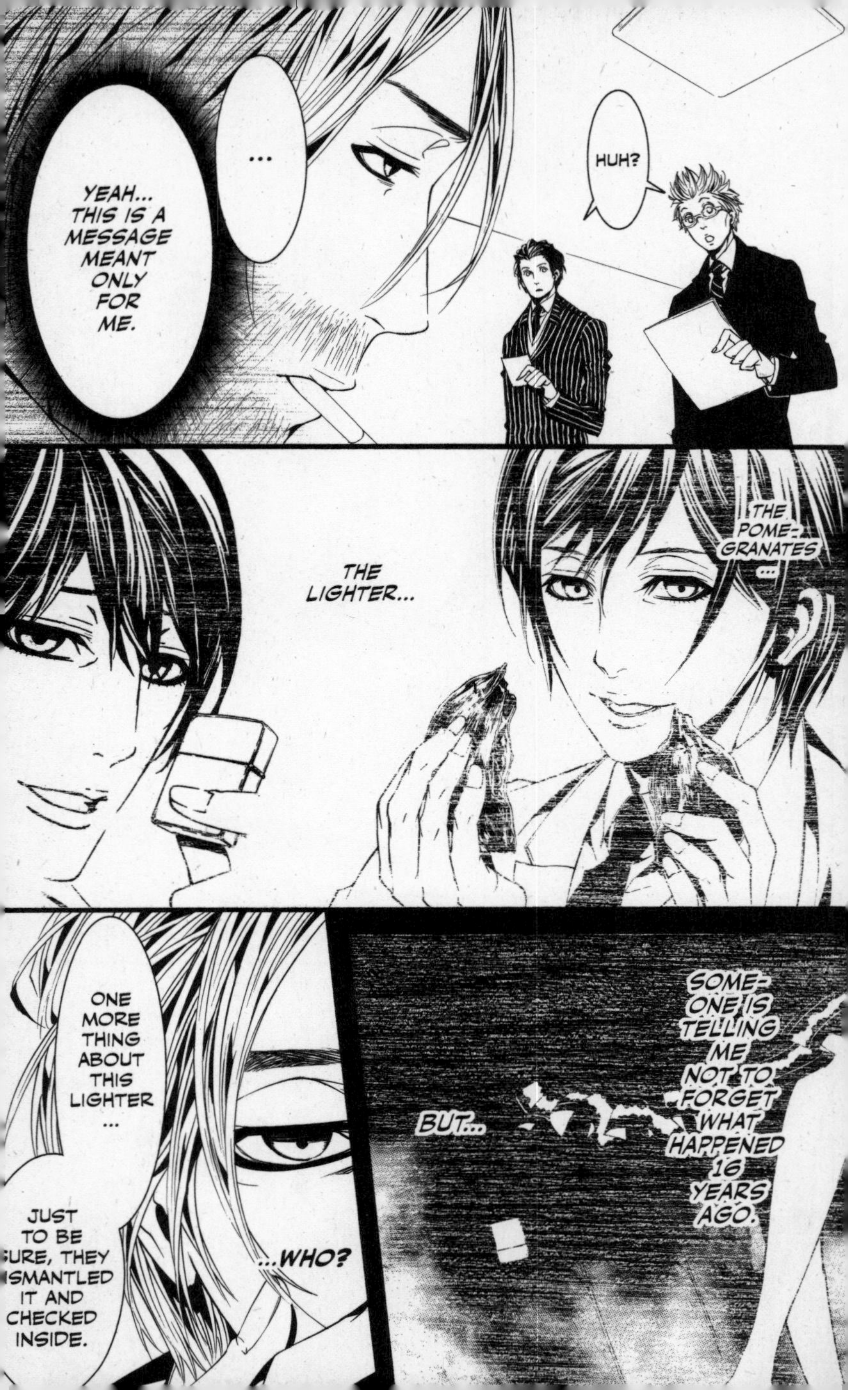
HUH?
...
YEAH... THIS IS A MESSAGE MEANT ONLY FOR ME.
THE POME-GRANATES ...
THE LIGHTER...
SOME-ONE IS TELLING ME NOT TO FORGET WHAT HAPPENED 16 YEARS AGO.
BUT...
...WHO?
ONE MORE THING ABOUT THIS LIGHTER ...
JUST TO BE URE, THEY ISMANTLED IT AND CHECKED INSIDE.

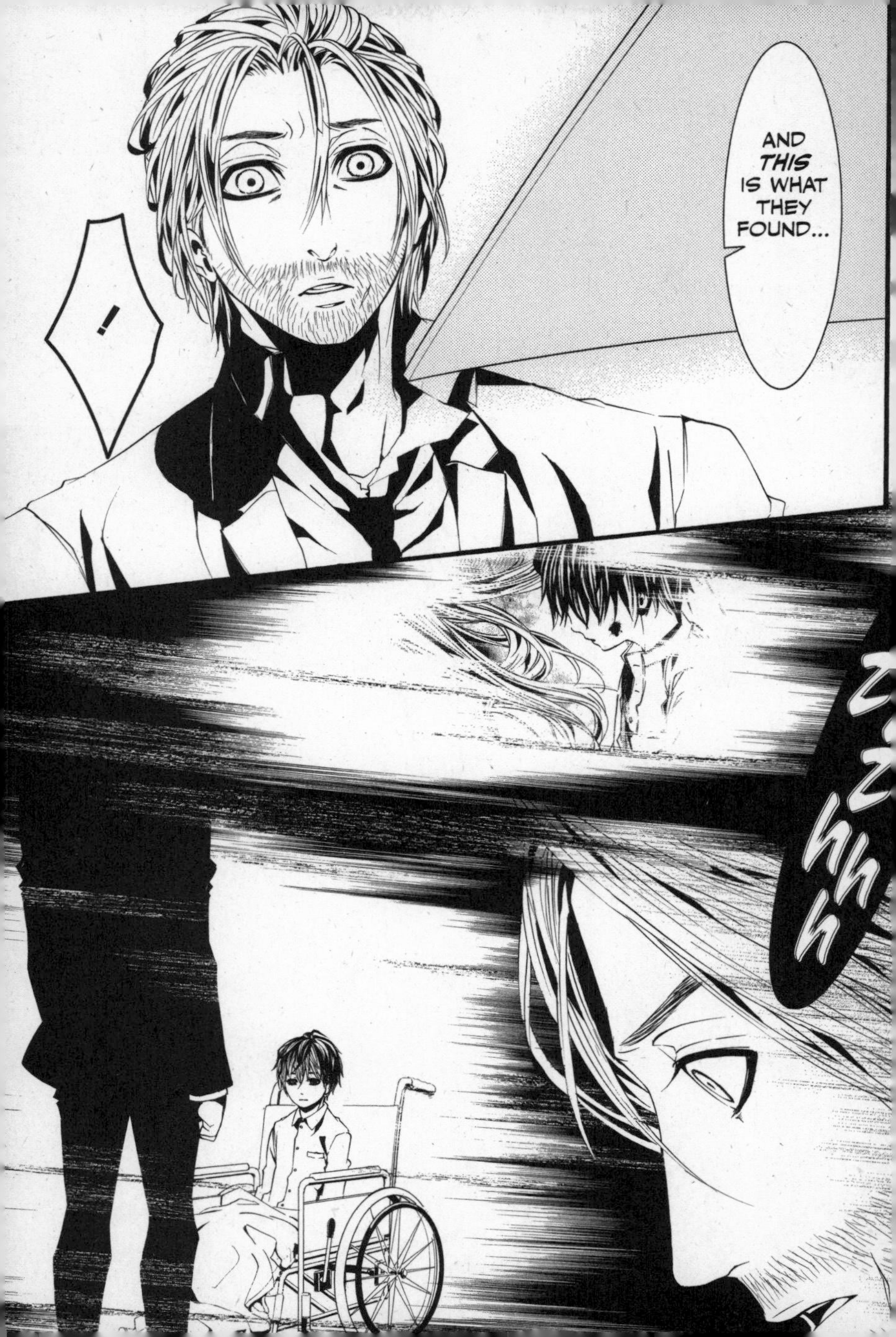
AND *THIS* IS WHAT THEY FOUND...
!

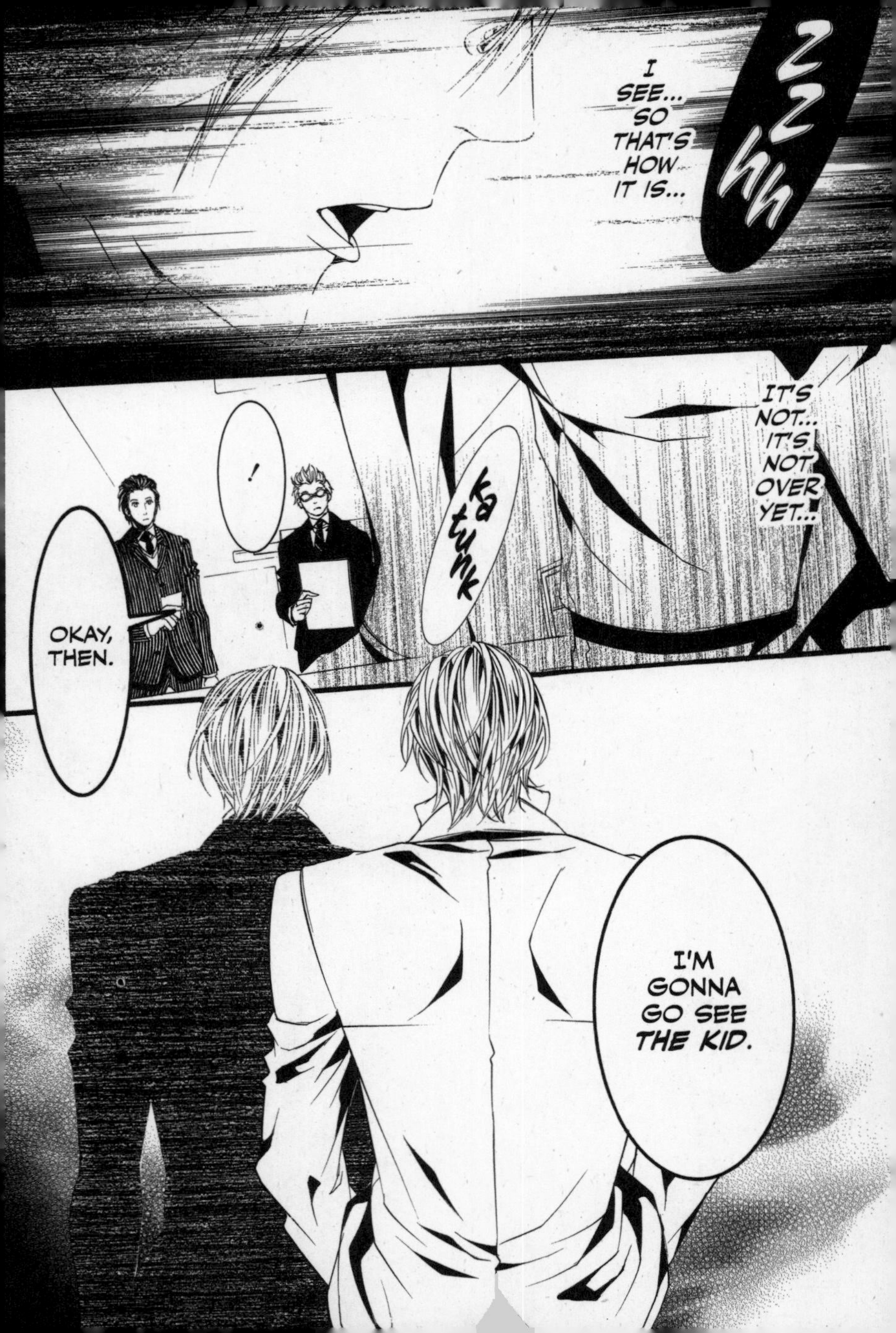
I SEE... SO THAT'S HOW IT IS...
IT'S NOT... IT'S NOT OVER YET...
ka tunk
!
OKAY, THEN.
I'M GONNA GO SEE *THE KID*.

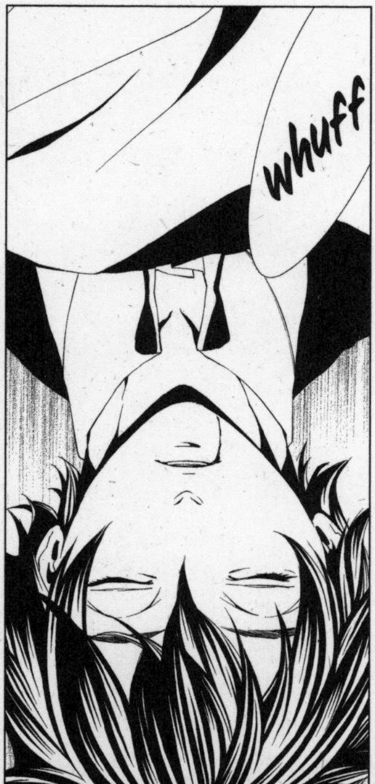
whuff

switch

naked ape : Saki Otoh & Nakamura Tomomi

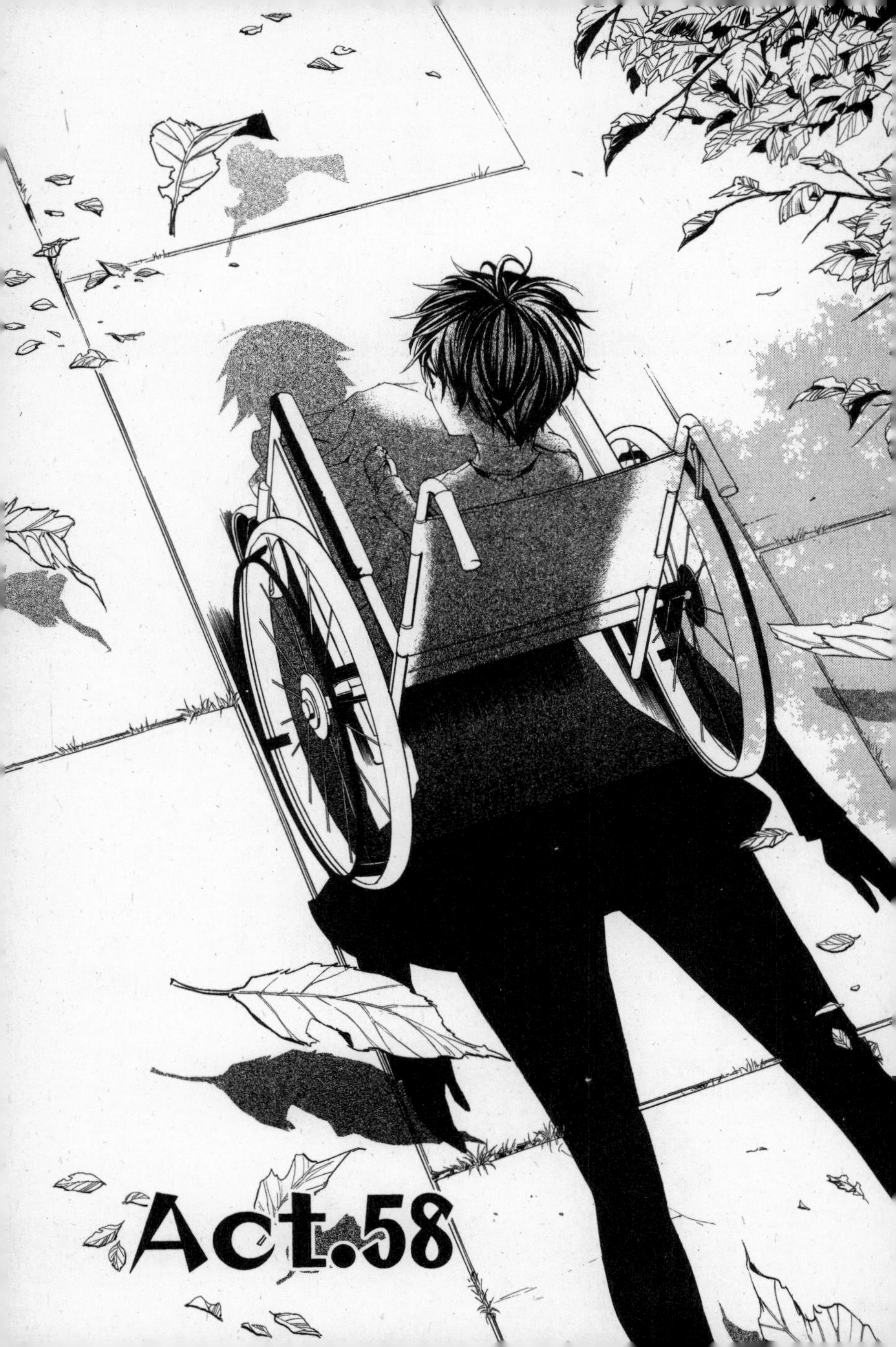
Act.58

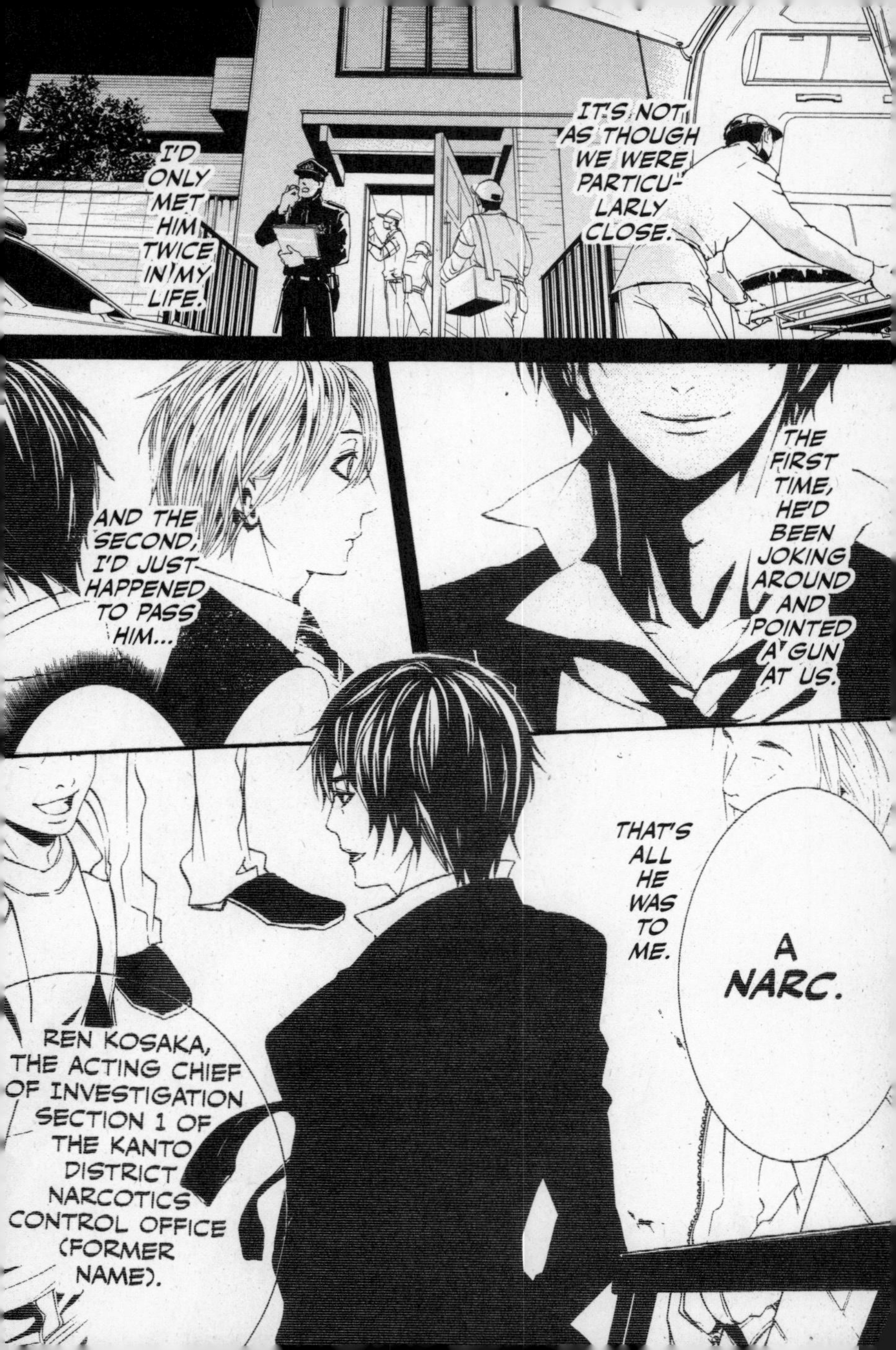
IT'S NOT AS THOUGH WE WERE PARTICU-LARLY CLOSE.
I'D ONLY MET HIM TWICE IN MY LIFE.
THE FIRST TIME, HE'D BEEN JOKING AROUND AND POINTED A GUN AT US.
AND THE SECOND, I'D JUST HAPPENED TO PASS HIM...
A NARC.
THAT'S ALL HE WAS TO ME.
REN KOSAKA, THE ACTING CHIEF OF INVESTIGATION SECTION 1 OF THE KANTO DISTRICT NARCOTICS CONTROL OFFICE (FORMER NAME).

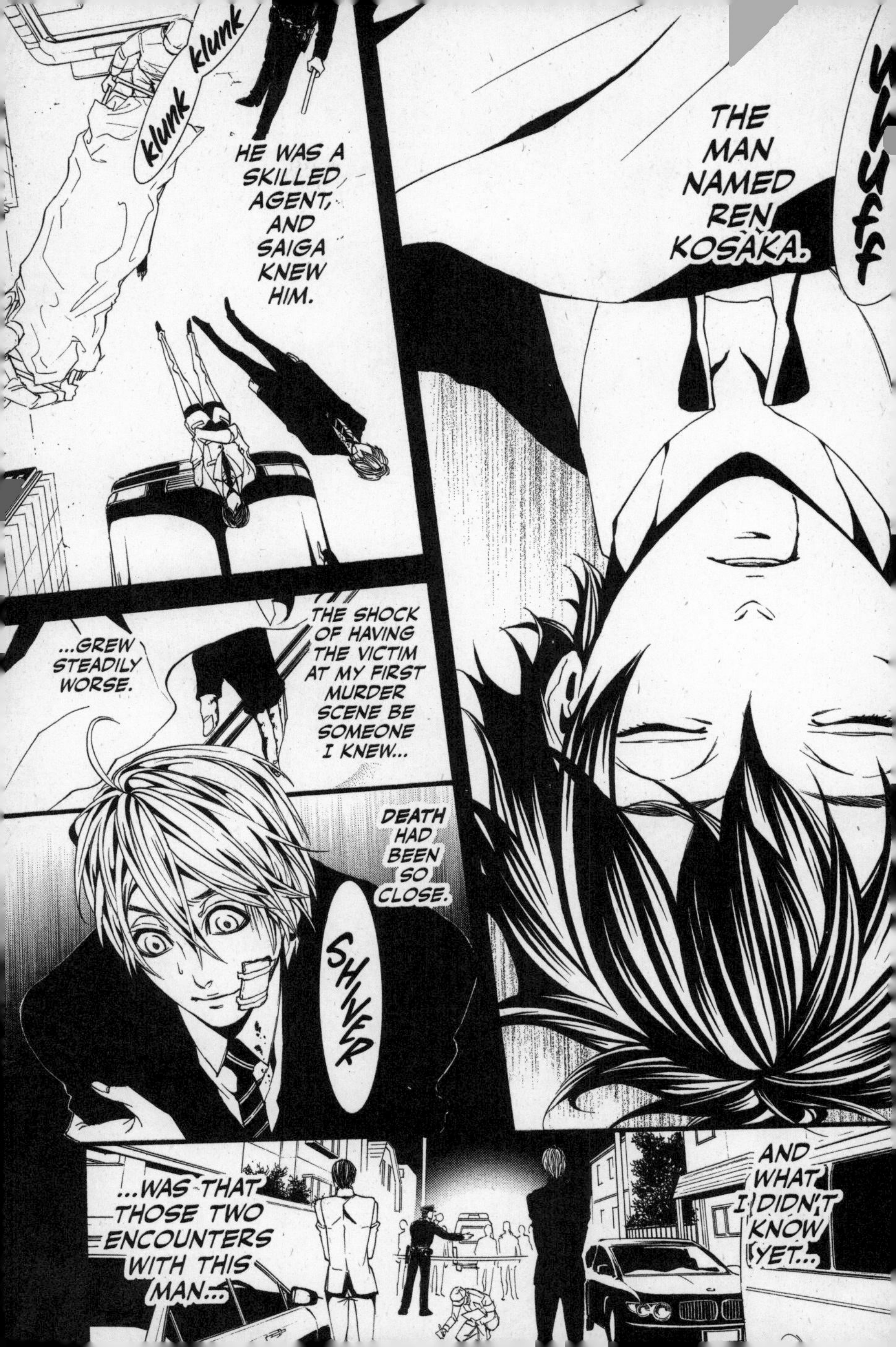
whuff
THE MAN NAMED REN KOSAKA.
klunk
klunk
HE WAS A SKILLED AGENT, AND SAIGA KNEW HIM.
THE SHOCK OF HAVING THE VICTIM AT MY FIRST MURDER SCENE BE SOMEONE I KNEW...
...GREW STEADILY WORSE.
DEATH HAD BEEN SO CLOSE.
SHIVER
AND WHAT I DIDN'T KNOW YET...
...WAS THAT THOSE TWO ENCOUNTERS WITH THIS MAN...

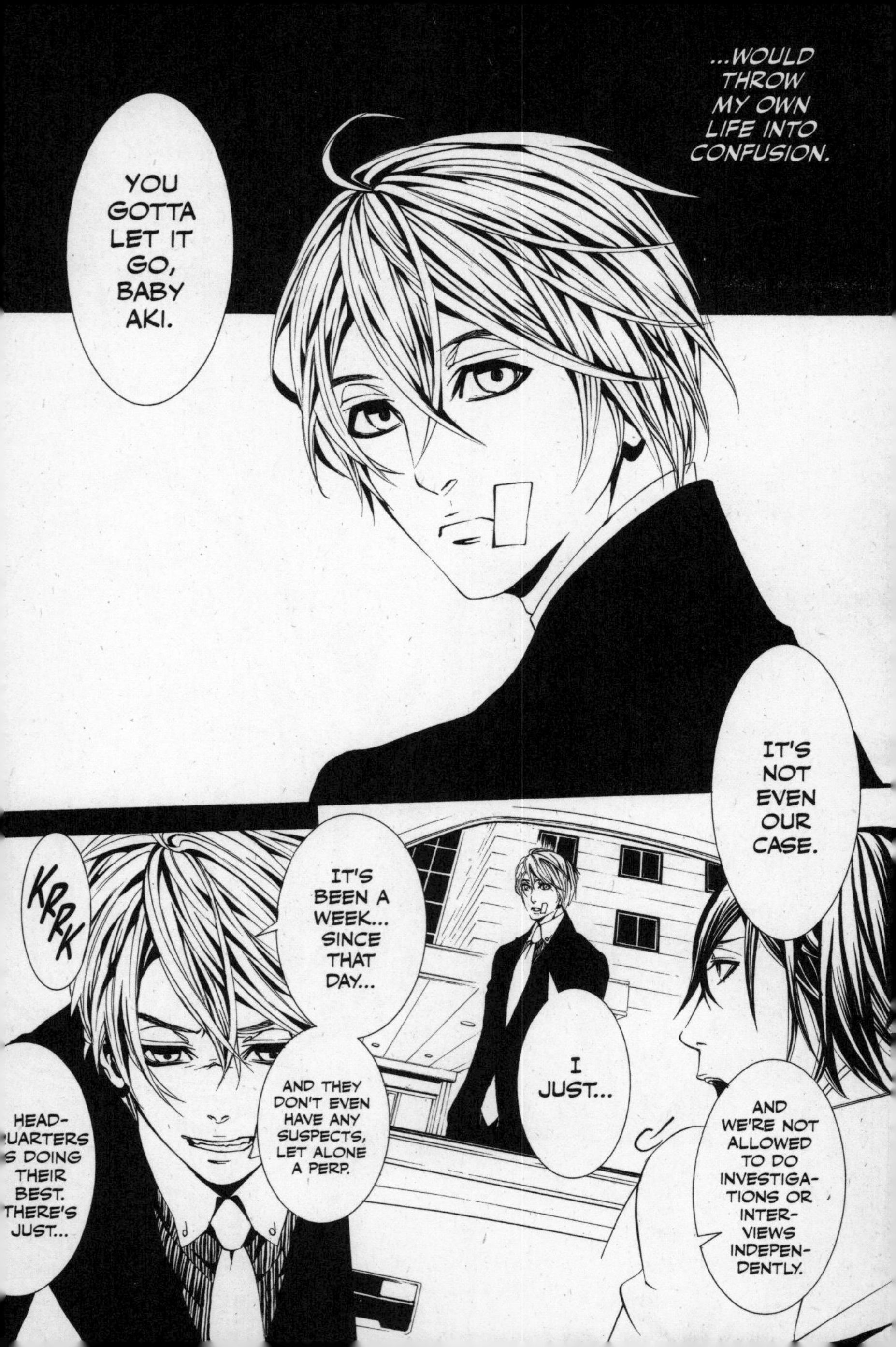
...WOULD THROW MY OWN LIFE INTO CONFUSION.
YOU GOTTA LET IT GO, BABY AKI.
IT'S NOT EVEN OUR CASE.
AND WE'RE NOT ALLOWED TO DO INVESTIGA-TIONS OR INTER-VIEWS INDEPEN-DENTLY.
I JUST...
IT'S BEEN A WEEK... SINCE THAT DAY...
AND THEY DON'T EVEN HAVE ANY SUSPECTS, LET ALONE A PERP.
KRRK
HEAD-UARTERS S DOING THEIR BEST. THERE'S JUST...

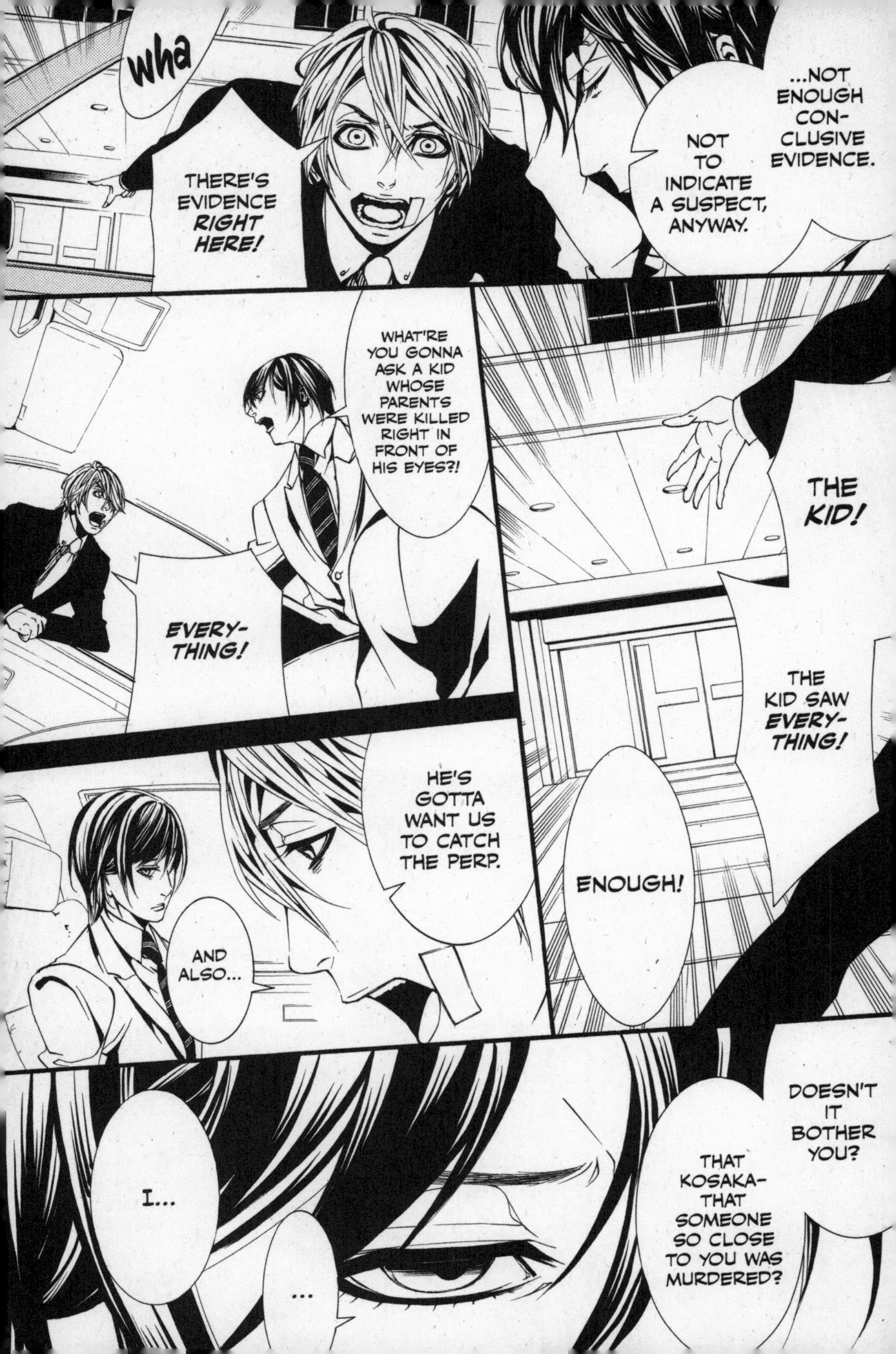
...NOT ENOUGH CON-CLUSIVE EVIDENCE.
NOT TO INDICATE A SUSPECT, ANYWAY.
wha
THERE'S EVIDENCE RIGHT HERE!
THE KID!
THE KID SAW EVERY-THING!
ENOUGH!
WHAT'RE YOU GONNA ASK A KID WHOSE PARENTS WERE KILLED RIGHT IN FRONT OF HIS EYES?!
EVERY-THING!
HE'S GOTTA WANT US TO CATCH THE PERP.
AND ALSO...
DOESN'T IT BOTHER YOU?
THAT KOSAKA-THAT SOMEONE SO CLOSE TO YOU WAS MURDERED?
I...
...

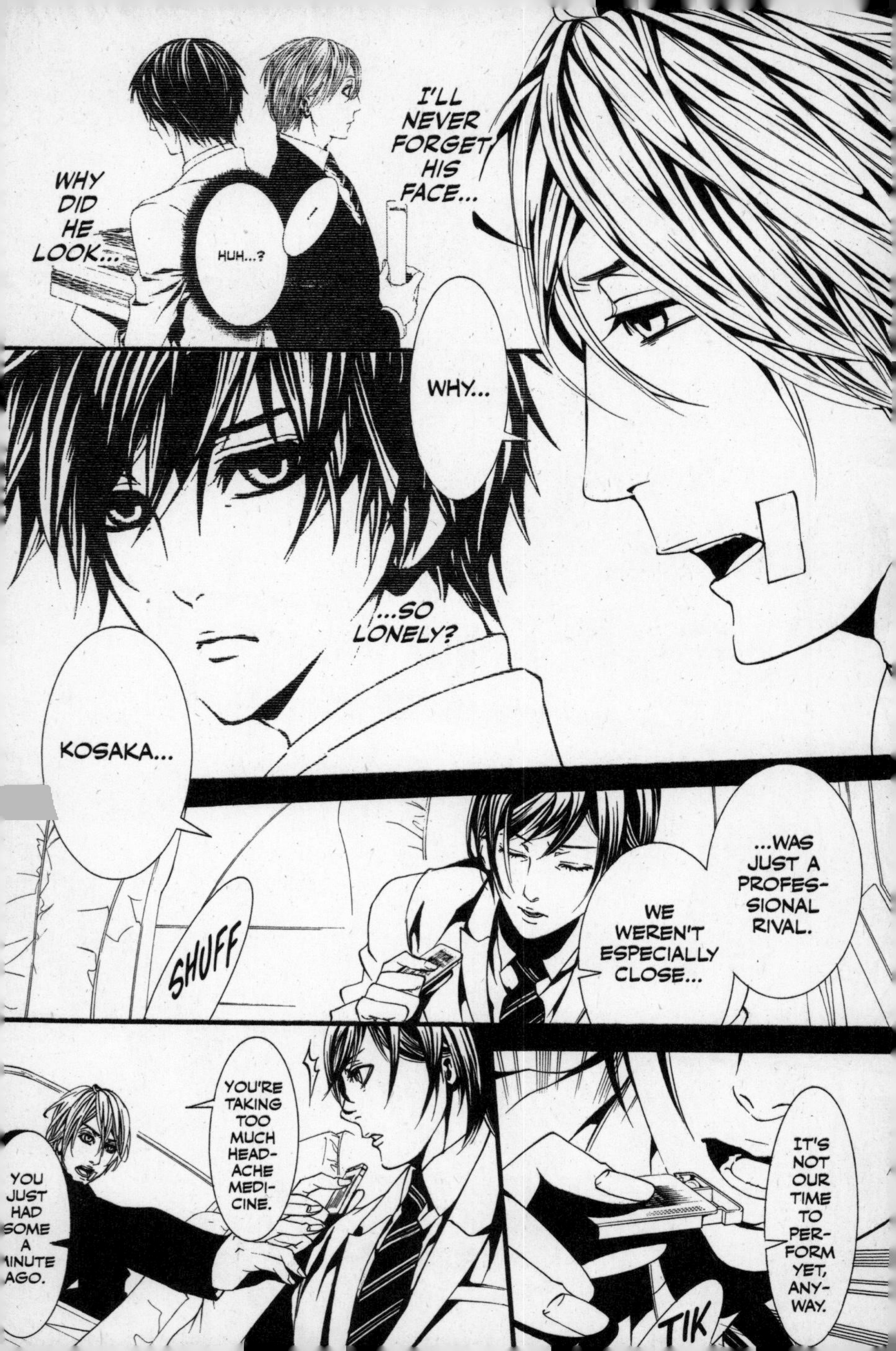
I'LL NEVER FORGET HIS FACE...
HUH...?
WHY DID HE LOOK...
WHY...
...SO LONELY?
KOSAKA...
...WAS JUST A PROFES-SIONAL RIVAL.
WE WEREN'T ESPECIALLY CLOSE...
SHUFF
IT'S NOT OUR TIME TO PER-FORM YET, ANY-WAY.
TIK
YOU'RE TAKING TOO MUCH HEAD-ACHE MEDI-CINE.
YOU JUST HAD SOME A INUTE AGO.

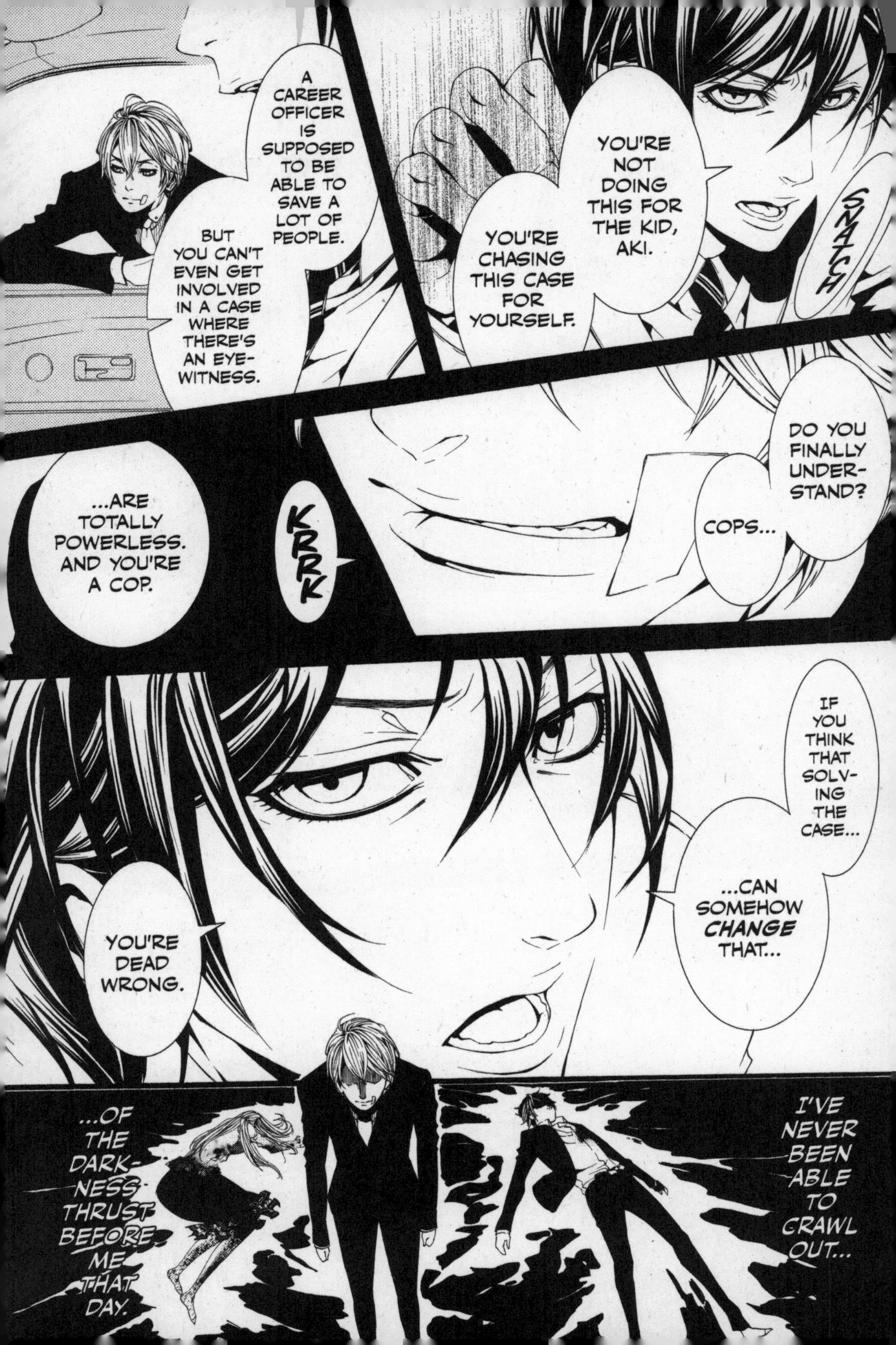
YOU'RE NOT DOING THIS FOR THE KID, AKI.
YOU'RE CHASING THIS CASE FOR YOURSELF.
SNATCH
A CAREER OFFICER IS SUPPOSED TO BE ABLE TO SAVE A LOT OF PEOPLE.
BUT YOU CAN'T EVEN GET INVOLVED IN A CASE WHERE THERE'S AN EYE-WITNESS.
DO YOU FINALLY UNDER-STAND?
COPS...
KRRK
...ARE TOTALLY POWERLESS. AND YOU'RE A COP.
IF YOU THINK THAT SOLVING THE CASE...
...CAN SOMEHOW *CHANGE* THAT...
YOU'RE DEAD WRONG.
I'VE NEVER BEEN ABLE TO CRAWL OUT...
...OF THE DARKNESS THRUST BEFORE ME THAT DAY.

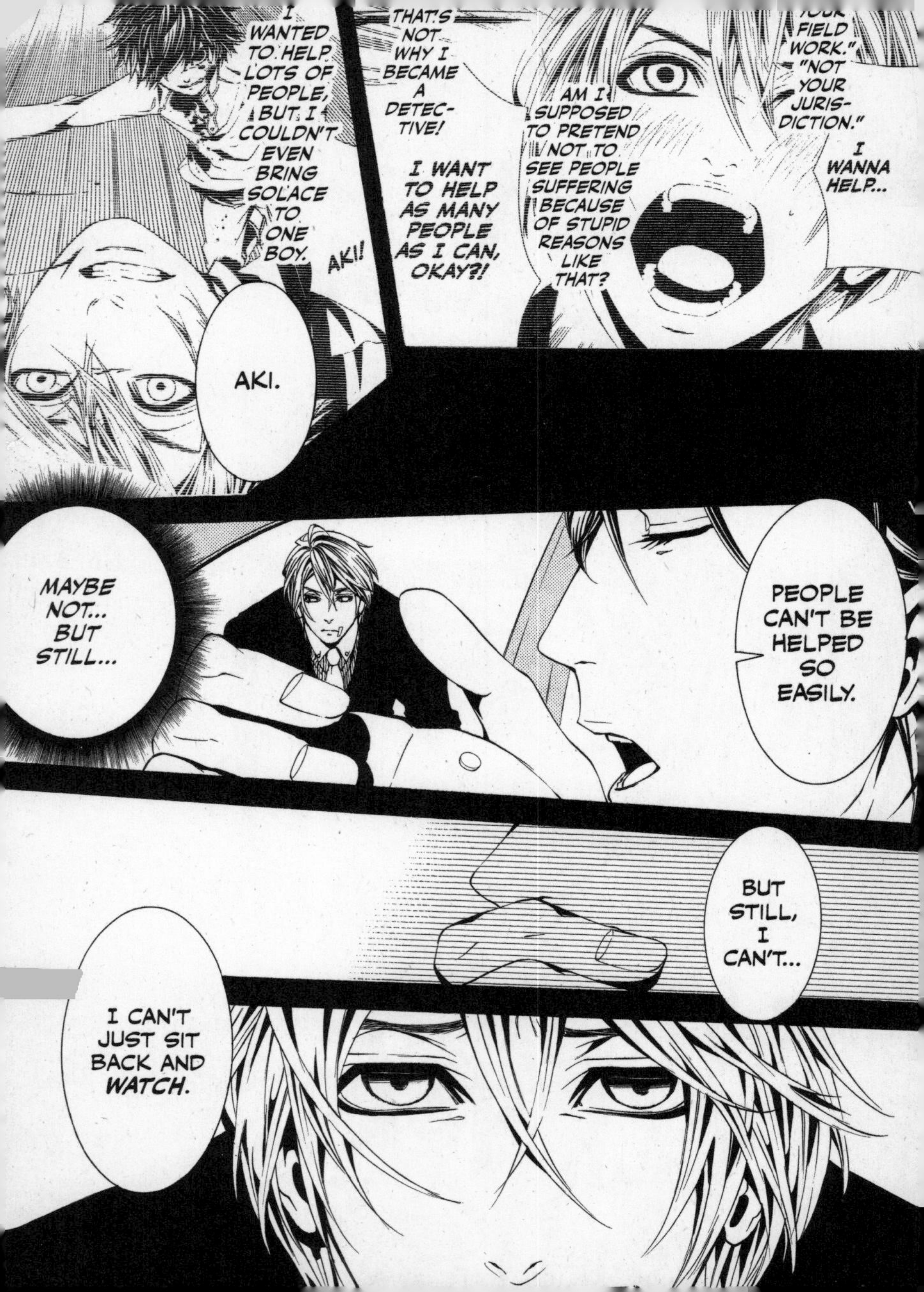
FIELD WORK." "NOT YOUR JURIS-DICTION."
I WANNA HELP...
AM I SUPPOSED TO PRETEND NOT TO SEE PEOPLE SUFFERING BECAUSE OF STUPID REASONS LIKE THAT?
THAT'S NOT WHY I BECAME A DETEC-TIVE!
I WANT TO HELP AS MANY PEOPLE AS I CAN, OKAY?!
I WANTED TO HELP LOTS OF PEOPLE, BUT I COULDN'T EVEN BRING SOLACE TO ONE BOY.
AKI!
AKI.
PEOPLE CAN'T BE HELPED SO EASILY.
MAYBE NOT... BUT STILL...
BUT STILL, I CAN'T...
I CAN'T JUST SIT BACK AND *WATCH*.

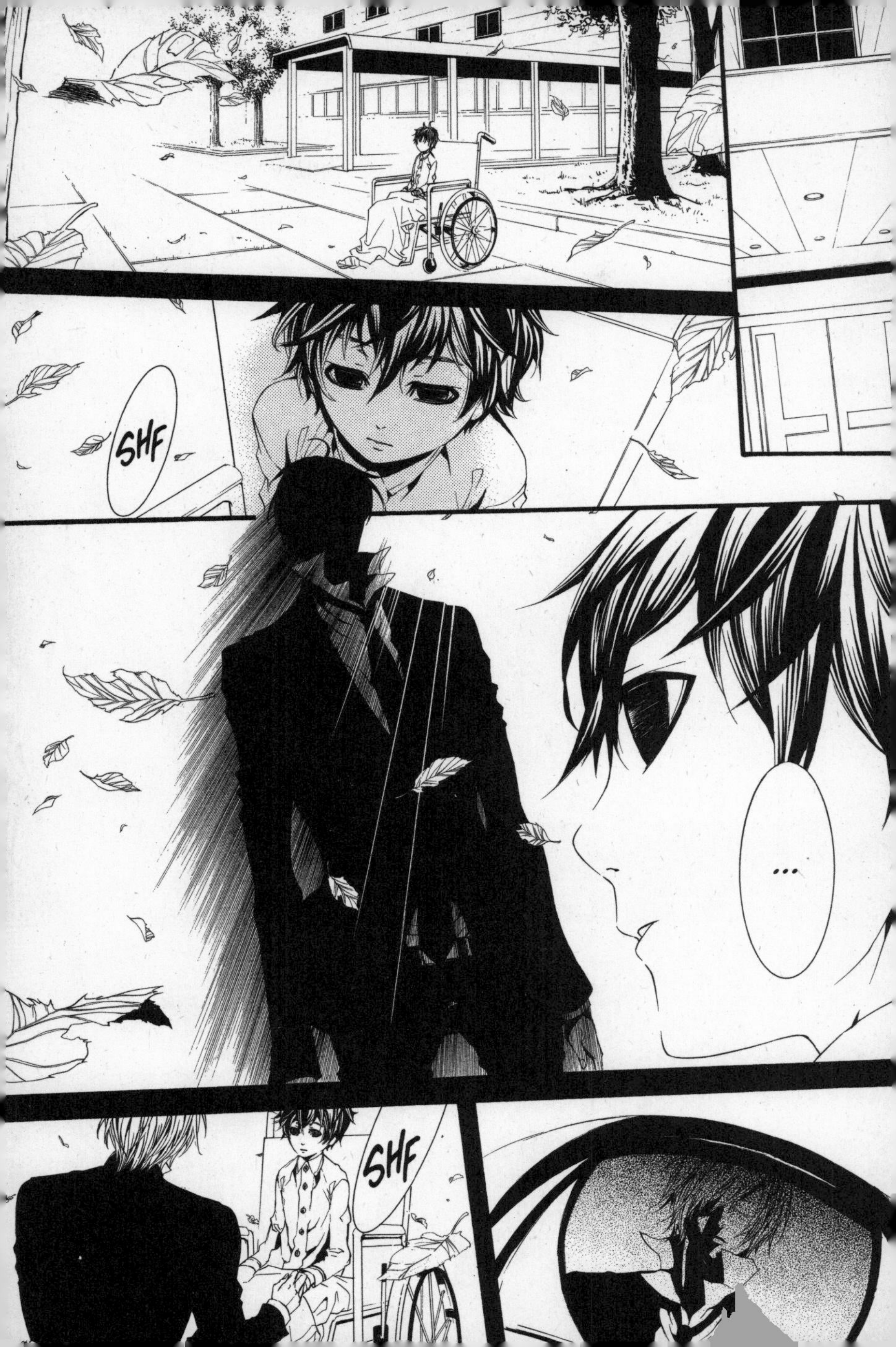
SHF
...
SHF

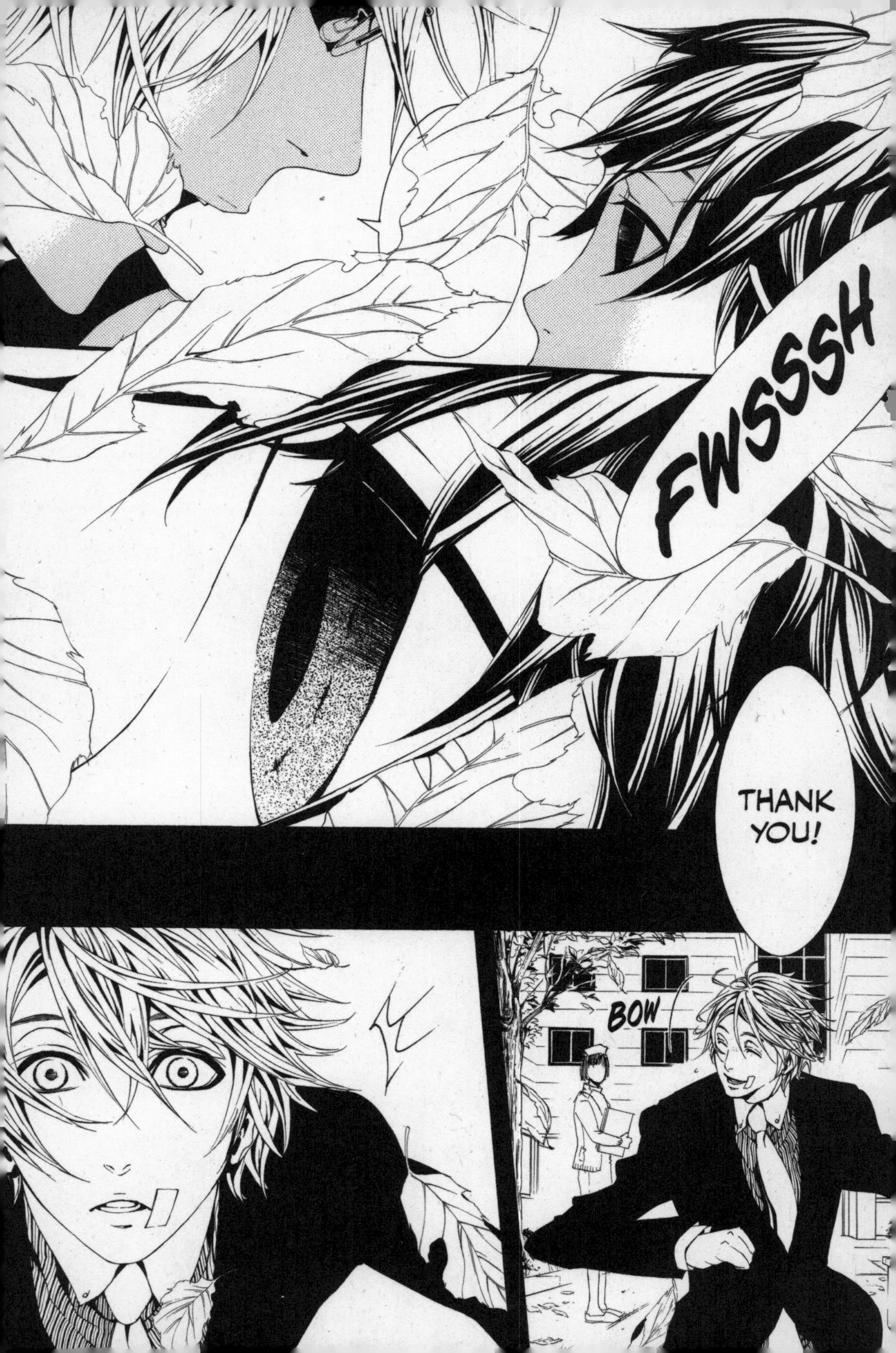
FWSSSH
THANK YOU!
BOW

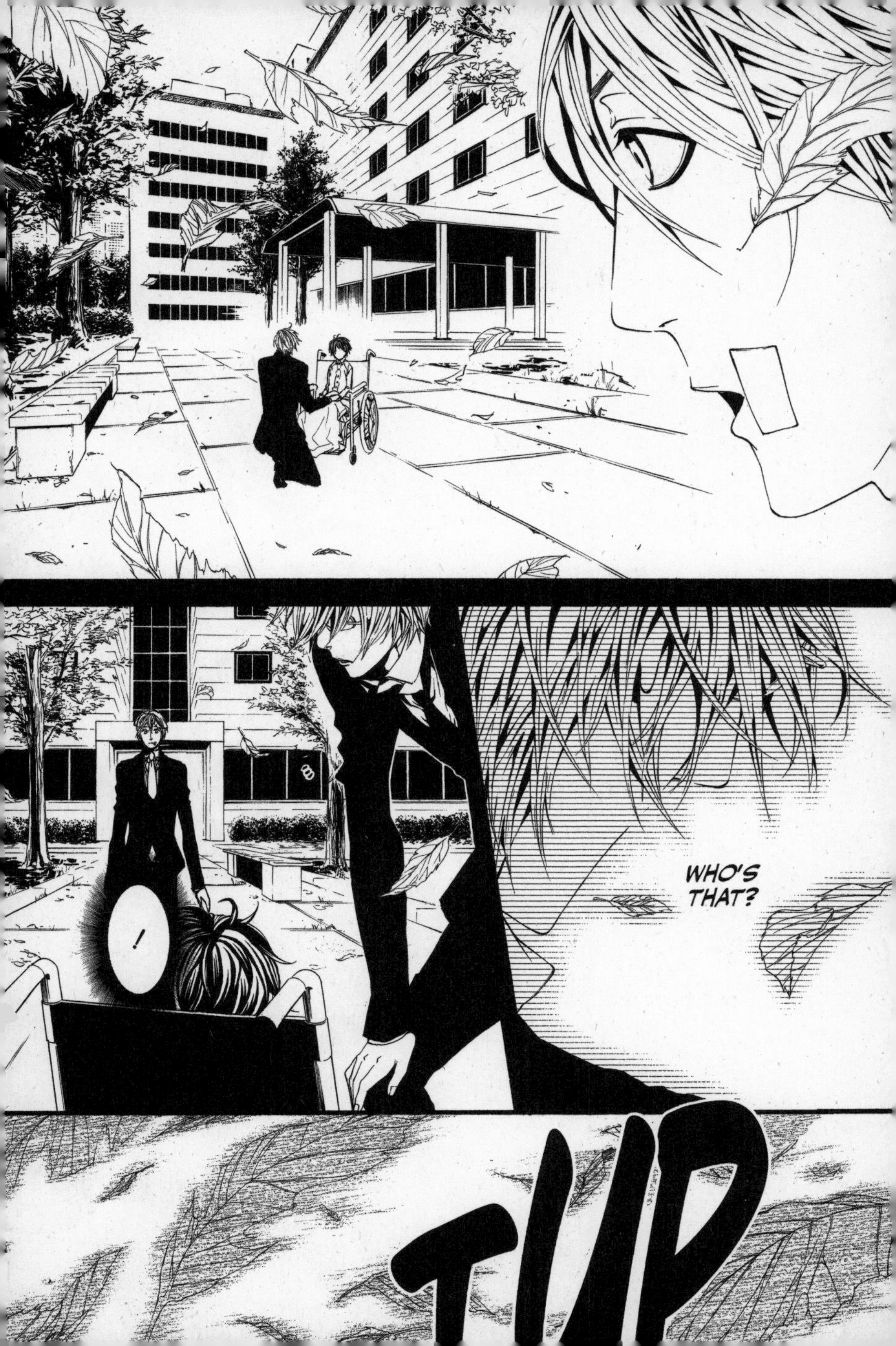
WHO'S THAT?
!
TMP

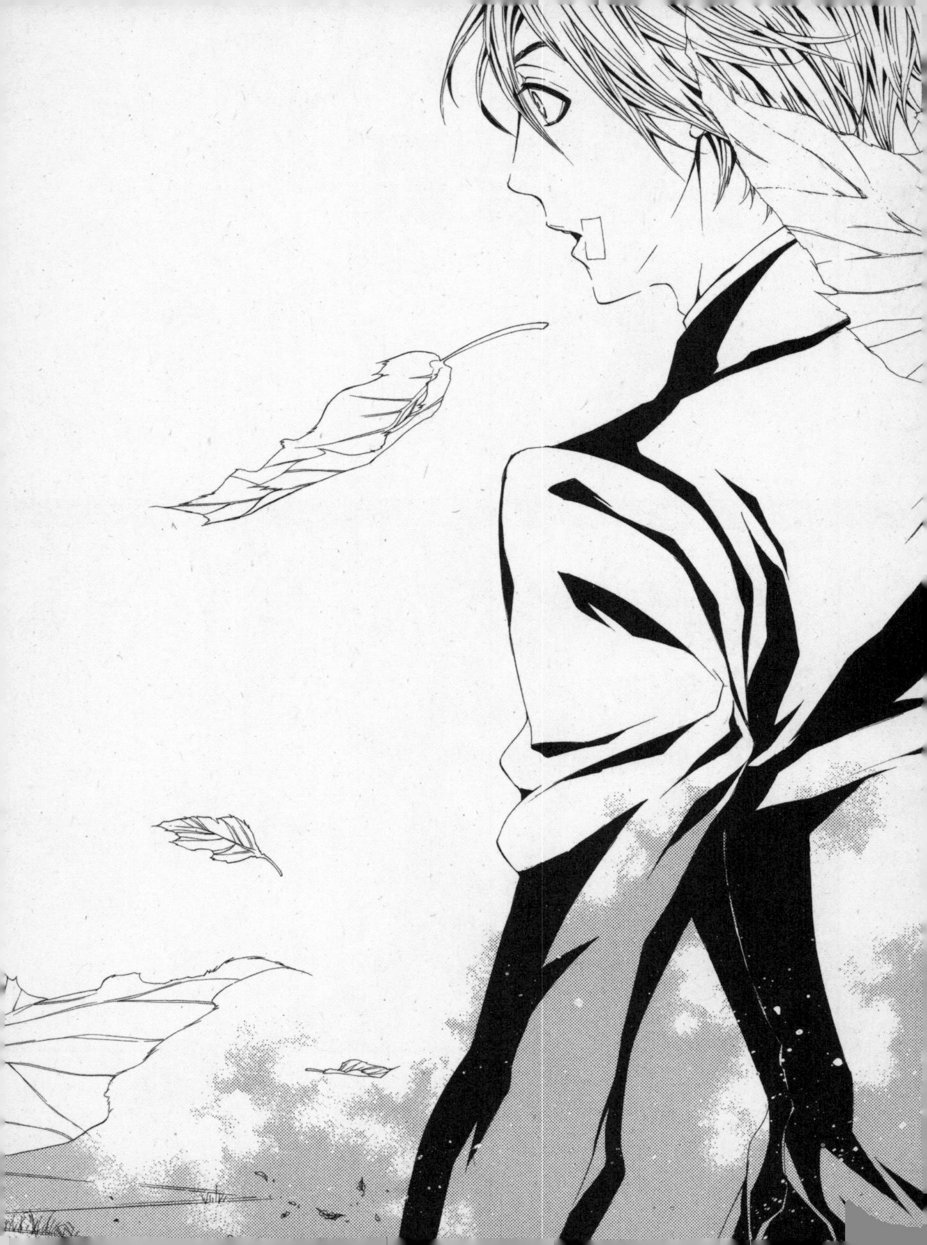

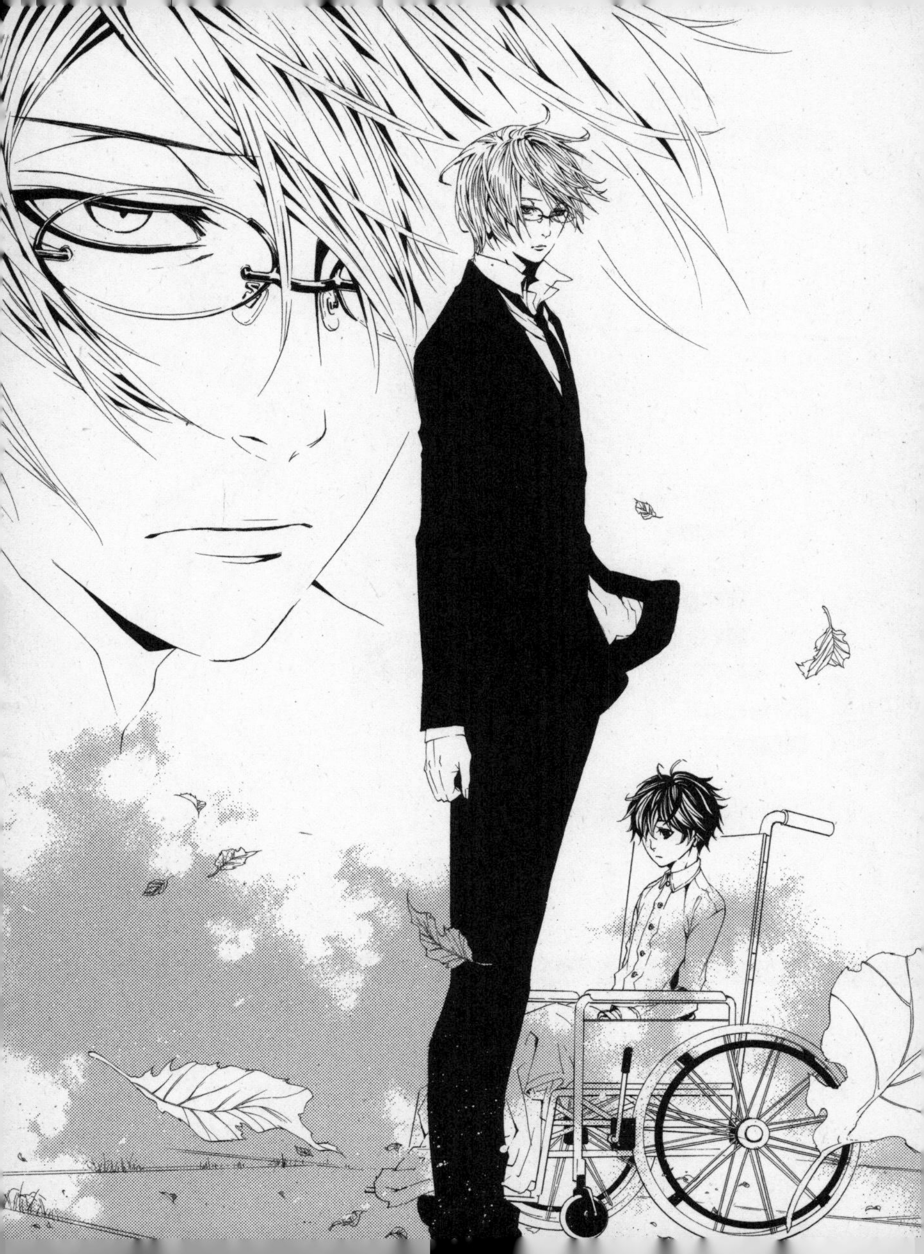

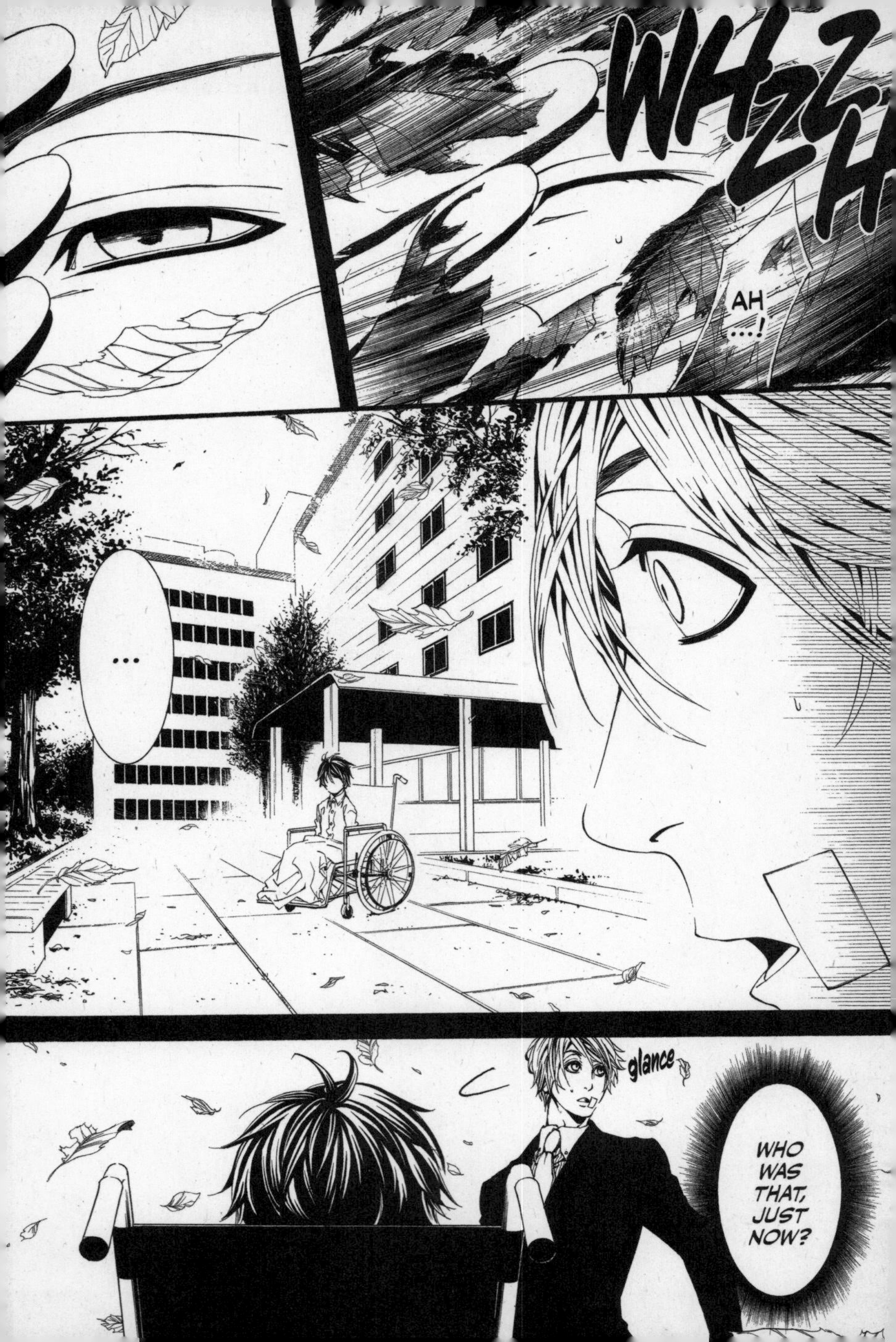
WHZZZH
AH ...!
...
glance
WHO WAS THAT, JUST NOW?

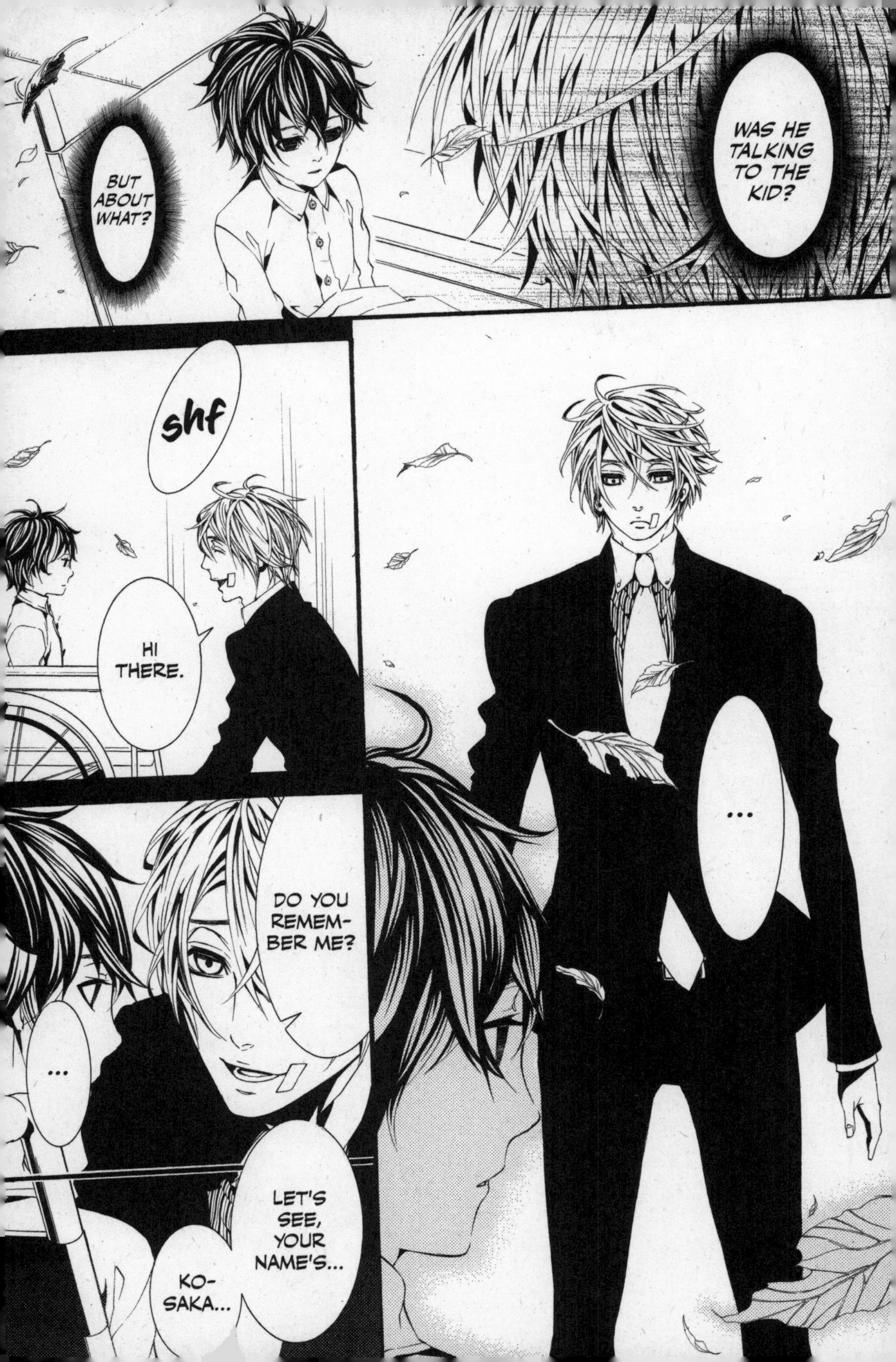
WAS HE TALKING TO THE KID?
BUT ABOUT WHAT?
...
shf
HI THERE.
DO YOU REMEMBER ME?
...
LET'S SEE, YOUR NAME'S...
KO-SAKA...

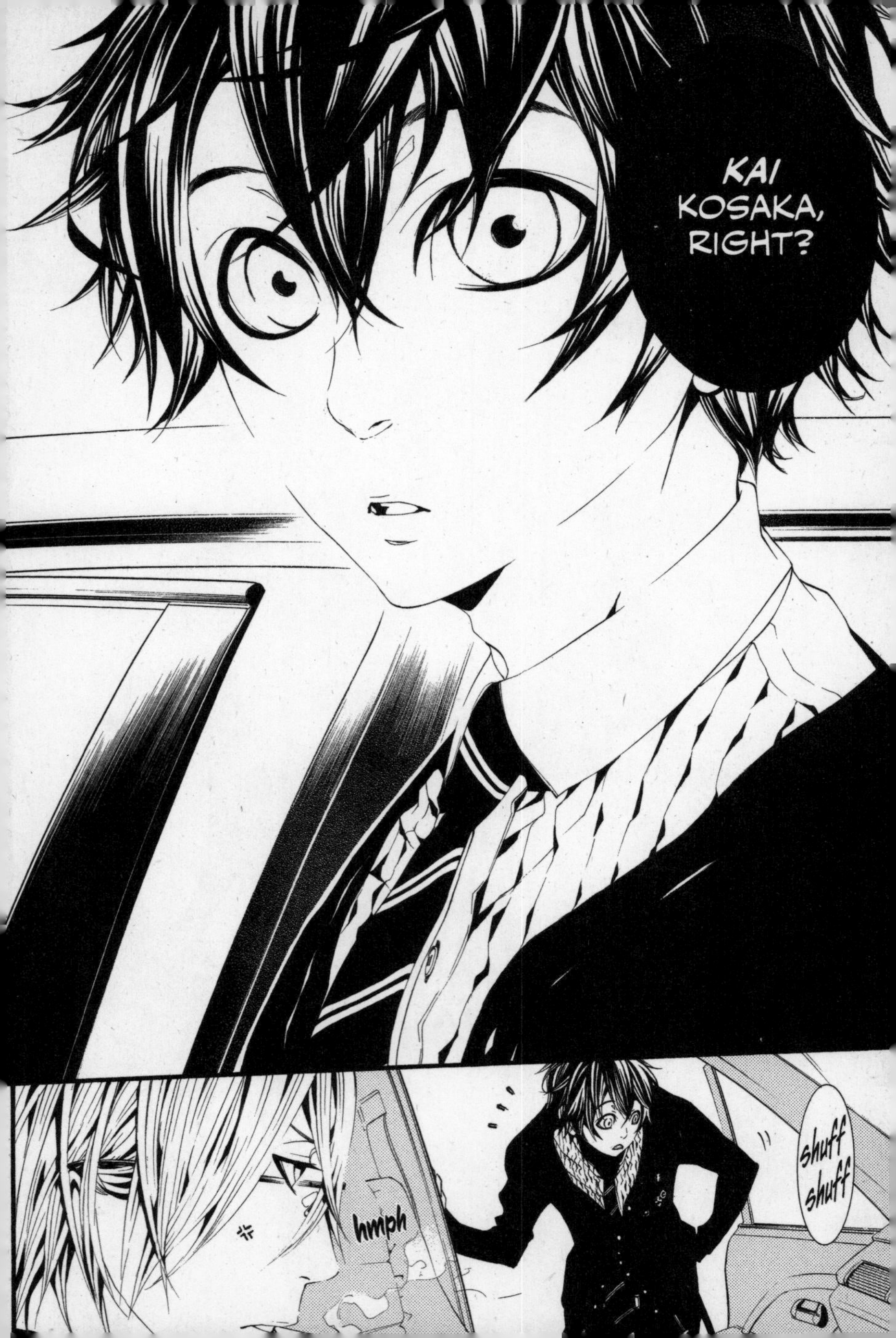
KAI KOSAKA, RIGHT?
shuff shuff
...
hmph

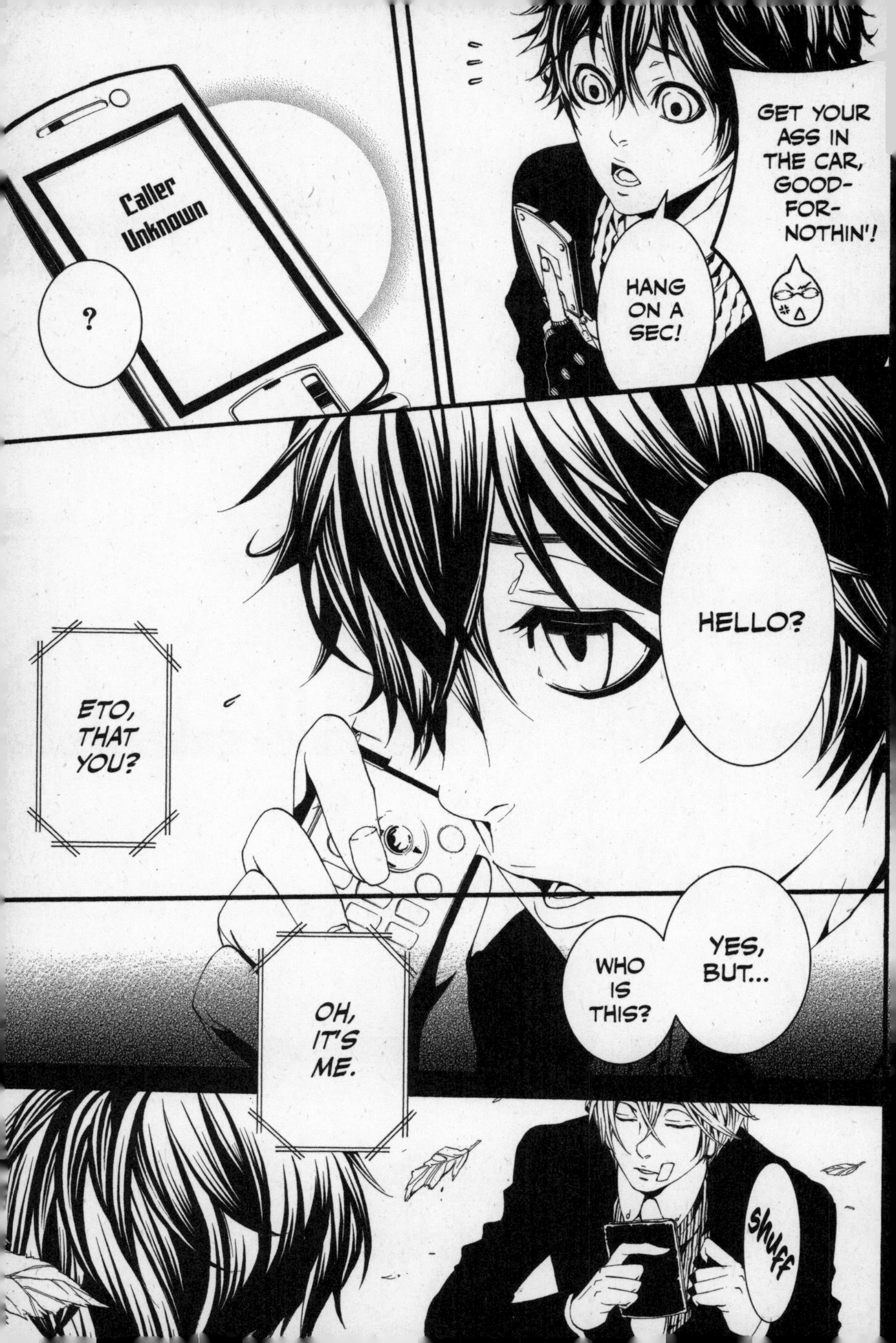
GET YOUR ASS IN THE CAR, GOOD-FOR-NOTHIN'!
HANG ON A SEC!
Caller Unknown
?
HELLO?
ETO, THAT YOU?
YES, BUT...
WHO IS THIS?
OH, IT'S ME.
shuff

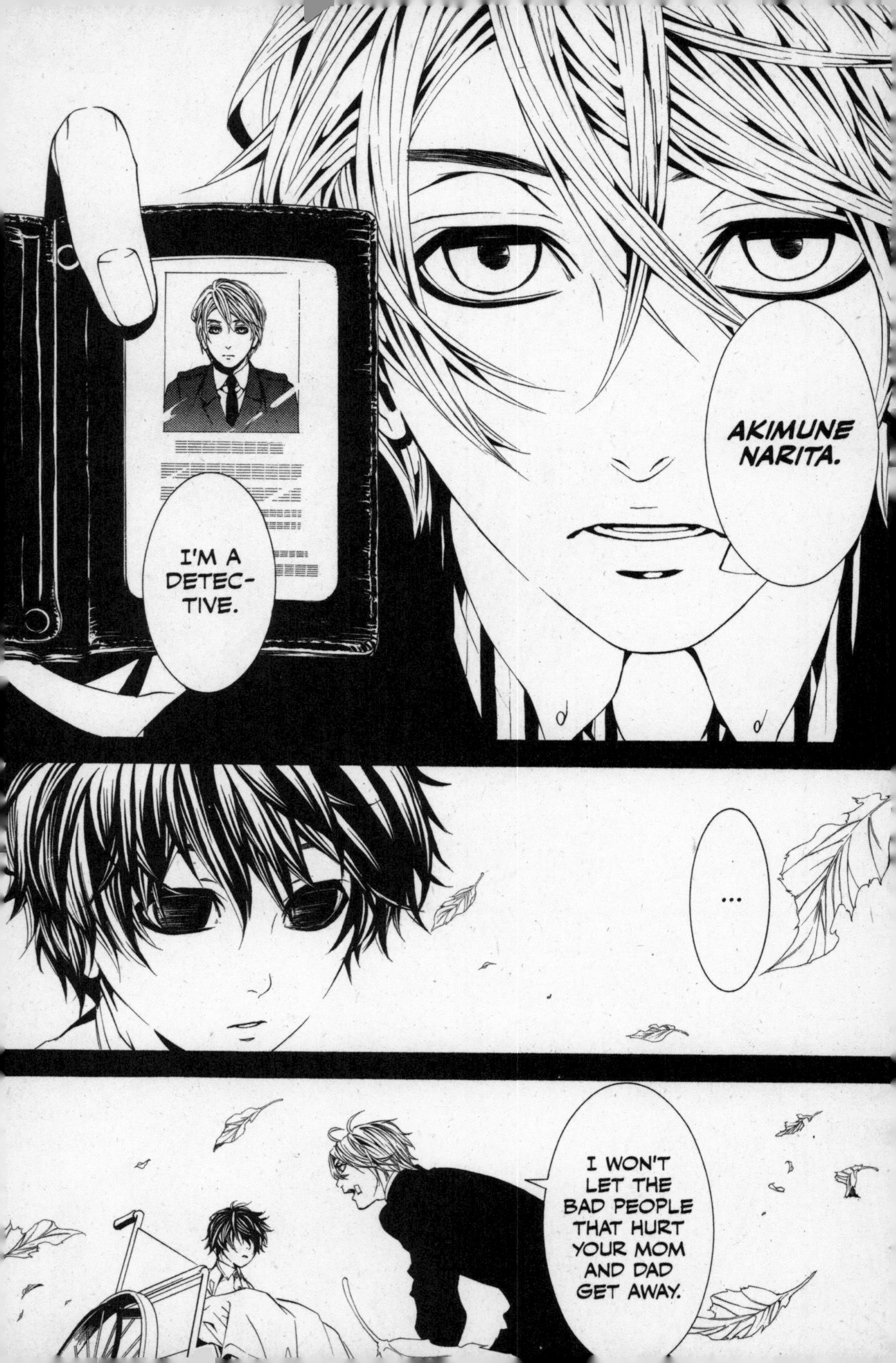
AKIMUNE NARITA.
I'M A DETECTIVE.
...
I WON'T LET THE BAD PEOPLE THAT HURT YOUR MOM AND DAD GET AWAY.

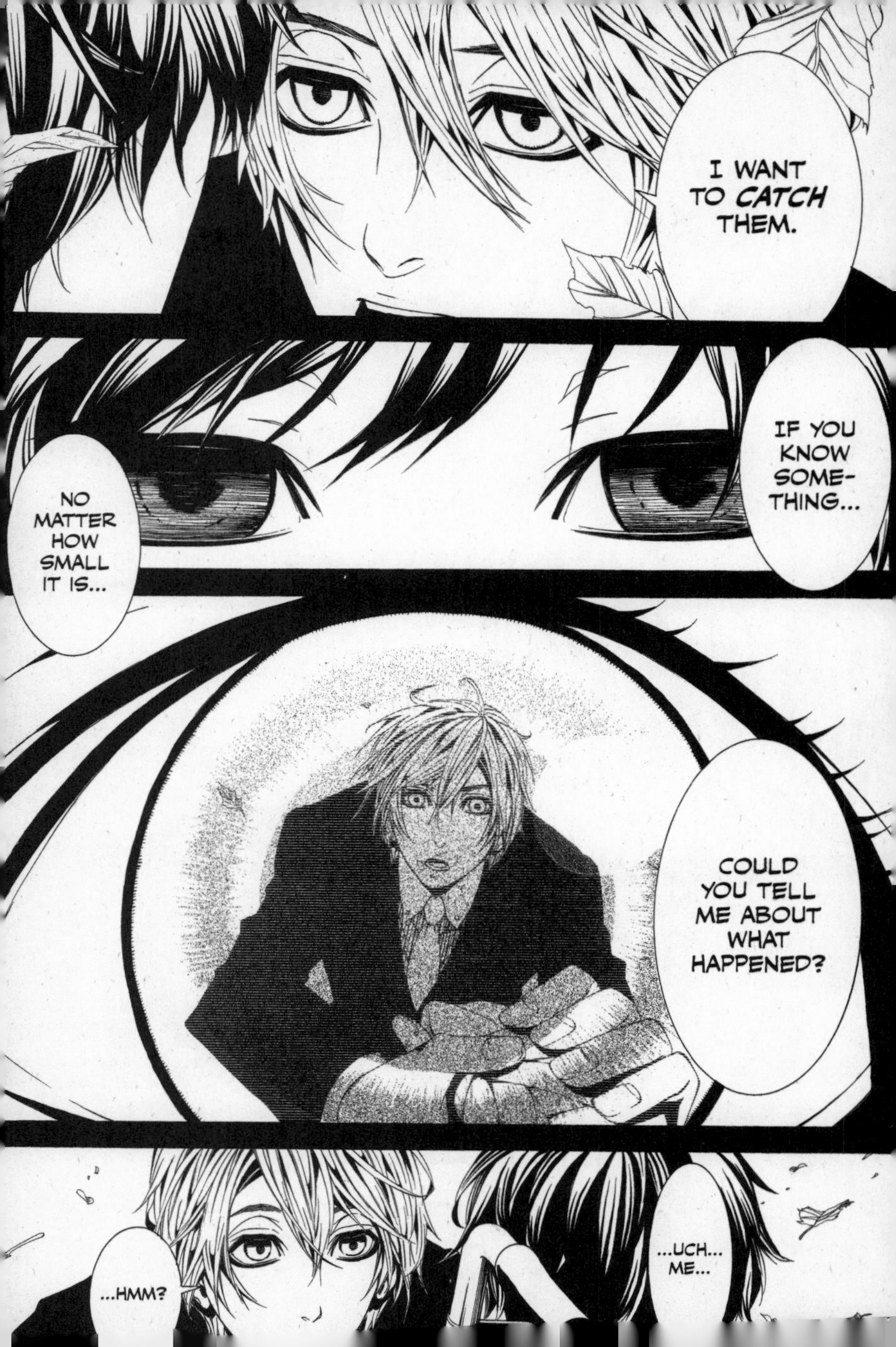
I WANT TO *CATCH* THEM.
IF YOU KNOW SOME-THING...
NO MATTER HOW SMALL IT IS...
COULD YOU TELL ME ABOUT WHAT HAPPENED?
...UCH... ME...
...HMM?

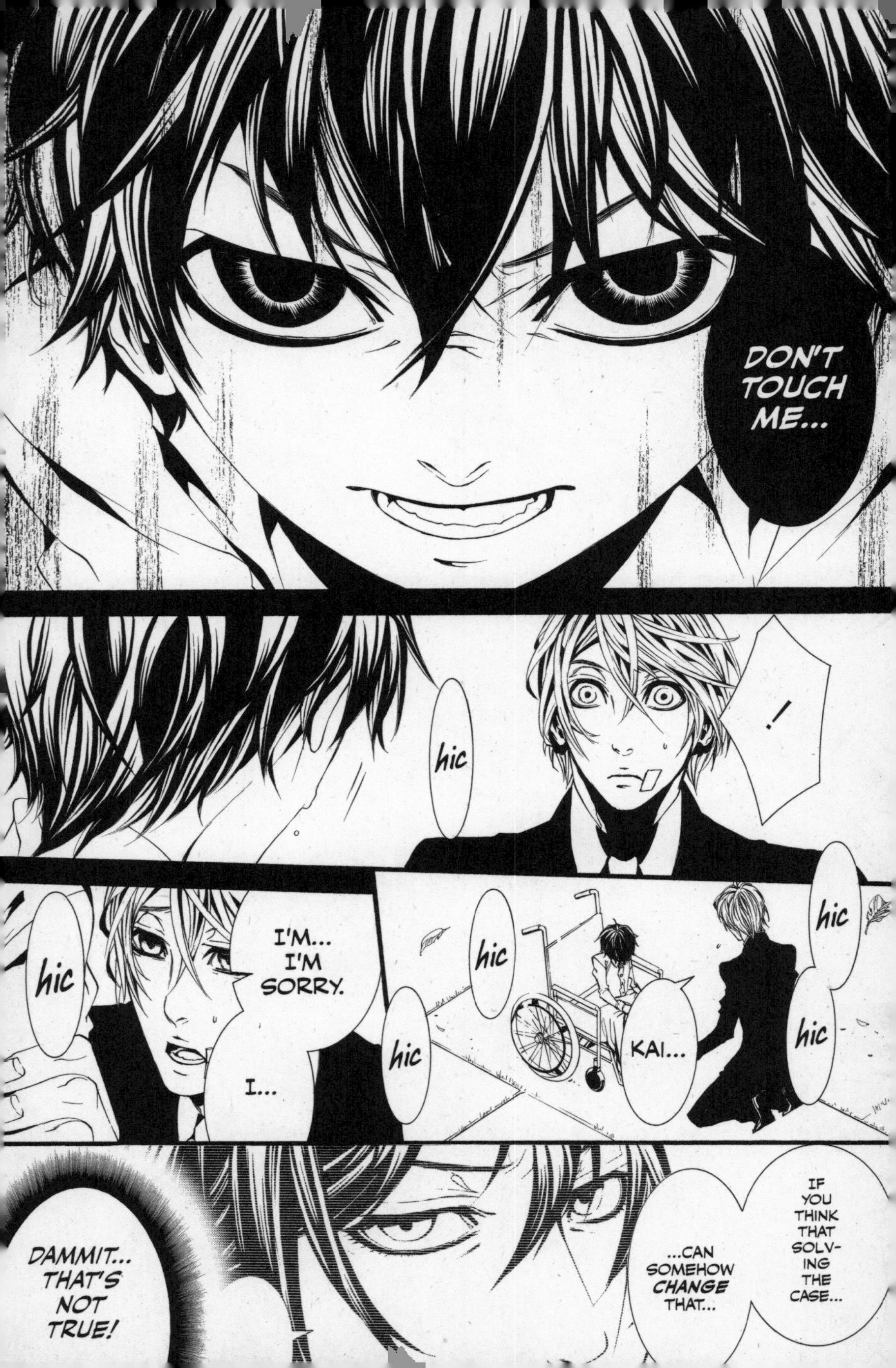
DON'T TOUCH ME...
!
hic
hic
hic
hic
KAI...
hic
I'M... I'M SORRY.
hic
I...
IF YOU THINK THAT SOLV-ING THE CASE...
...CAN SOMEHOW CHANGE THAT...
DAMMIT... THAT'S NOT TRUE!

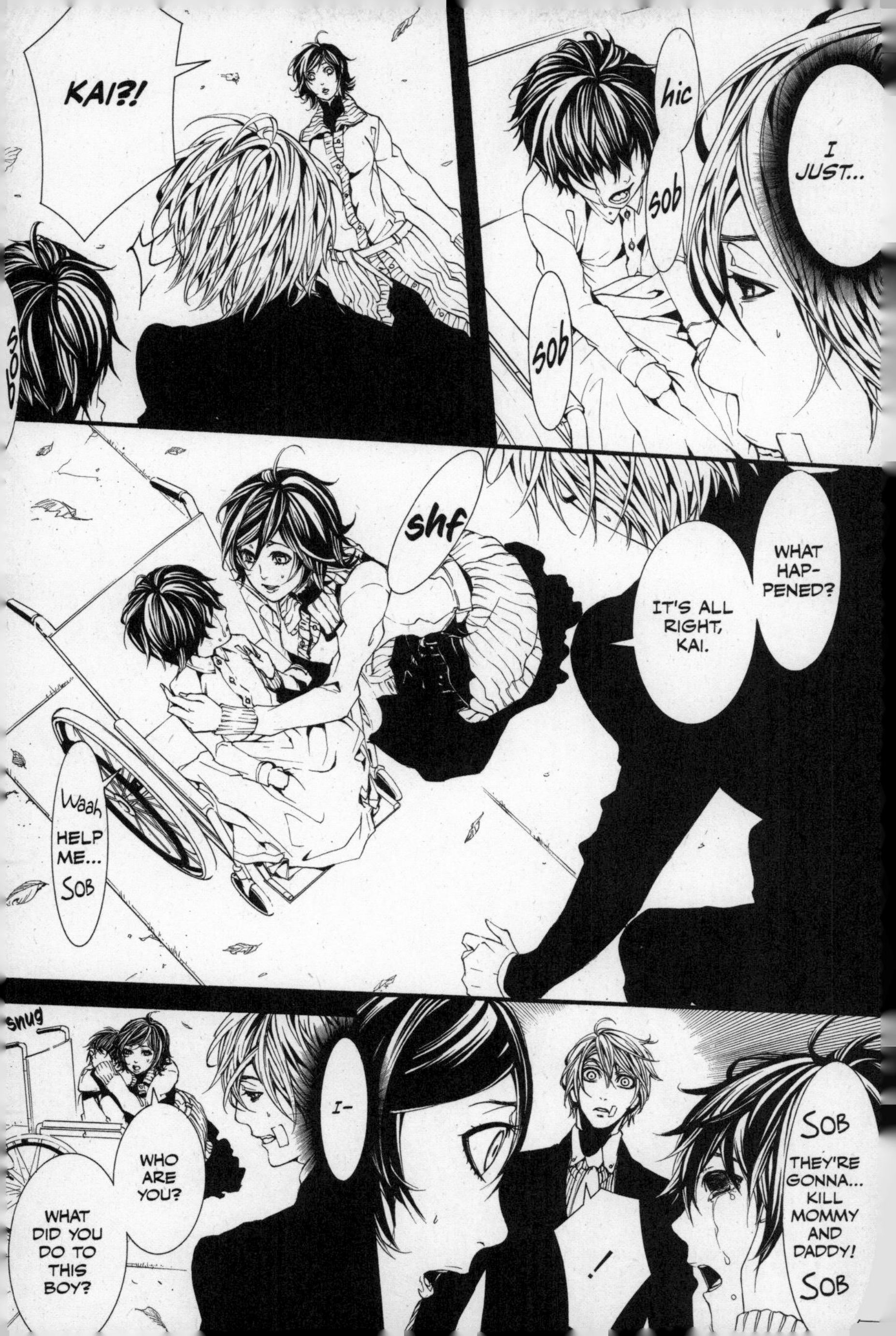
I JUST...
hic
sob
sob
KAI?!
sob
WHAT HAP-PENED?
IT'S ALL RIGHT, KAI.
shf
Waah HELP ME... SOB
SOB THEY'RE GONNA... KILL MOMMY AND DADDY! SOB
!
I-
WHO ARE YOU?
WHAT DID YOU DO TO THIS BOY?
snug

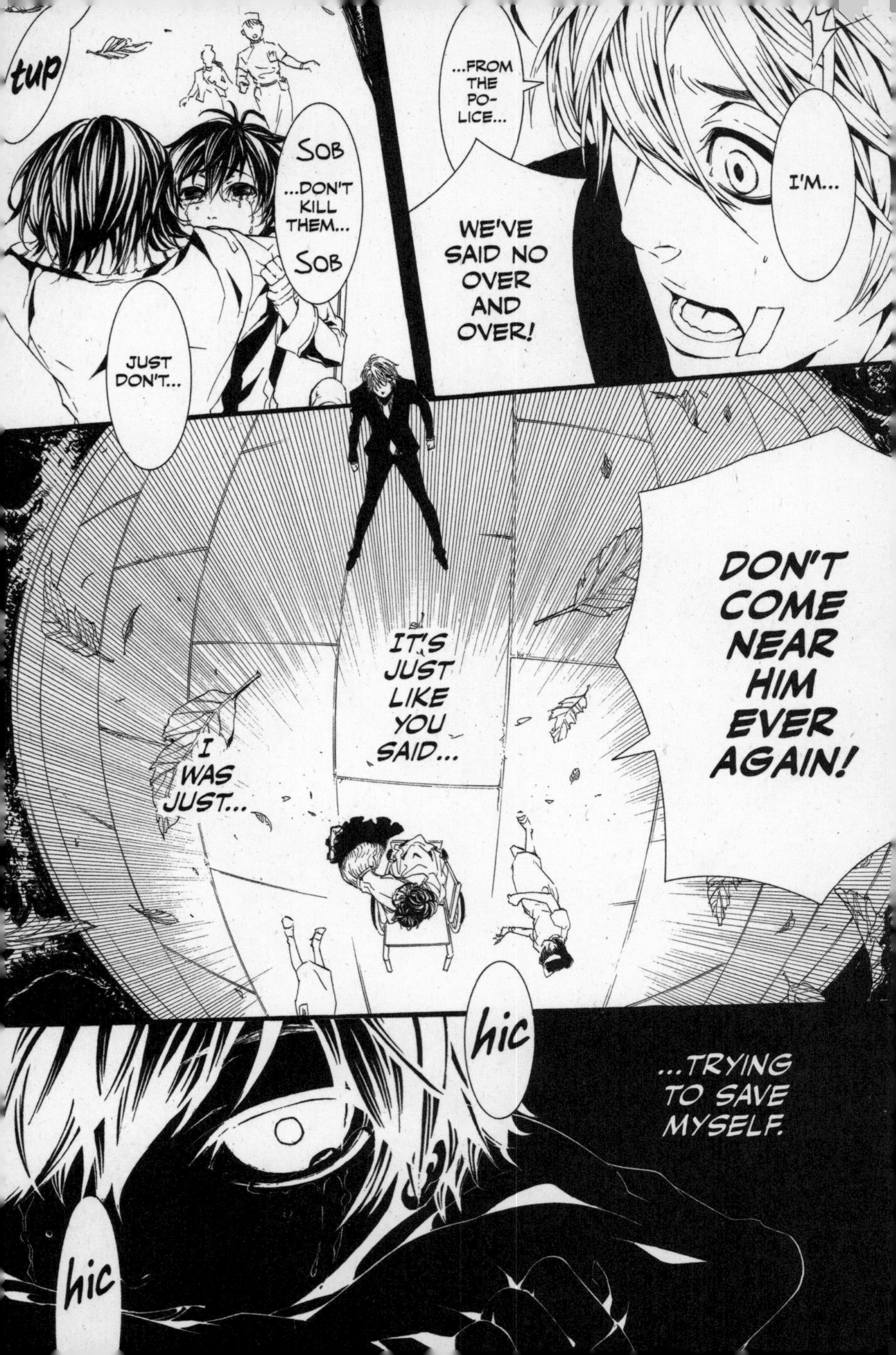
I'M...
...FROM THE POLICE...
WE'VE SAID NO OVER AND OVER!
tup
SOB
...DON'T KILL THEM...
SOB
JUST DON'T...
DON'T COME NEAR HIM EVER AGAIN!
IT'S JUST LIKE YOU SAID...
I WAS JUST...
hic
...TRYING TO SAVE MYSELF.
hic

switch

naked ape : Saki Otoh & Nakamura Tomomi

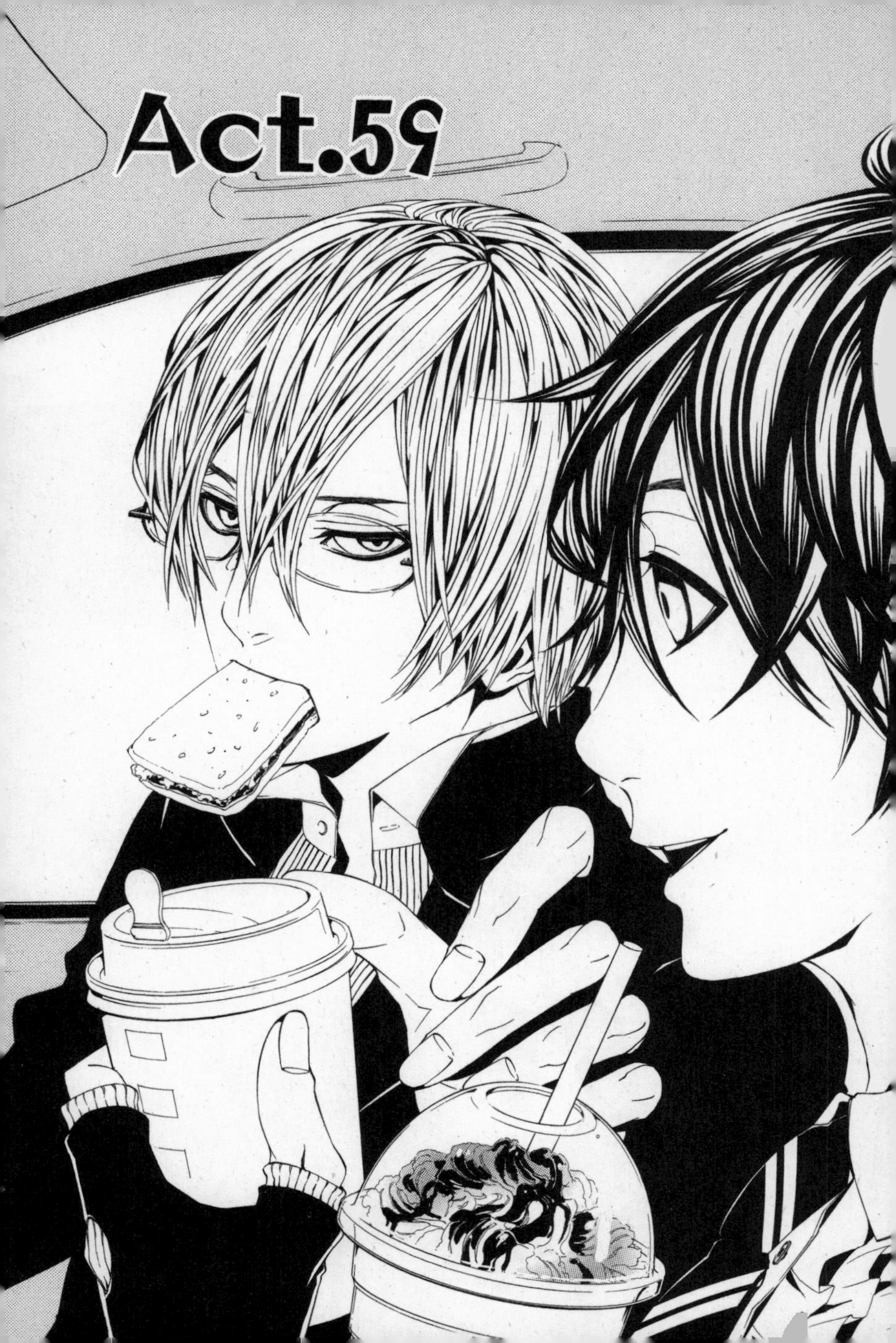
Act.59

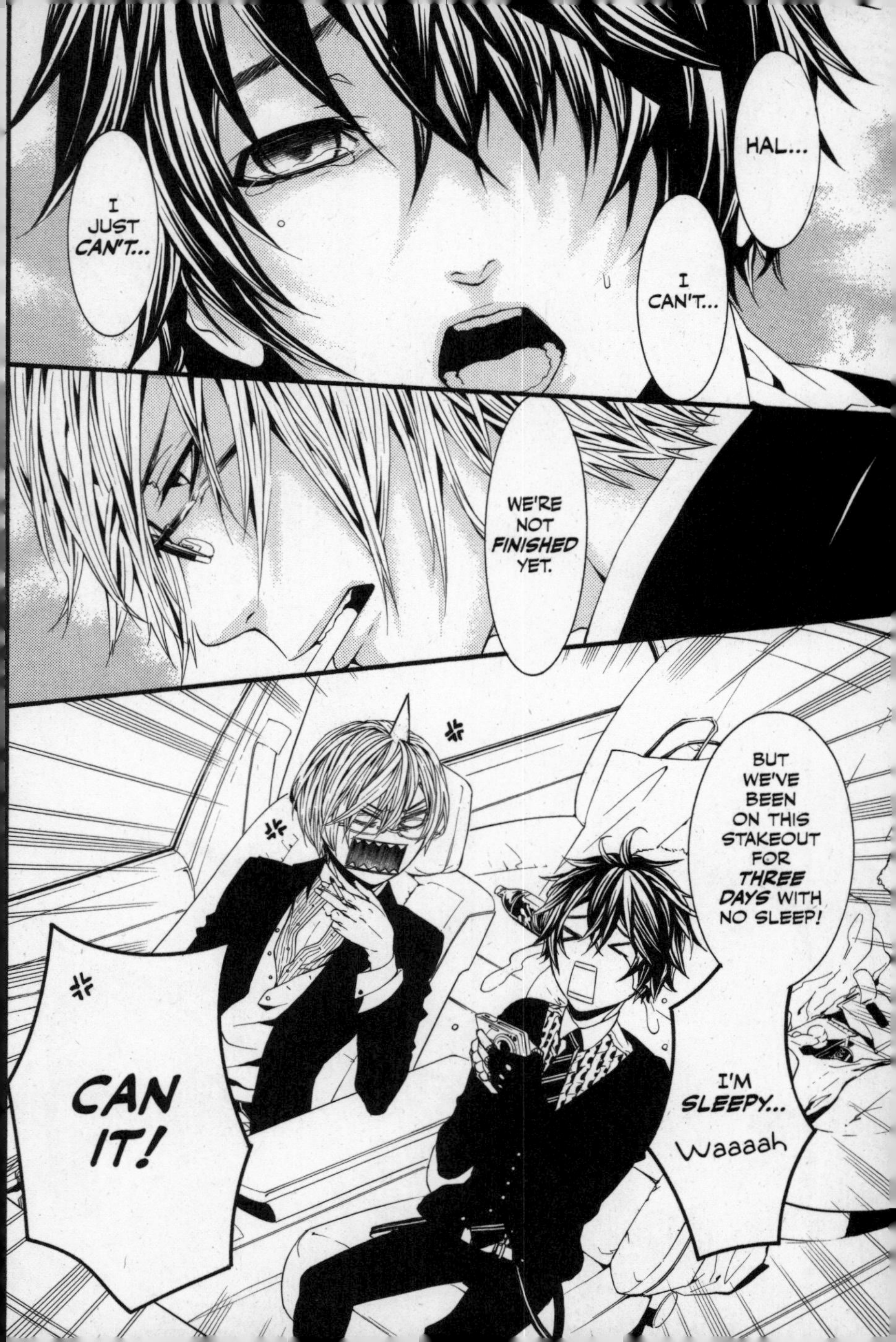
HAL...
I CAN'T...
I JUST *CAN'T*...
WE'RE NOT *FINISHED* YET.
BUT WE'VE BEEN ON THIS STAKEOUT FOR *THREE DAYS* WITH NO SLEEP!
I'M *SLEEPY*...
Waaaah
CAN IT!

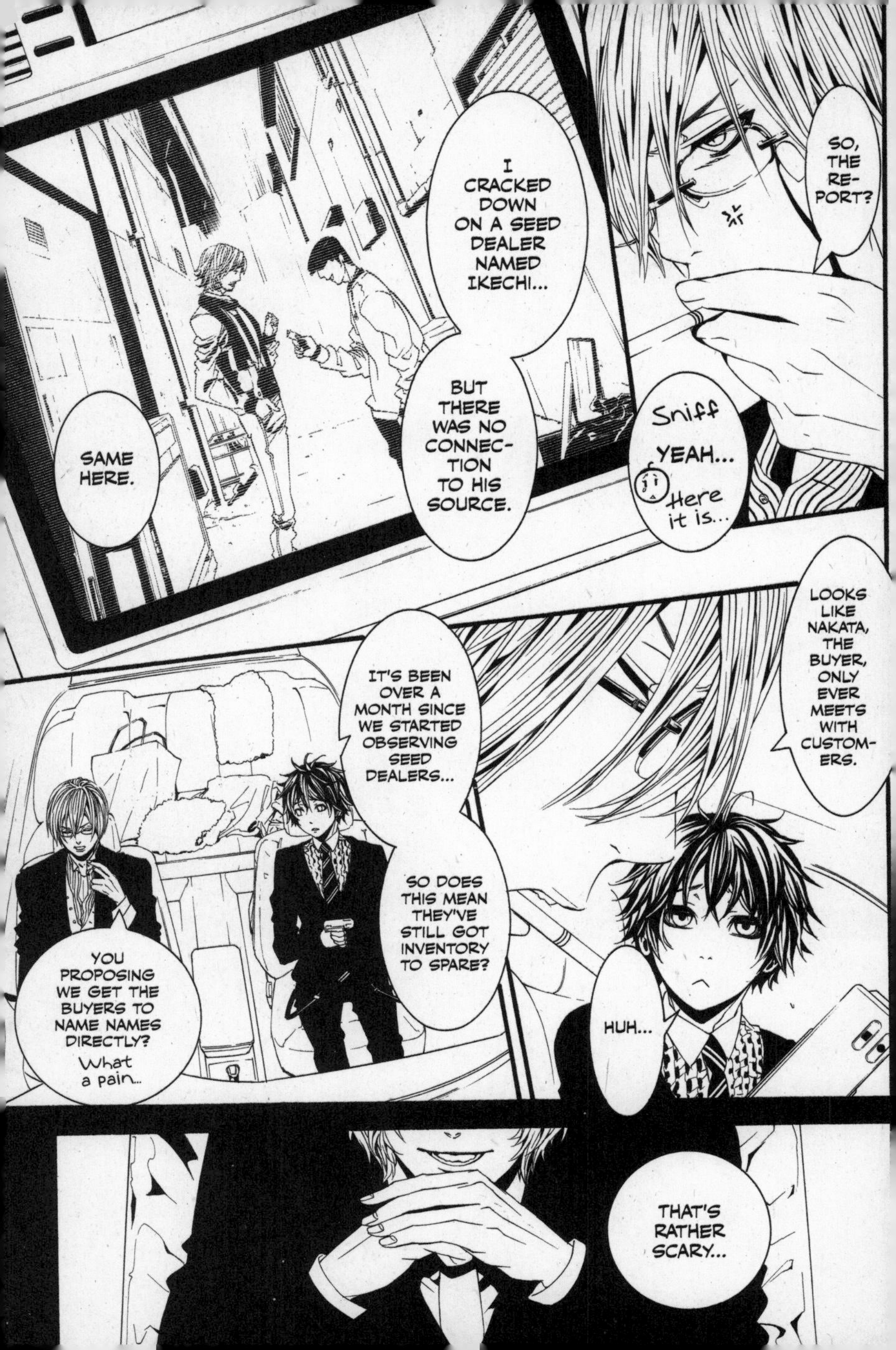
SO, THE RE-PORT?
Sniff YEAH... Here it is...
I CRACKED DOWN ON A SEED DEALER NAMED IKECHI...
BUT THERE WAS NO CONNECTION TO HIS SOURCE.
SAME HERE.
LOOKS LIKE NAKATA, THE BUYER, ONLY EVER MEETS WITH CUSTOMERS.
HUH...
IT'S BEEN OVER A MONTH SINCE WE STARTED OBSERVING SEED DEALERS...
SO DOES THIS MEAN THEY'VE STILL GOT INVENTORY TO SPARE?
YOU PROPOSING WE GET THE BUYERS TO NAME NAMES DIRECTLY? What a pain...
THAT'S RATHER SCARY...

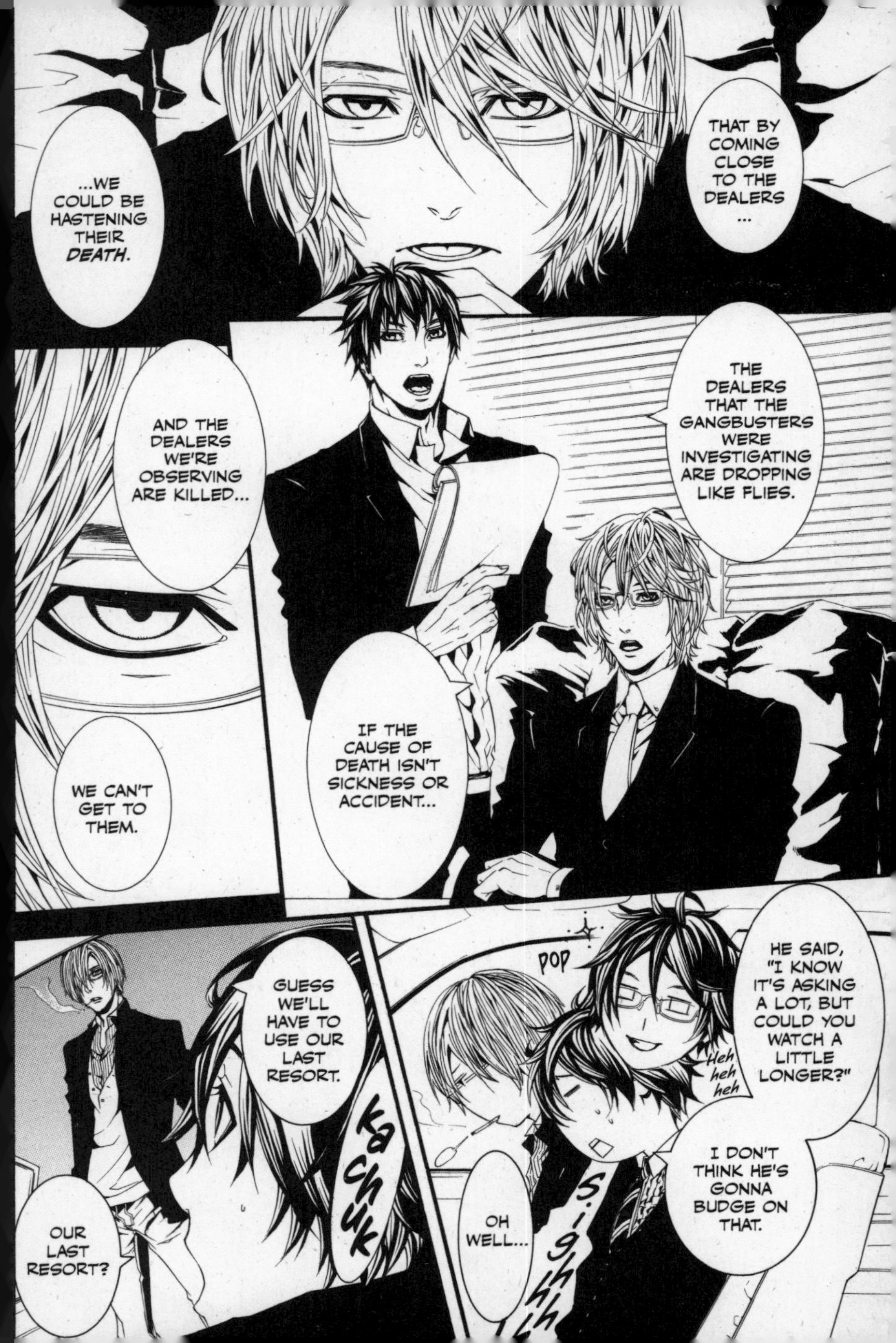
THAT BY COMING CLOSE TO THE DEALERS ...
...WE COULD BE HASTENING THEIR DEATH.
THE DEALERS THAT THE GANGBUSTERS WERE INVESTIGATING ARE DROPPING LIKE FLIES.
IF THE CAUSE OF DEATH ISN'T SICKNESS OR ACCIDENT...
AND THE DEALERS WE'RE OBSERVING ARE KILLED...
WE CAN'T GET TO THEM.
POP
HE SAID, "I KNOW IT'S ASKING A LOT, BUT COULD YOU WATCH A LITTLE LONGER?"
Heh heh heh
I DON'T THINK HE'S GONNA BUDGE ON THAT.
OH WELL...
Sighhh
GUESS WE'LL HAVE TO USE OUR LAST RESORT.
kachuk
OUR LAST RESORT?

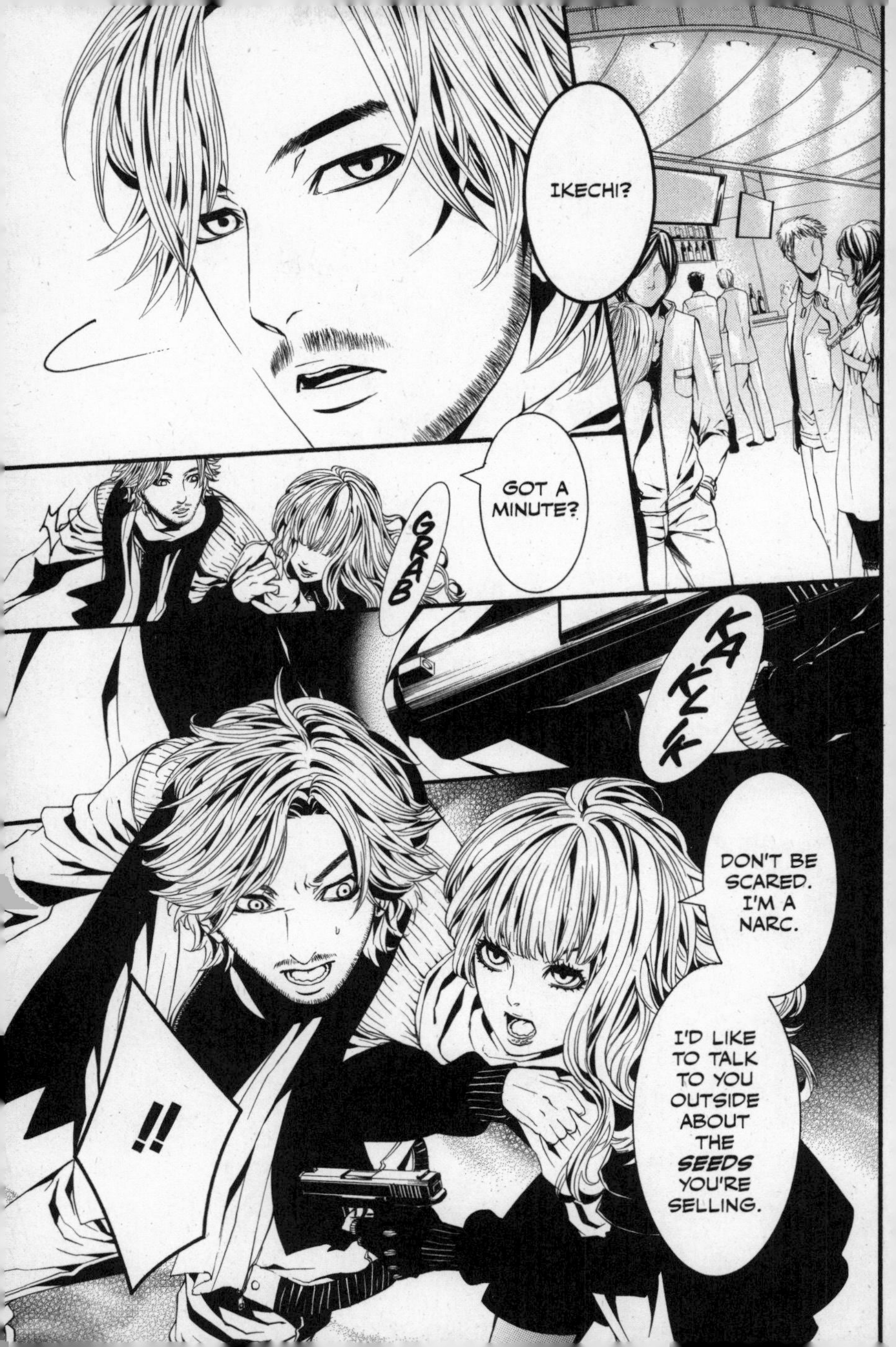

IKECHI?
GOT A MINUTE?
GRAB
KA-KLIK
DON'T BE SCARED. I'M A NARC.
I'D LIKE TO TALK TO YOU OUTSIDE ABOUT THE *SEEDS* YOU'RE SELLING.
!!

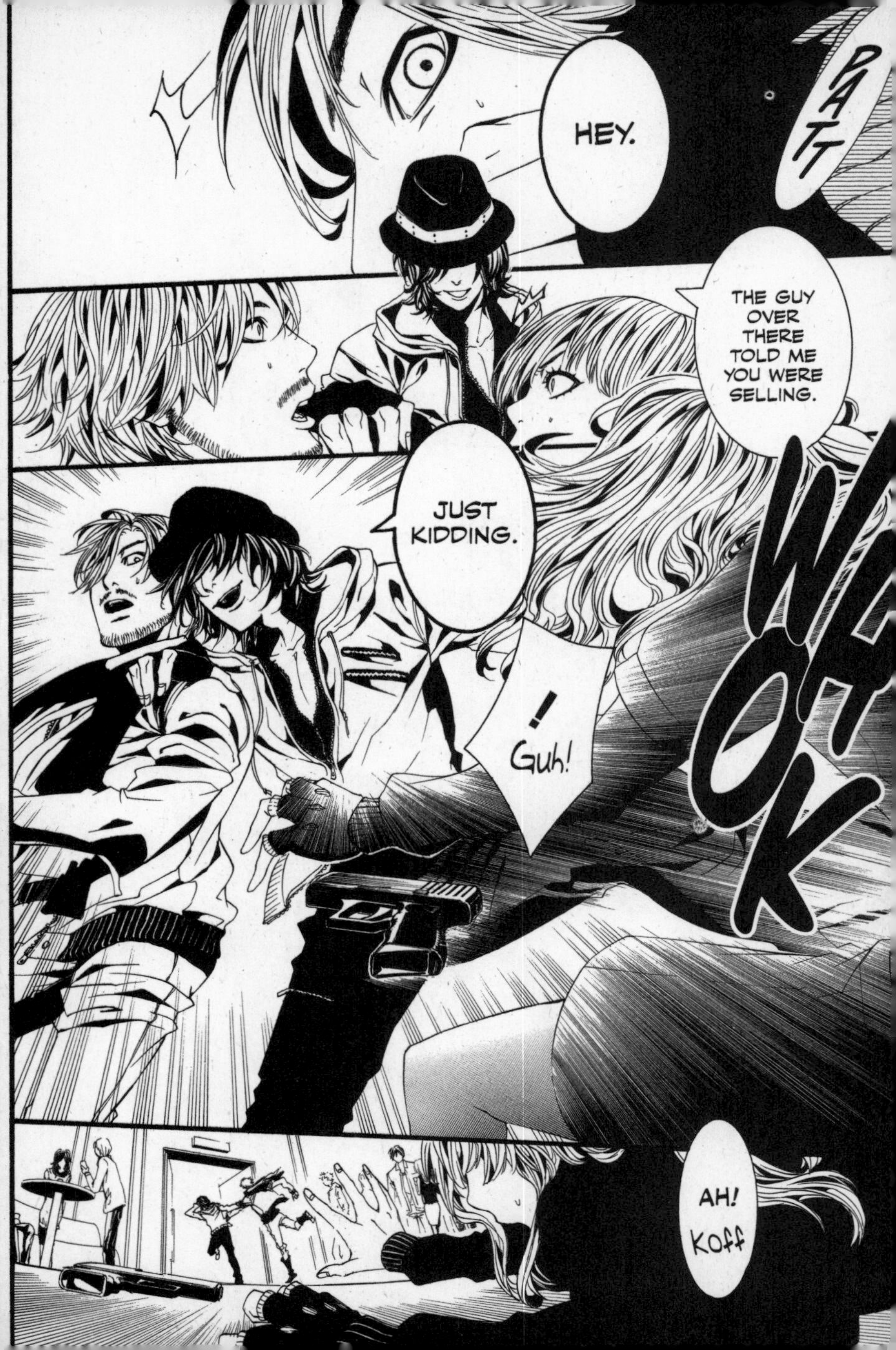
PATT
HEY.
THE GUY OVER THERE TOLD ME YOU WERE SELLING.
JUST KIDDING.
WHOCK
! Guh!
AH! Koff

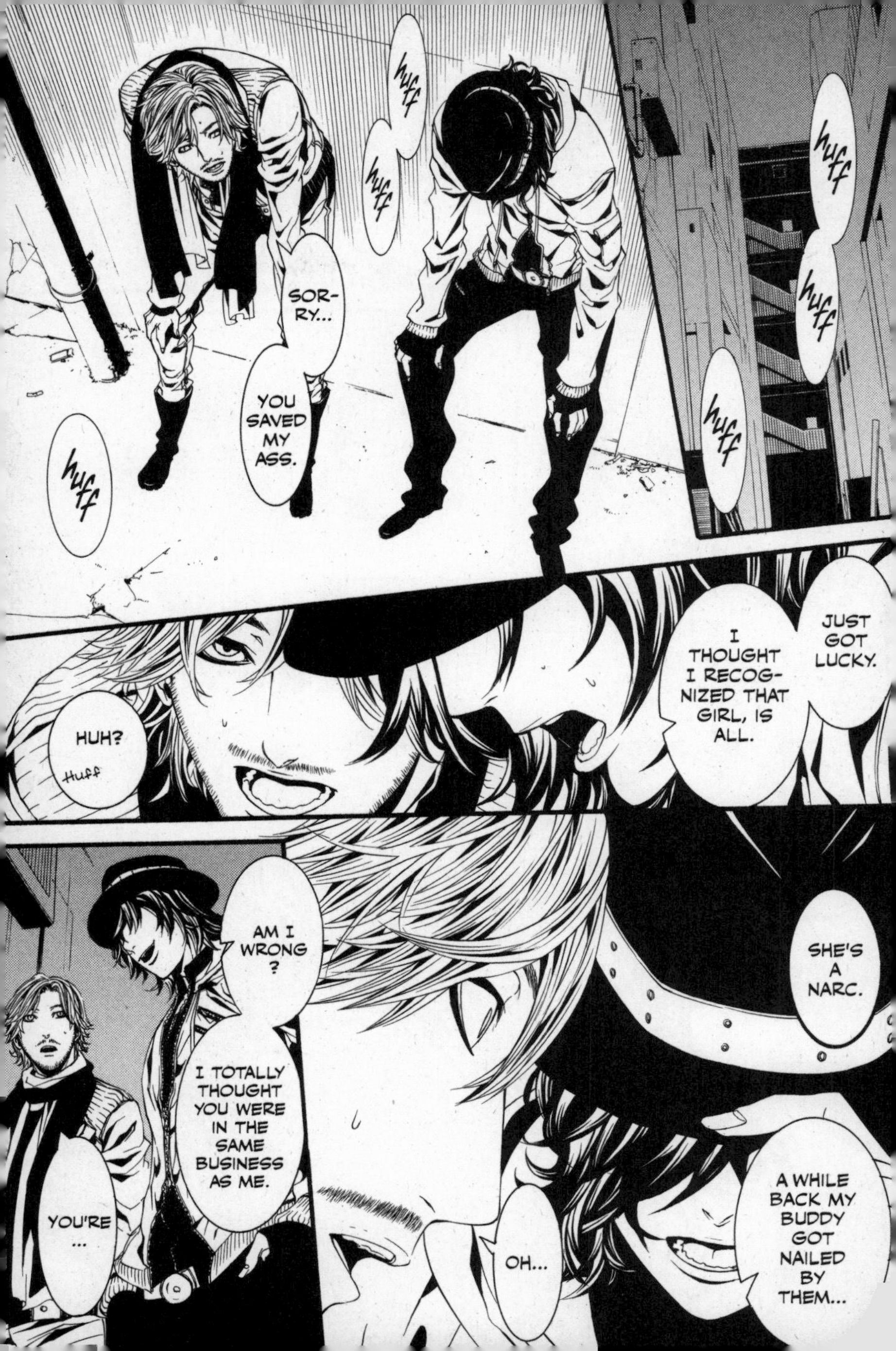
huff
huff
huff
huff
huff
SOR-RY...
YOU SAVED MY ASS.
huff
JUST GOT LUCKY.
I THOUGHT I RECOG-NIZED THAT GIRL, IS ALL.
HUH?
Huff
SHE'S A NARC.
A WHILE BACK MY BUDDY GOT NAILED BY THEM...
OH...
AM I WRONG?
I TOTALLY THOUGHT YOU WERE IN THE SAME BUSINESS AS ME.
YOU'RE ...

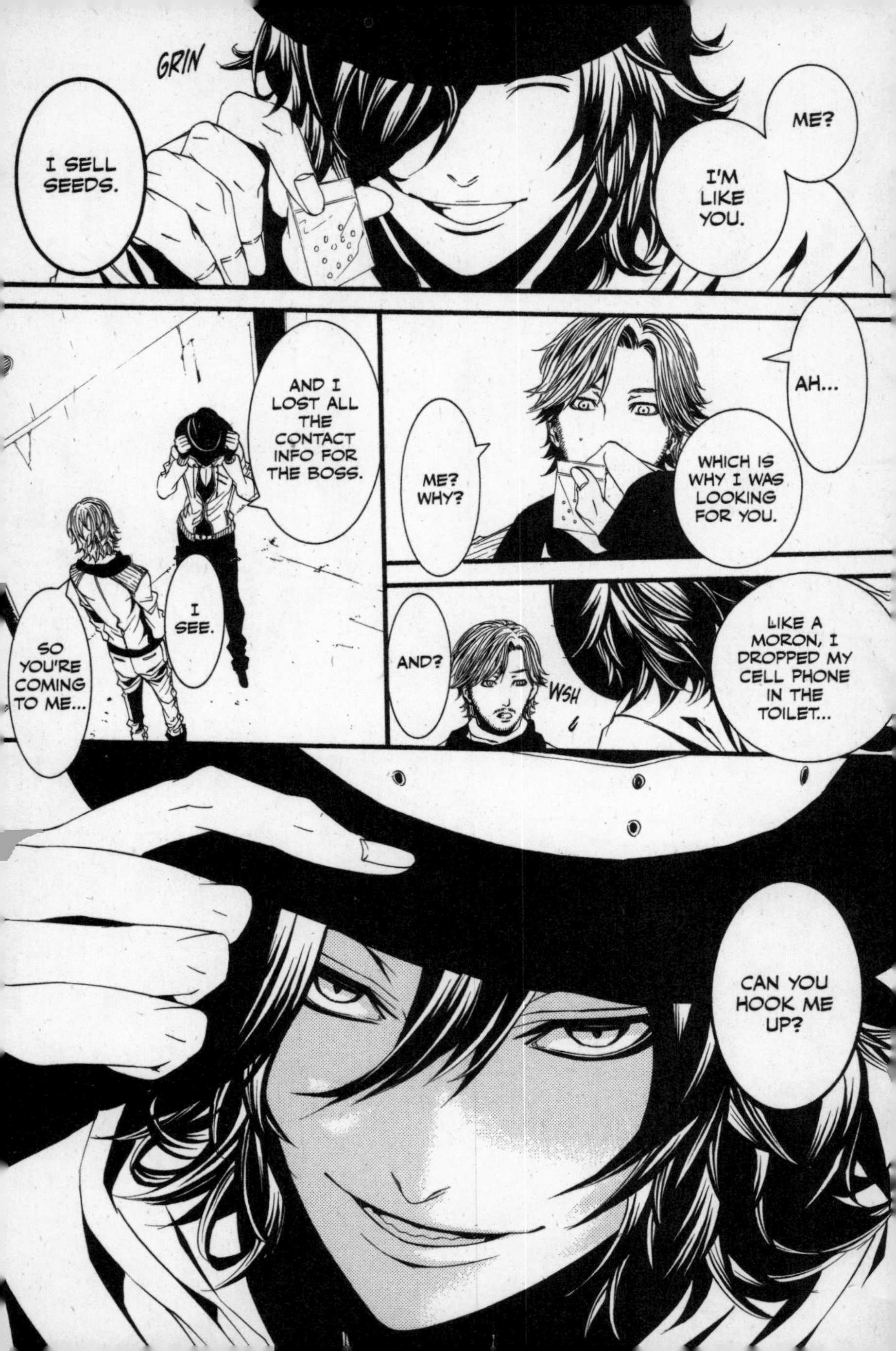
ME?
I'M LIKE YOU.
GRIN
I SELL SEEDS.
AH...
WHICH IS WHY I WAS LOOKING FOR YOU.
ME? WHY?
LIKE A MORON, I DROPPED MY CELL PHONE IN THE TOILET...
WSH
AND?
AND I LOST ALL THE CONTACT INFO FOR THE BOSS.
I SEE.
SO YOU'RE COMING TO ME...
CAN YOU HOOK ME UP?

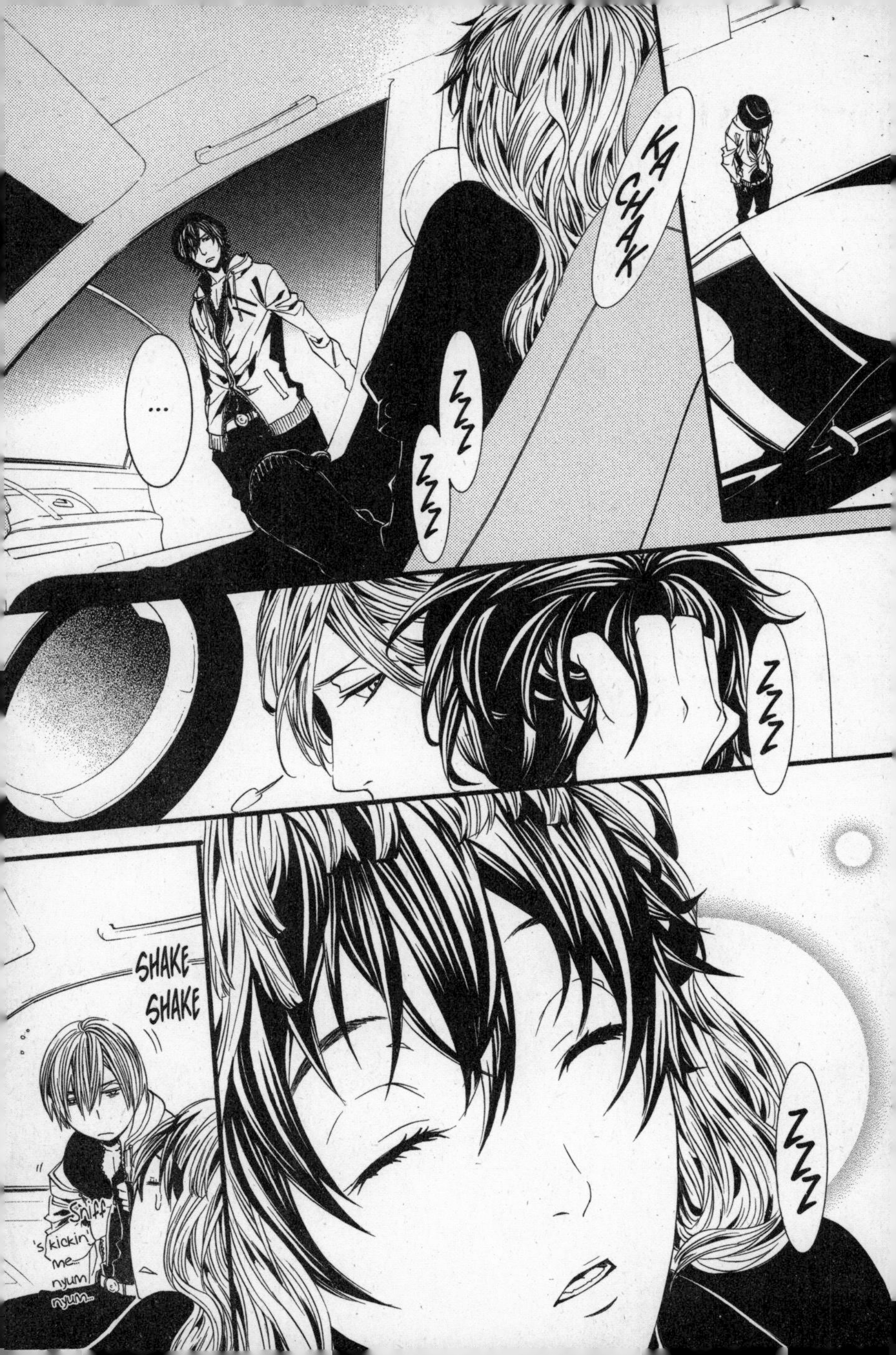
KA CHAK
ZZZ
ZZZ
...
ZZZ
ZZZ
SHAKE SHAKE
Sniff
'S kickin' me... nyum nyum...

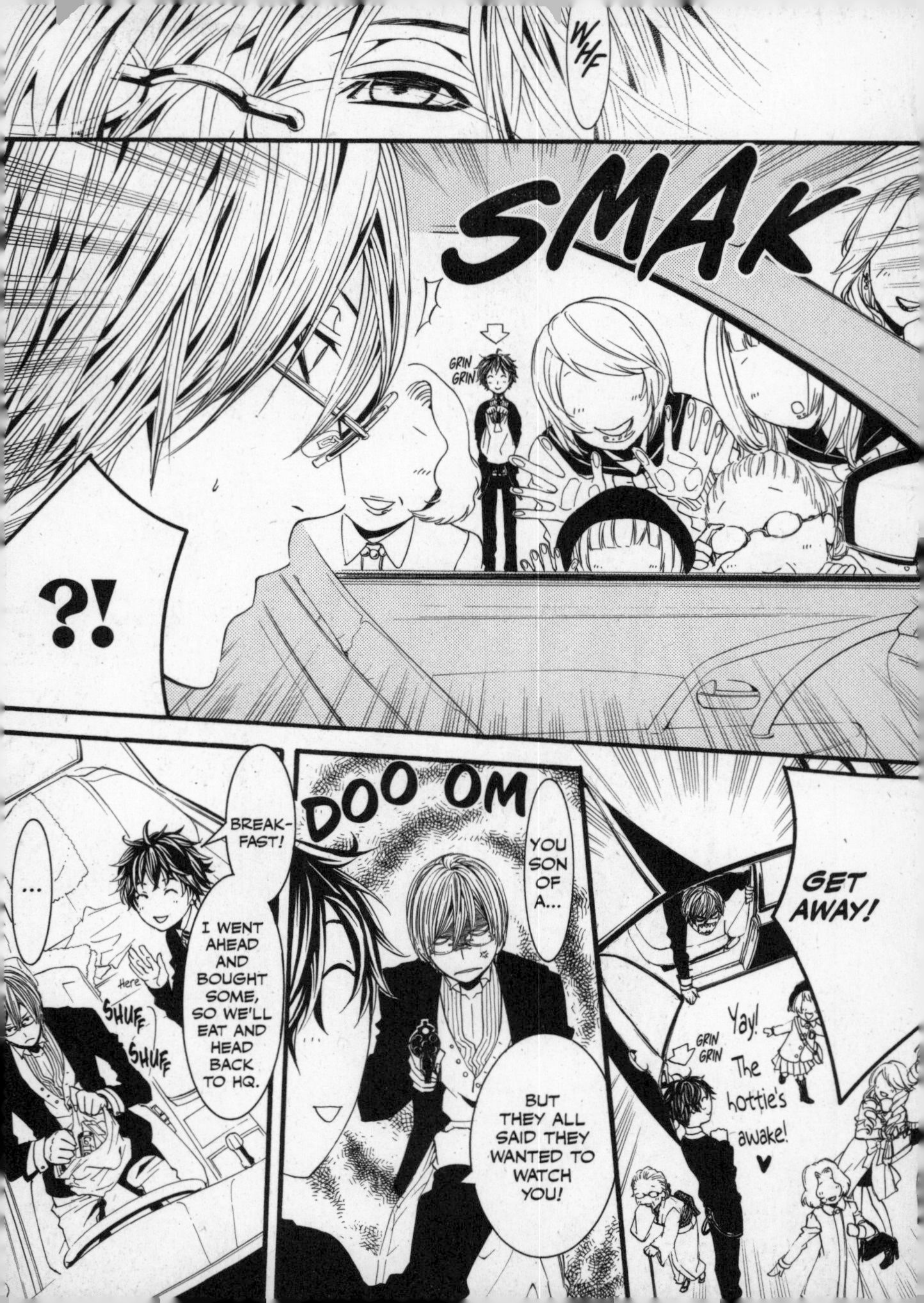
WHF
SMAK
GRIN GRIN
?!
GET AWAY!
GRIN GRIN
Yay! The hottie's awake! ♥
DOO OM
YOU SON OF A...
BUT THEY ALL SAID THEY WANTED TO WATCH YOU!
BREAK-FAST!
...
I WENT AHEAD AND BOUGHT SOME, SO WE'LL EAT AND HEAD BACK TO HQ.
Here
SHUFF SHUFF

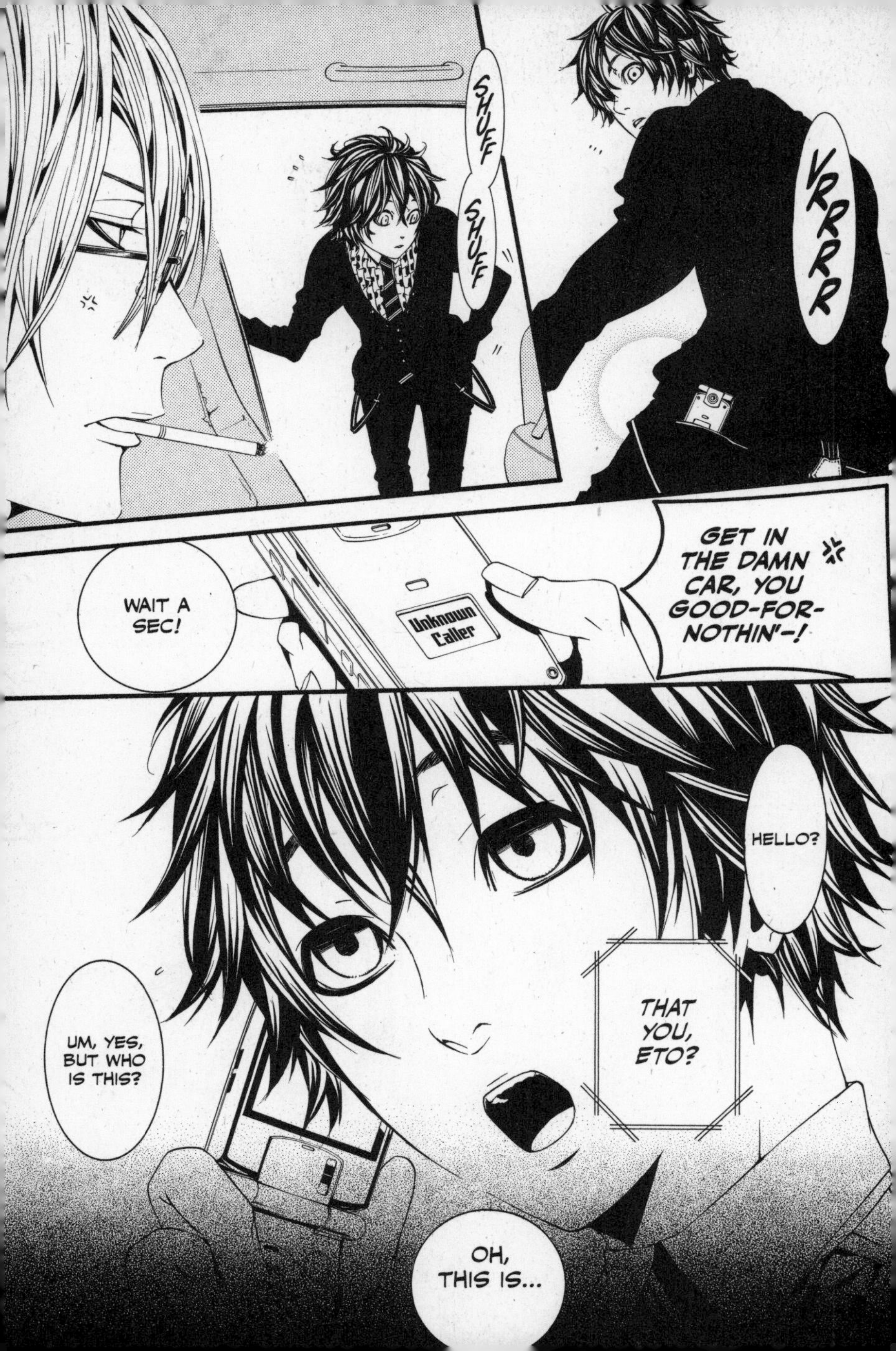
VRRRR
SHUFF
SHUFF
GET IN THE DAMN CAR, YOU GOOD-FOR-NOTHIN'-!
Unknown Caller
WAIT A SEC!
HELLO?
THAT YOU, ETO?
UM, YES, BUT WHO IS THIS?
OH, THIS IS...

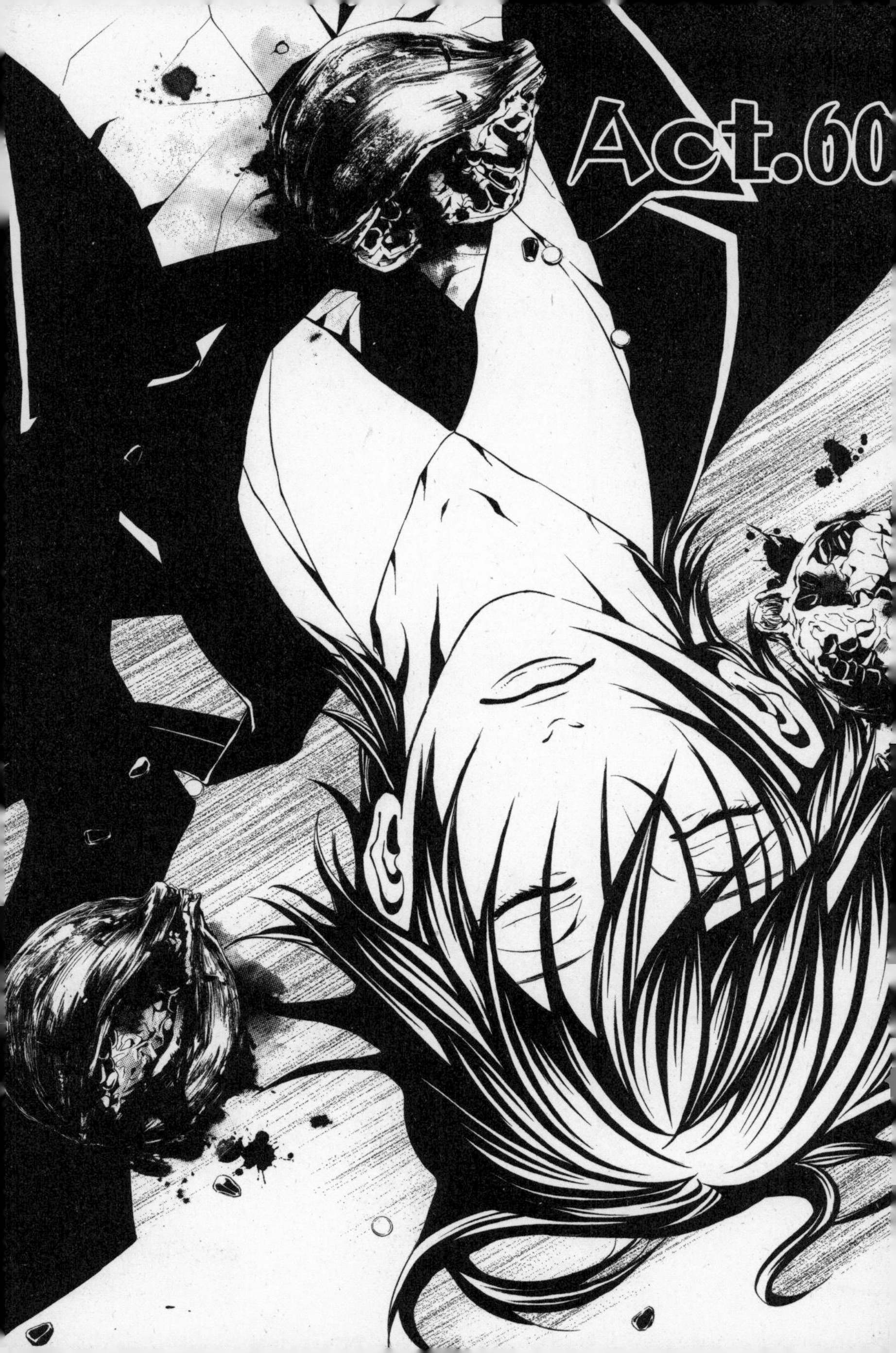
Act.60

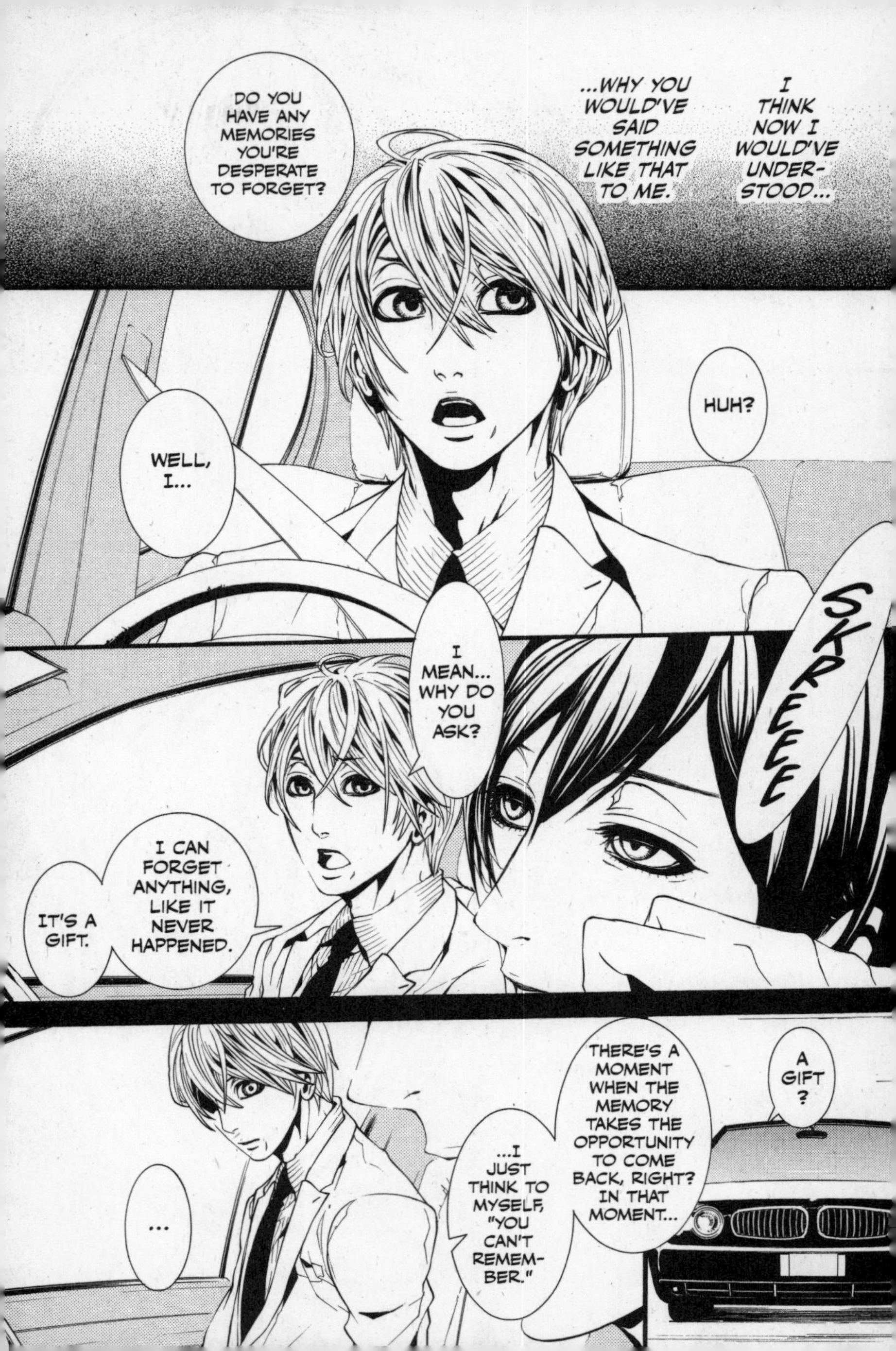
I THINK NOW I WOULD'VE UNDER-STOOD...
...WHY YOU WOULD'VE SAID SOMETHING LIKE THAT TO ME.
DO YOU HAVE ANY MEMORIES YOU'RE DESPERATE TO FORGET?
HUH?
WELL, I...
SKREEE
I MEAN... WHY DO YOU ASK?
I CAN FORGET ANYTHING, LIKE IT NEVER HAPPENED.
IT'S A GIFT.
A GIFT?
THERE'S A MOMENT WHEN THE MEMORY TAKES THE OPPORTUNITY TO COME BACK, RIGHT? IN THAT MOMENT...
...I JUST THINK TO MYSELF, "YOU CAN'T REMEM-BER."
...

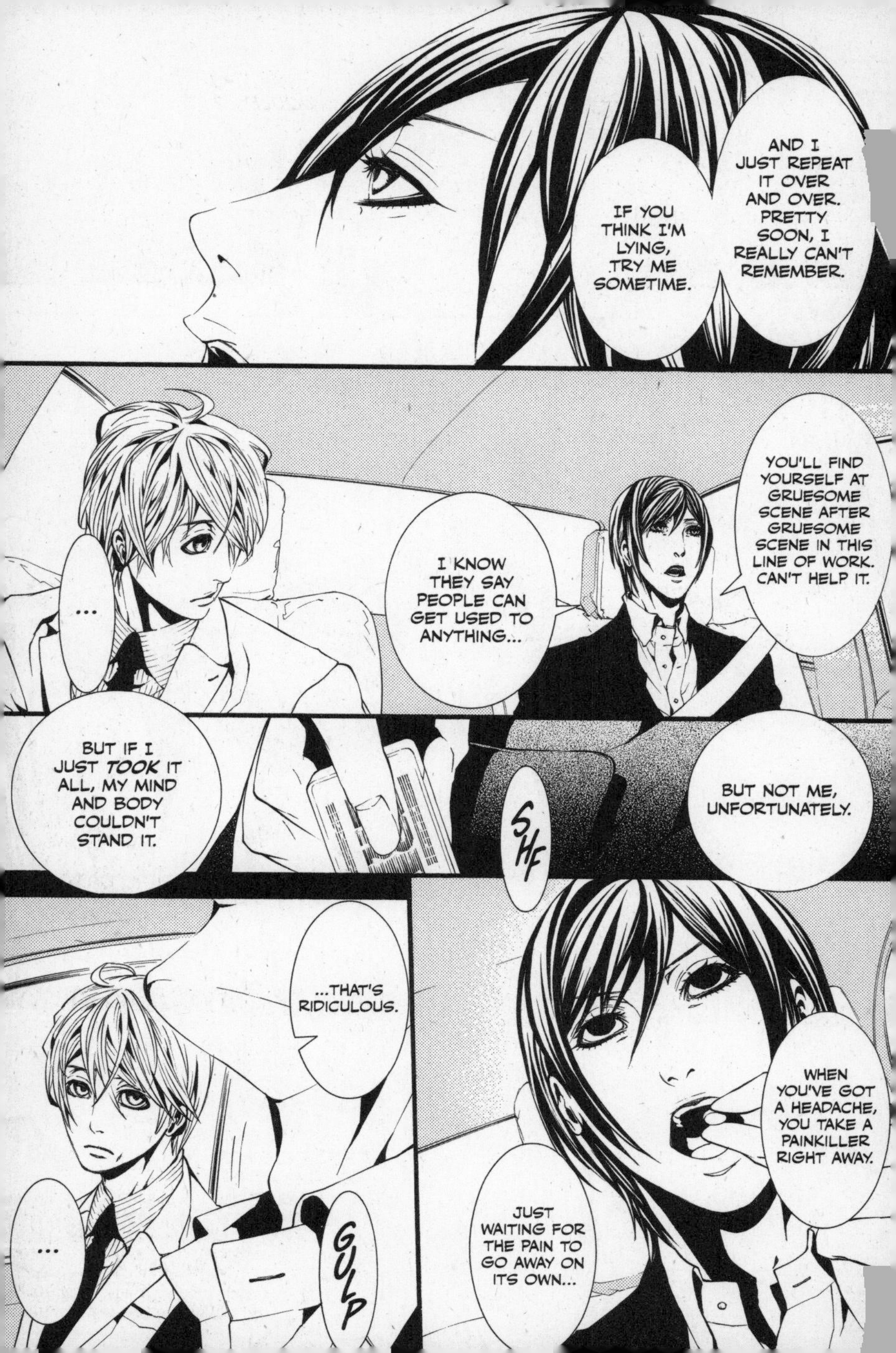
AND I JUST REPEAT IT OVER AND OVER. PRETTY SOON, I REALLY CAN'T REMEMBER.
IF YOU THINK I'M LYING, TRY ME SOMETIME.
YOU'LL FIND YOURSELF AT GRUESOME SCENE AFTER GRUESOME SCENE IN THIS LINE OF WORK. CAN'T HELP IT.
I KNOW THEY SAY PEOPLE CAN GET USED TO ANYTHING...
...
BUT NOT ME, UNFORTUNATELY.
SHF
BUT IF I JUST *TOOK* IT ALL, MY MIND AND BODY COULDN'T STAND IT.
WHEN YOU'VE GOT A HEADACHE, YOU TAKE A PAINKILLER RIGHT AWAY.
JUST WAITING FOR THE PAIN TO GO AWAY ON ITS OWN...
...THAT'S RIDICULOUS.
GULP
...

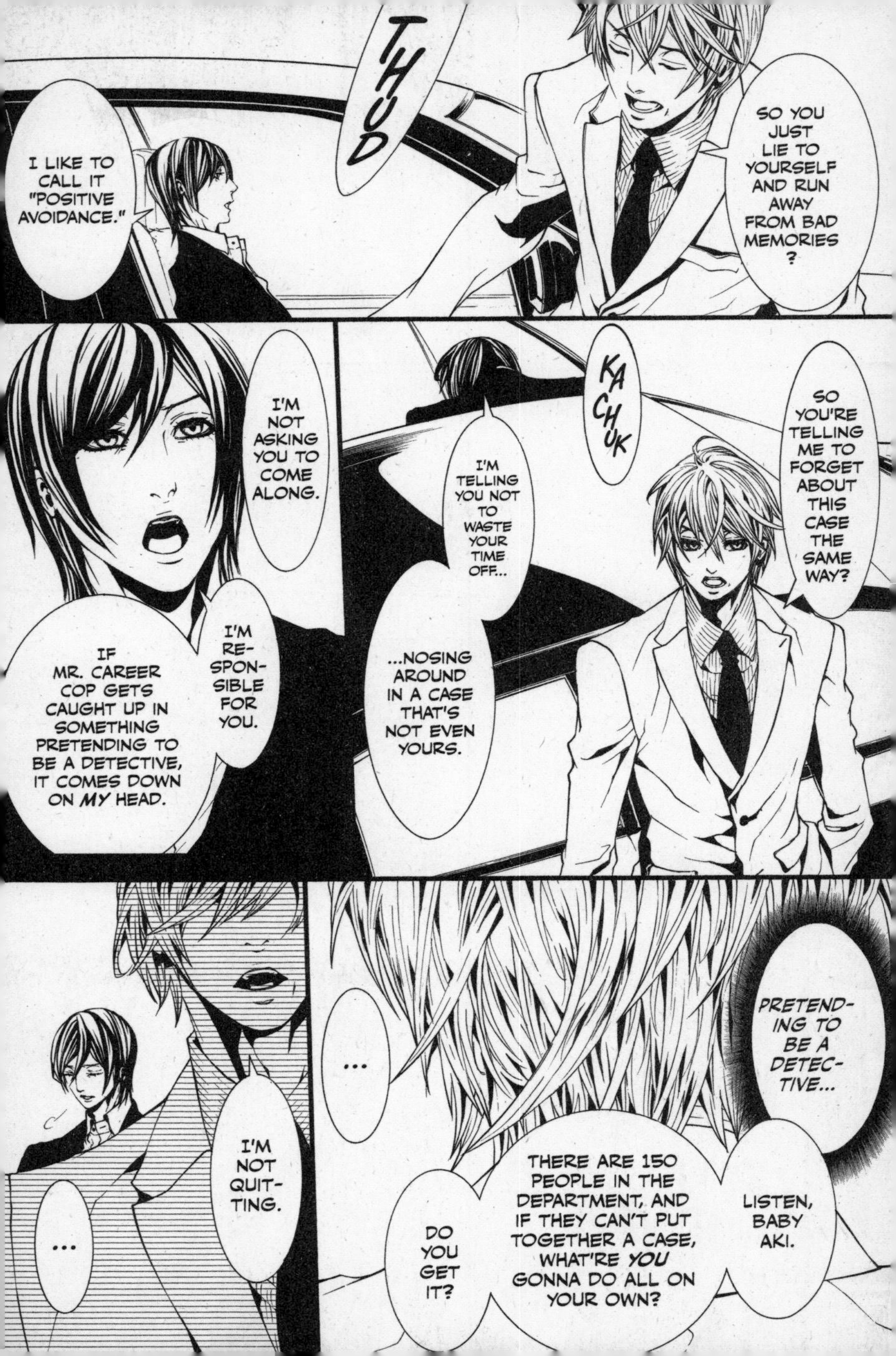
SO YOU JUST LIE TO YOURSELF AND RUN AWAY FROM BAD MEMORIES?
THUD
I LIKE TO CALL IT "POSITIVE AVOIDANCE."
SO YOU'RE TELLING ME TO FORGET ABOUT THIS CASE THE SAME WAY?
KACHUK
I'M TELLING YOU NOT TO WASTE YOUR TIME OFF...
...NOSING AROUND IN A CASE THAT'S NOT EVEN YOURS.
I'M NOT ASKING YOU TO COME ALONG.
I'M RESPONSIBLE FOR YOU.
IF MR. CAREER COP GETS CAUGHT UP IN SOMETHING PRETENDING TO BE A DETECTIVE, IT COMES DOWN ON *MY* HEAD.
PRETENDING TO BE A DETECTIVE...
...
LISTEN, BABY AKI.
THERE ARE 150 PEOPLE IN THE DEPARTMENT, AND IF THEY CAN'T PUT TOGETHER A CASE, WHAT'RE *YOU* GONNA DO ALL ON YOUR OWN?
DO YOU GET IT?
I'M NOT QUITTING.
...

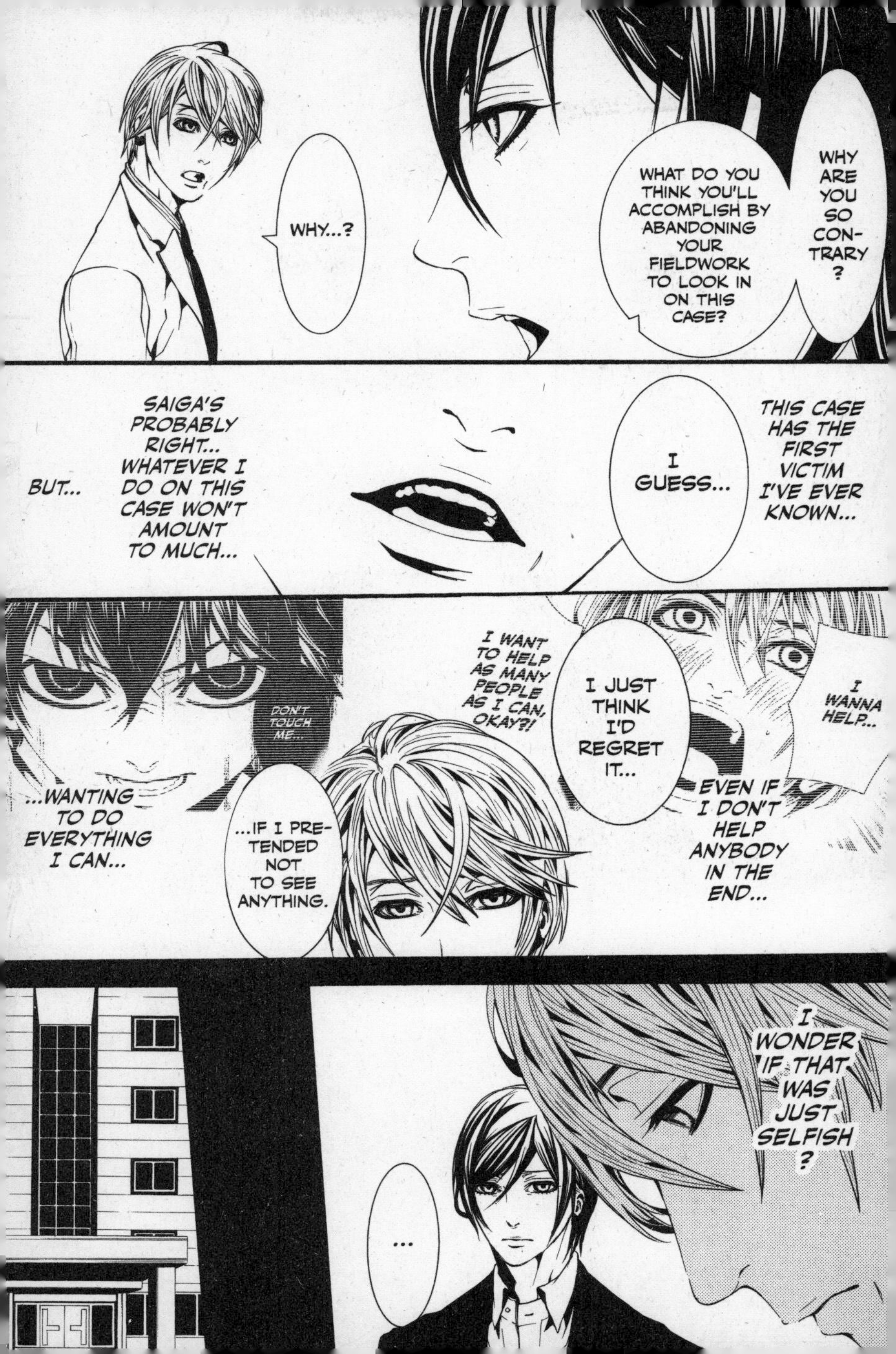
WHY ARE YOU SO CONTRARY?
WHAT DO YOU THINK YOU'LL ACCOMPLISH BY ABANDONING YOUR FIELDWORK TO LOOK IN ON THIS CASE?
WHY...?
THIS CASE HAS THE FIRST VICTIM I'VE EVER KNOWN...
I GUESS...
SAIGA'S PROBABLY RIGHT... WHATEVER I DO ON THIS CASE WON'T AMOUNT TO MUCH...
BUT...
I WANNA HELP...
EVEN IF I DON'T HELP ANYBODY IN THE END...
I JUST THINK I'D REGRET IT...
I WANT TO HELP AS MANY PEOPLE AS I CAN, OKAY?!
DON'T TOUCH ME...
...IF I PRETENDED NOT TO SEE ANYTHING.
...WANTING TO DO EVERYTHING I CAN...
I WONDER IF THAT WAS JUST SELFISH?
...

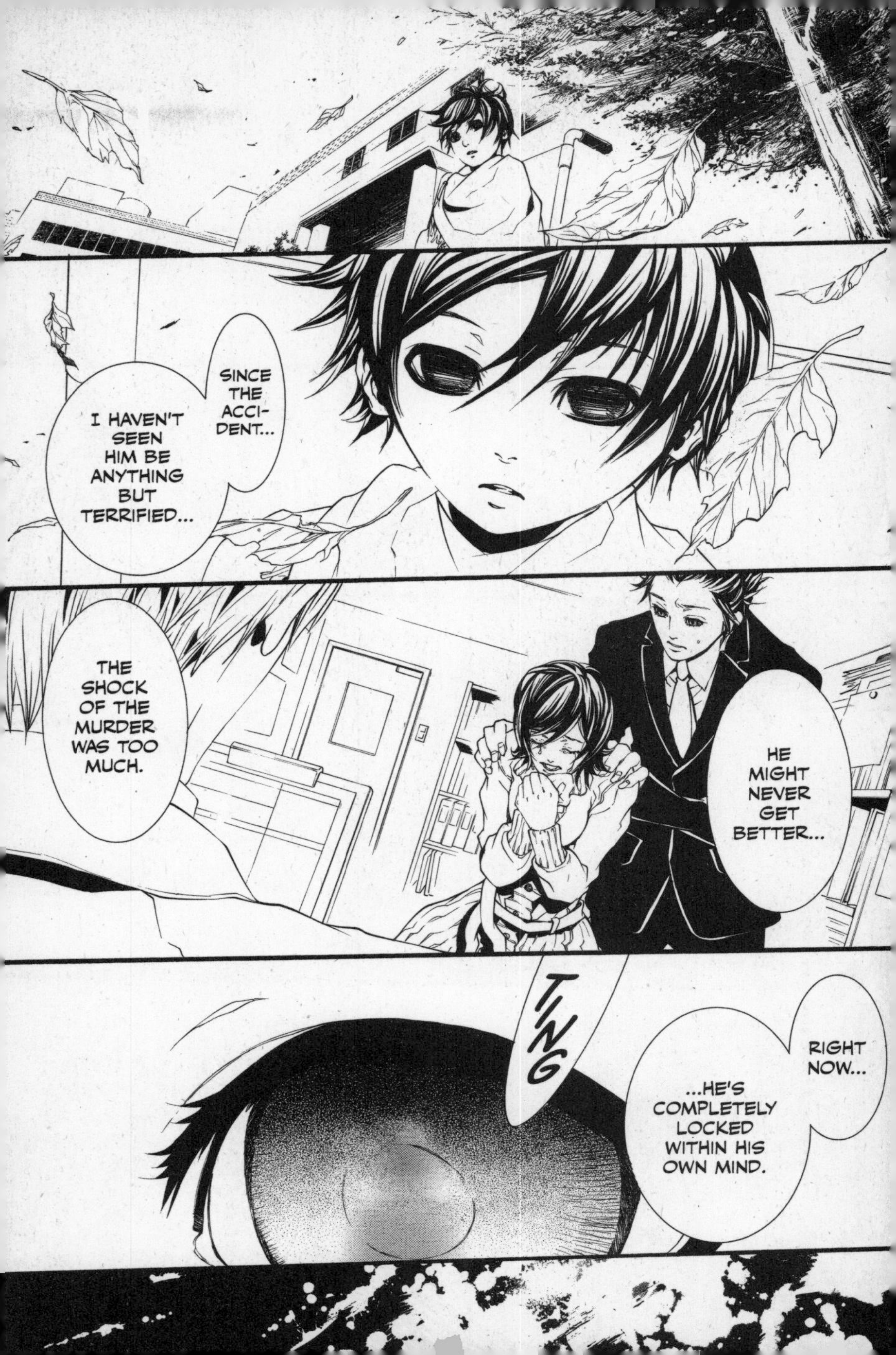
SINCE THE ACCI-DENT...
I HAVEN'T SEEN HIM BE ANYTHING BUT TERRIFIED...
HE MIGHT NEVER GET BETTER...
THE SHOCK OF THE MURDER WAS TOO MUCH.
RIGHT NOW...
...HE'S COMPLETELY LOCKED WITHIN HIS OWN MIND.
TING

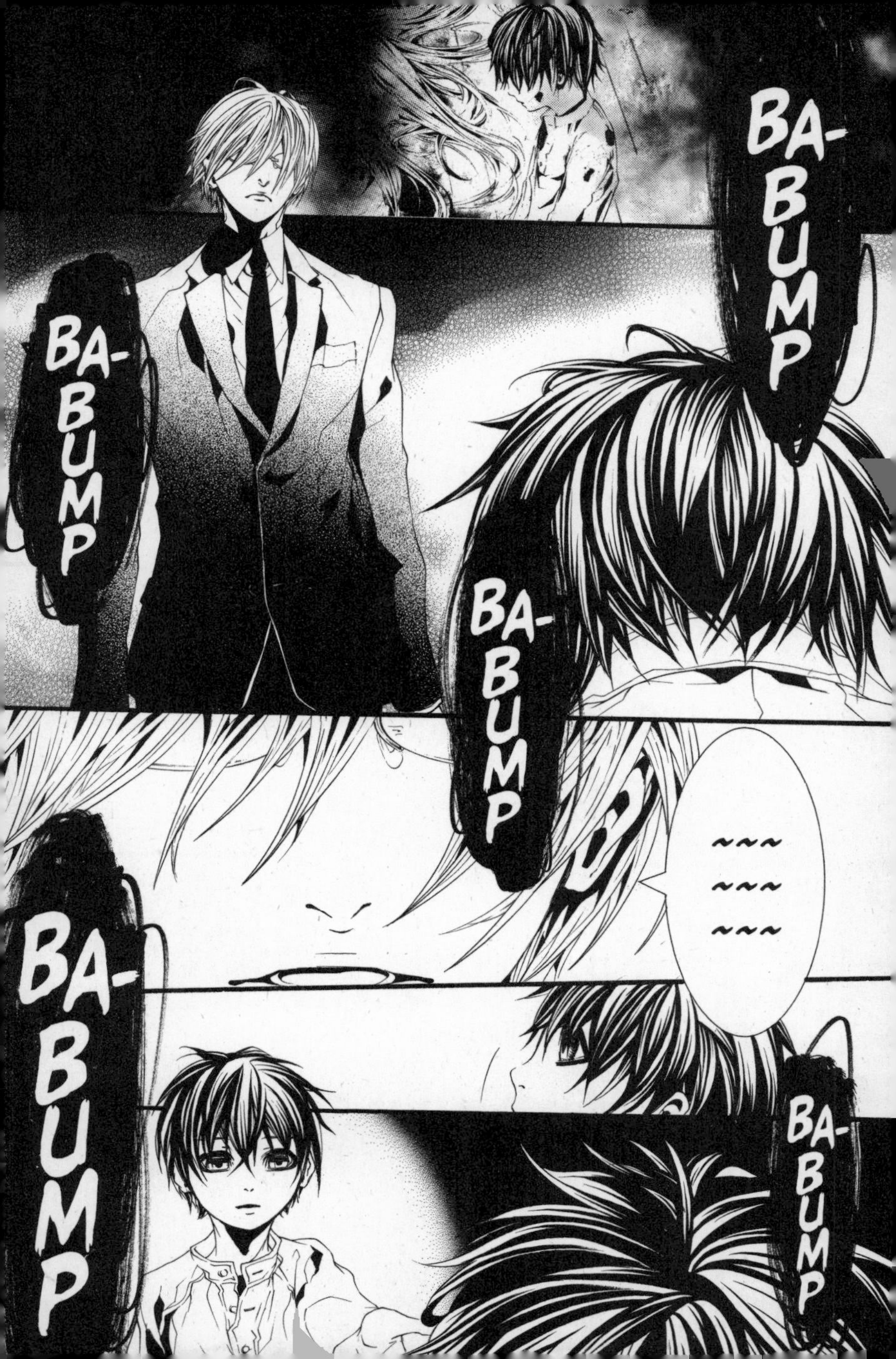
BA-BUMP
BA-BUMP
BA-BUMP
~~~ ~~~ ~~~
BA-BUMP
BA-BUMP
~~~

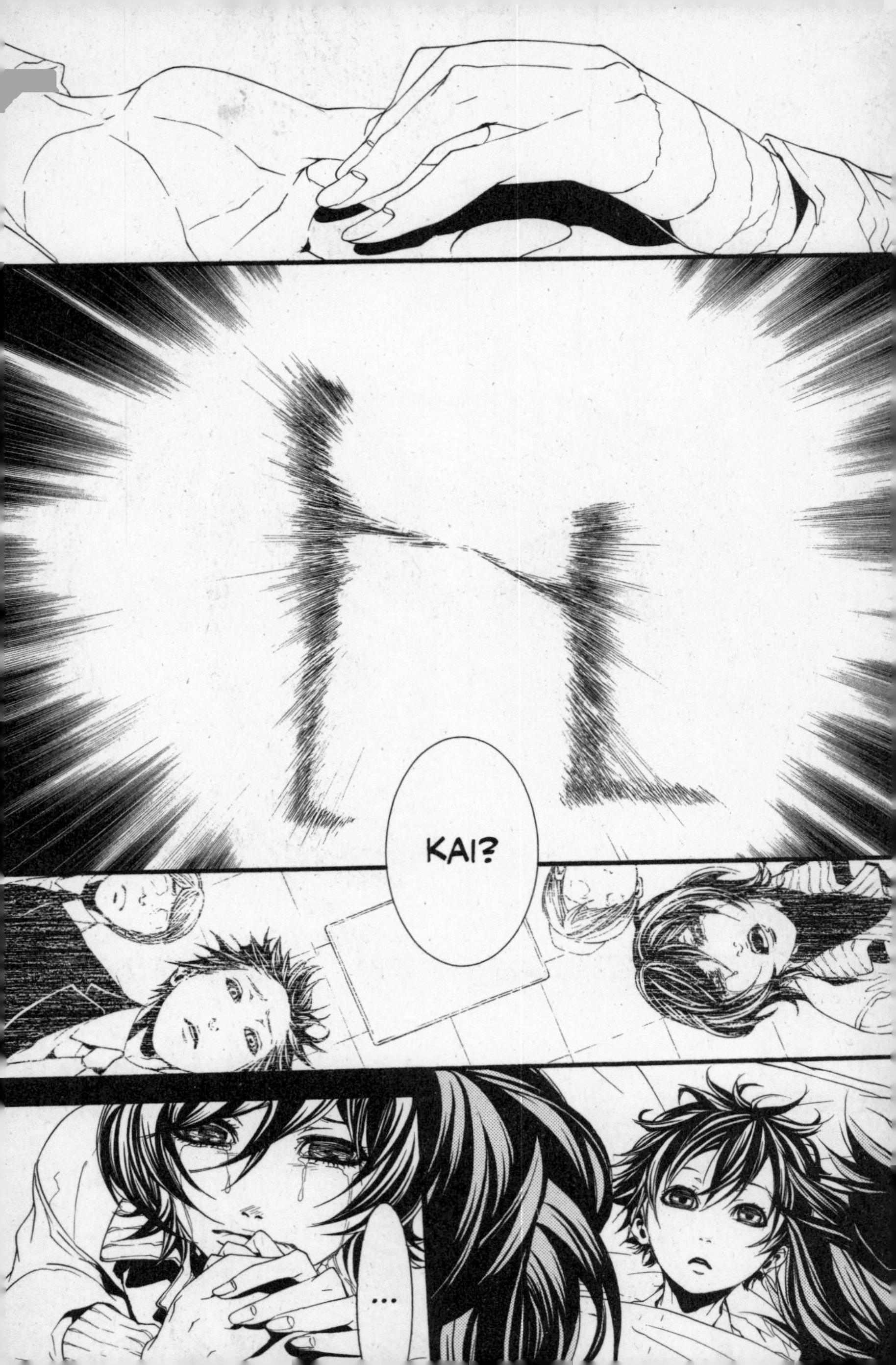
KAI?
...

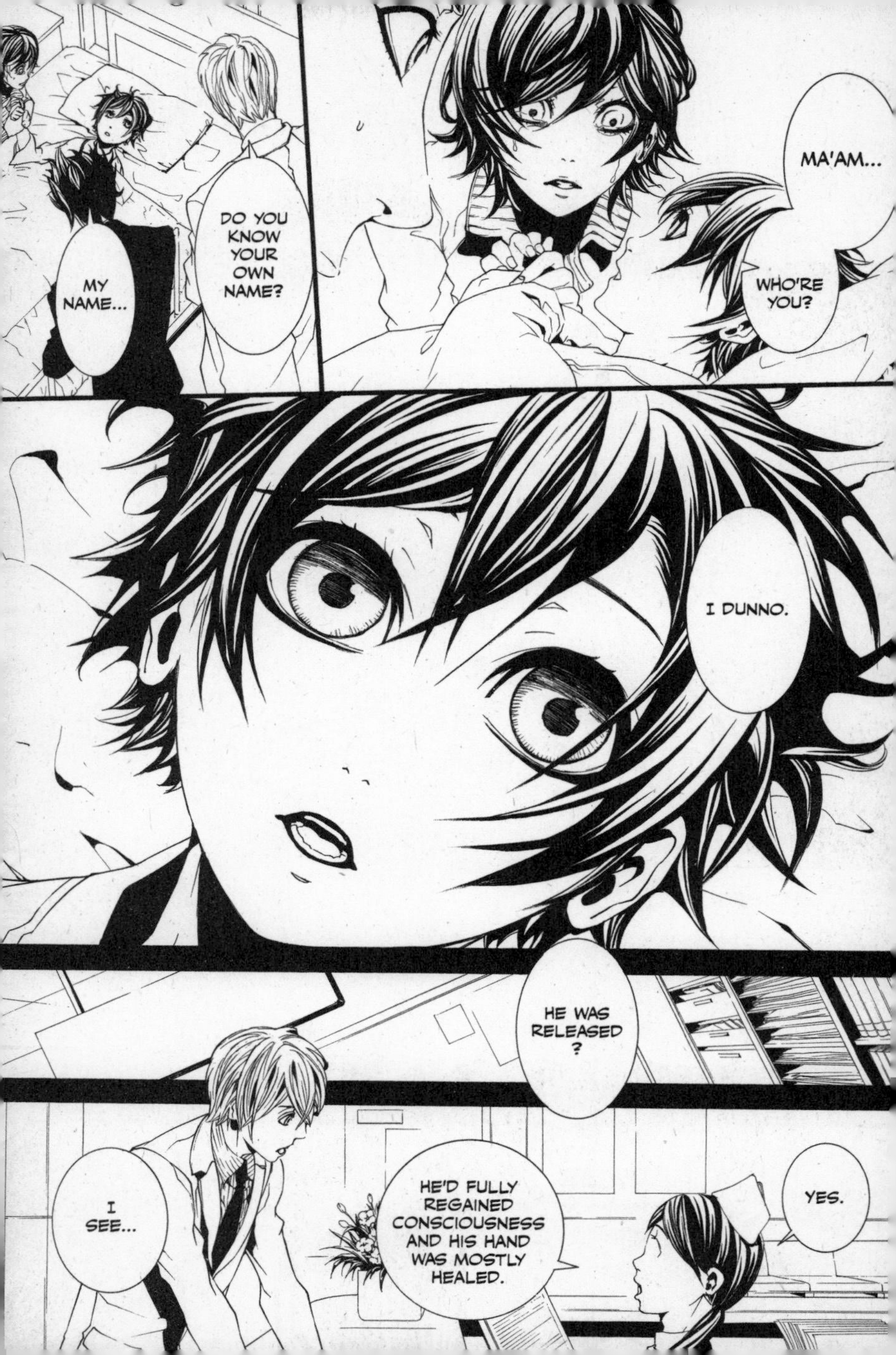
MA'AM...
WHO'RE YOU?
DO YOU KNOW YOUR OWN NAME?
MY NAME...
I DUNNO.
HE WAS RELEASED?
YES.
HE'D FULLY REGAINED CONSCIOUSNESS AND HIS HAND WAS MOSTLY HEALED.
I SEE...

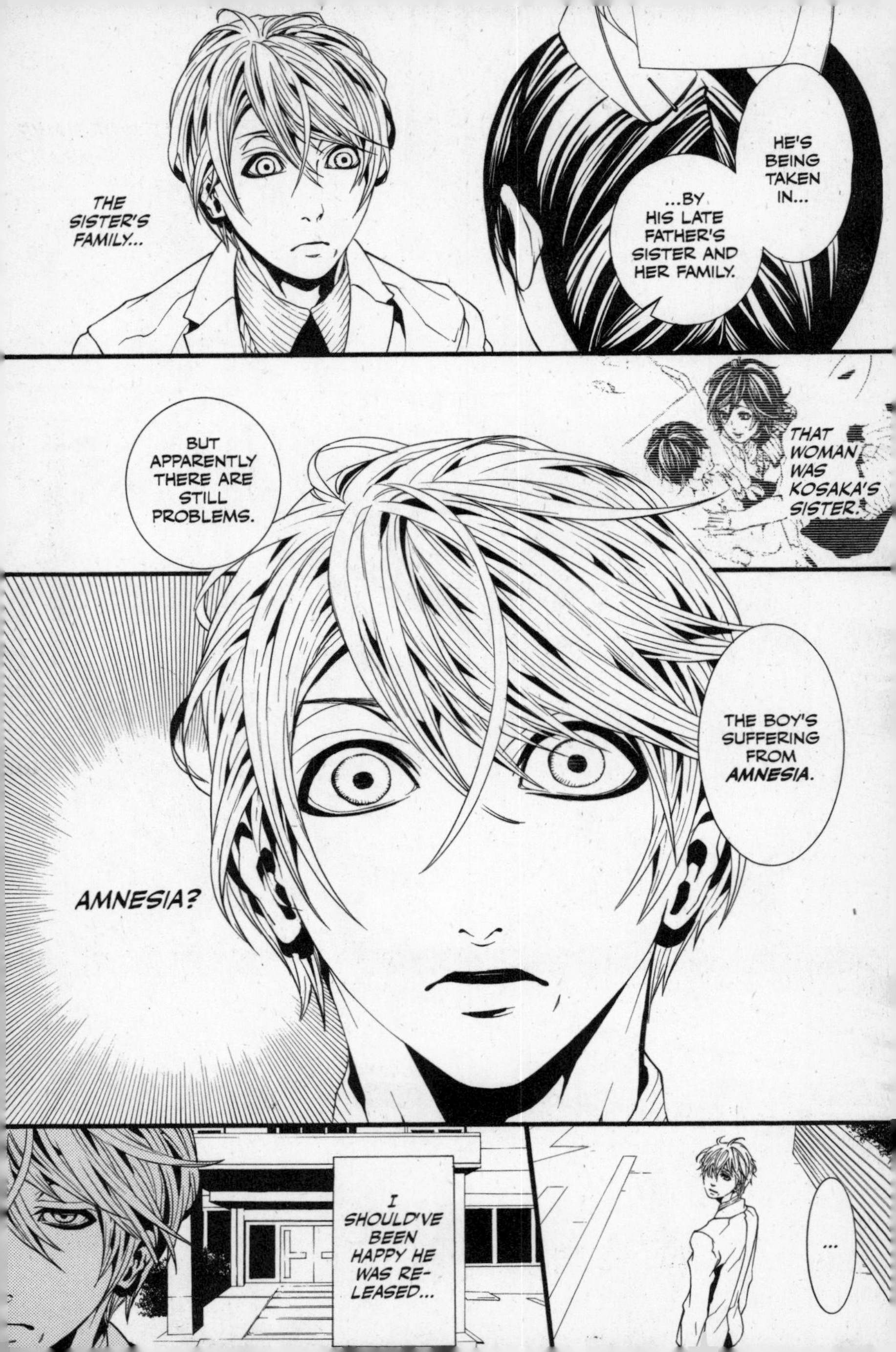
HE'S BEING TAKEN IN...
...BY HIS LATE FATHER'S SISTER AND HER FAMILY.
THE SISTER'S FAMILY...
THAT WOMAN WAS KOSAKA'S SISTER.
BUT APPARENTLY THERE ARE STILL PROBLEMS.
THE BOY'S SUFFERING FROM *AMNESIA*.
AMNESIA?
...
I SHOULD'VE BEEN HAPPY HE WAS RE-LEASED...

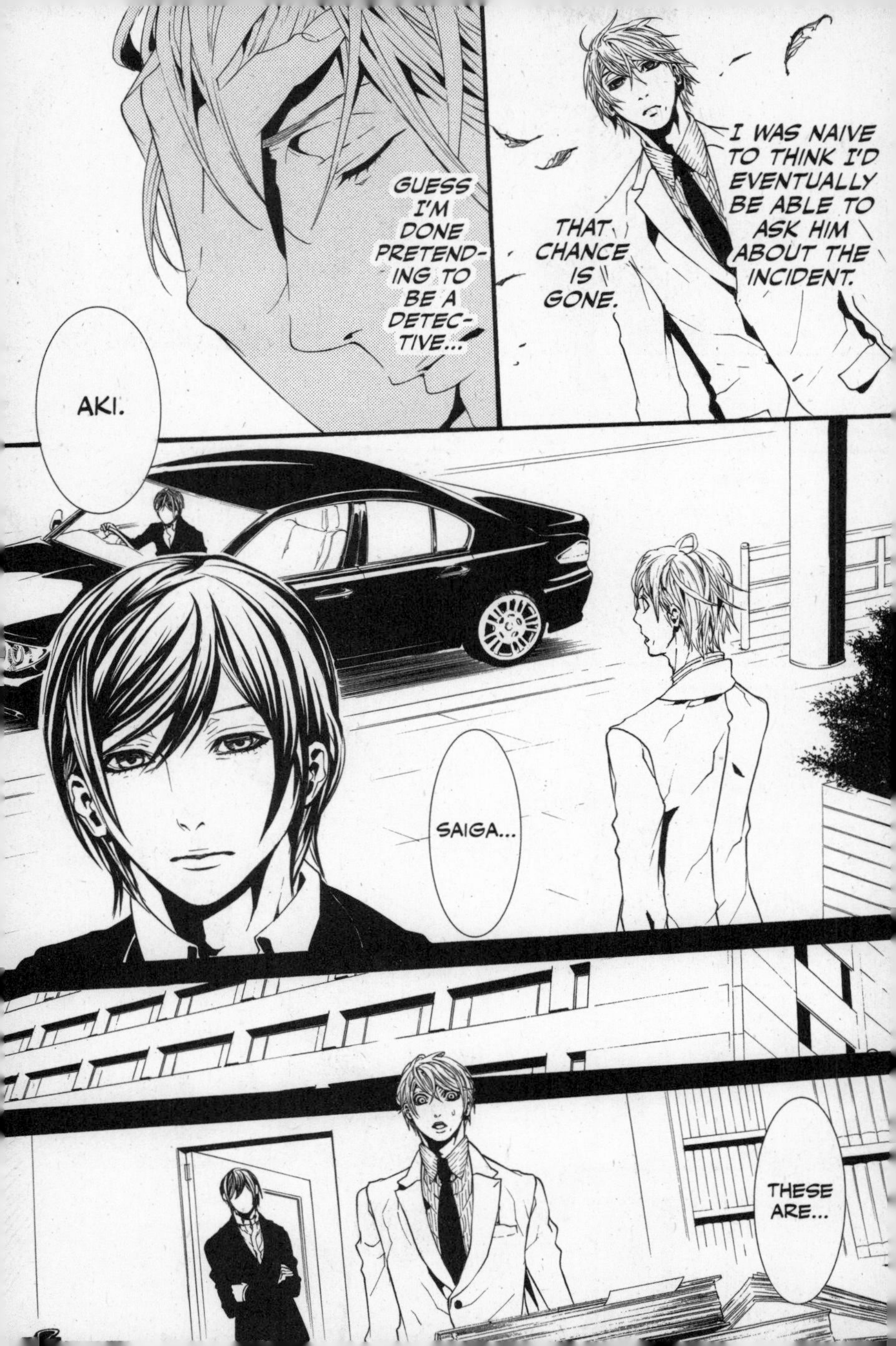
I WAS NAIVE TO THINK I'D EVENTUALLY BE ABLE TO ASK HIM ABOUT THE INCIDENT.
THAT CHANCE IS GONE.
GUESS I'M DONE PRETENDING TO BE A DETECTIVE...
AKI.
SAIGA...
THESE ARE...

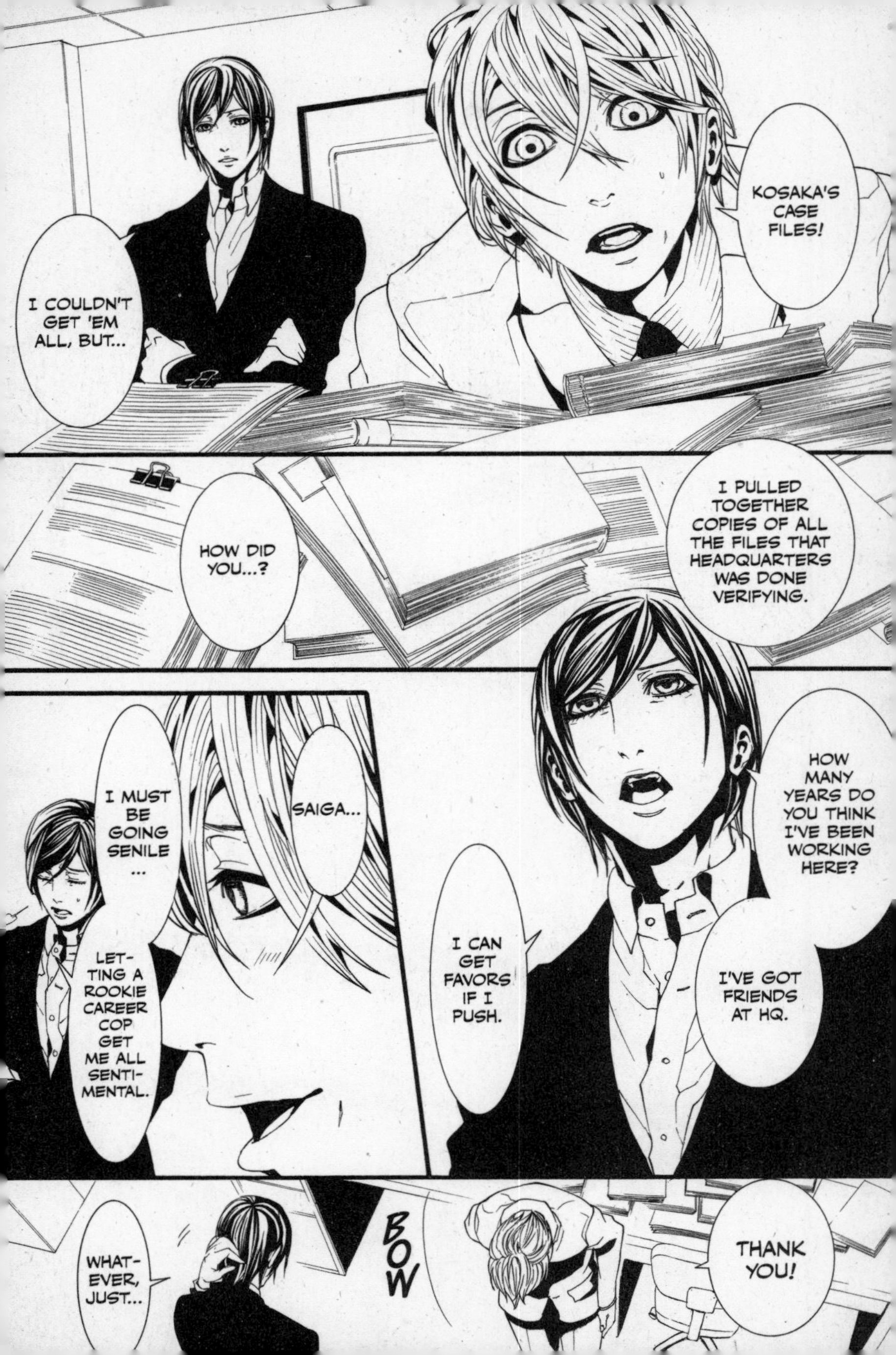
KOSAKA'S CASE FILES!
I COULDN'T GET 'EM ALL, BUT...
I PULLED TOGETHER COPIES OF ALL THE FILES THAT HEADQUARTERS WAS DONE VERIFYING.
HOW DID YOU...?
HOW MANY YEARS DO YOU THINK I'VE BEEN WORKING HERE?
I'VE GOT FRIENDS AT HQ.
I CAN GET FAVORS IF I PUSH.
SAIGA...
I MUST BE GOING SENILE...
LETTING A ROOKIE CAREER COP GET ME ALL SENTIMENTAL.
THANK YOU!
BOW
WHATEVER, JUST...

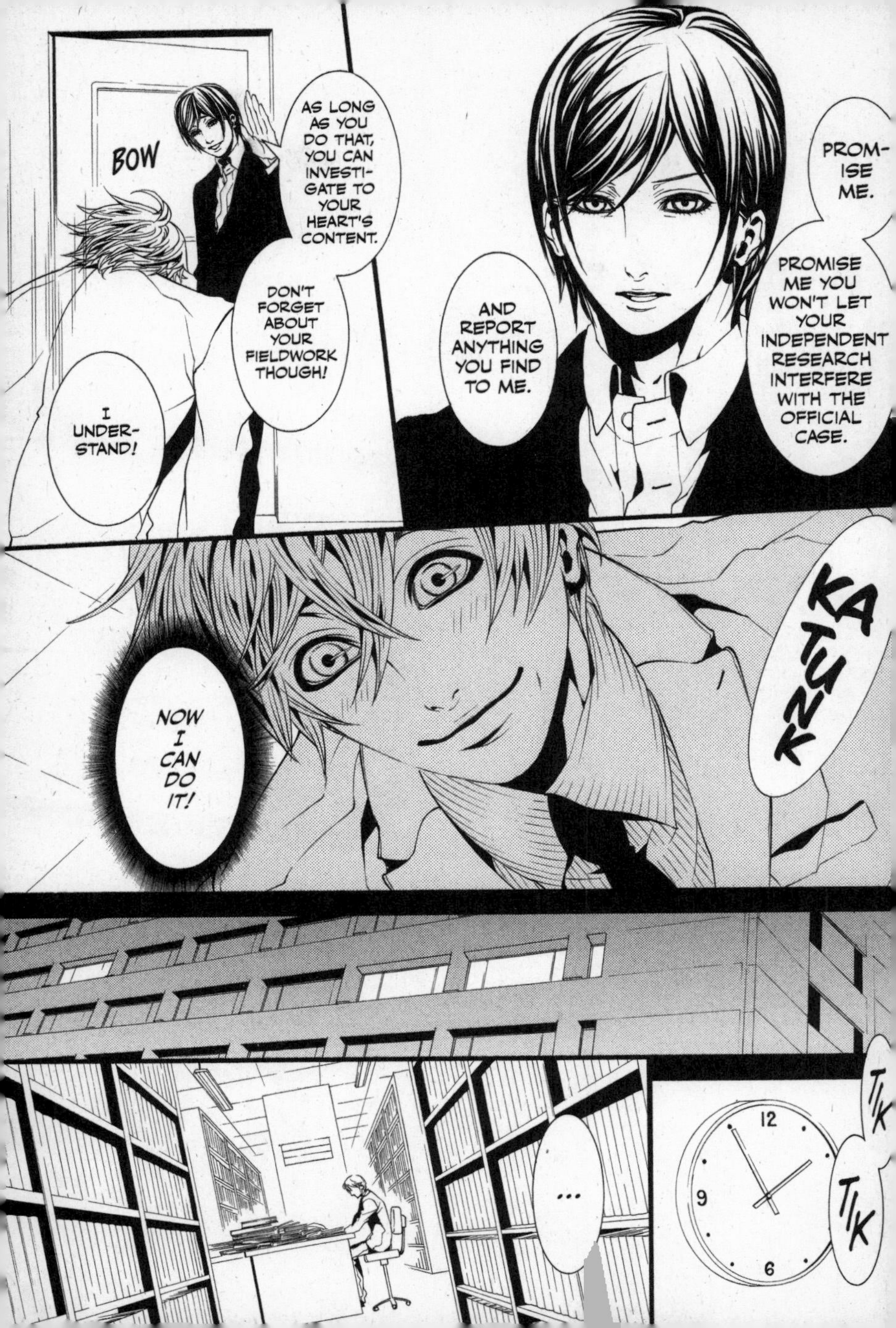
PROMISE ME.
PROMISE ME YOU WON'T LET YOUR INDEPENDENT RESEARCH INTERFERE WITH THE OFFICIAL CASE.
AND REPORT ANYTHING YOU FIND TO ME.
AS LONG AS YOU DO THAT, YOU CAN INVESTIGATE TO YOUR HEART'S CONTENT.
BOW
DON'T FORGET ABOUT YOUR FIELDWORK THOUGH!
I UNDERSTAND!
KATUNK
NOW I CAN DO IT!
TIK
TIK
...

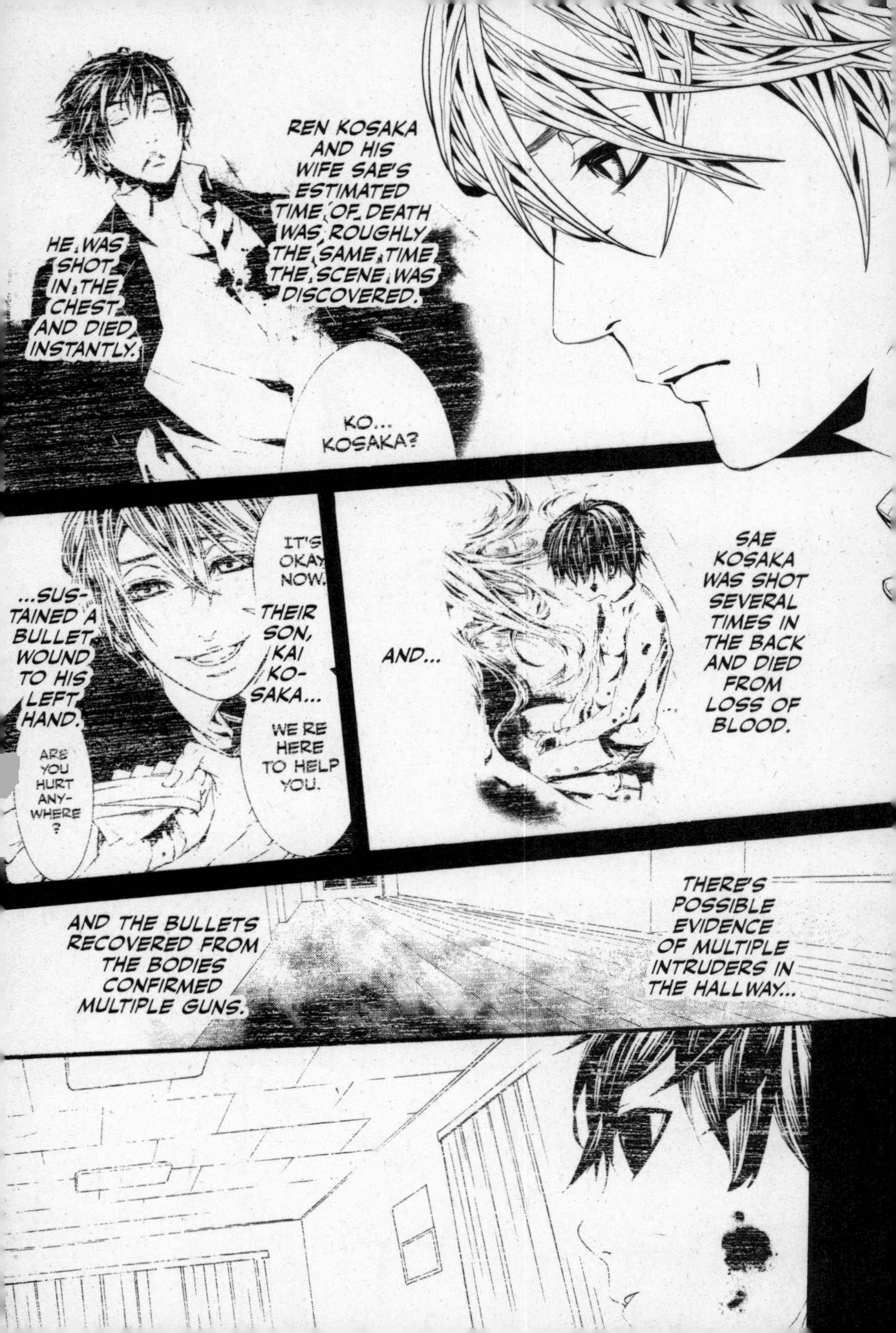
REN KOSAKA AND HIS WIFE SAE'S ESTIMATED TIME OF DEATH WAS ROUGHLY THE SAME TIME THE SCENE WAS DISCOVERED.
HE WAS SHOT IN THE CHEST AND DIED INSTANTLY.
KO... KOSAKA?
SAE KOSAKA WAS SHOT SEVERAL TIMES IN THE BACK AND DIED FROM LOSS OF BLOOD.
...
AND...
IT'S OKAY NOW.
THEIR SON, KAI KO-SAKA...
...SUS-TAINED A BULLET WOUND TO HIS LEFT HAND.
WE RE HERE TO HELP YOU.
ARE YOU HURT ANY-WHERE?
THERE'S POSSIBLE EVIDENCE OF MULTIPLE INTRUDERS IN THE HALLWAY...
AND THE BULLETS RECOVERED FROM THE BODIES CONFIRMED MULTIPLE GUNS.

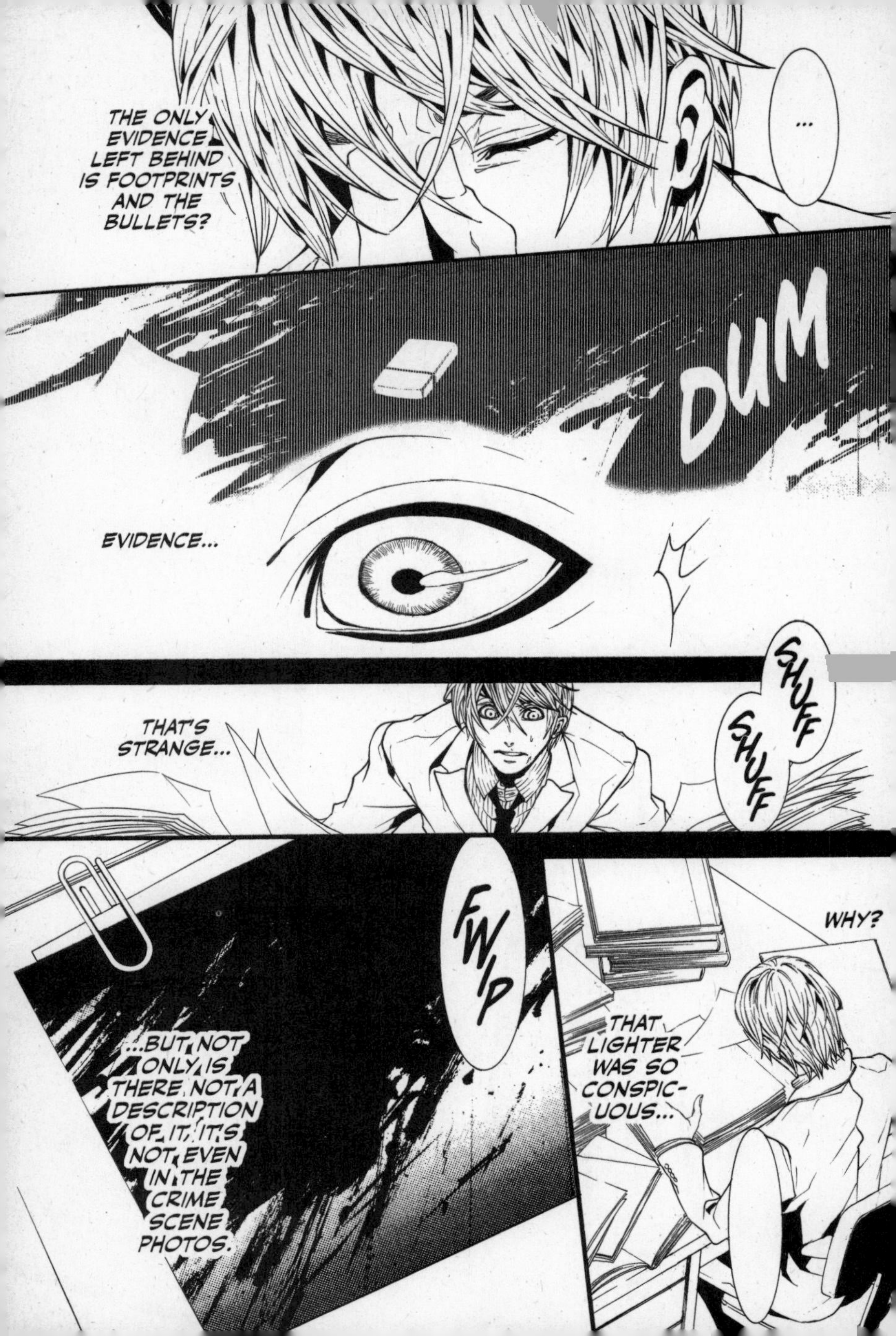
...
THE ONLY EVIDENCE LEFT BEHIND IS FOOTPRINTS AND THE BULLETS?
DUM
EVIDENCE...
SHUFF SHUFF
THAT'S STRANGE...
WHY?
THAT LIGHTER WAS SO CONSPICUOUS...
FWIP
...BUT NOT ONLY IS THERE NOT A DESCRIPTION OF IT, IT'S NOT EVEN IN THE CRIME SCENE PHOTOS.

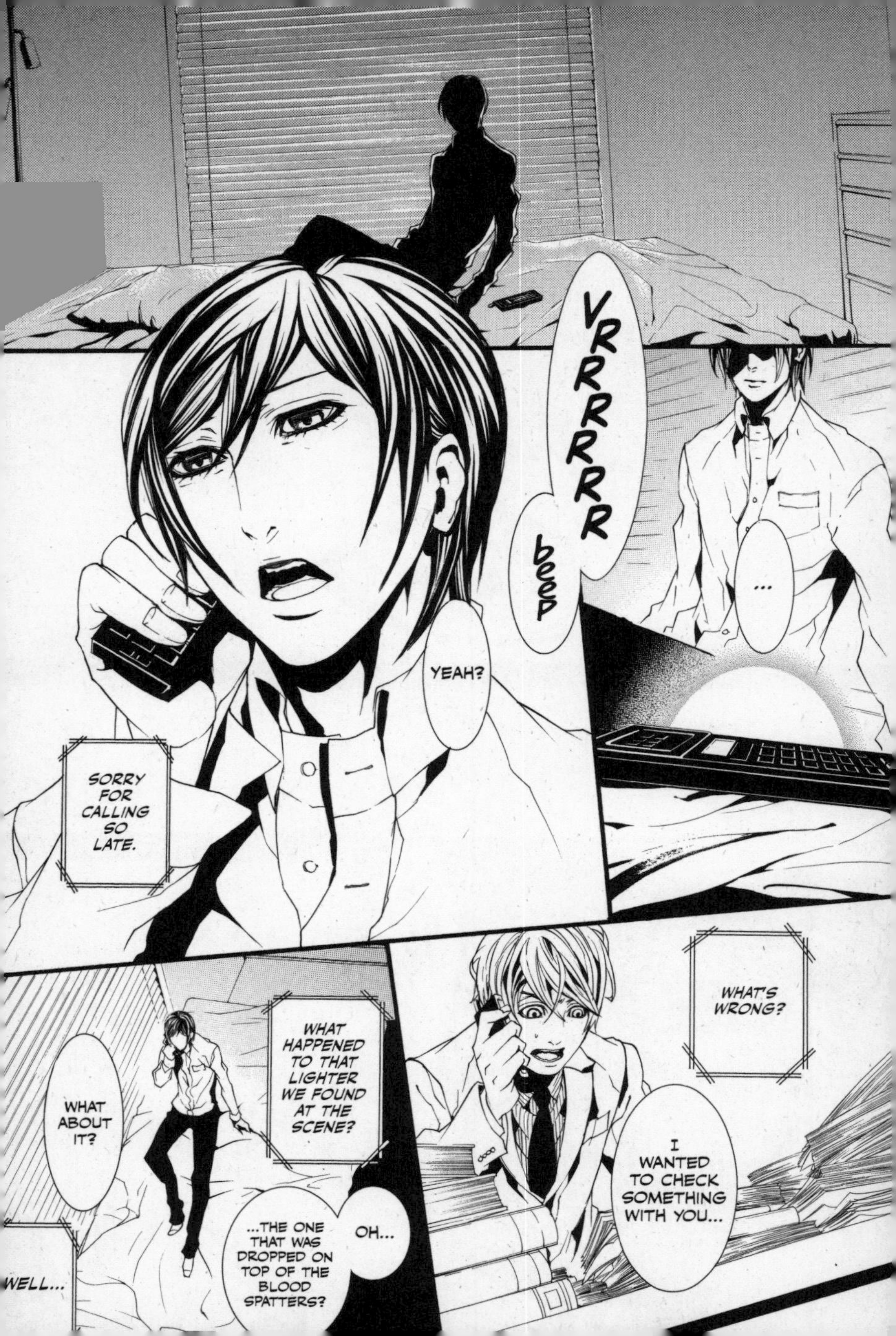

VRRRRRR
beep
...
YEAH?
SORRY FOR CALLING SO LATE.
WHAT'S WRONG?
I WANTED TO CHECK SOMETHING WITH YOU...
WHAT HAPPENED TO THAT LIGHTER WE FOUND AT THE SCENE?
OH...
...THE ONE THAT WAS DROPPED ON TOP OF THE BLOOD SPATTERS?
WHAT ABOUT IT?
WELL...

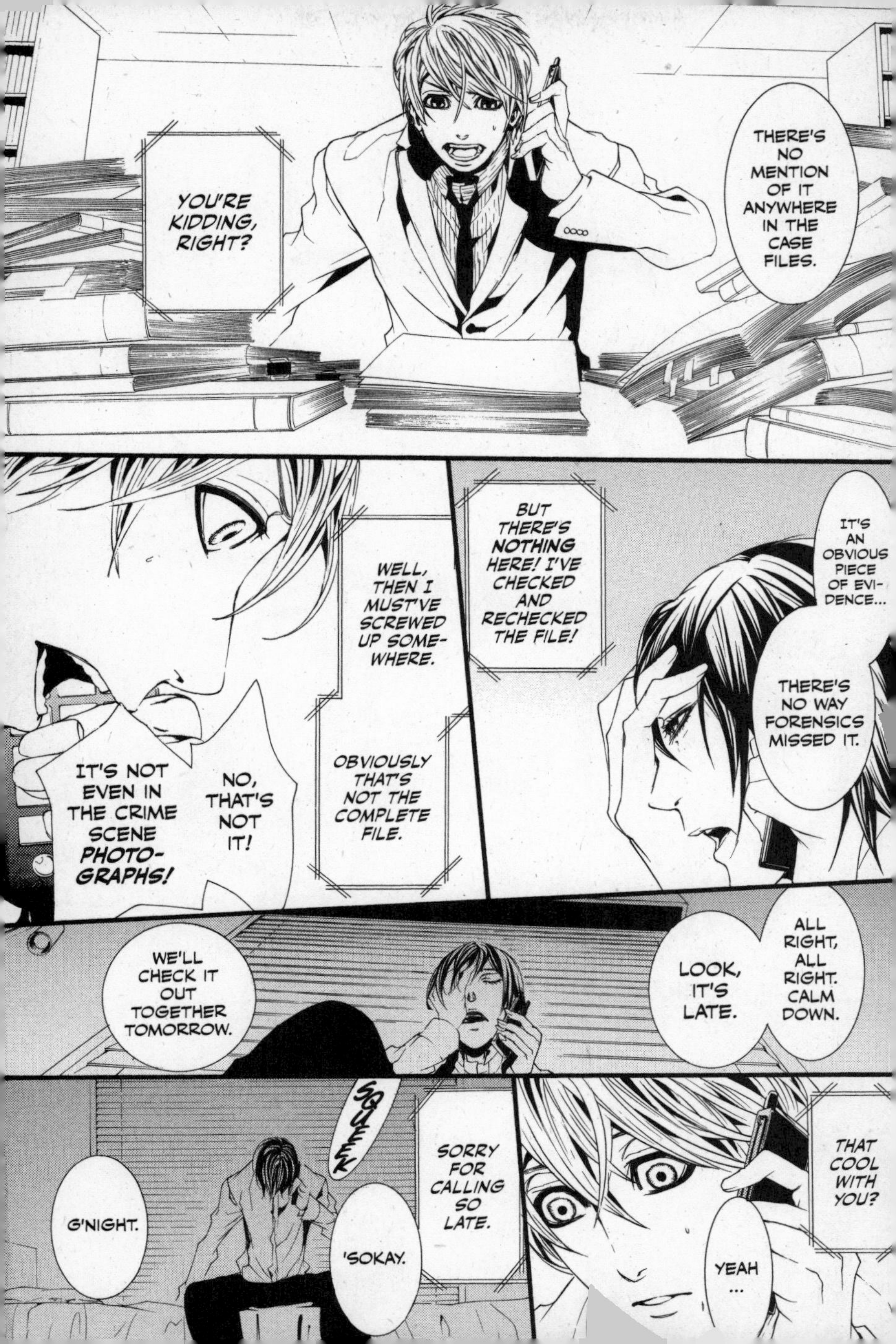
THERE'S NO MENTION OF IT ANYWHERE IN THE CASE FILES.
YOU'RE KIDDING, RIGHT?
IT'S AN OBVIOUS PIECE OF EVI-DENCE...
THERE'S NO WAY FORENSICS MISSED IT.
BUT THERE'S NOTHING HERE! I'VE CHECKED AND RECHECKED THE FILE!
WELL, THEN I MUST'VE SCREWED UP SOME-WHERE.
OBVIOUSLY THAT'S NOT THE COMPLETE FILE.
NO, THAT'S NOT IT!
IT'S NOT EVEN IN THE CRIME SCENE PHOTO-GRAPHS!
ALL RIGHT, ALL RIGHT. CALM DOWN.
LOOK, IT'S LATE.
WE'LL CHECK IT OUT TOGETHER TOMORROW.
THAT COOL WITH YOU?
YEAH ...
SORRY FOR CALLING SO LATE.
SQUEEEK
'SOKAY.
G'NIGHT.

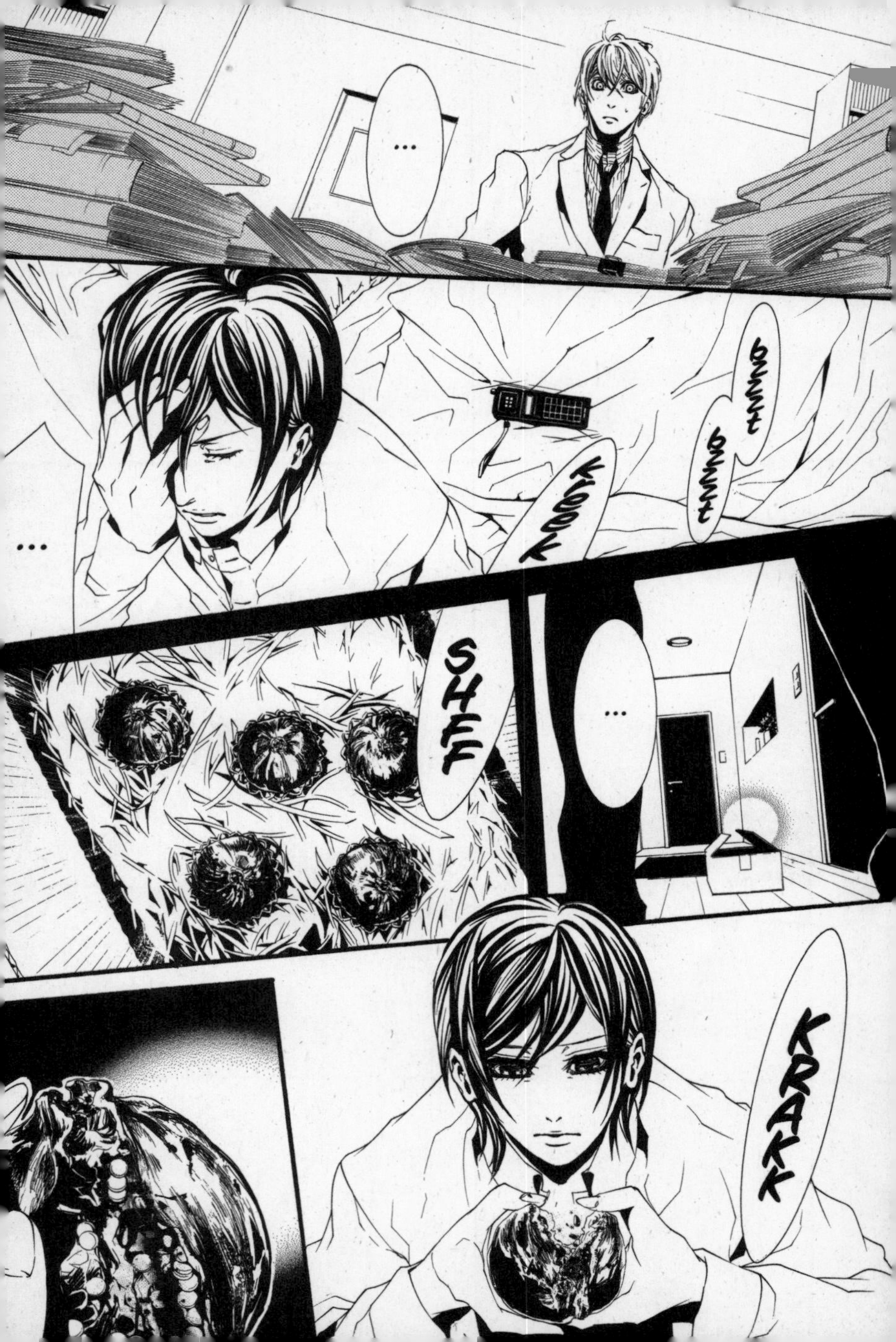
...
bzzzt
bzzzt
kleek
...
...
SHEFF
KRAKK

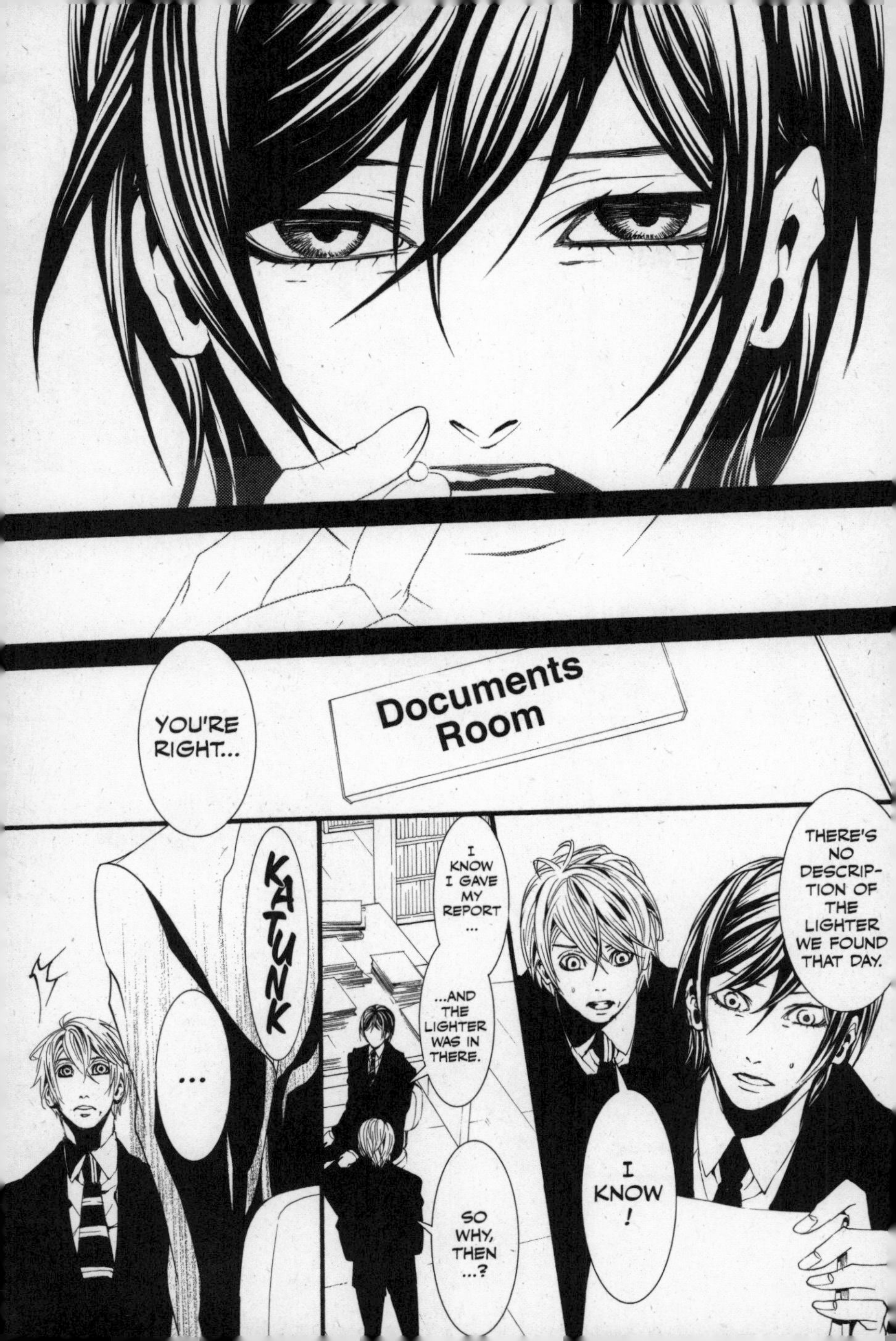
Documents Room
YOU'RE RIGHT...
THERE'S NO DESCRIP- TION OF THE LIGHTER WE FOUND THAT DAY.
I KNOW I GAVE MY REPORT...
...AND THE LIGHTER WAS IN THERE.
I KNOW!
SO WHY, THEN...?
KATUNK
...

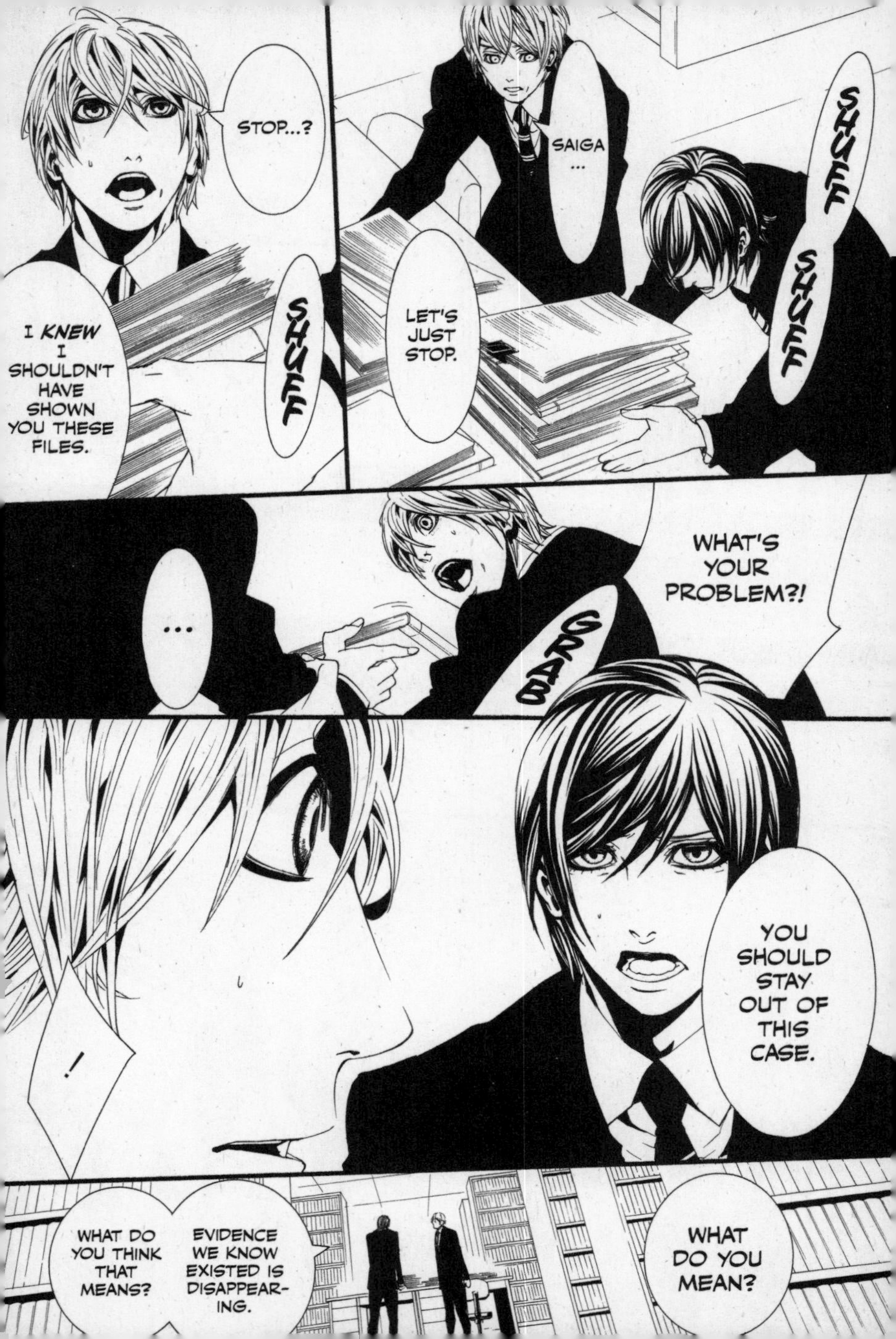
SHUFF
SHUFF
SAIGA ...
LET'S JUST STOP.
STOP...?
SHUFF
I KNEW I SHOULDN'T HAVE SHOWN YOU THESE FILES.
WHAT'S YOUR PROBLEM?!
GRAB
...
YOU SHOULD STAY OUT OF THIS CASE.
!
WHAT DO YOU MEAN?
EVIDENCE WE KNOW EXISTED IS DISAPPEAR-ING.
WHAT DO YOU THINK THAT MEANS?

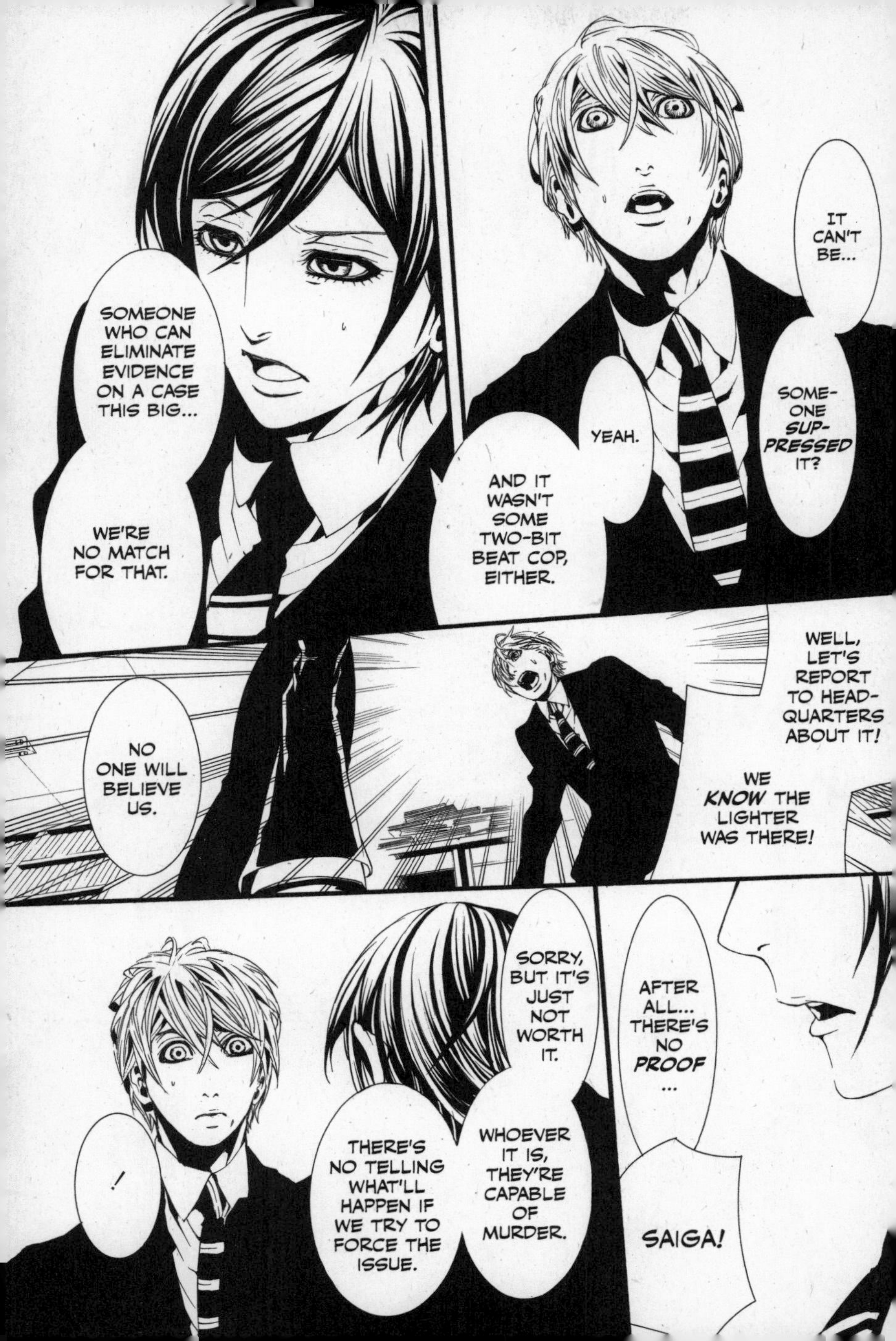
IT CAN'T BE...
SOMEONE *SUPPRESSED* IT?
YEAH.
AND IT WASN'T SOME TWO-BIT BEAT COP, EITHER.
SOMEONE WHO CAN ELIMINATE EVIDENCE ON A CASE THIS BIG...
WE'RE NO MATCH FOR THAT.
WELL, LET'S REPORT TO HEADQUARTERS ABOUT IT!
WE *KNOW* THE LIGHTER WAS THERE!
NO ONE WILL BELIEVE US.
AFTER ALL... THERE'S NO *PROOF* ...
SAIGA!
SORRY, BUT IT'S JUST NOT WORTH IT.
WHOEVER IT IS, THEY'RE CAPABLE OF MURDER.
THERE'S NO TELLING WHAT'LL HAPPEN IF WE TRY TO FORCE THE ISSUE.
!

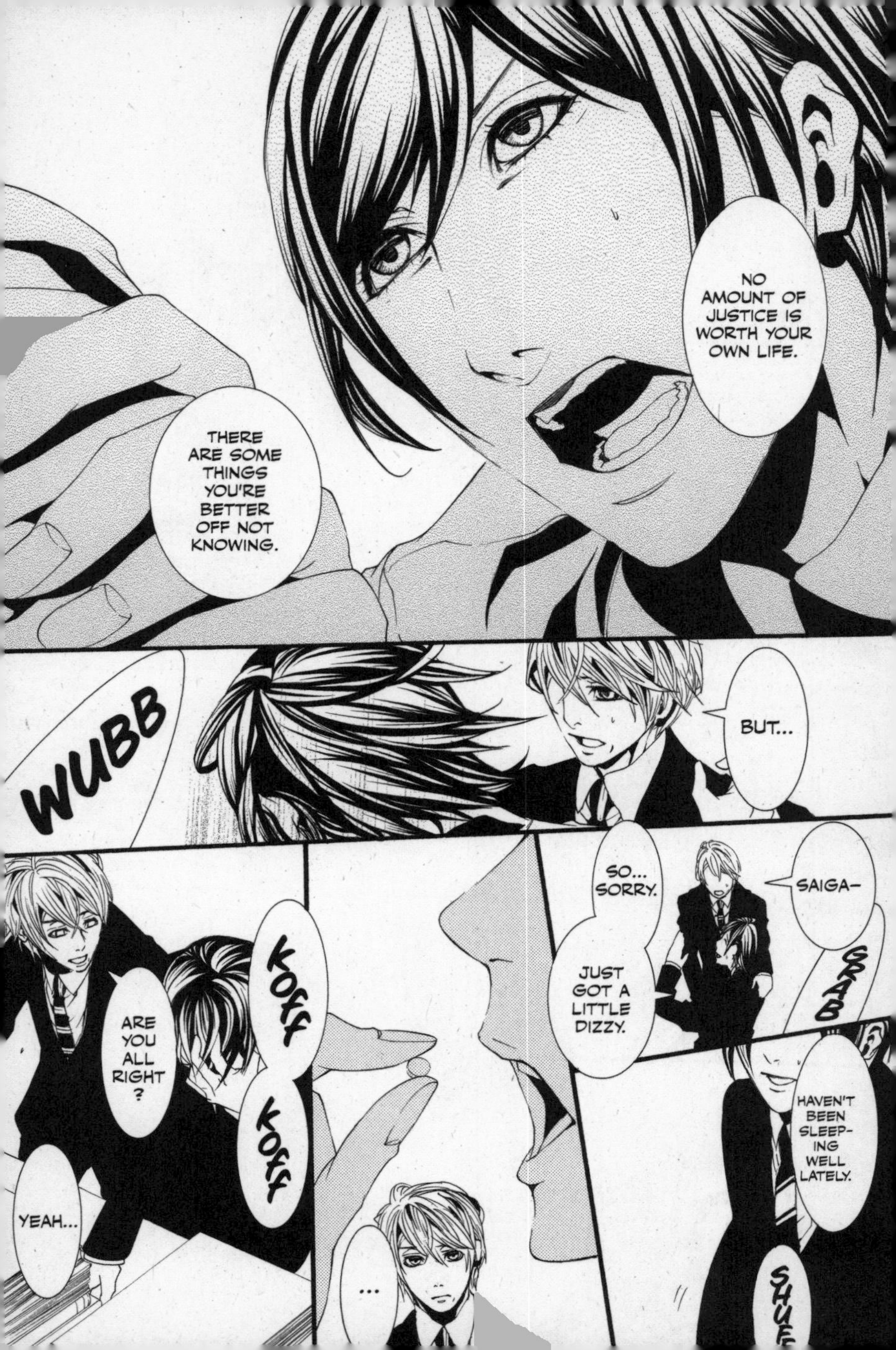
NO AMOUNT OF JUSTICE IS WORTH YOUR OWN LIFE.
THERE ARE SOME THINGS YOU'RE BETTER OFF NOT KNOWING.
BUT...
WUBB
SAIGA-
GRAB
SO... SORRY.
JUST GOT A LITTLE DIZZY.
HAVEN'T BEEN SLEEP-ING WELL LATELY.
SHUFF
...
KOFF
KOFF
ARE YOU ALL RIGHT?
YEAH...

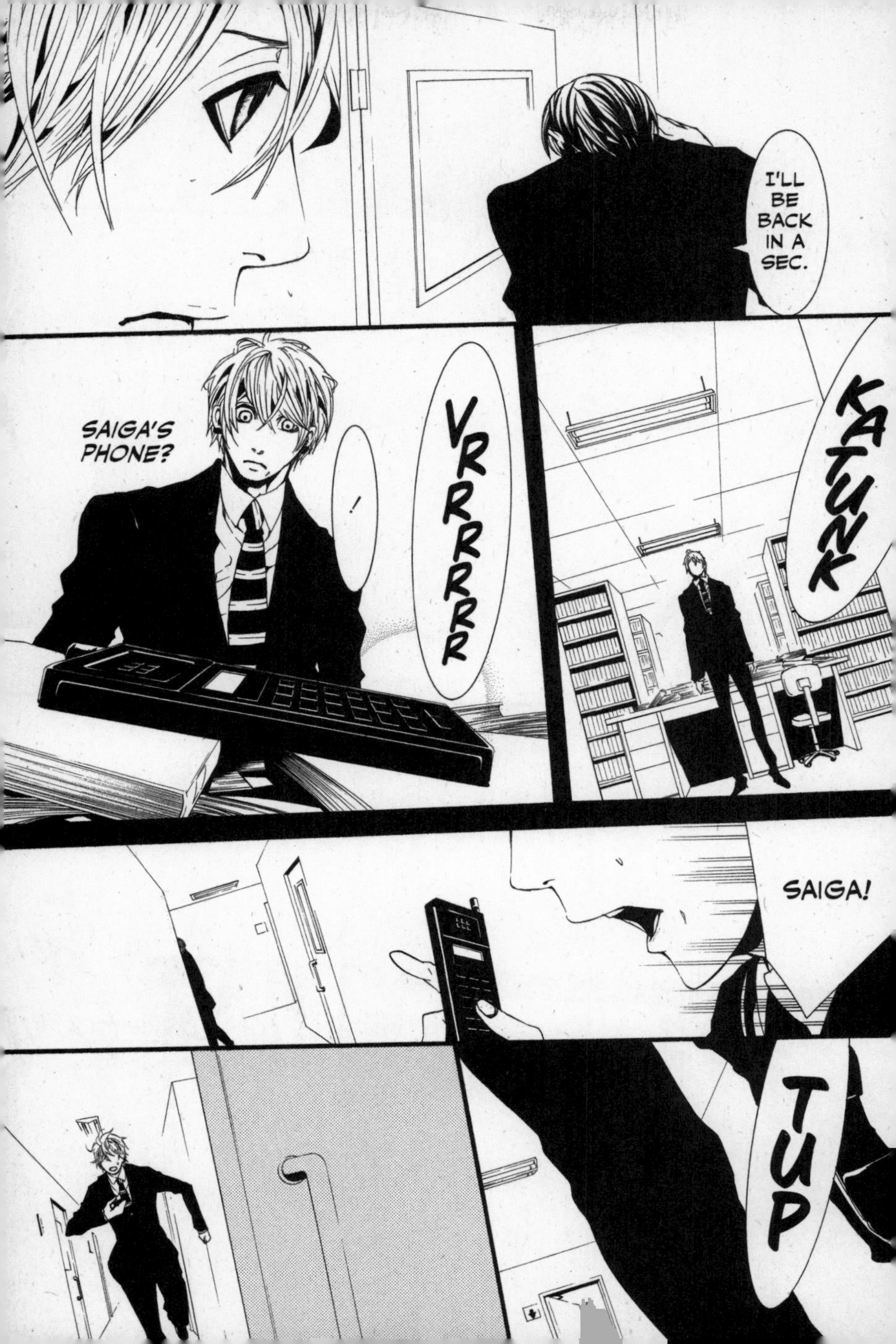
I'LL BE BACK IN A SEC.
KATUNK
VRRRRRR
!
SAIGA'S PHONE?
SAIGA!
TUP

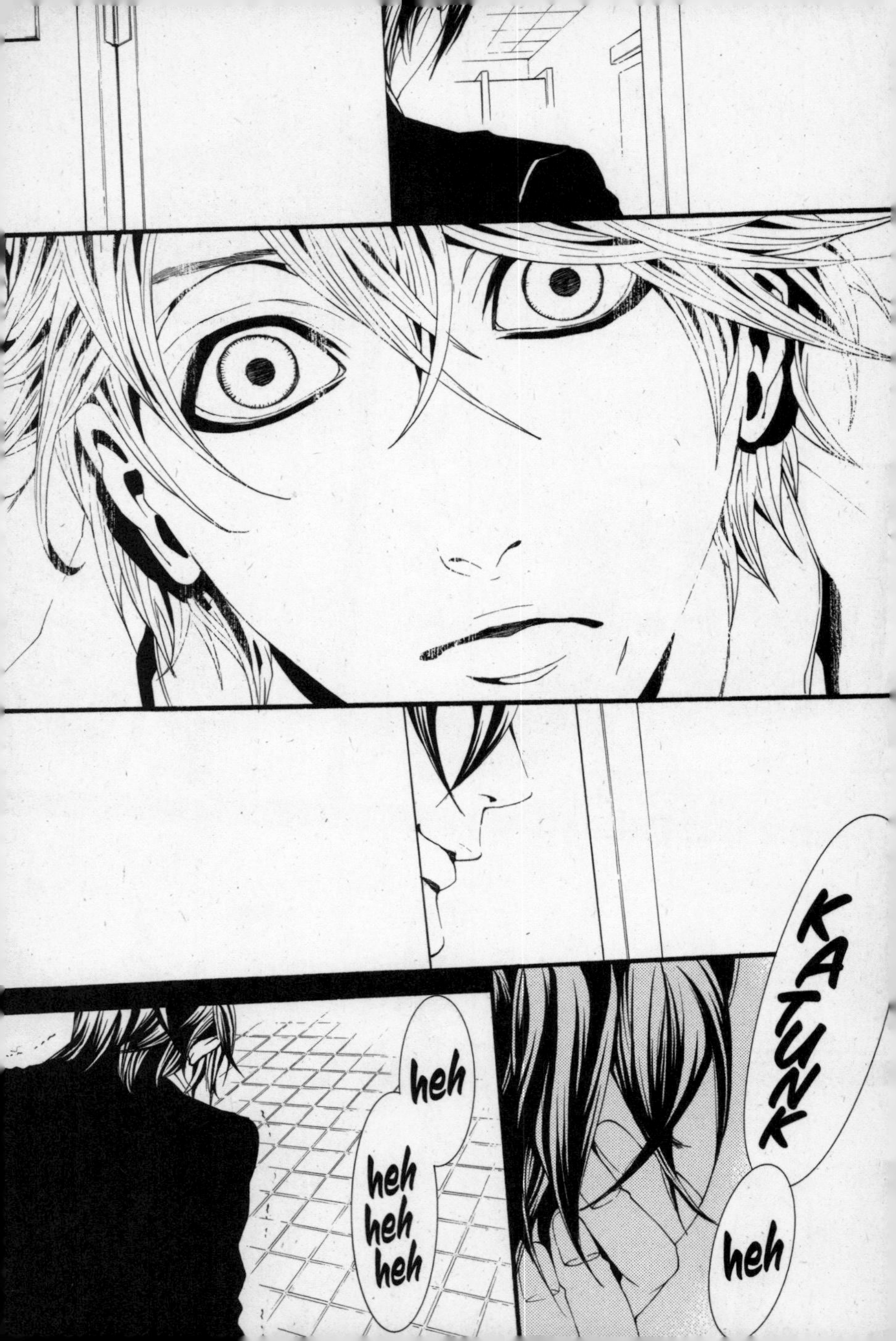
KATUNK
heh
heh
heh heh heh

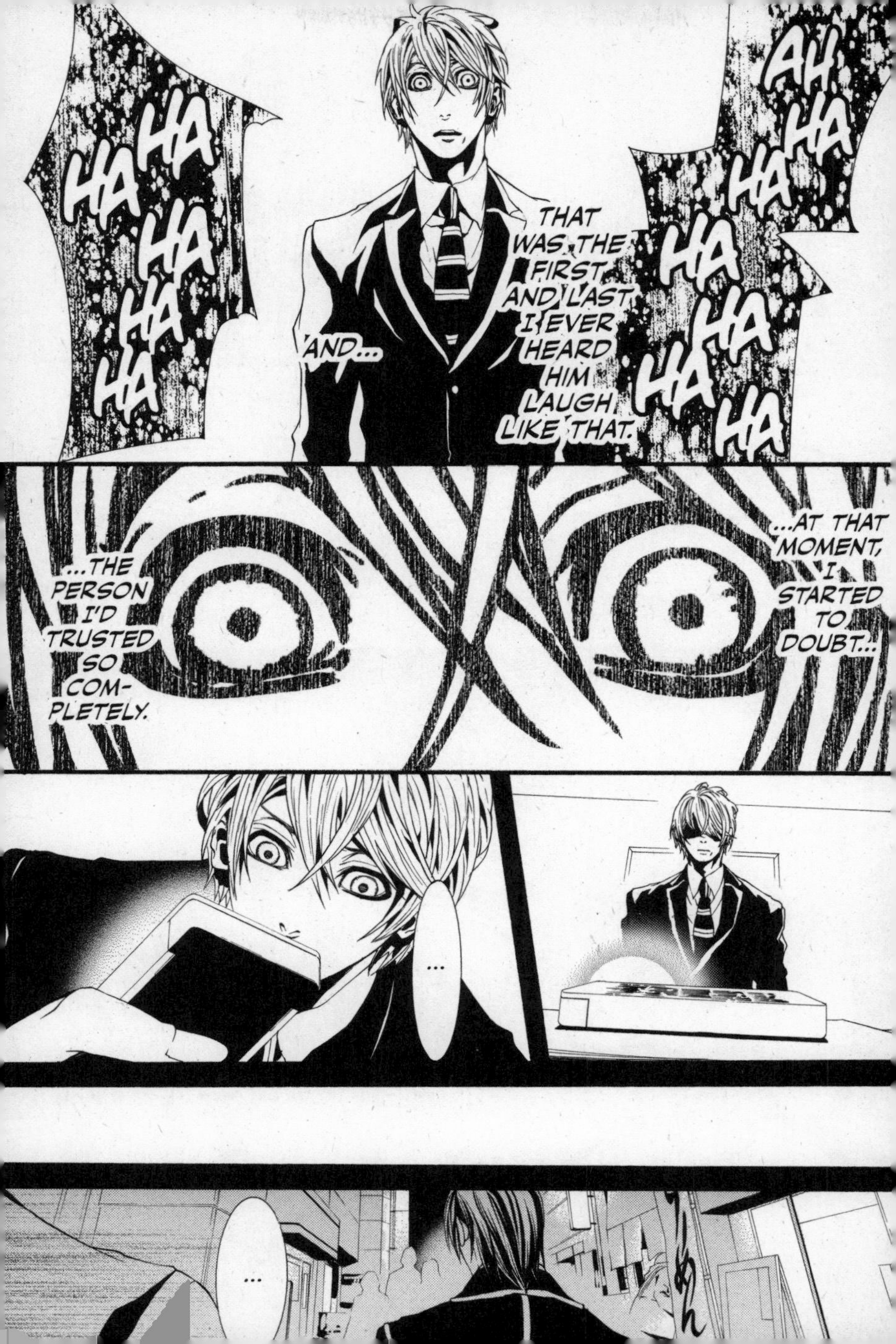
AH HA HA HA HA HA HA HA
THAT WAS THE FIRST AND LAST I EVER HEARD HIM LAUGH LIKE THAT.
AND...
HA HA HA HA HA HA
...AT THAT MOMENT, I STARTED TO DOUBT...
...THE PERSON I'D TRUSTED SO COM-PLETELY.
...
...

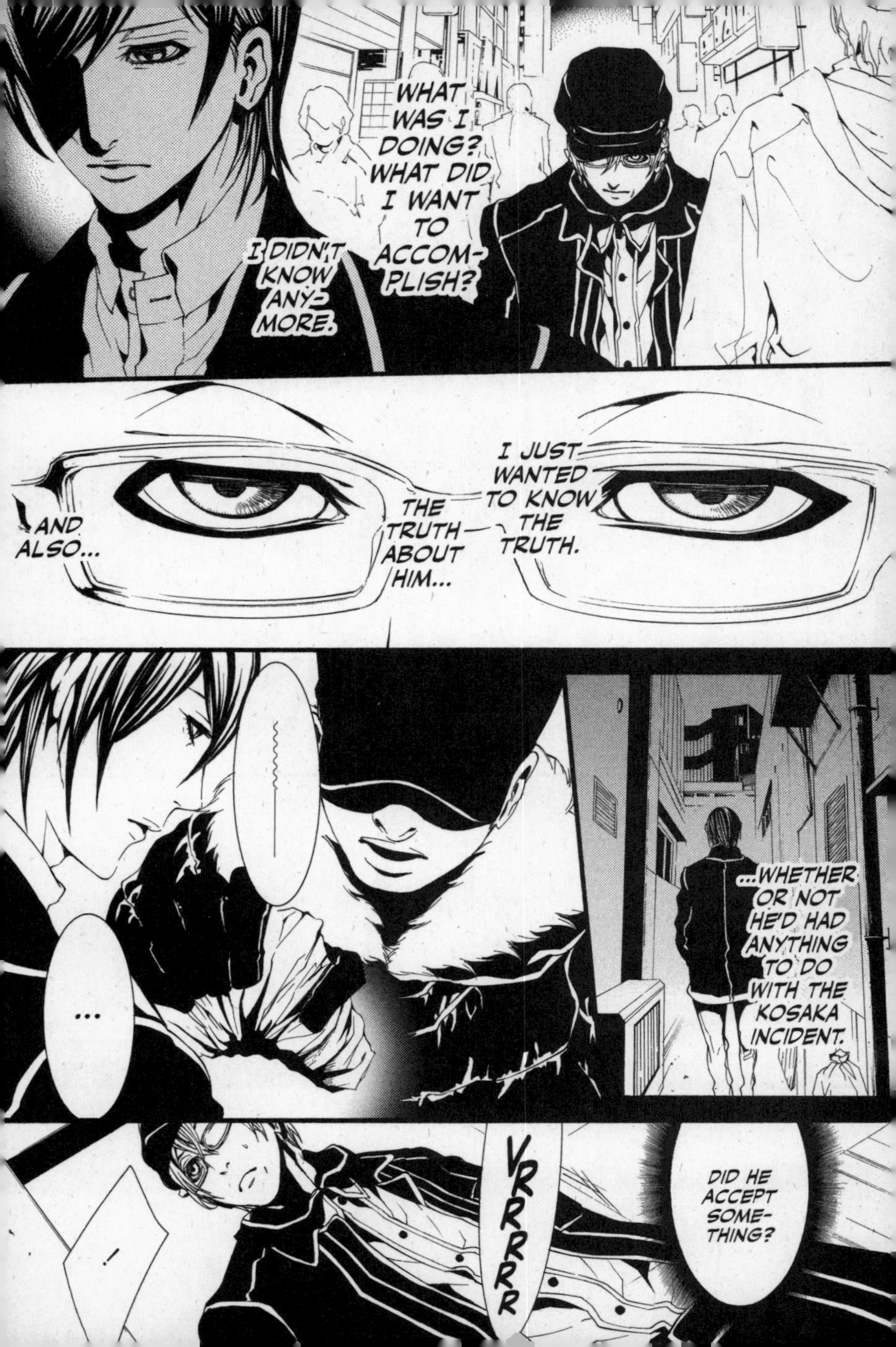
WHAT WAS I DOING? WHAT DID I WANT TO ACCOMPLISH?
I DIDN'T KNOW ANYMORE.
I JUST WANTED TO KNOW THE TRUTH.
THE TRUTH ABOUT HIM...
AND ALSO...
...WHETHER OR NOT HE'D HAD ANYTHING TO DO WITH THE KOSAKA INCIDENT.
...
DID HE ACCEPT SOMETHING?
VRRRRR
!

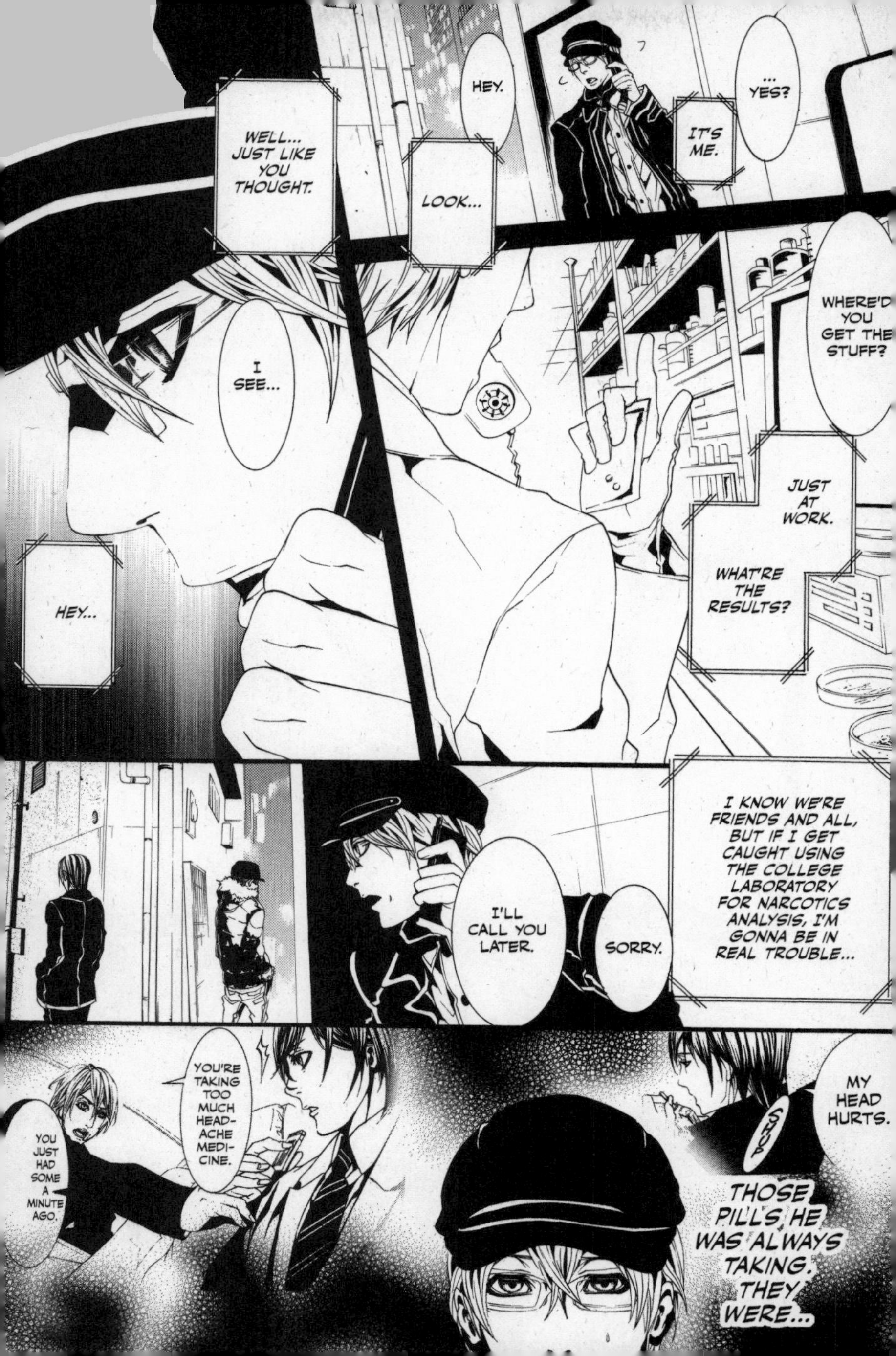
...YES?
IT'S ME.
HEY.
LOOK...
WELL... JUST LIKE YOU THOUGHT.
WHERE'D YOU GET THE STUFF?
JUST AT WORK.
WHAT'RE THE RESULTS?
I SEE...
HEY...
I KNOW WE'RE FRIENDS AND ALL, BUT IF I GET CAUGHT USING THE COLLEGE LABORATORY FOR NARCOTICS ANALYSIS, I'M GONNA BE IN REAL TROUBLE...
SORRY.
I'LL CALL YOU LATER.
MY HEAD HURTS.
SHUP
YOU'RE TAKING TOO MUCH HEAD-ACHE MEDI-CINE.
YOU JUST HAD SOME A MINUTE AGO.
THOSE PILLS HE WAS ALWAYS TAKING. THEY WERE...

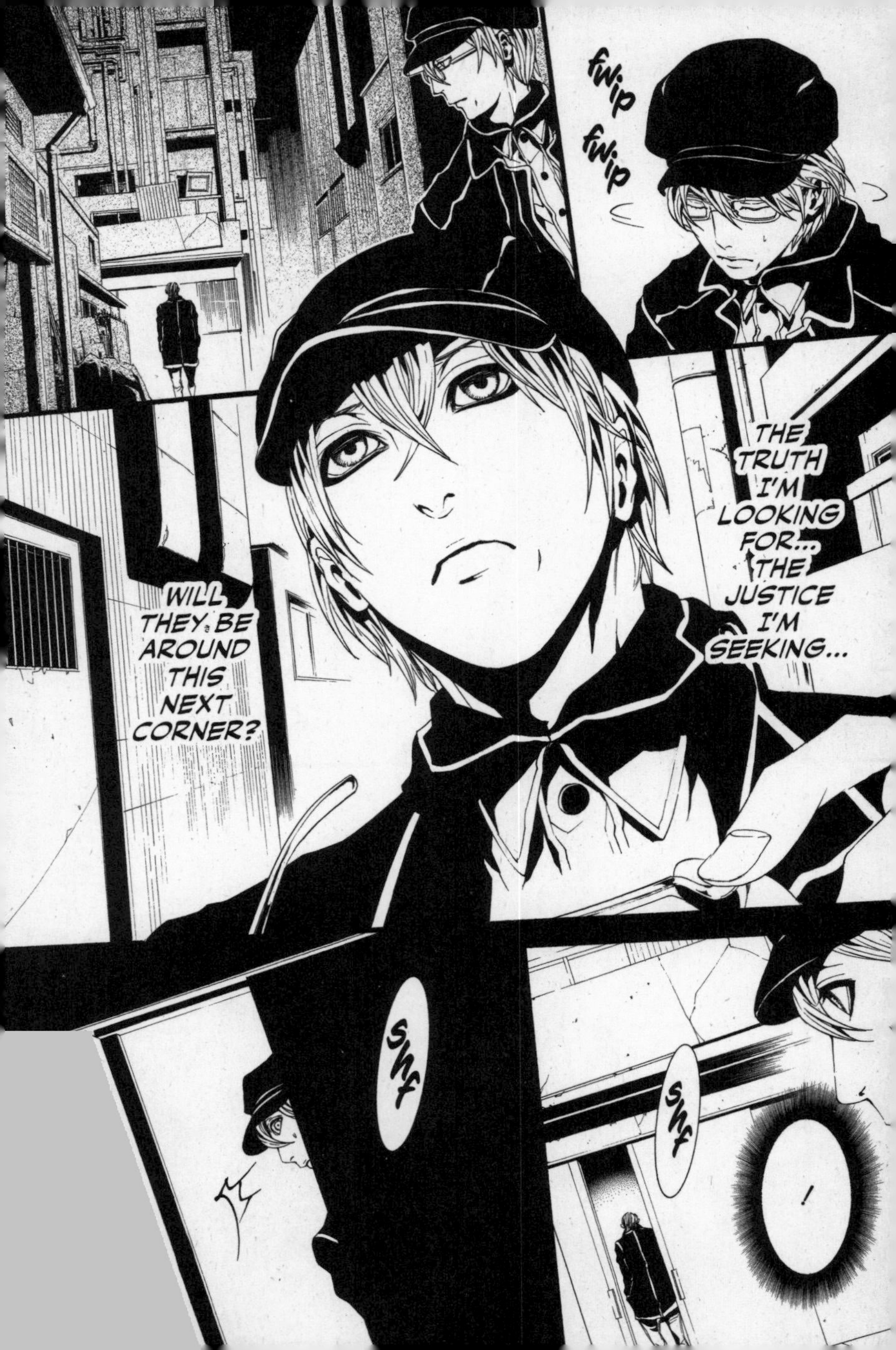
fwip fwip
THE TRUTH I'M LOOKING FOR... THE JUSTICE I'M SEEKING...
WILL THEY BE AROUND THIS NEXT CORNER?
snf
!
snf

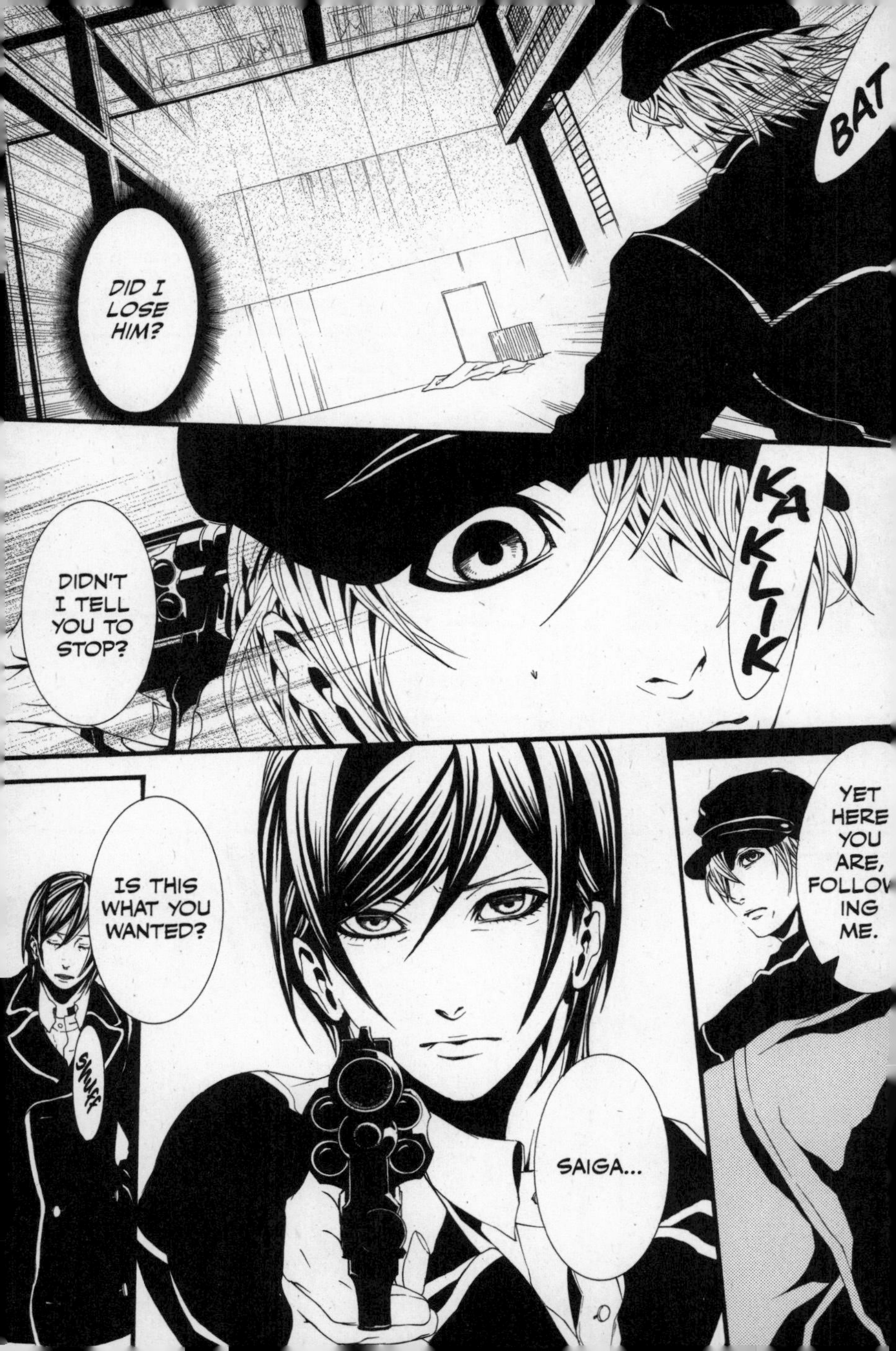

BAT
DID I LOSE HIM?
KAKLIK
DIDN'T I TELL YOU TO STOP?
YET HERE YOU ARE, FOLLOWING ME.
IS THIS WHAT YOU WANTED?
SAIGA...
SNUFF

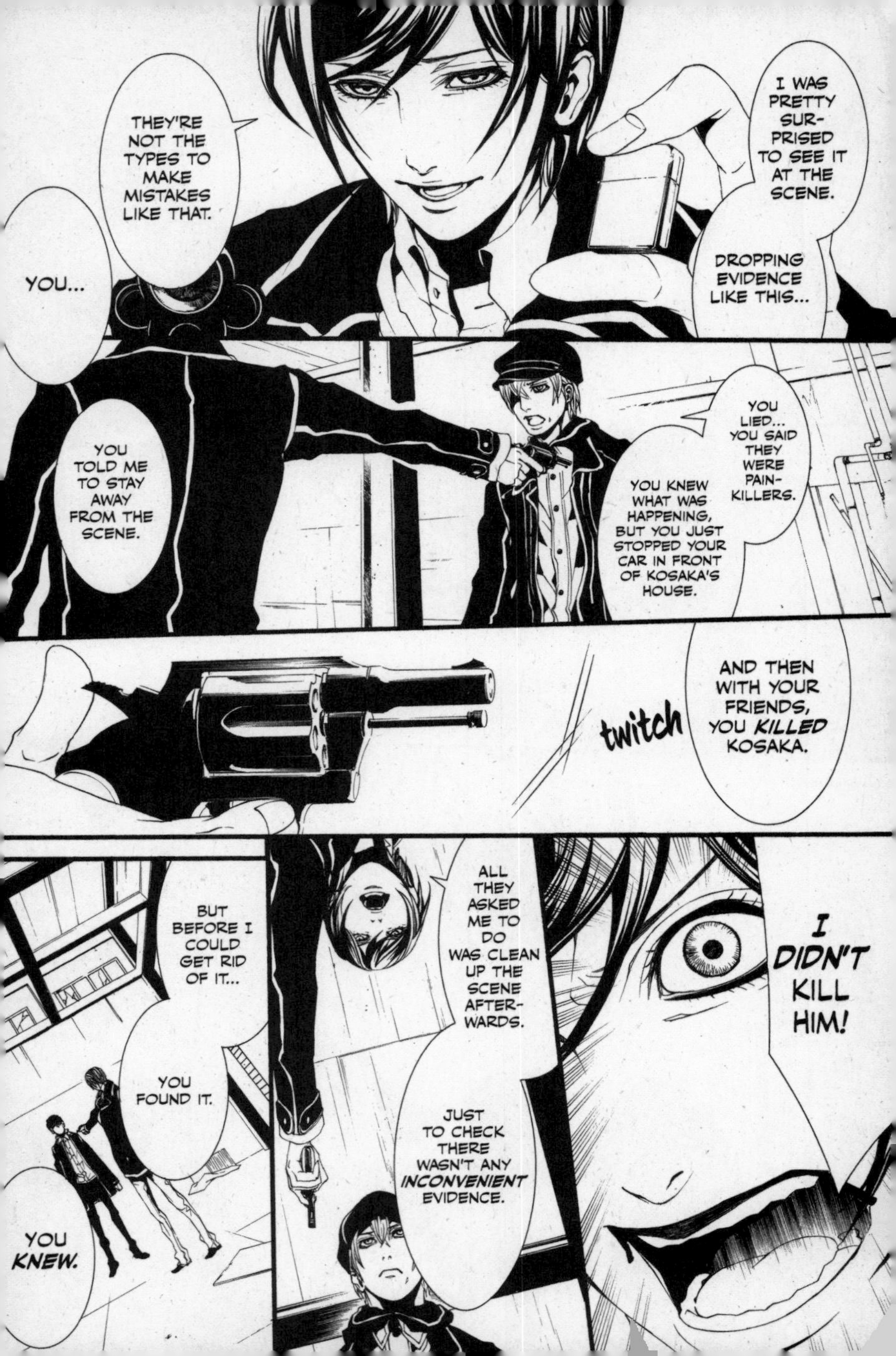
I WAS PRETTY SUR-PRISED TO SEE IT AT THE SCENE.
DROPPING EVIDENCE LIKE THIS...
THEY'RE NOT THE TYPES TO MAKE MISTAKES LIKE THAT.
YOU...
YOU LIED... YOU SAID THEY WERE PAIN-KILLERS.
YOU KNEW WHAT WAS HAPPENING, BUT YOU JUST STOPPED YOUR CAR IN FRONT OF KOSAKA'S HOUSE.
YOU TOLD ME TO STAY AWAY FROM THE SCENE.
AND THEN WITH YOUR FRIENDS, YOU *KILLED* KOSAKA.
twitch
I DIDN'T KILL HIM!
ALL THEY ASKED ME TO DO WAS CLEAN UP THE SCENE AFTER-WARDS.
JUST TO CHECK THERE WASN'T ANY *INCONVENIENT* EVIDENCE.
BUT BEFORE I COULD GET RID OF IT...
YOU FOUND IT.
YOU *KNEW.*

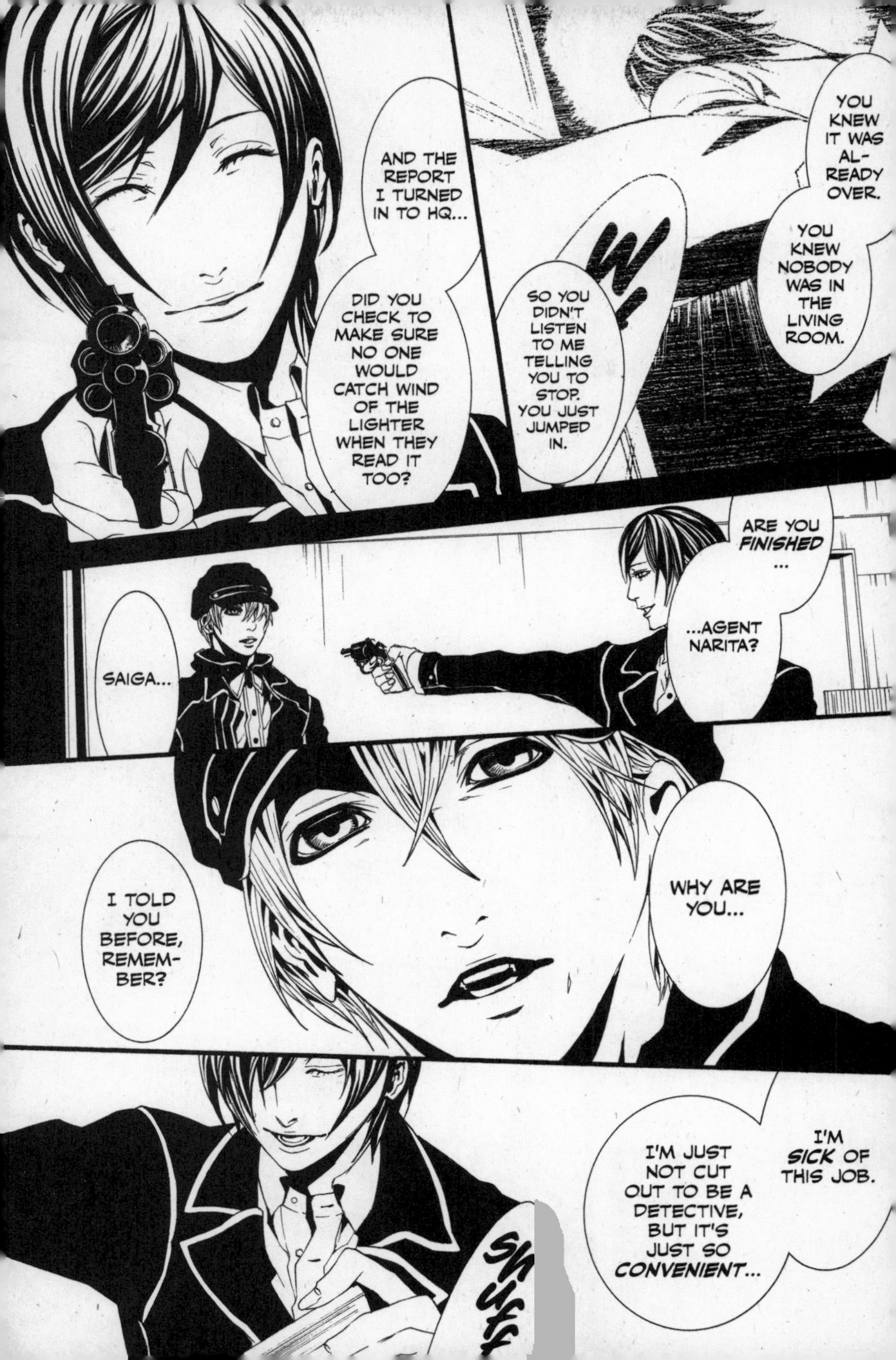

YOU KNEW IT WAS AL-READY OVER.
YOU KNEW NOBODY WAS IN THE LIVING ROOM.
SO YOU DIDN'T LISTEN TO ME TELLING YOU TO STOP. YOU JUST JUMPED IN.
AND THE REPORT I TURNED IN TO HQ...
DID YOU CHECK TO MAKE SURE NO ONE WOULD CATCH WIND OF THE LIGHTER WHEN THEY READ IT TOO?
ARE YOU *FINISHED*...
...AGENT NARITA?
SAIGA...
WHY ARE YOU...
I TOLD YOU BEFORE, REMEM-BER?
I'M *SICK* OF THIS JOB.
I'M JUST NOT CUT OUT TO BE A DETECTIVE, BUT IT'S JUST SO *CONVENIENT*...

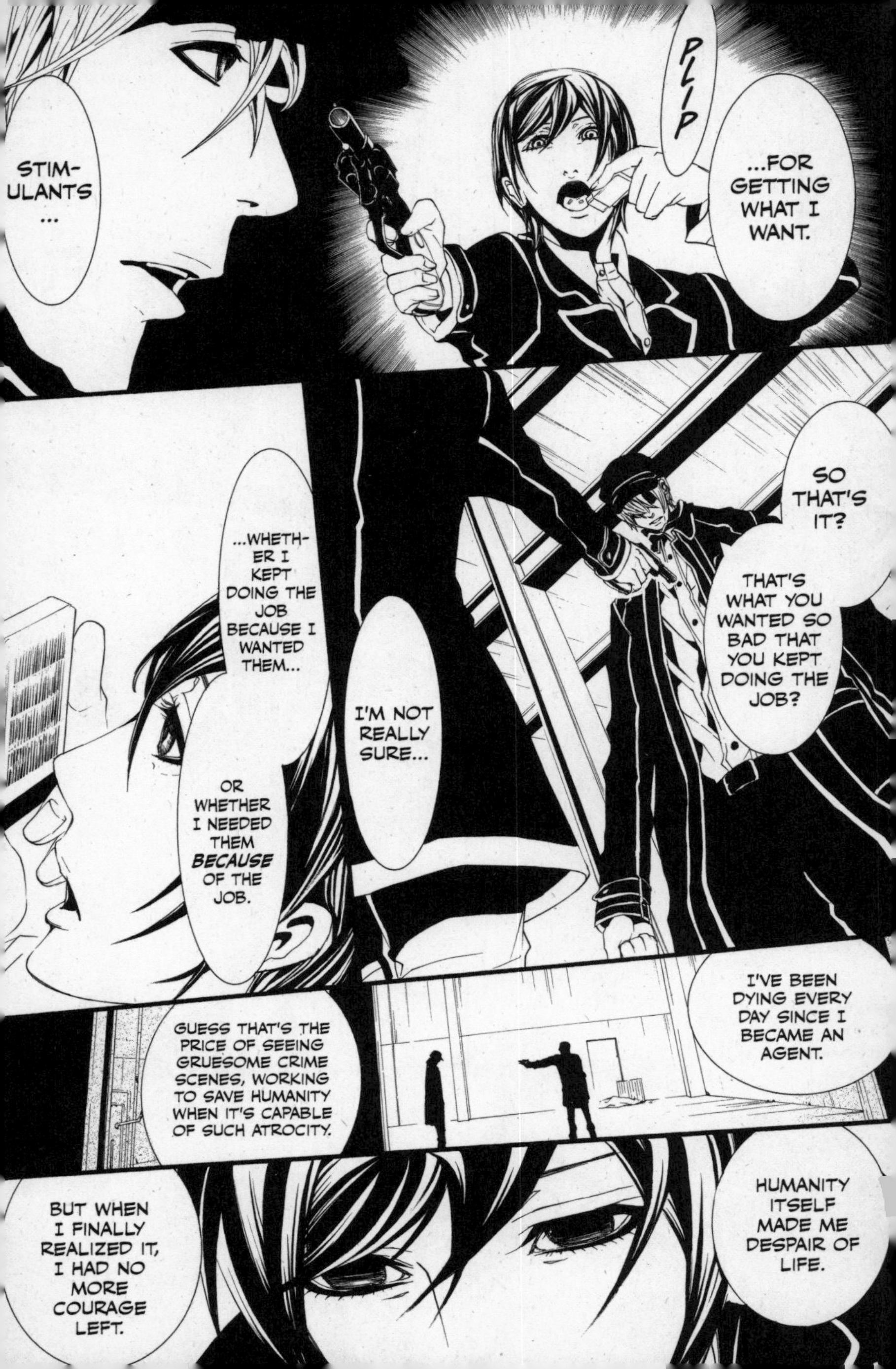
PLIP
...FOR GETTING WHAT I WANT.
STIM-ULANTS ...
SO THAT'S IT?
THAT'S WHAT YOU WANTED SO BAD THAT YOU KEPT DOING THE JOB?
I'M NOT REALLY SURE...
...WHETH-ER I KEPT DOING THE JOB BECAUSE I WANTED THEM...
OR WHETHER I NEEDED THEM *BECAUSE* OF THE JOB.
I'VE BEEN DYING EVERY DAY SINCE I BECAME AN AGENT.
GUESS THAT'S THE PRICE OF SEEING GRUESOME CRIME SCENES, WORKING TO SAVE HUMANITY WHEN IT'S CAPABLE OF SUCH ATROCITY.
HUMANITY ITSELF MADE ME DESPAIR OF LIFE.
BUT WHEN I FINALLY REALIZED IT, I HAD NO MORE COURAGE LEFT.

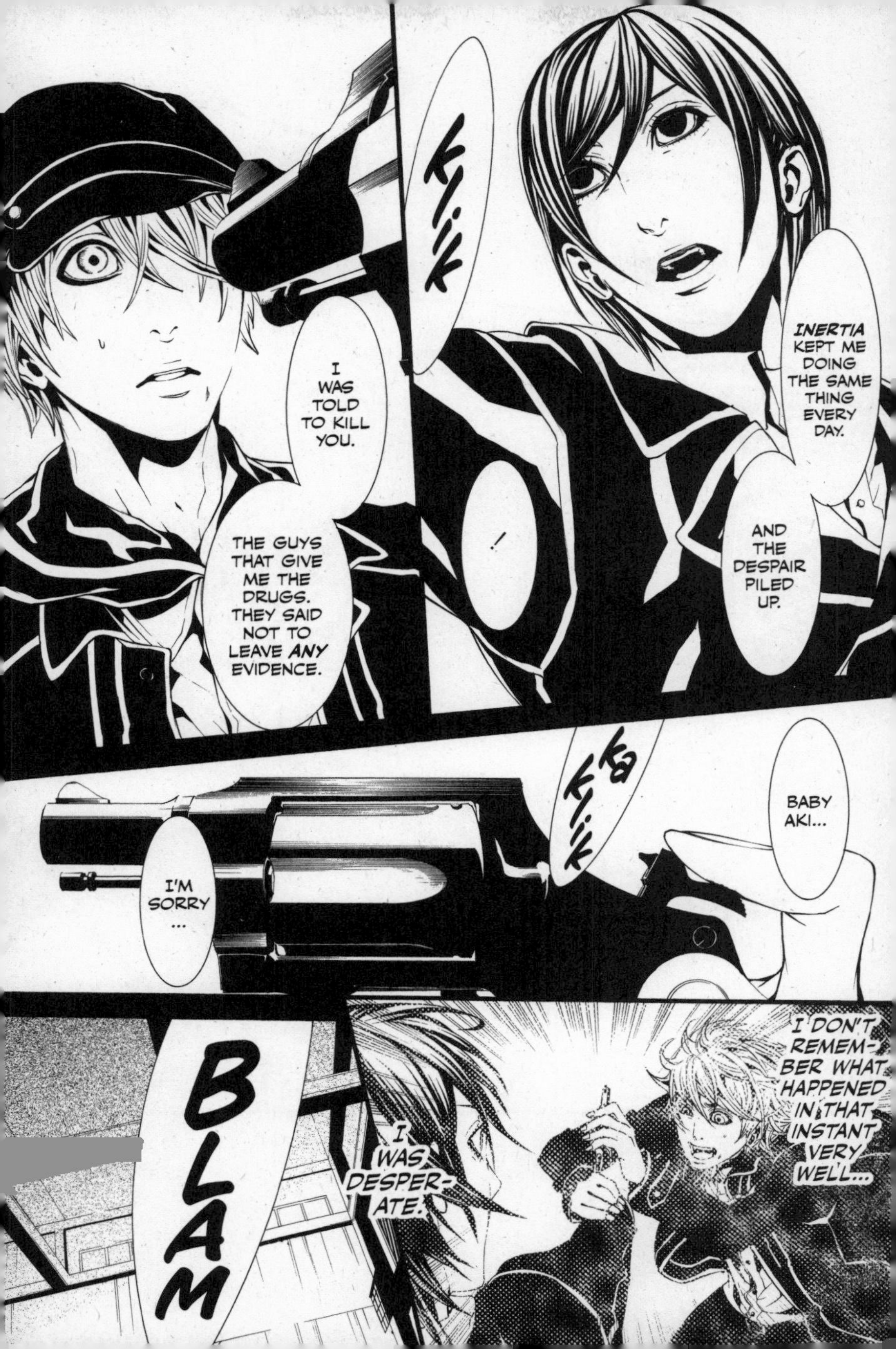
INERTIA KEPT ME DOING THE SAME THING EVERY DAY.
AND THE DESPAIR PILED UP.
Kliik
!
I WAS TOLD TO KILL YOU.
THE GUYS THAT GIVE ME THE DRUGS. THEY SAID NOT TO LEAVE ANY EVIDENCE.
BABY AKI...
ka kliik
I'M SORRY ...
I DON'T REMEM-BER WHAT HAPPENED IN THAT INSTANT VERY WELL...
I WAS DESPER-ATE.
BLAM

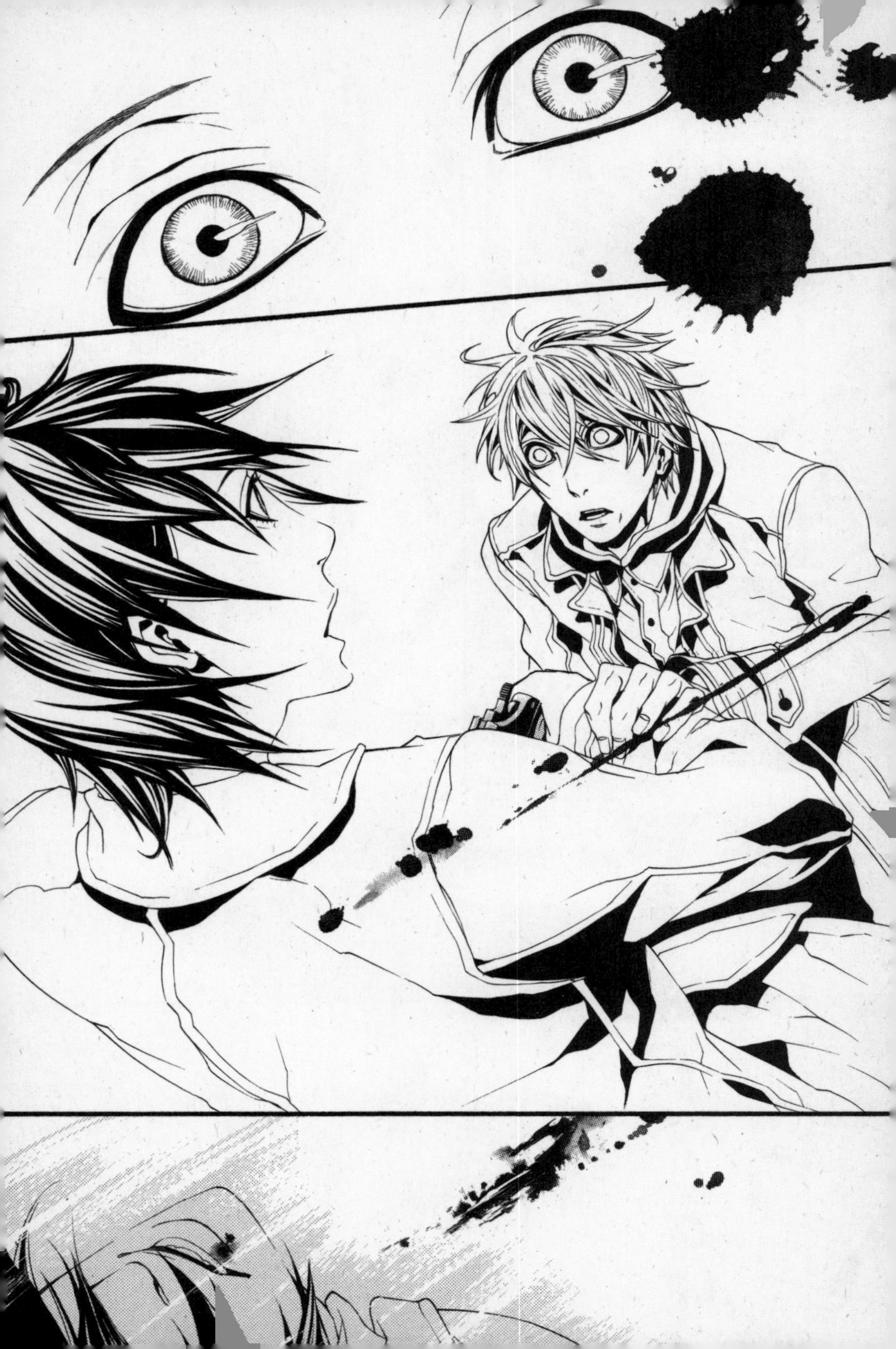

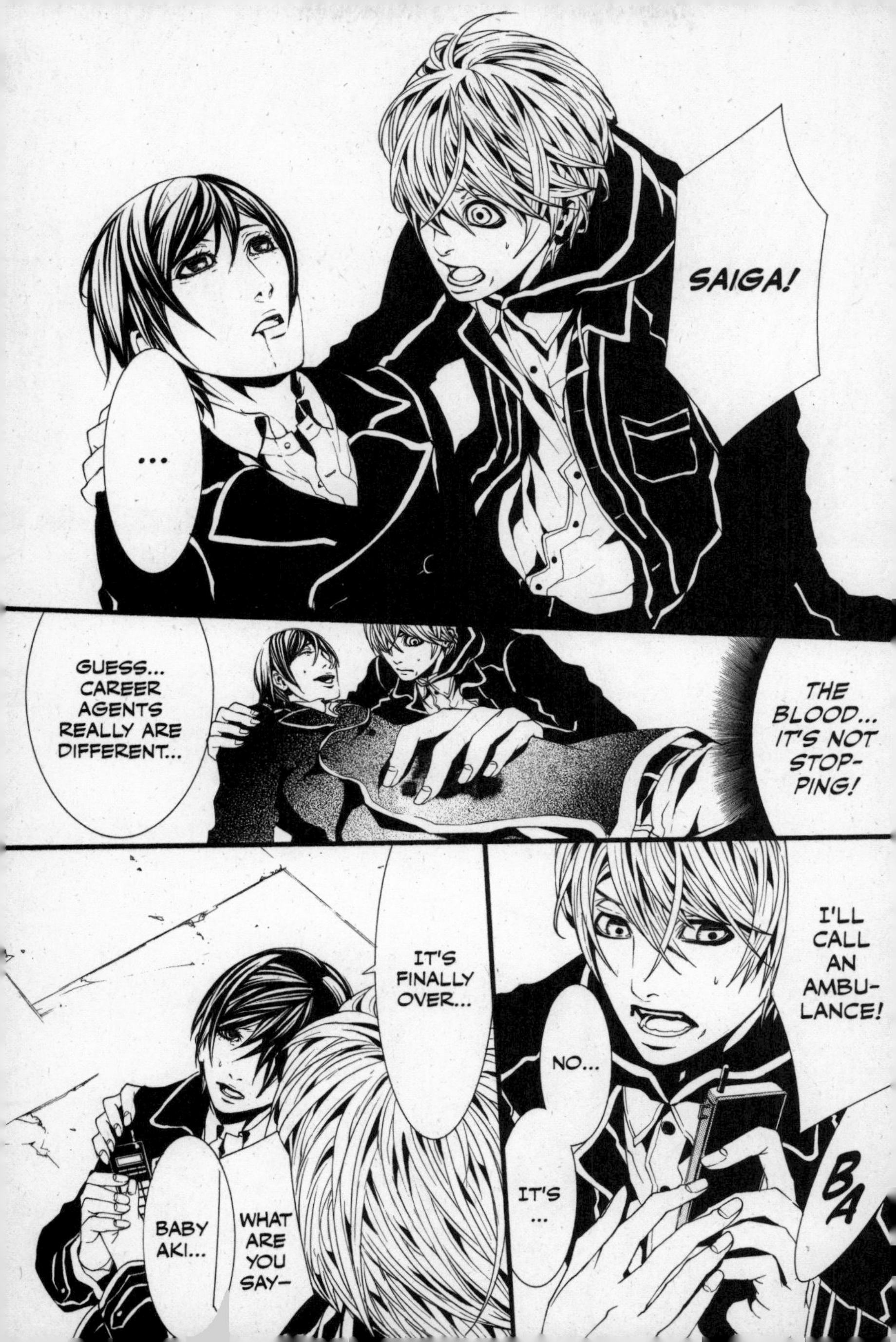
SAIGA!
...
THE BLOOD... IT'S NOT STOP-PING!
GUESS... CAREER AGENTS REALLY ARE DIFFERENT...
I'LL CALL AN AMBU-LANCE!
NO...
BA
IT'S ...
IT'S FINALLY OVER...
WHAT ARE YOU SAY-
BABY AKI...

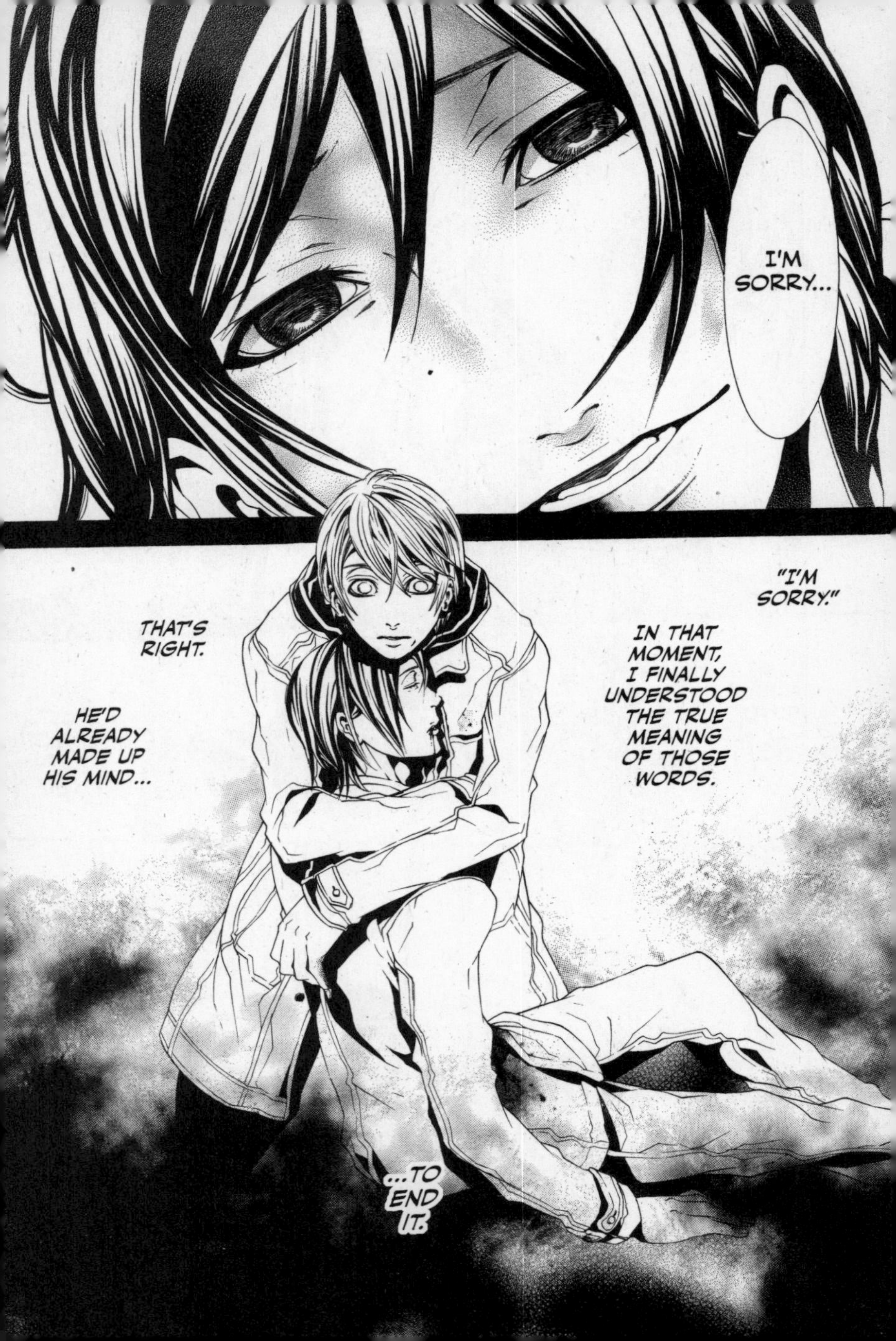
I'M SORRY...
"I'M SORRY."
IN THAT MOMENT, I FINALLY UNDERSTOOD THE TRUE MEANING OF THOSE WORDS.
THAT'S RIGHT.
HE'D ALREADY MADE UP HIS MIND...
...TO END IT.

naked ape : Saki Otoh & Nakamura Tomomi

switch

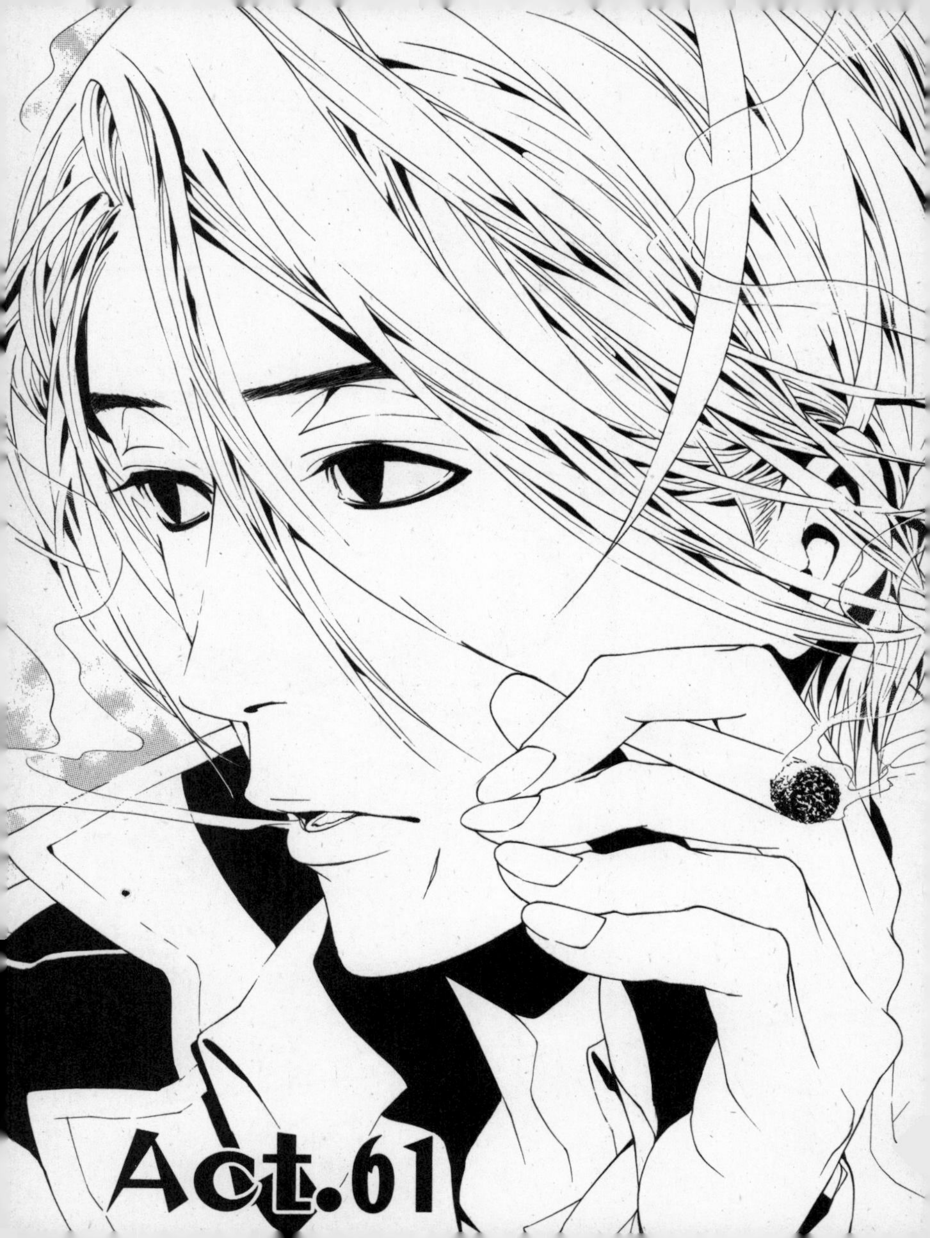
Act.61

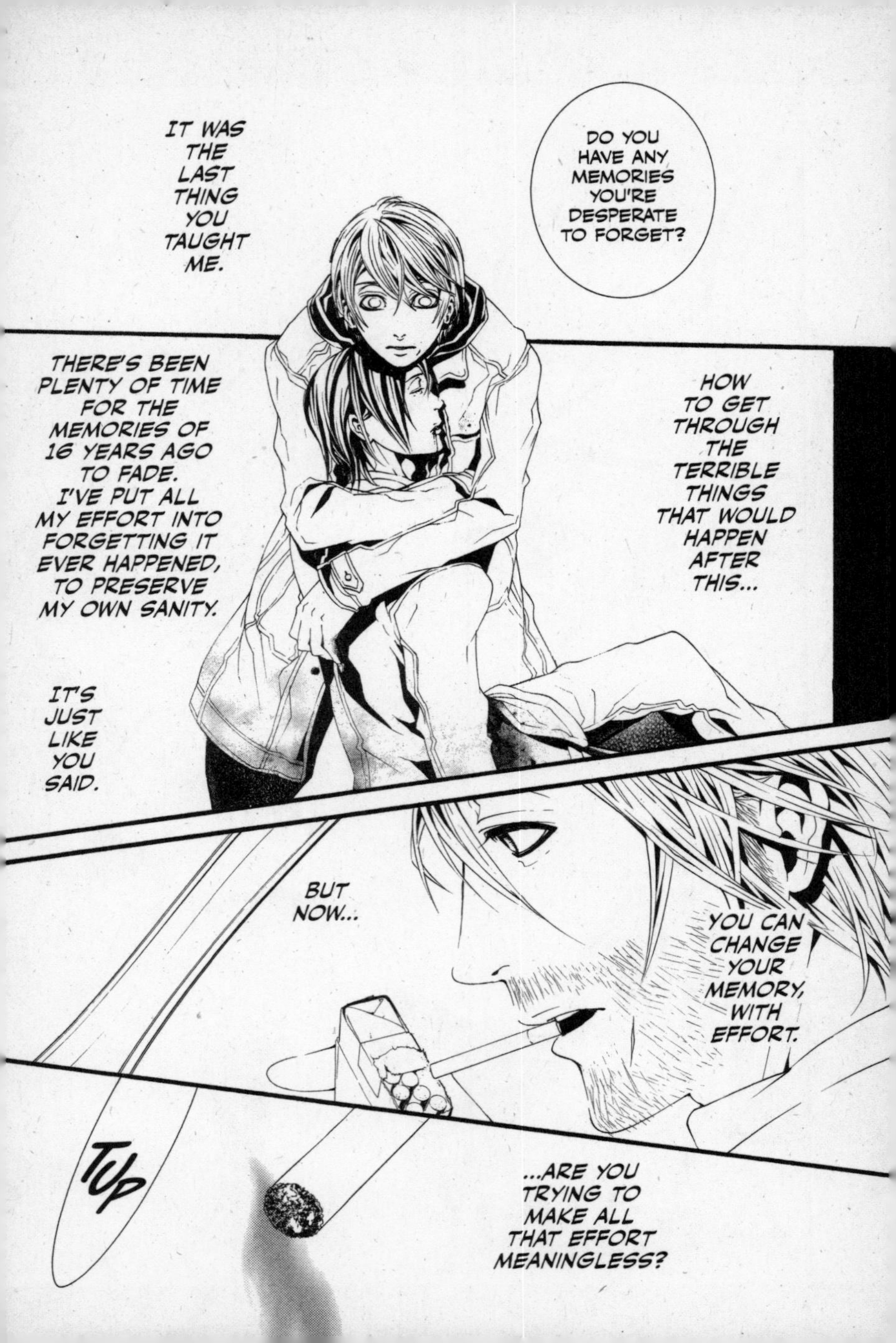
DO YOU HAVE ANY MEMORIES YOU'RE DESPERATE TO FORGET?
IT WAS THE LAST THING YOU TAUGHT ME.
HOW TO GET THROUGH THE TERRIBLE THINGS THAT WOULD HAPPEN AFTER THIS...
THERE'S BEEN PLENTY OF TIME FOR THE MEMORIES OF 16 YEARS AGO TO FADE. I'VE PUT ALL MY EFFORT INTO FORGETTING IT EVER HAPPENED, TO PRESERVE MY OWN SANITY.
IT'S JUST LIKE YOU SAID.
YOU CAN CHANGE YOUR MEMORY, WITH EFFORT.
BUT NOW...
...ARE YOU TRYING TO MAKE ALL THAT EFFORT MEANINGLESS?
TUP

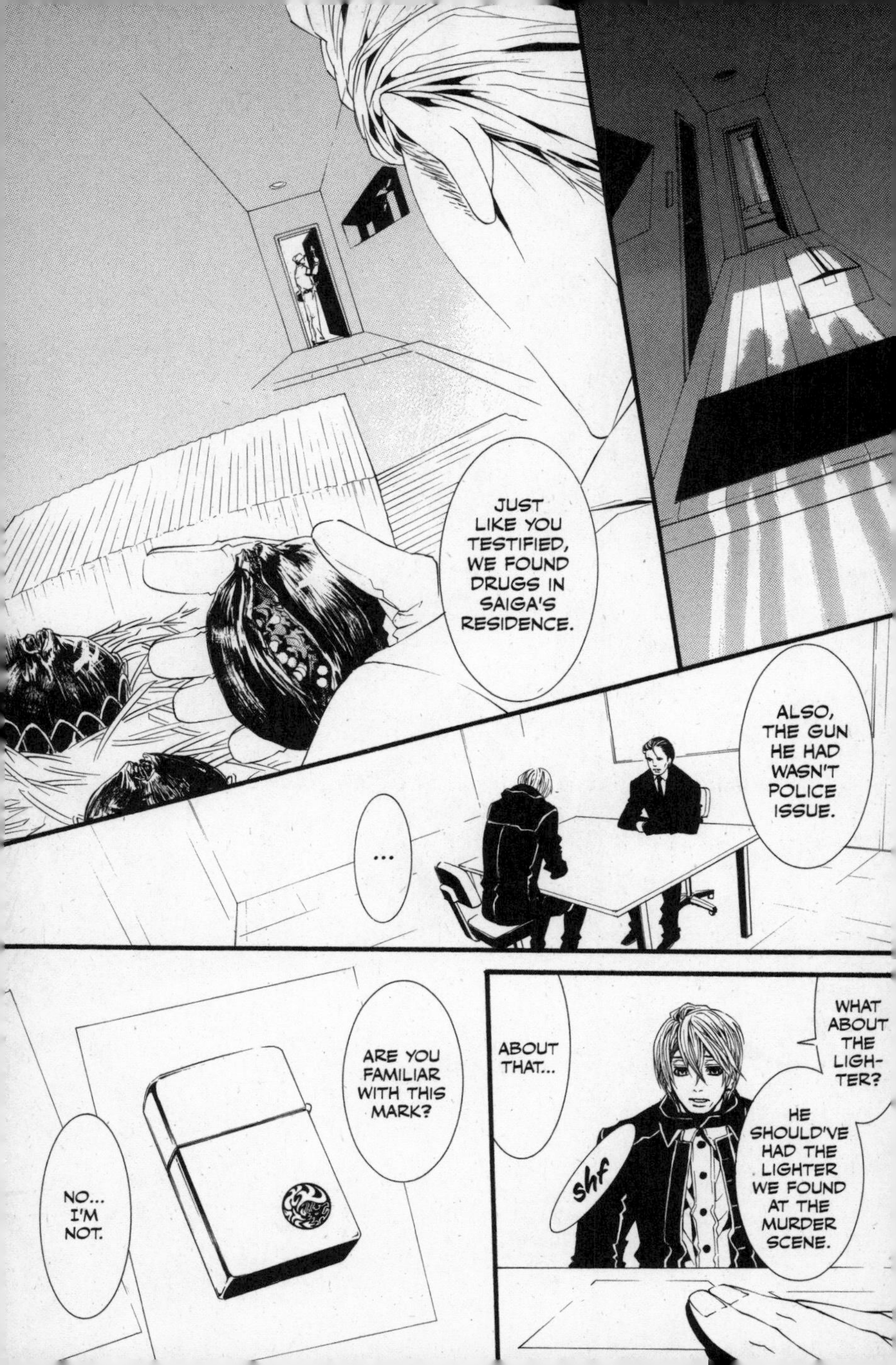
JUST LIKE YOU TESTIFIED, WE FOUND DRUGS IN SAIGA'S RESIDENCE.
ALSO, THE GUN HE HAD WASN'T POLICE ISSUE.
...
WHAT ABOUT THE LIGH-TER?
HE SHOULD'VE HAD THE LIGHTER WE FOUND AT THE MURDER SCENE.
shf
ABOUT THAT...
ARE YOU FAMILIAR WITH THIS MARK?
NO... I'M NOT.

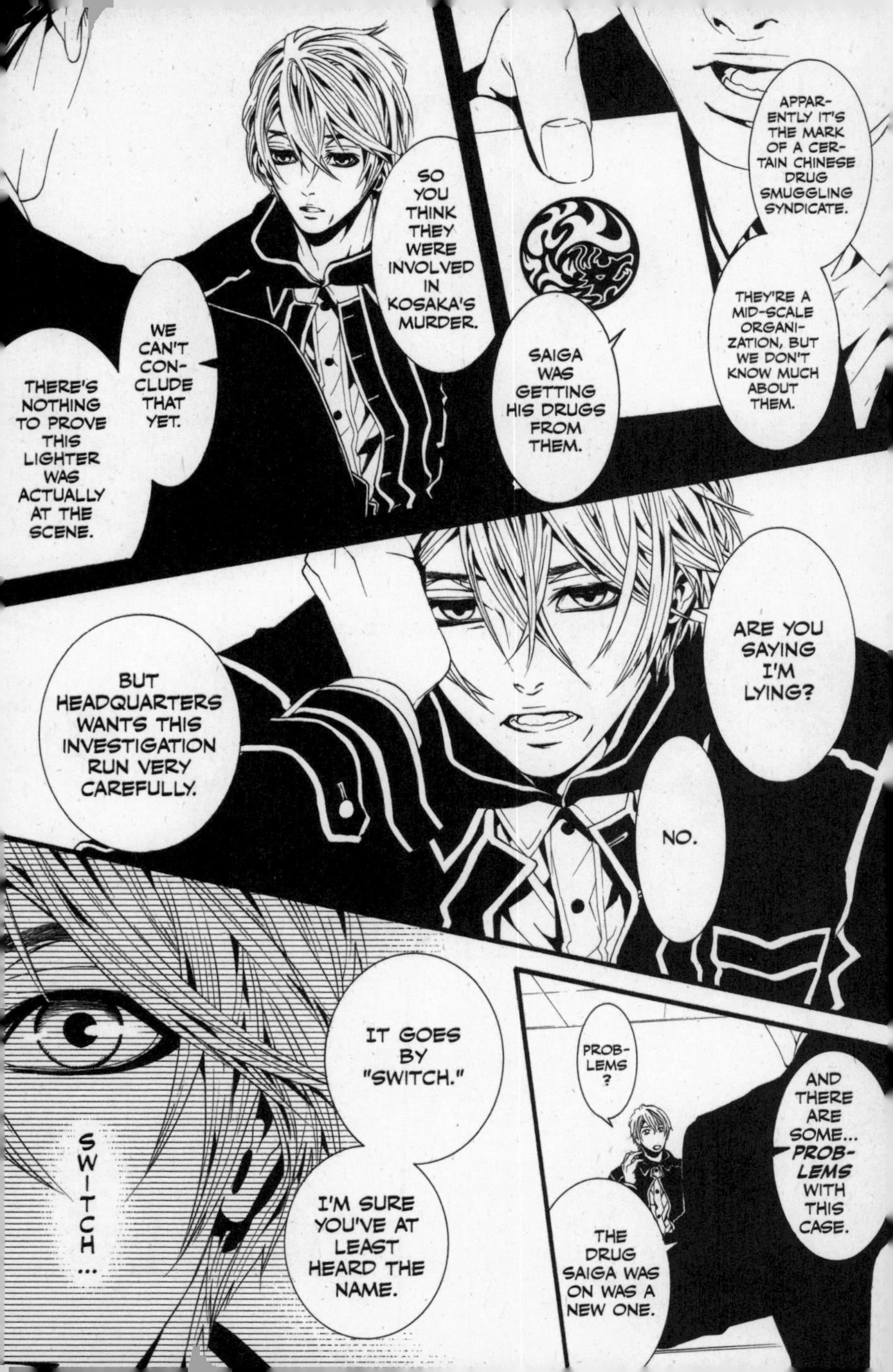
APPARENTLY IT'S THE MARK OF A CERTAIN CHINESE DRUG SMUGGLING SYNDICATE.
THEY'RE A MID-SCALE ORGANIZATION, BUT WE DON'T KNOW MUCH ABOUT THEM.
SAIGA WAS GETTING HIS DRUGS FROM THEM.
SO YOU THINK THEY WERE INVOLVED IN KOSAKA'S MURDER.
WE CAN'T CONCLUDE THAT YET.
THERE'S NOTHING TO PROVE THIS LIGHTER WAS ACTUALLY AT THE SCENE.
ARE YOU SAYING I'M LYING?
NO.
BUT HEADQUARTERS WANTS THIS INVESTIGATION RUN VERY CAREFULLY.
AND THERE ARE SOME... *PROBLEMS* WITH THIS CASE.
PROBLEMS?
THE DRUG SAIGA WAS ON WAS A NEW ONE.
IT GOES BY "SWITCH."
I'M SURE YOU'VE AT LEAST HEARD THE NAME.
SWITCH...

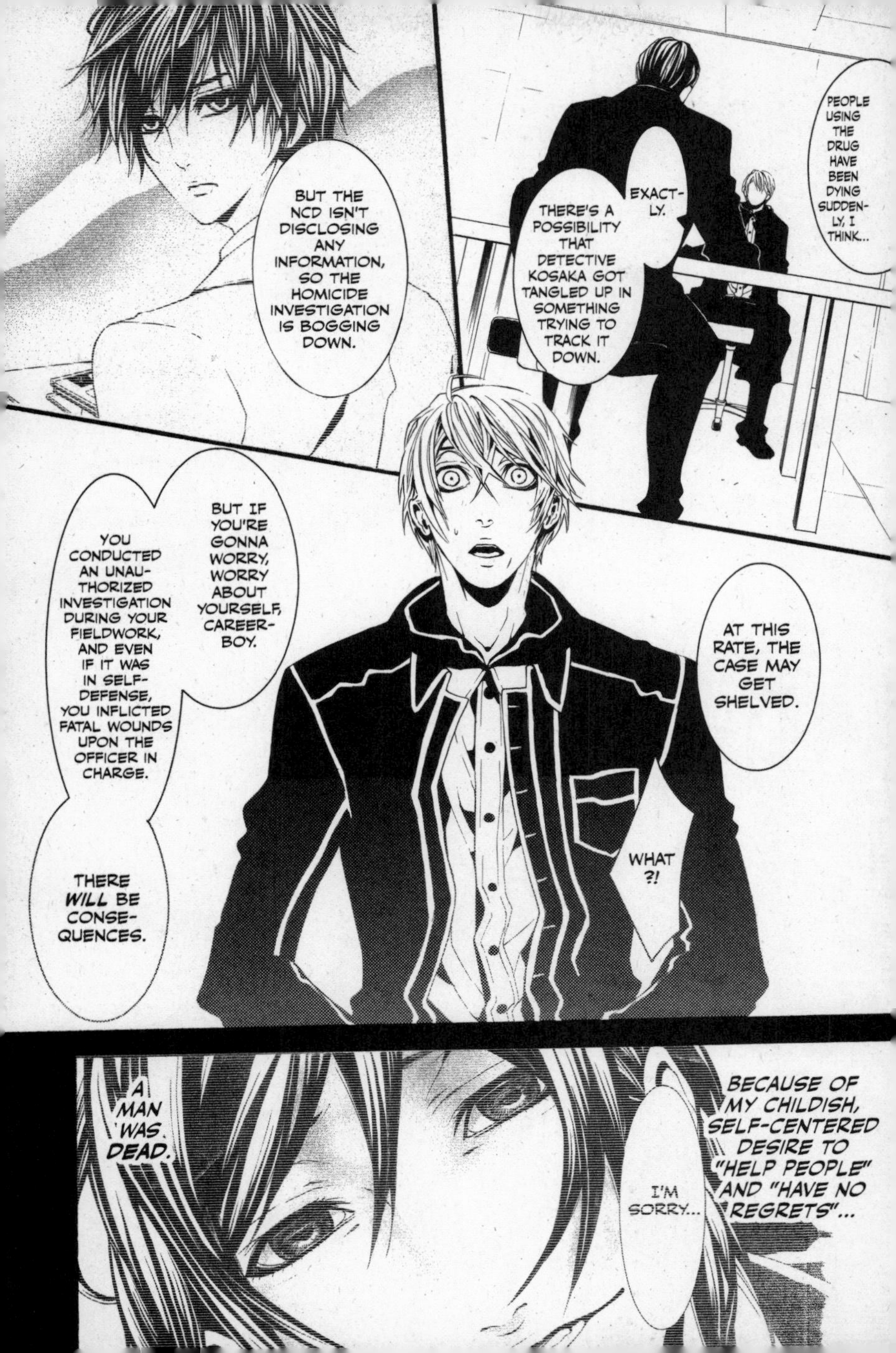
PEOPLE USING THE DRUG HAVE BEEN DYING SUDDEN-LY, I THINK...
EXACT-LY.
THERE'S A POSSIBILITY THAT DETECTIVE KOSAKA GOT TANGLED UP IN SOMETHING TRYING TO TRACK IT DOWN.
BUT THE NCD ISN'T DISCLOSING ANY INFORMATION, SO THE HOMICIDE INVESTIGATION IS BOGGING DOWN.
AT THIS RATE, THE CASE MAY GET SHELVED.
WHAT ?!
BUT IF YOU'RE GONNA WORRY, WORRY ABOUT YOURSELF, CAREER-BOY.
YOU CONDUCTED AN UNAU-THORIZED INVESTIGATION DURING YOUR FIELDWORK, AND EVEN IF IT WAS IN SELF-DEFENSE, YOU INFLICTED FATAL WOUNDS UPON THE OFFICER IN CHARGE.
THERE *WILL* BE CONSE-QUENCES.
BECAUSE OF MY CHILDISH, SELF-CENTERED DESIRE TO "HELP PEOPLE" AND "HAVE NO REGRETS"...
I'M SORRY...
A MAN WAS *DEAD*.

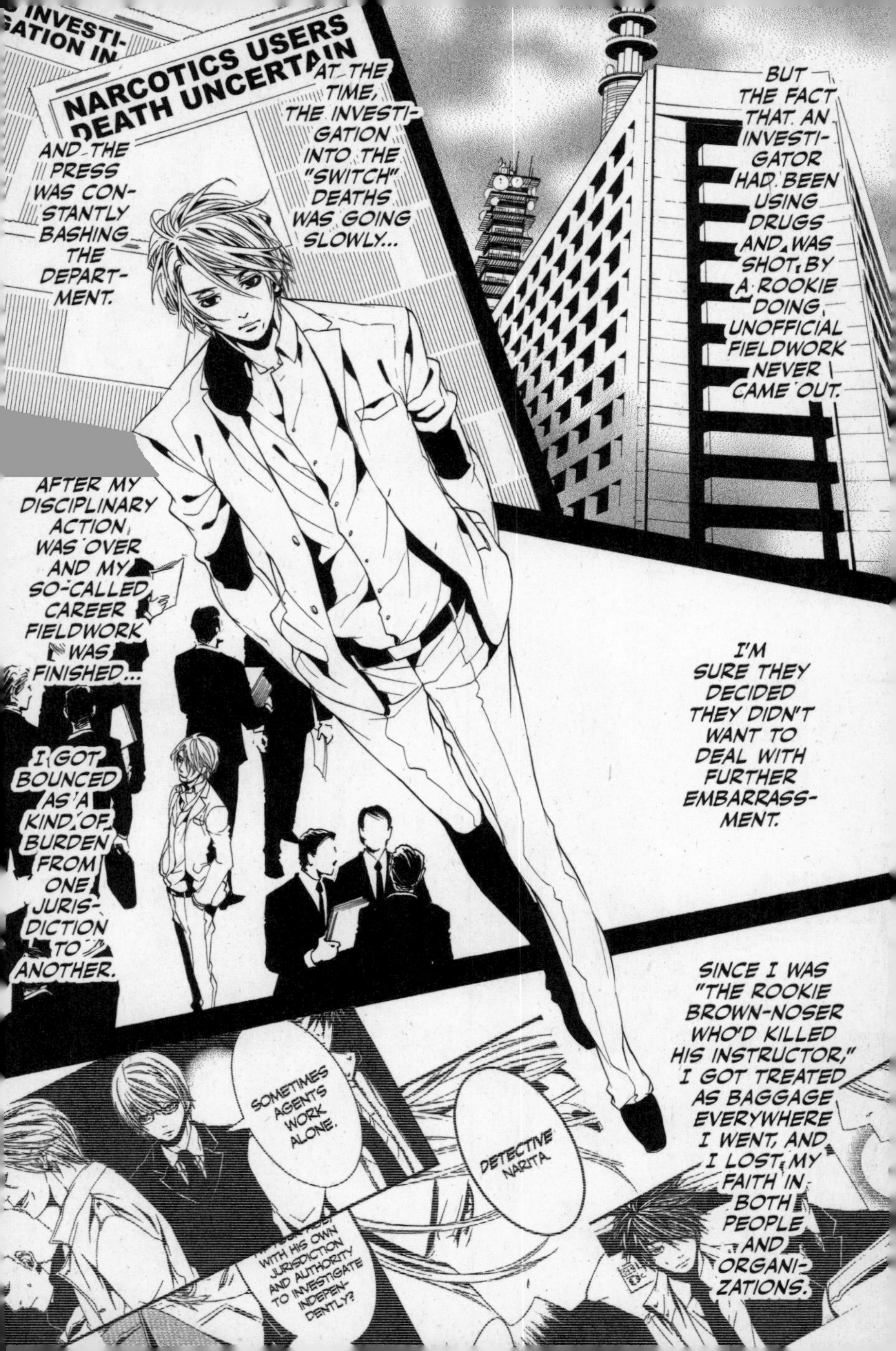
INVESTI-GATION IN
NARCOTICS USERS DEATH UNCERTAIN
AT THE TIME, THE INVESTIGATION INTO THE "SWITCH" DEATHS WAS GOING SLOWLY...
AND THE PRESS WAS CONSTANTLY BASHING THE DEPARTMENT.
BUT THE FACT THAT AN INVESTIGATOR HAD BEEN USING DRUGS AND WAS SHOT BY A ROOKIE DOING UNOFFICIAL FIELDWORK NEVER CAME OUT.
AFTER MY DISCIPLINARY ACTION WAS OVER AND MY SO-CALLED CAREER FIELDWORK WAS FINISHED...
I GOT BOUNCED AS A KIND OF BURDEN FROM ONE JURISDICTION TO ANOTHER.
I'M SURE THEY DECIDED THEY DIDN'T WANT TO DEAL WITH FURTHER EMBARRASSMENT.
SINCE I WAS "THE ROOKIE BROWN-NOSER WHO'D KILLED HIS INSTRUCTOR," I GOT TREATED AS BAGGAGE EVERYWHERE I WENT, AND I LOST MY FAITH IN BOTH PEOPLE AND ORGANIZATIONS.
DETECTIVE NARITA.
SOMETIMES AGENTS WORK ALONE.
WITH HIS OWN JURISDICTION AND AUTHORITY TO INVESTIGATE INDEPENDENTLY?

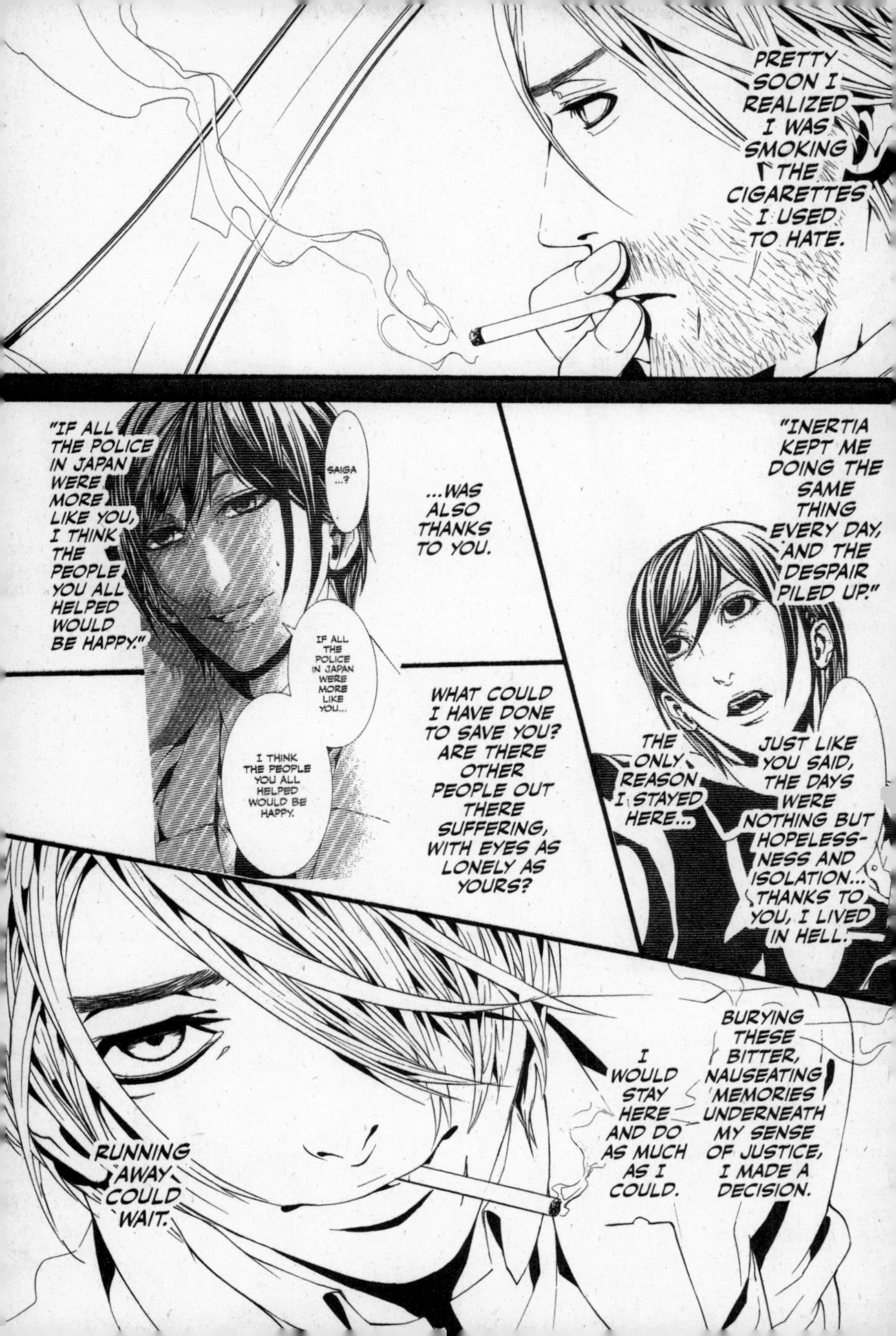
PRETTY SOON I REALIZED I WAS SMOKING THE CIGARETTES I USED TO HATE.
"INERTIA KEPT ME DOING THE SAME THING EVERY DAY, AND THE DESPAIR PILED UP."
JUST LIKE YOU SAID, THE DAYS WERE NOTHING BUT HOPELESS-NESS AND ISOLATION... THANKS TO YOU, I LIVED IN HELL.
THE ONLY REASON I STAYED HERE...
...WAS ALSO THANKS TO YOU.
SAIGA ...?
"IF ALL THE POLICE IN JAPAN WERE MORE LIKE YOU, I THINK THE PEOPLE YOU ALL HELPED WOULD BE HAPPY."
IF ALL THE POLICE IN JAPAN WERE MORE LIKE YOU...
I THINK THE PEOPLE YOU ALL HELPED WOULD BE HAPPY.
WHAT COULD I HAVE DONE TO SAVE YOU? ARE THERE OTHER PEOPLE OUT THERE SUFFERING, WITH EYES AS LONELY AS YOURS?
BURYING THESE BITTER, NAUSEATING MEMORIES UNDERNEATH MY SENSE OF JUSTICE, I MADE A DECISION.
I WOULD STAY HERE AND DO AS MUCH AS I COULD.
RUNNING AWAY COULD WAIT.

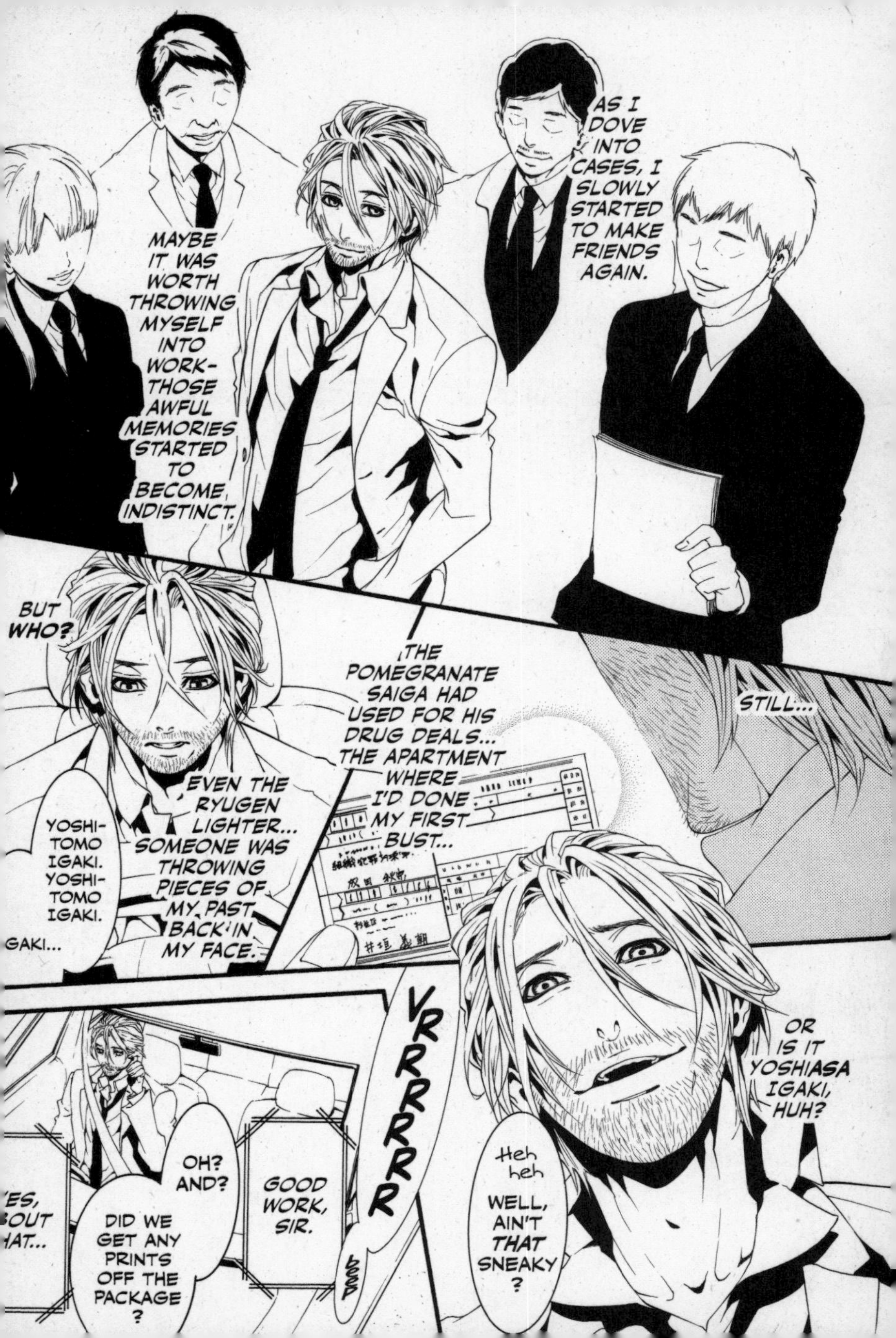
AS I DOVE INTO CASES, I SLOWLY STARTED TO MAKE FRIENDS AGAIN.
MAYBE IT WAS WORTH THROWING MYSELF INTO WORK- THOSE AWFUL MEMORIES STARTED TO BECOME INDISTINCT.
STILL...
THE POMEGRANATE SAIGA HAD USED FOR HIS DRUG DEALS... THE APARTMENT WHERE I'D DONE MY FIRST BUST...
BUT WHO?
EVEN THE RYUGEN LIGHTER... SOMEONE WAS THROWING PIECES OF MY PAST BACK IN MY FACE.
YOSHI-TOMO IGAKI. YOSHI-TOMO IGAKI.
GAKI...
OR IS IT YOSHIASA IGAKI, HUH?
Heh heh
WELL, AIN'T *THAT* SNEAKY?
VRRRRRR
beep
GOOD WORK, SIR.
OH? AND?
DID WE GET ANY PRINTS OFF THE PACKAGE?
ES, BOUT HAT...

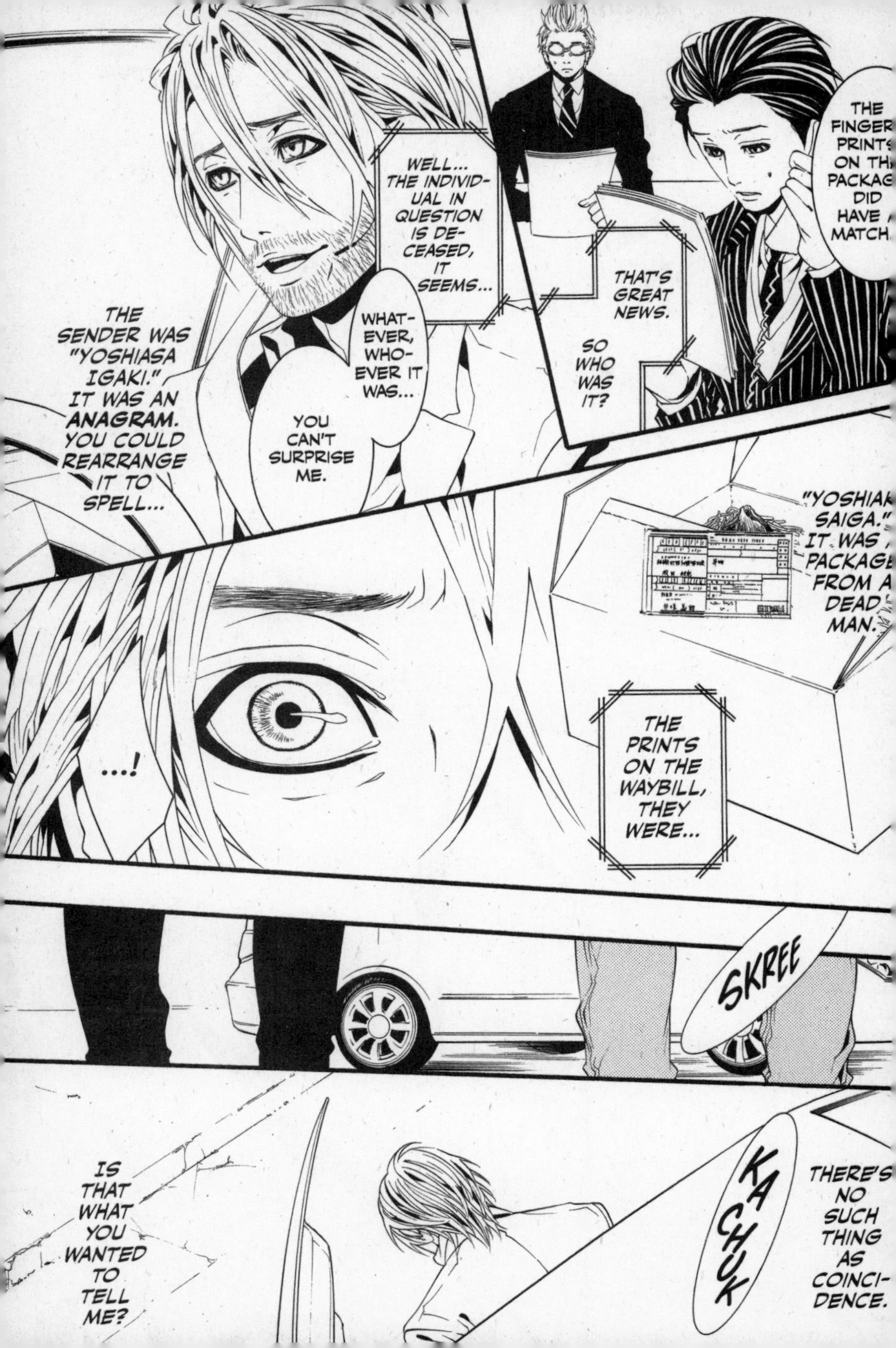
THE FINGERPRINTS ON TH PACKAG DID HAVE MATCH.
THAT'S GREAT NEWS.
SO WHO WAS IT?
WELL... THE INDIVIDUAL IN QUESTION IS DECEASED, IT SEEMS...
WHATEVER, WHOEVER IT WAS...
YOU CAN'T SURPRISE ME.
THE SENDER WAS "YOSHIASA IGAKI." IT WAS AN ANAGRAM. YOU COULD REARRANGE IT TO SPELL...
"YOSHIAK SAIGA." IT WAS PACKAGE FROM A DEAD MAN.
THE PRINTS ON THE WAYBILL, THEY WERE...
...!
SKREE
THERE'S NO SUCH THING AS COINCIDENCE.
KACHUK
IS THAT WHAT YOU WANTED TO TELL ME?

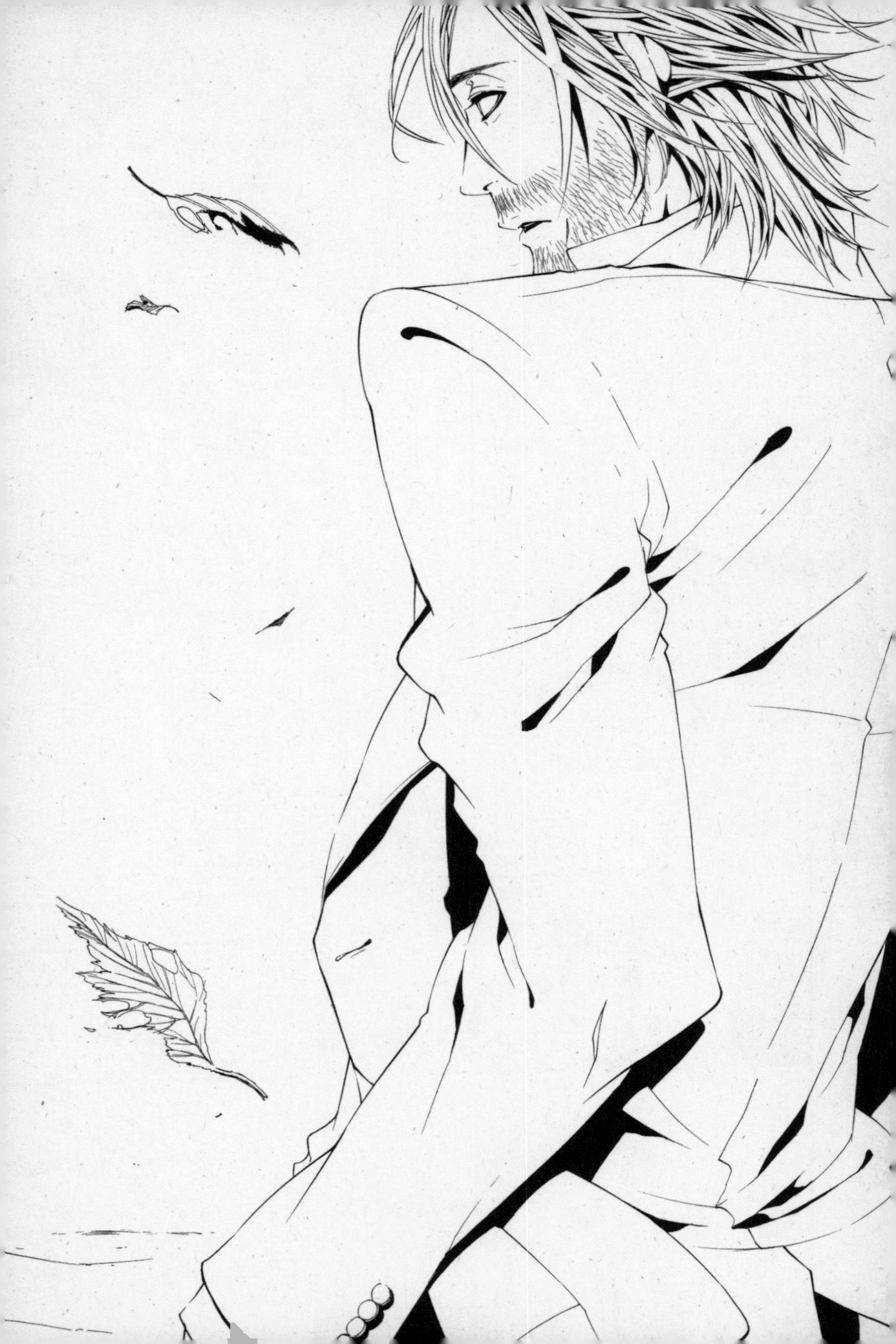

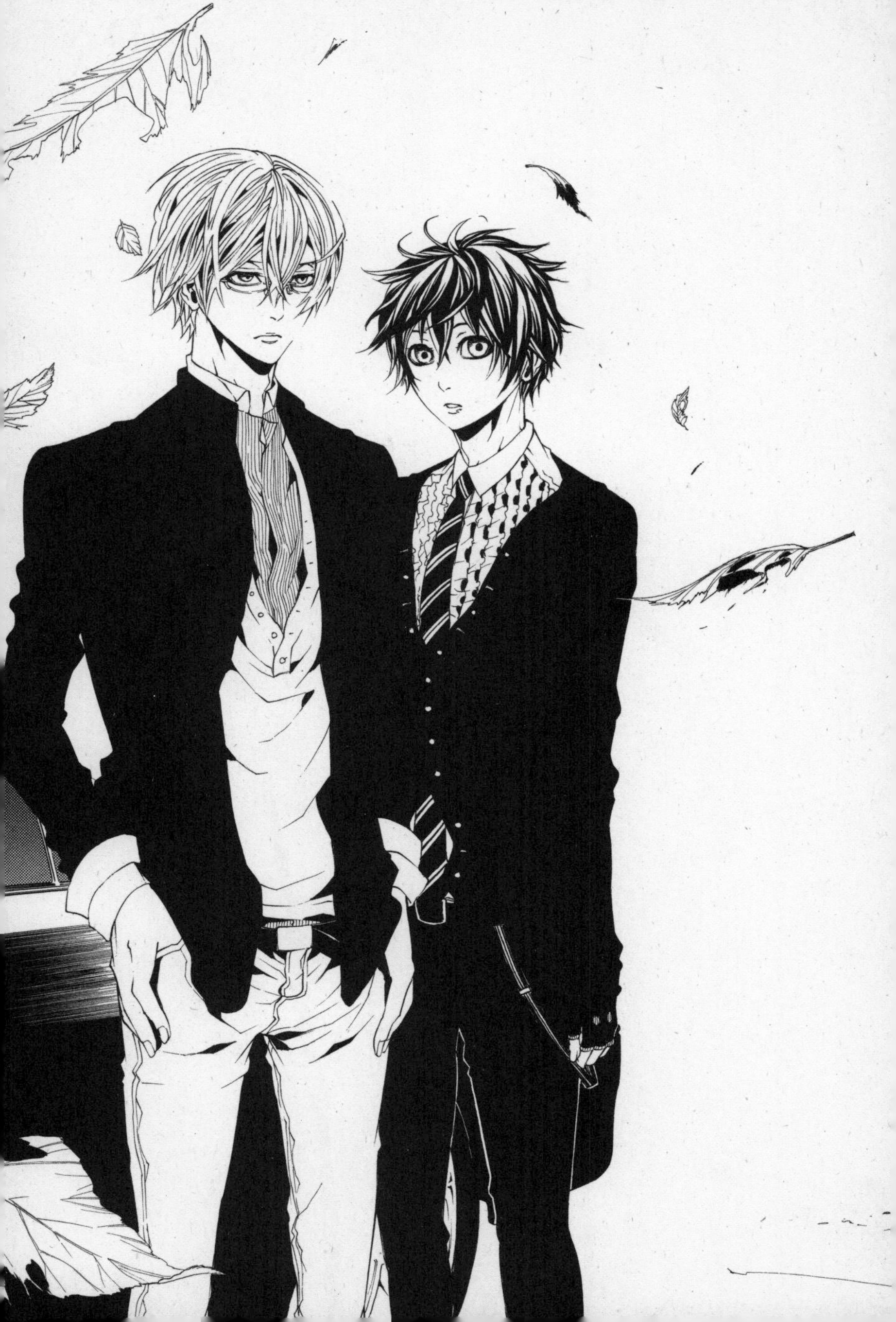

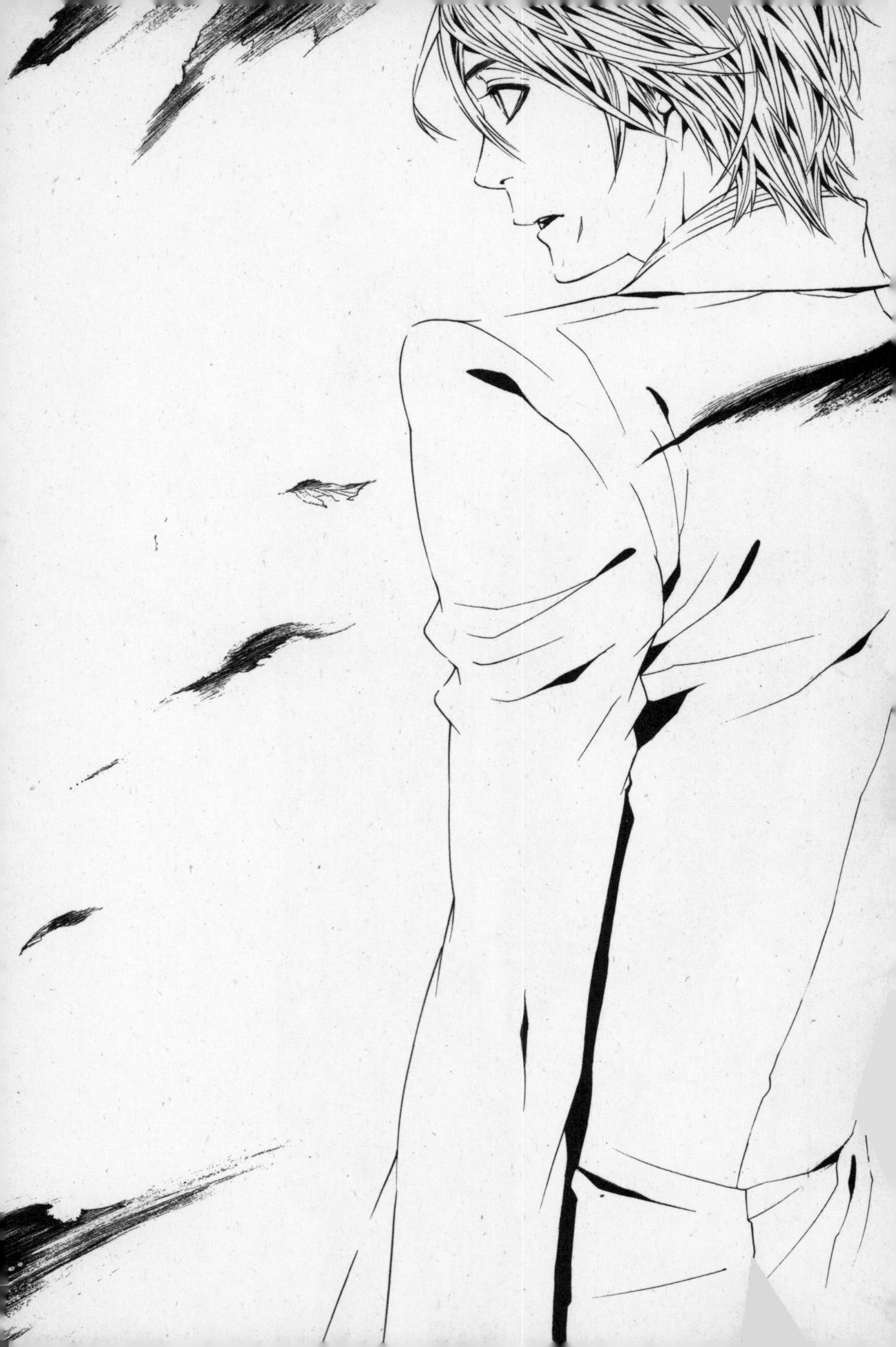

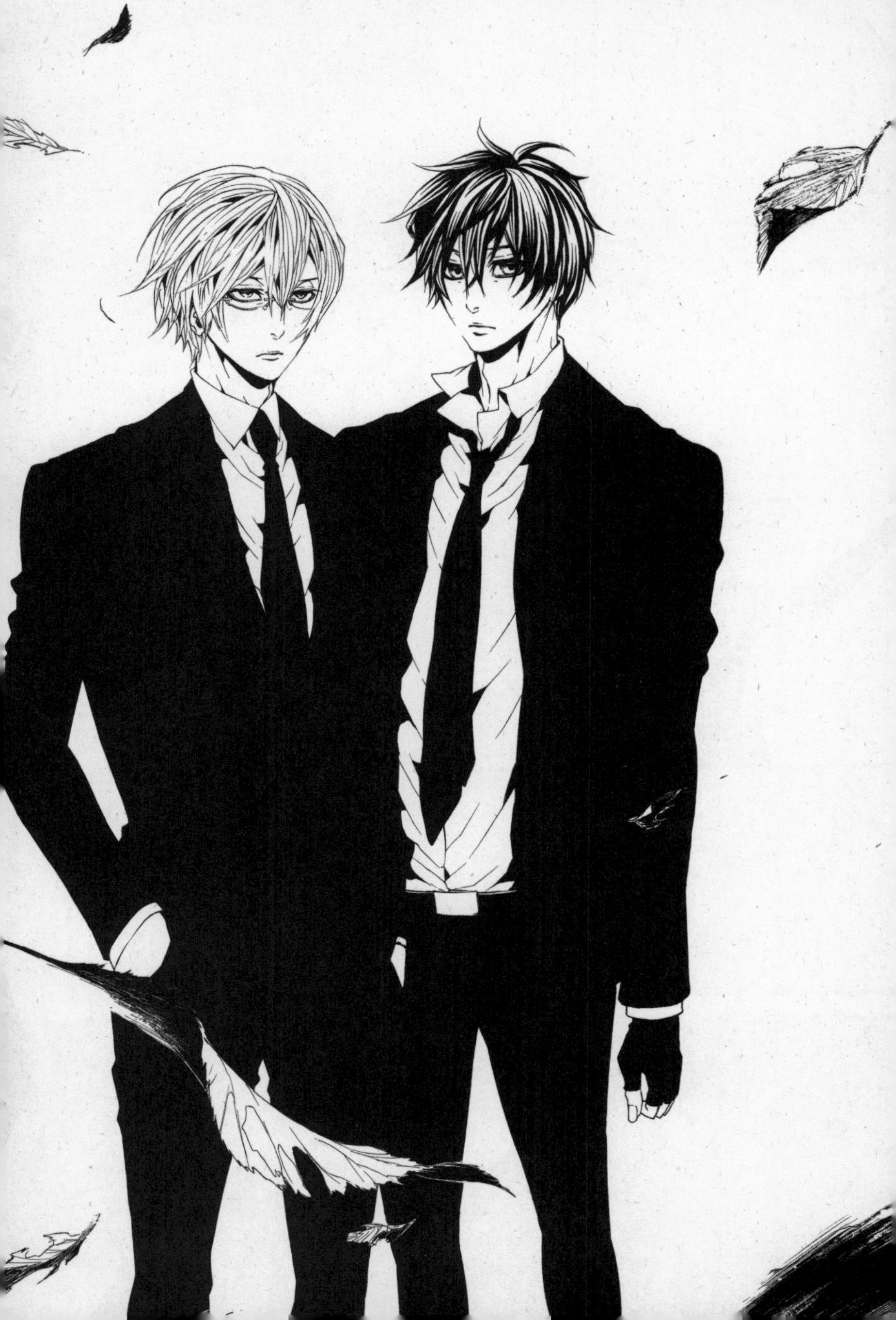

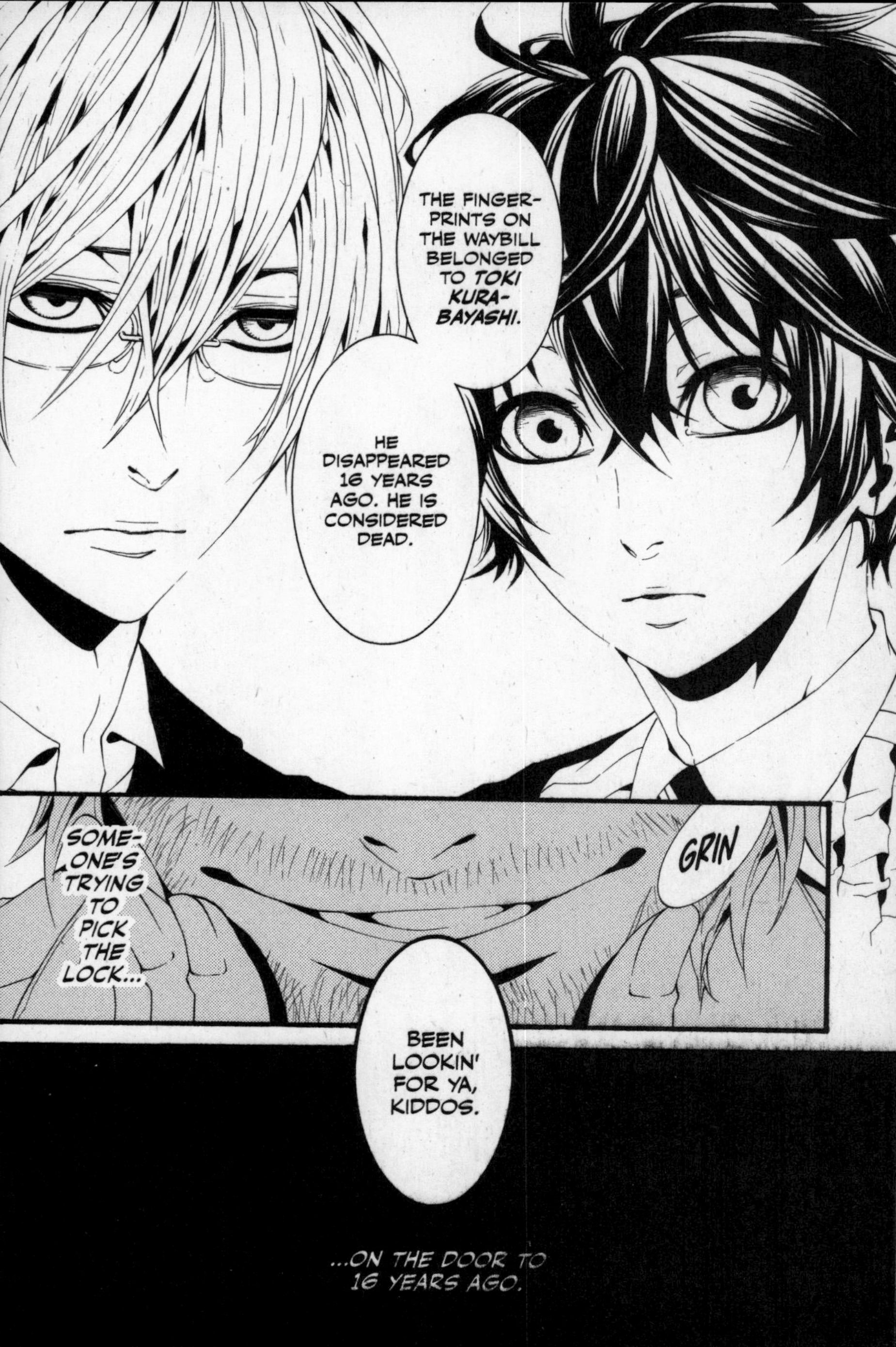
THE FINGER-PRINTS ON THE WAYBILL BELONGED TO *TOKI KURA-BAYASHI*.
HE DISAPPEARED 16 YEARS AGO. HE IS CONSIDERED DEAD.
GRIN
SOME-ONE'S TRYING TO PICK THE LOCK...
BEEN LOOKIN' FOR YA, KIDDOS.
...ON THE DOOR TO 16 YEARS AGO.

switch

naked ape : Saki Otoh & Nakamura Tomomi

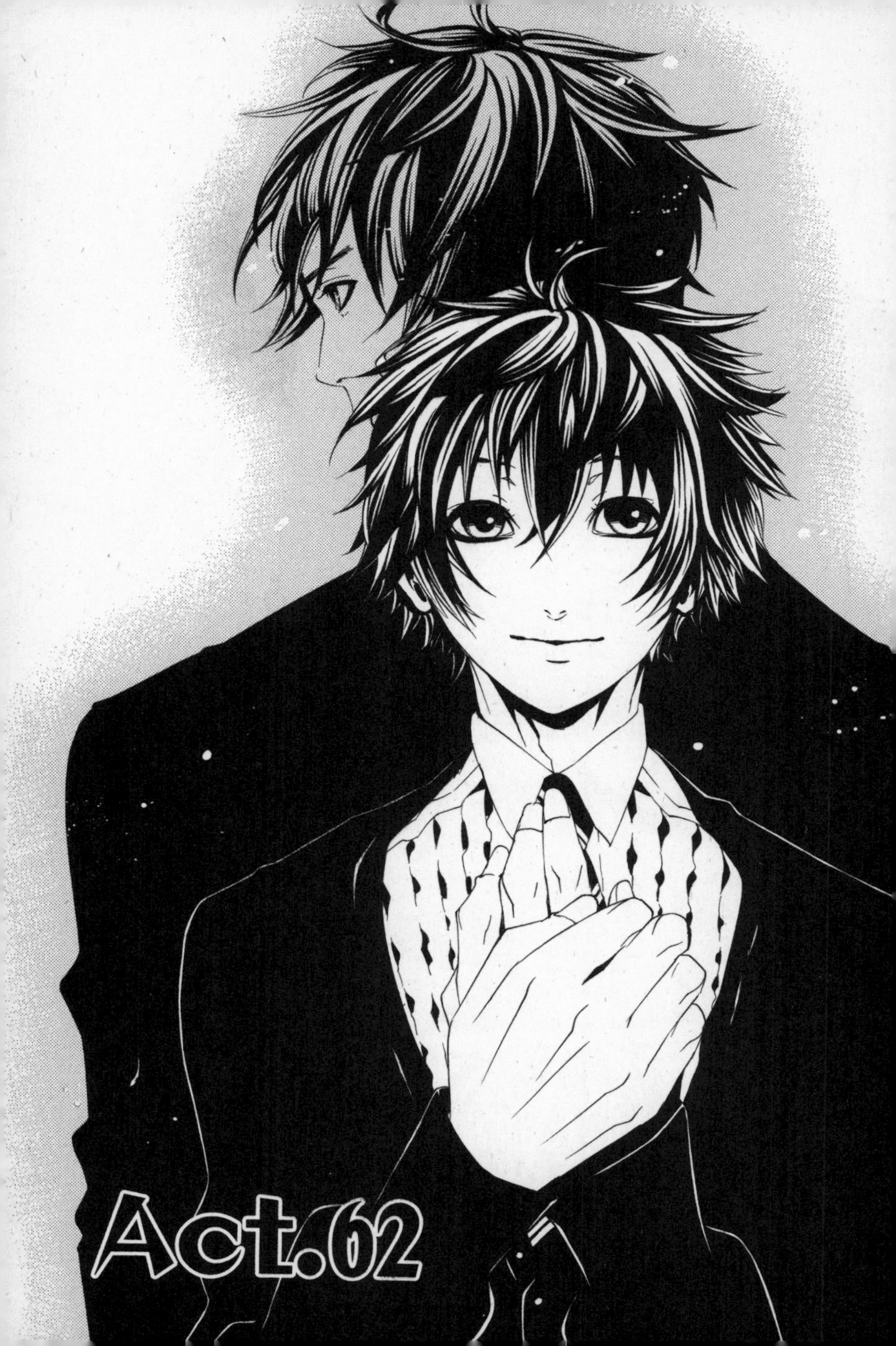
Act.62

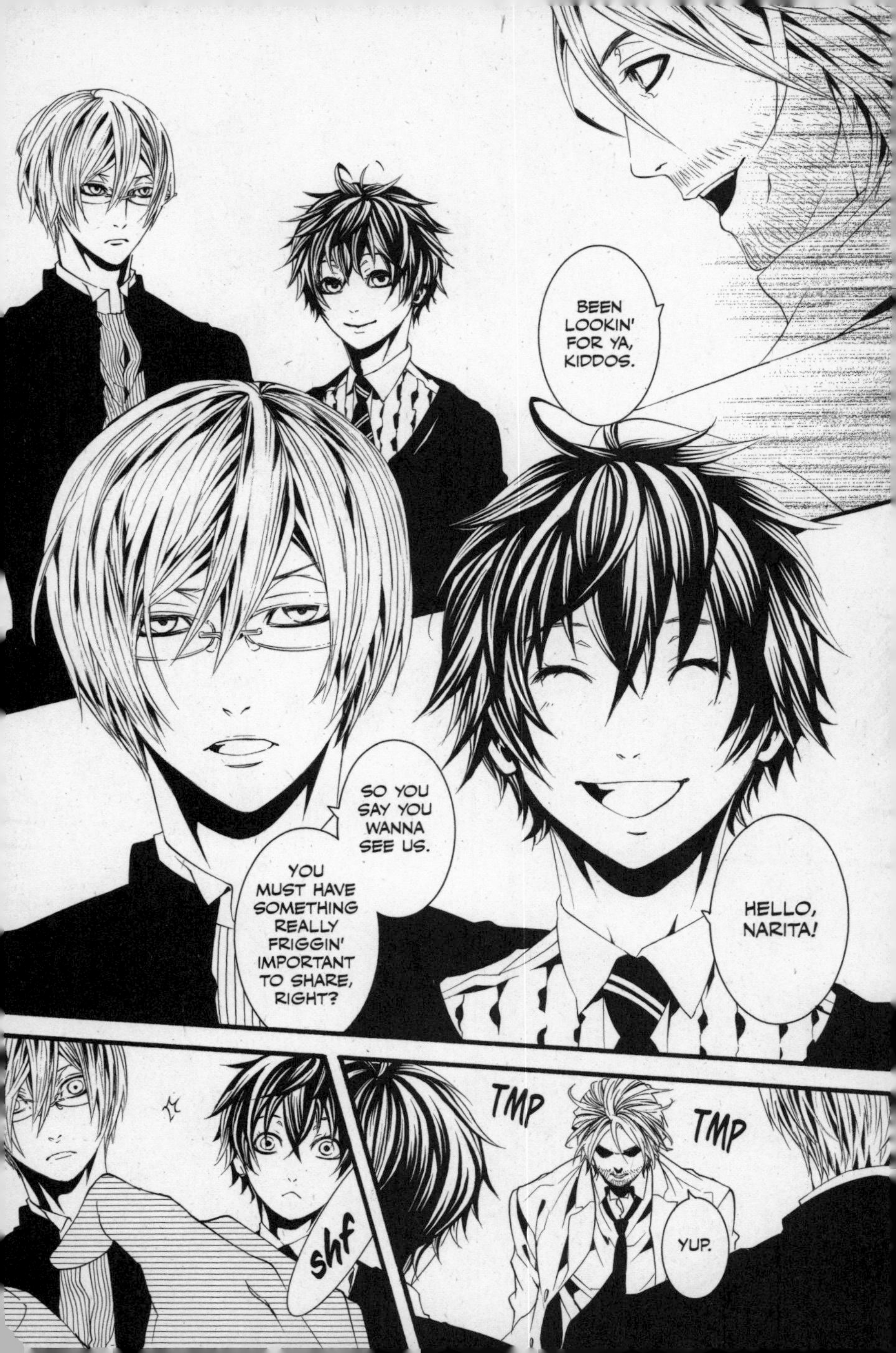
BEEN LOOKIN' FOR YA, KIDDOS.
HELLO, NARITA!
SO YOU SAY YOU WANNA SEE US.
YOU MUST HAVE SOMETHING REALLY FRIGGIN' IMPORTANT TO SHARE, RIGHT?
TMP
TMP
YUP.
shf

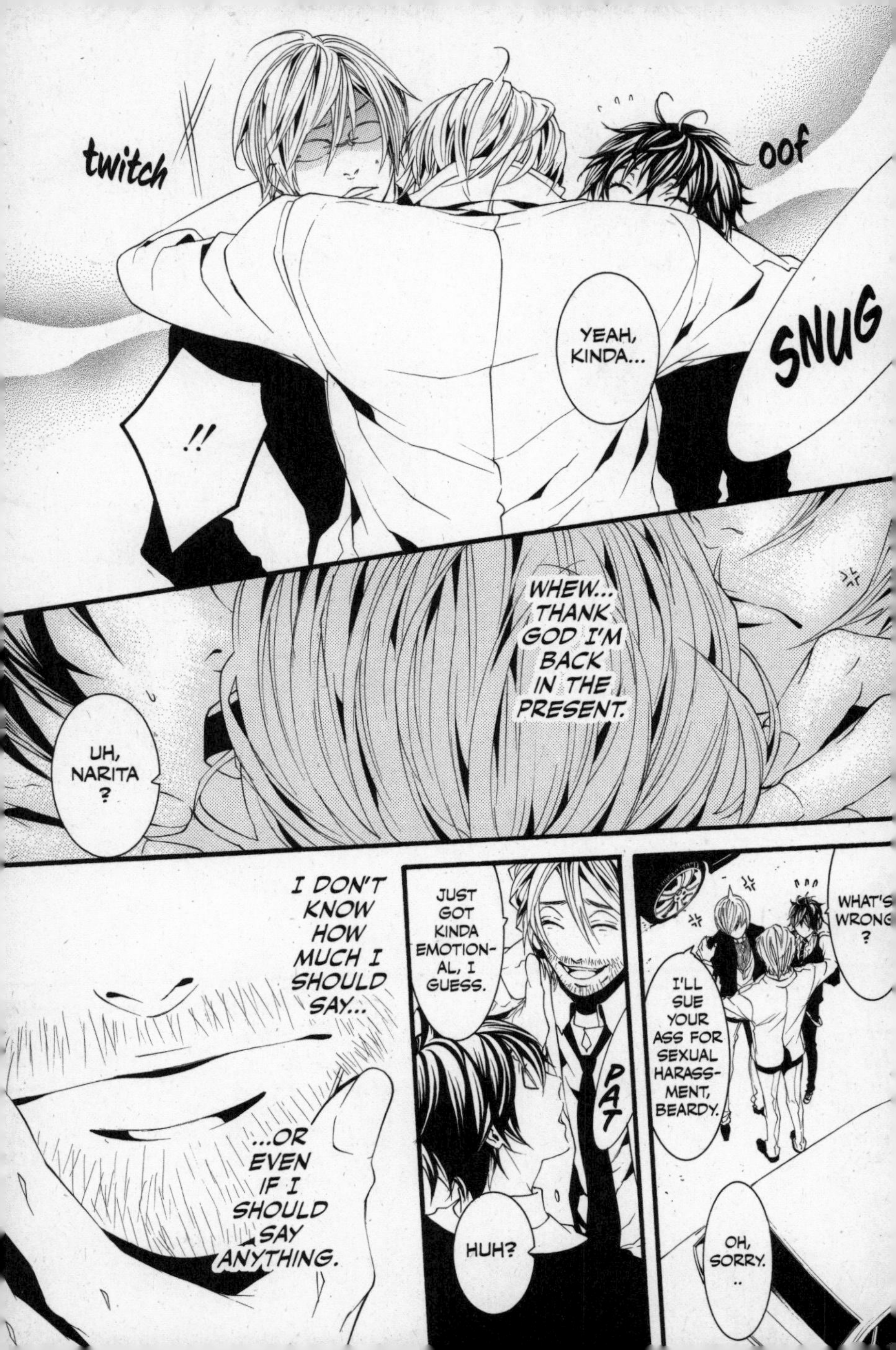
oof
SNUG
YEAH, KINDA...
twitch
!!
WHEW... THANK GOD I'M BACK IN THE PRESENT.
UH, NARITA?
WHAT'S WRONG?
I'LL SUE YOUR ASS FOR SEXUAL HARASSMENT, BEARDY.
OH, SORRY...
JUST GOT KINDA EMOTIONAL, I GUESS.
PAT
HUH?
I DON'T KNOW HOW MUCH I SHOULD SAY...
...OR EVEN IF I SHOULD SAY ANYTHING.

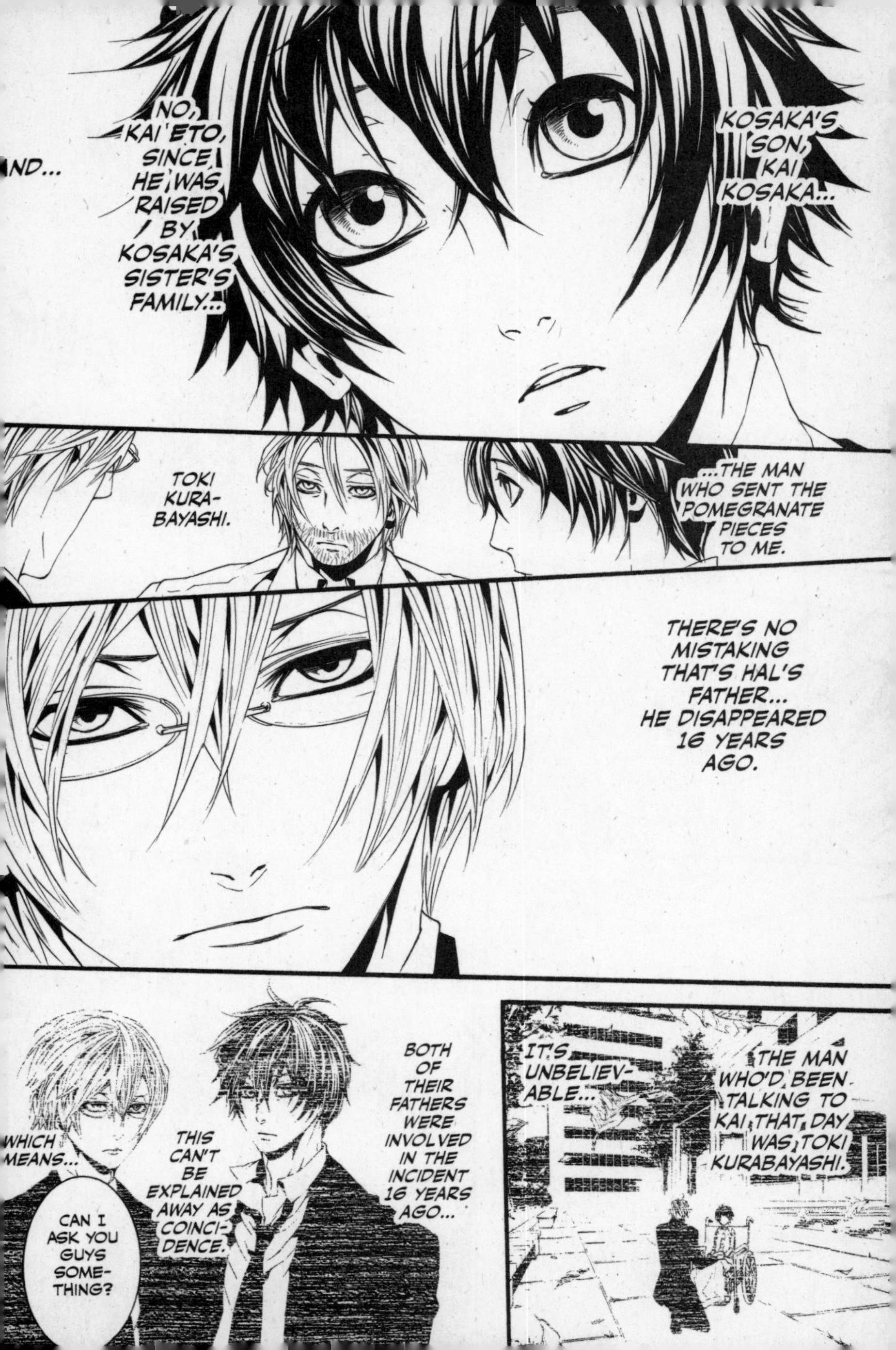
KOSAKA'S SON, KAI KOSAKA...
NO, KAI ETO, SINCE HE WAS RAISED BY KOSAKA'S SISTER'S FAMILY...
ND...
...THE MAN WHO SENT THE POMEGRANATE PIECES TO ME.
TOKI KURA-BAYASHI.
THERE'S NO MISTAKING THAT'S HAL'S FATHER... HE DISAPPEARED 16 YEARS AGO.
THE MAN WHO'D BEEN TALKING TO KAI THAT DAY WAS TOKI KURABAYASHI.
IT'S UNBELIEV-ABLE...
BOTH OF THEIR FATHERS WERE INVOLVED IN THE INCIDENT 16 YEARS AGO...
THIS CAN'T BE EXPLAINED AWAY AS COINCI-DENCE.
WHICH MEANS...
CAN I ASK YOU GUYS SOME-THING?

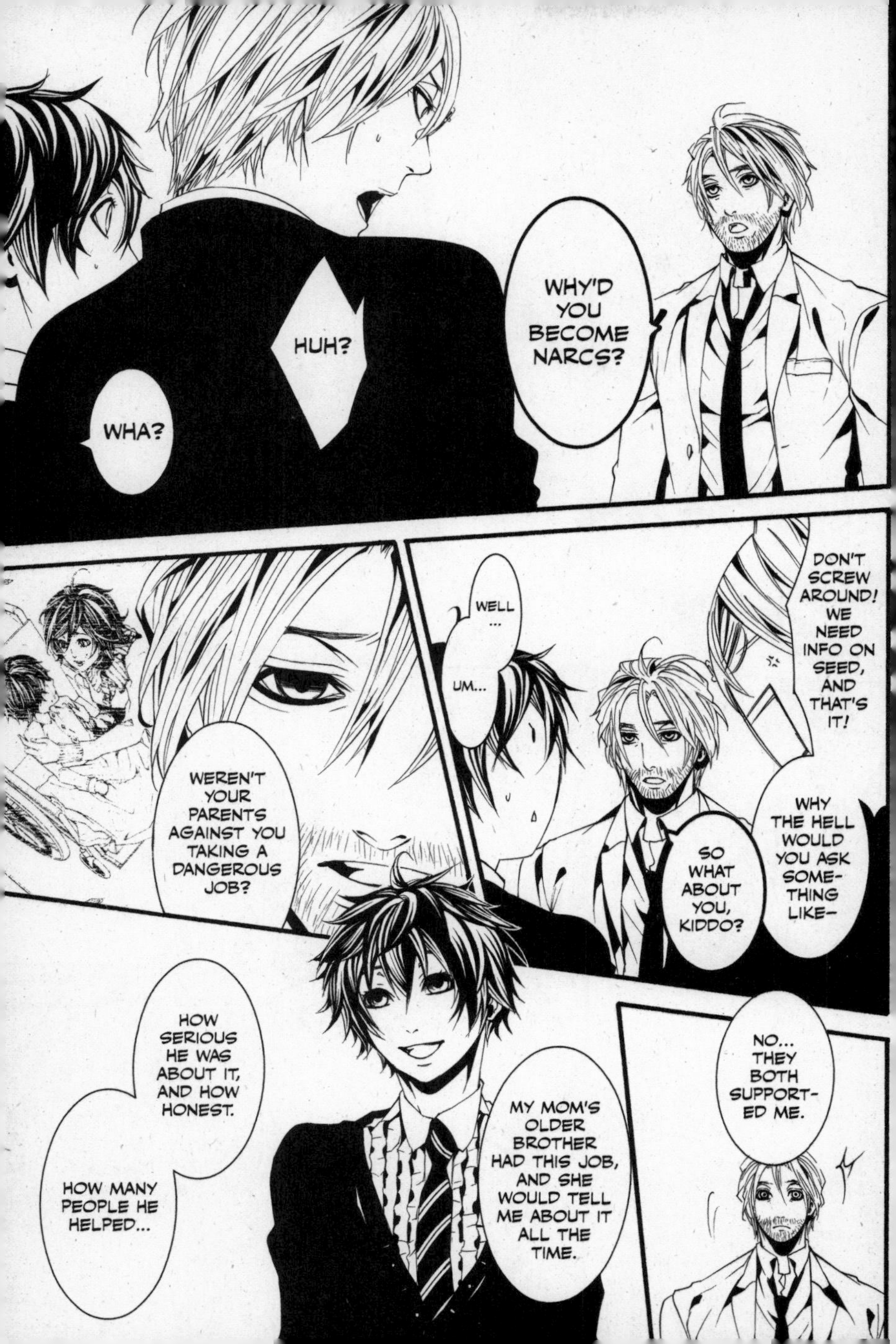
WHY'D YOU BECOME NARCS?
HUH?
WHA?
DON'T SCREW AROUND! WE NEED INFO ON SEED, AND THAT'S IT!
WELL...
UM...
WHY THE HELL WOULD YOU ASK SOME-THING LIKE-
SO WHAT ABOUT YOU, KIDDO?
WEREN'T YOUR PARENTS AGAINST YOU TAKING A DANGEROUS JOB?
NO... THEY BOTH SUPPORT-ED ME.
MY MOM'S OLDER BROTHER HAD THIS JOB, AND SHE WOULD TELL ME ABOUT IT ALL THE TIME.
HOW SERIOUS HE WAS ABOUT IT, AND HOW HONEST.
HOW MANY PEOPLE HE HELPED...

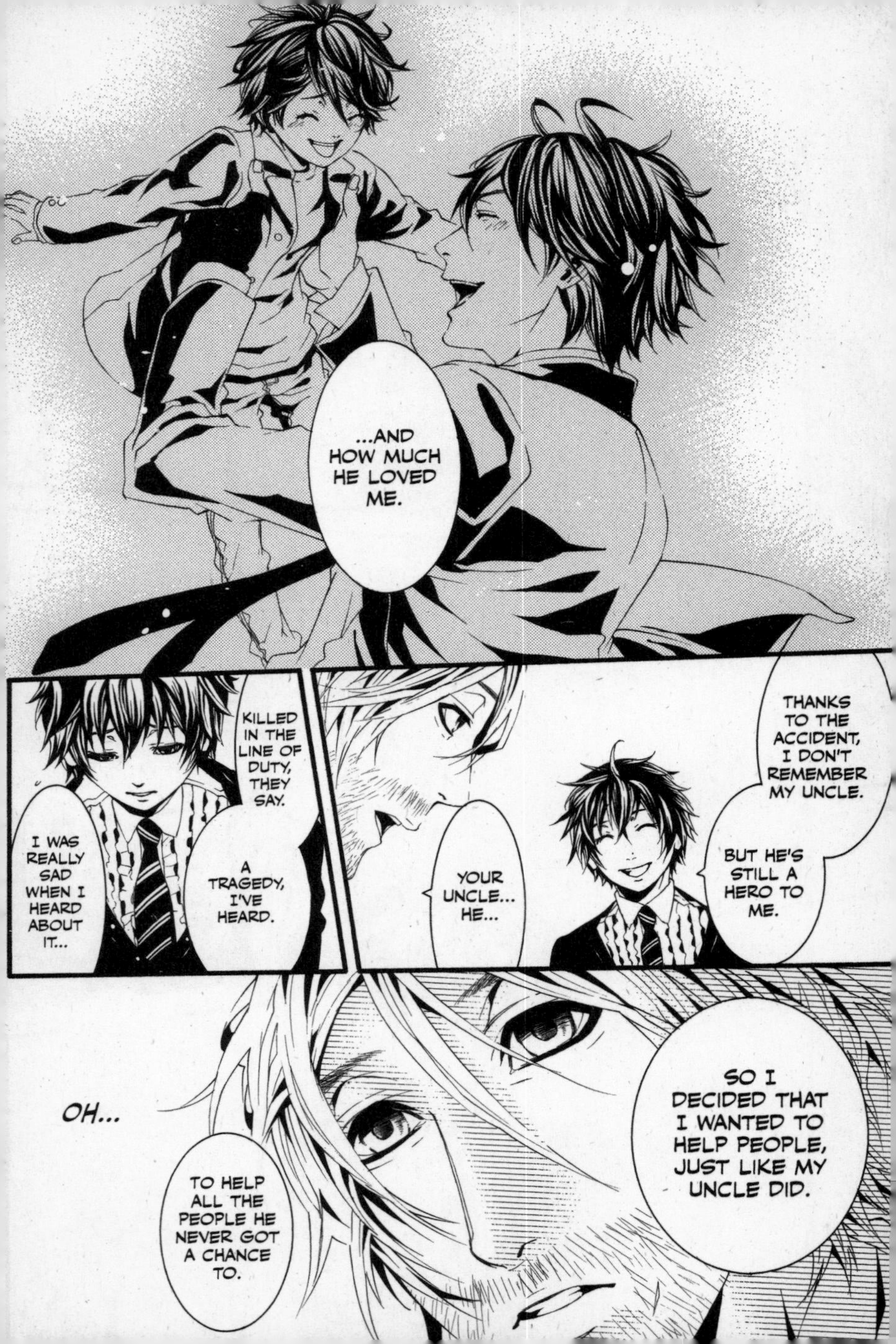
...AND HOW MUCH HE LOVED ME.
THANKS TO THE ACCIDENT, I DON'T REMEMBER MY UNCLE.
BUT HE'S STILL A HERO TO ME.
YOUR UNCLE... HE...
KILLED IN THE LINE OF DUTY, THEY SAY.
A TRAGEDY, I'VE HEARD.
I WAS REALLY SAD WHEN I HEARD ABOUT IT...
SO I DECIDED THAT I WANTED TO HELP PEOPLE, JUST LIKE MY UNCLE DID.
TO HELP ALL THE PEOPLE HE NEVER GOT A CHANCE TO.
OH...

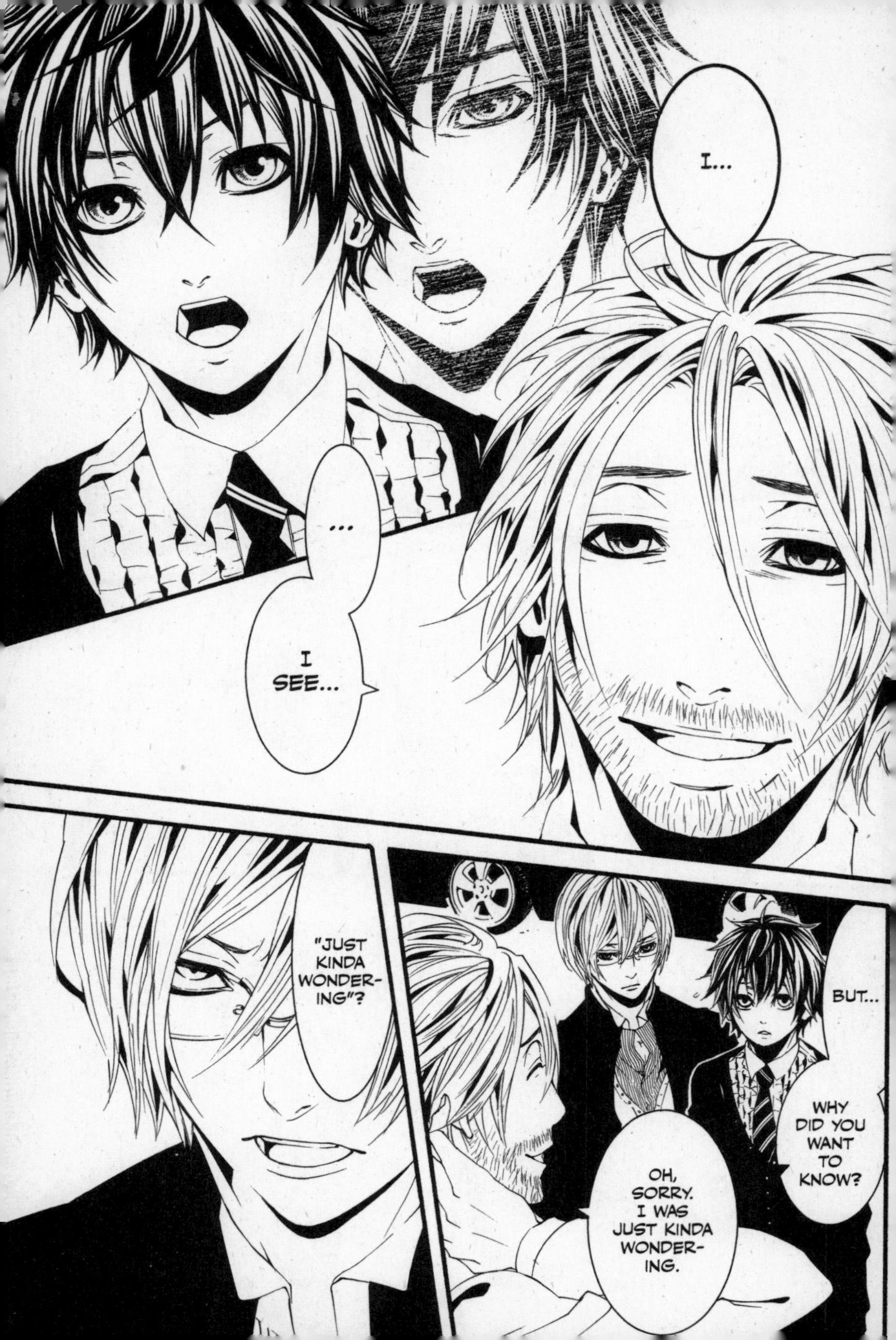
I...
...
I SEE...
BUT...
WHY DID YOU WANT TO KNOW?
OH, SORRY. I WAS JUST KINDA WONDERING.
"JUST KINDA WONDERING"?

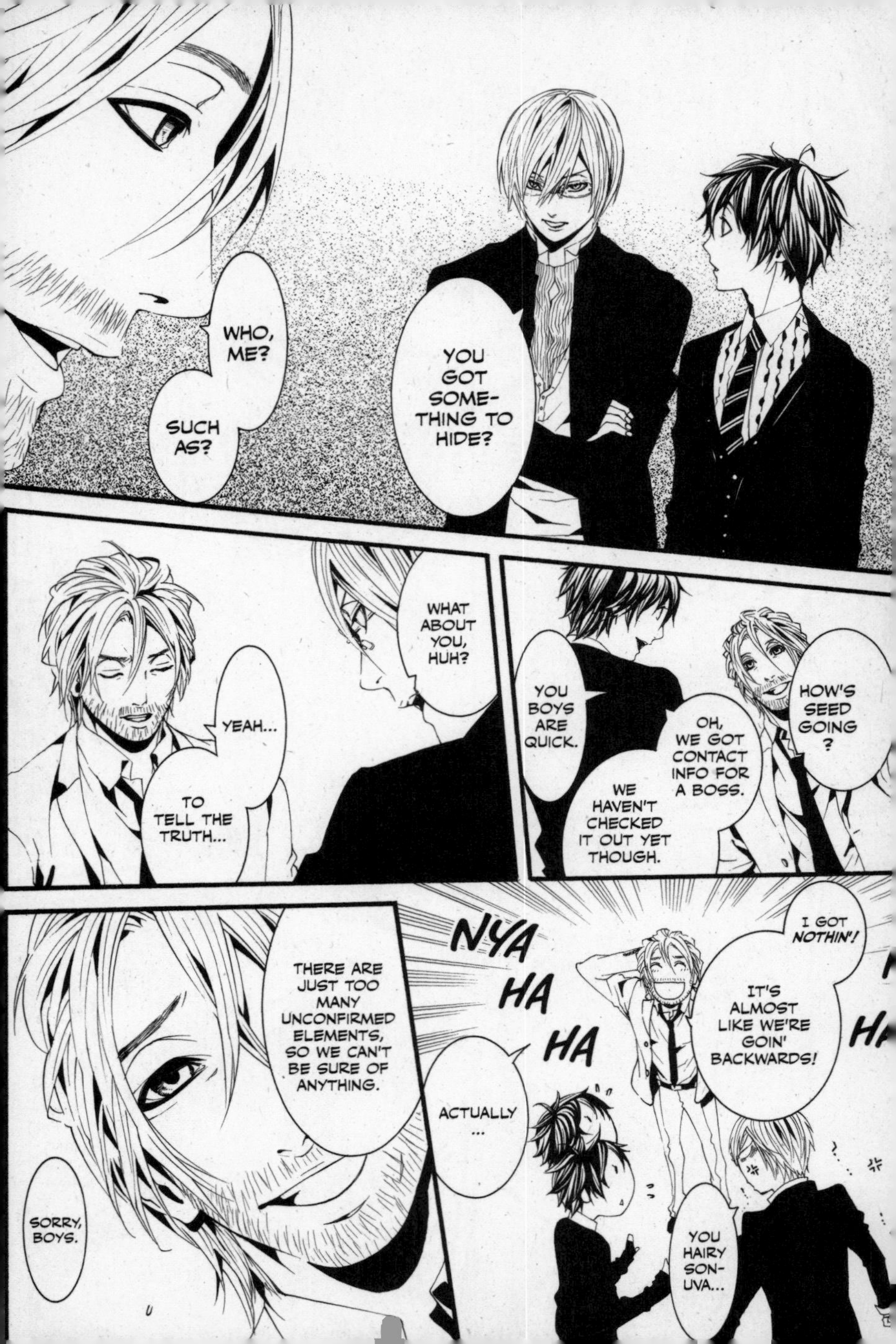
YOU GOT SOMETHING TO HIDE?
WHO, ME?
SUCH AS?
HOW'S SEED GOING?
OH, WE GOT CONTACT INFO FOR A BOSS.
WE HAVEN'T CHECKED IT OUT YET THOUGH.
YOU BOYS ARE QUICK.
WHAT ABOUT YOU, HUH?
YEAH...
TO TELL THE TRUTH...
I GOT NOTHIN'!
IT'S ALMOST LIKE WE'RE GOIN' BACKWARDS!
NYA HA HA
YOU HAIRY SONUVA...
ACTUALLY...
THERE ARE JUST TOO MANY UNCONFIRMED ELEMENTS, SO WE CAN'T BE SURE OF ANYTHING.
SORRY, BOYS.

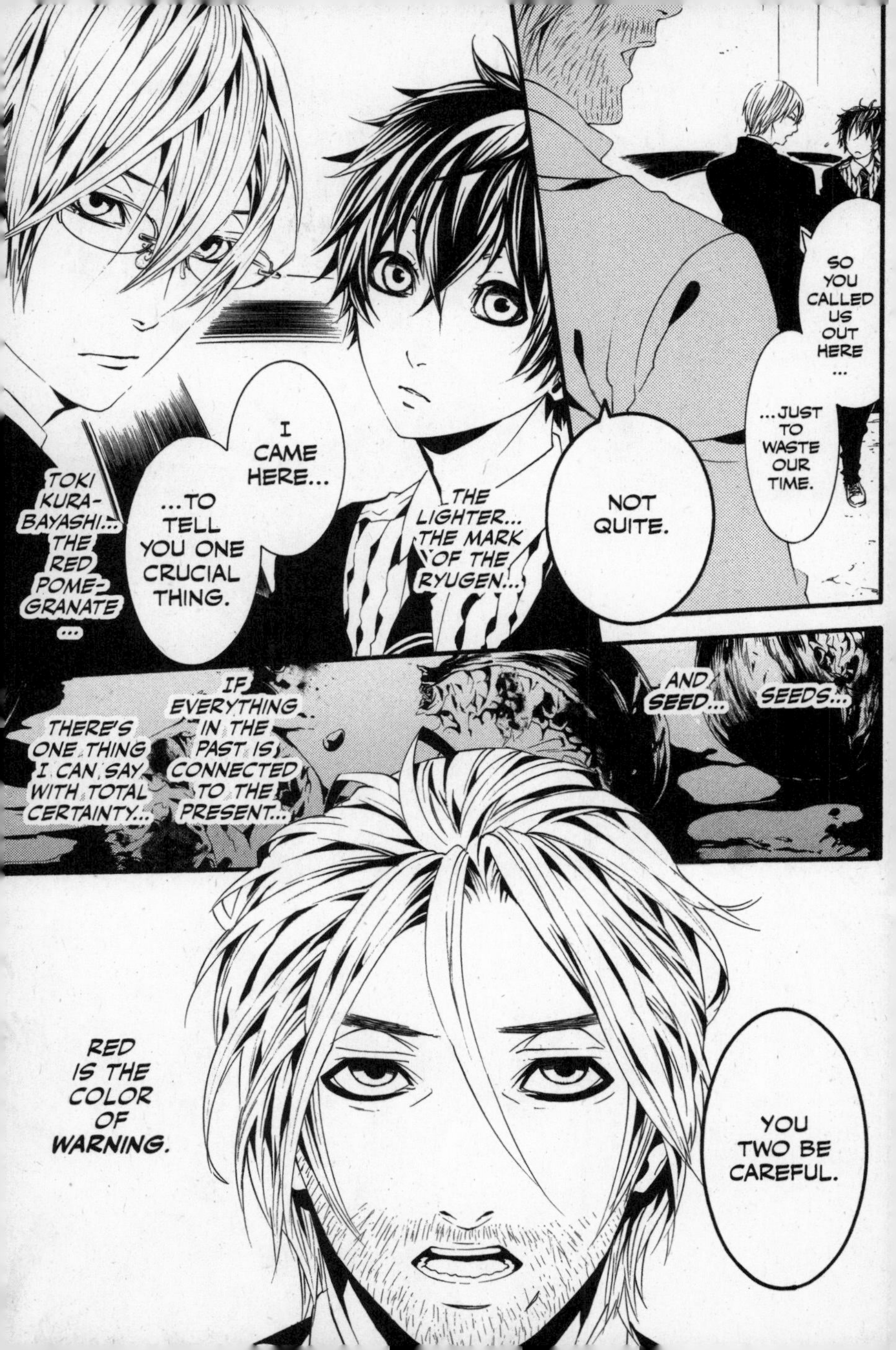
SO YOU CALLED US OUT HERE...
...JUST TO WASTE OUR TIME.
NOT QUITE.
THE LIGHTER... THE MARK OF THE RYUGEN...
I CAME HERE...
...TO TELL YOU ONE CRUCIAL THING.
TOKI KURA-BAYASHI... THE RED POME-GRANATE...
SEEDS...
AND SEED...
IF EVERYTHING IN THE PAST IS CONNECTED TO THE PRESENT...
THERE'S ONE THING I CAN SAY WITH TOTAL CERTAINTY...
YOU TWO BE CAREFUL.
RED IS THE COLOR OF WARNING.

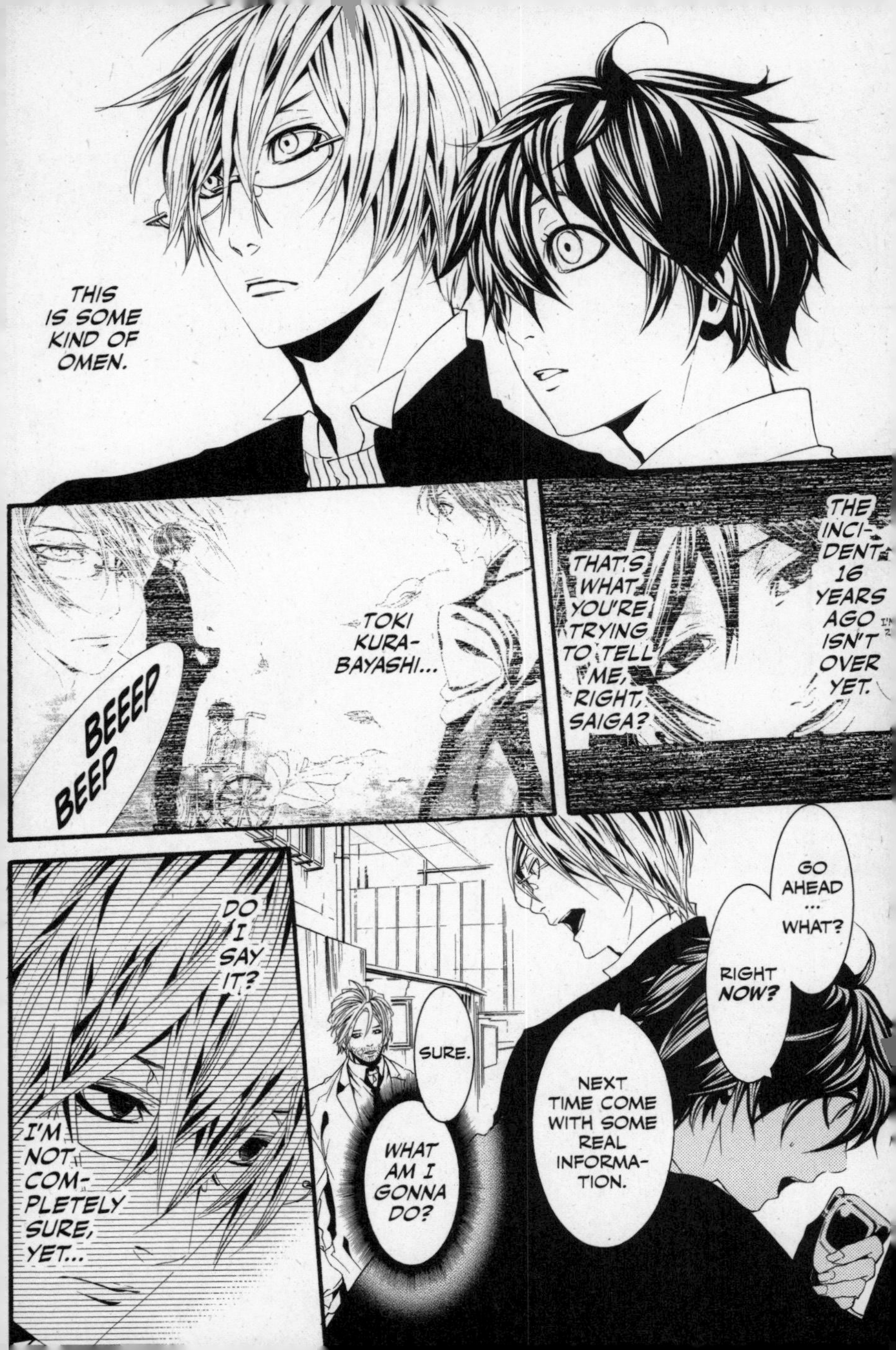
THIS IS SOME KIND OF OMEN.
THE INCI-DENT 16 YEARS AGO ISN'T OVER YET.
THAT'S WHAT YOU'RE TRYING TO TELL ME, RIGHT, SAIGA?
TOKI KURA-BAYASHI...
BEEEP BEEP
GO AHEAD ... WHAT?
RIGHT NOW?
SURE.
NEXT TIME COME WITH SOME REAL INFORMA-TION.
WHAT AM I GONNA DO?
DO I SAY IT?
I'M NOT COM-PLETELY SURE, YET...

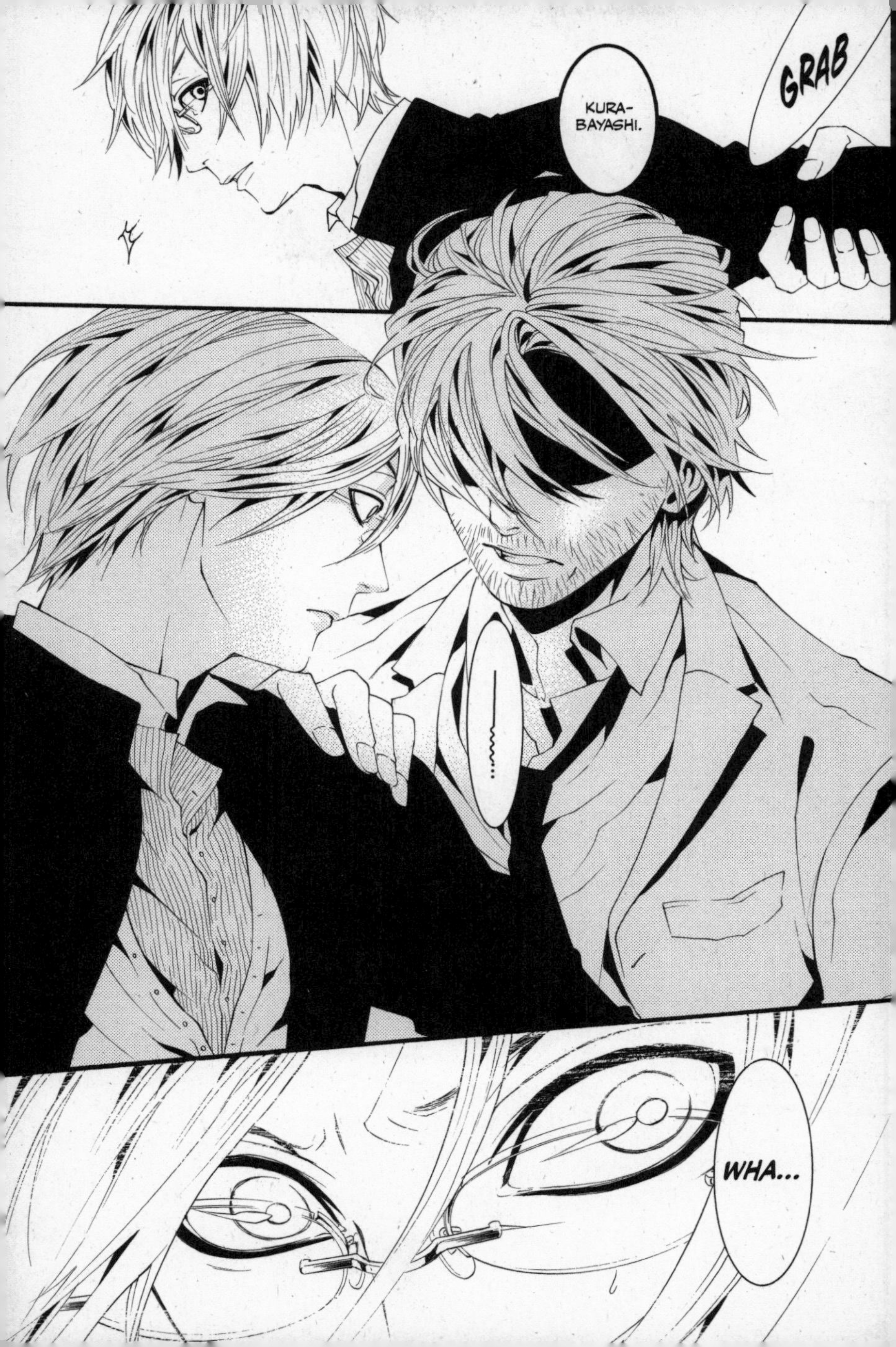
GRAB
KURA-BAYASHI.
......
WHA...

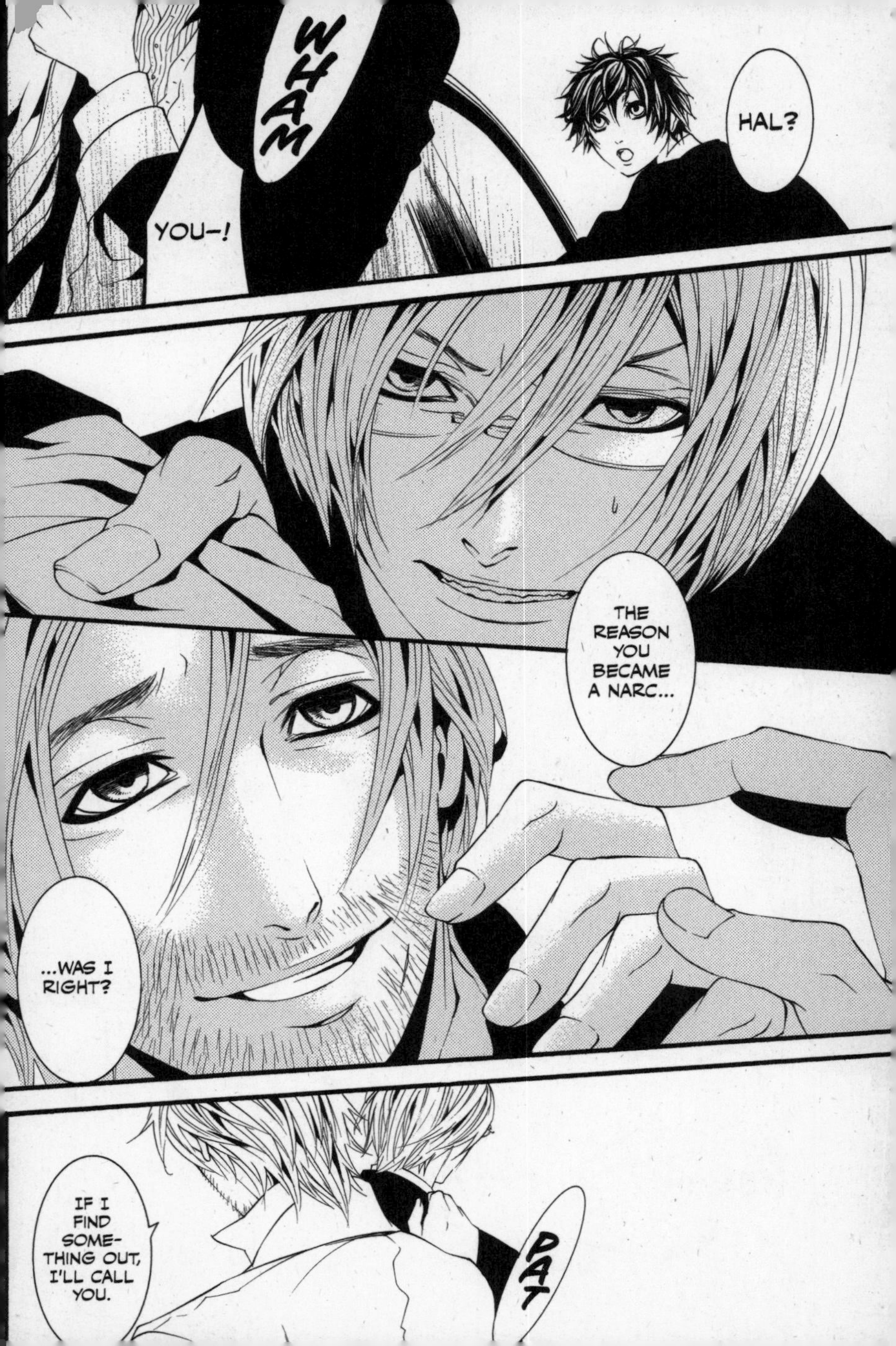
HAL?
WHAM
YOU—!
THE REASON YOU BECAME A NARC...
...WAS I RIGHT?
PAT
IF I FIND SOME-THING OUT, I'LL CALL YOU.

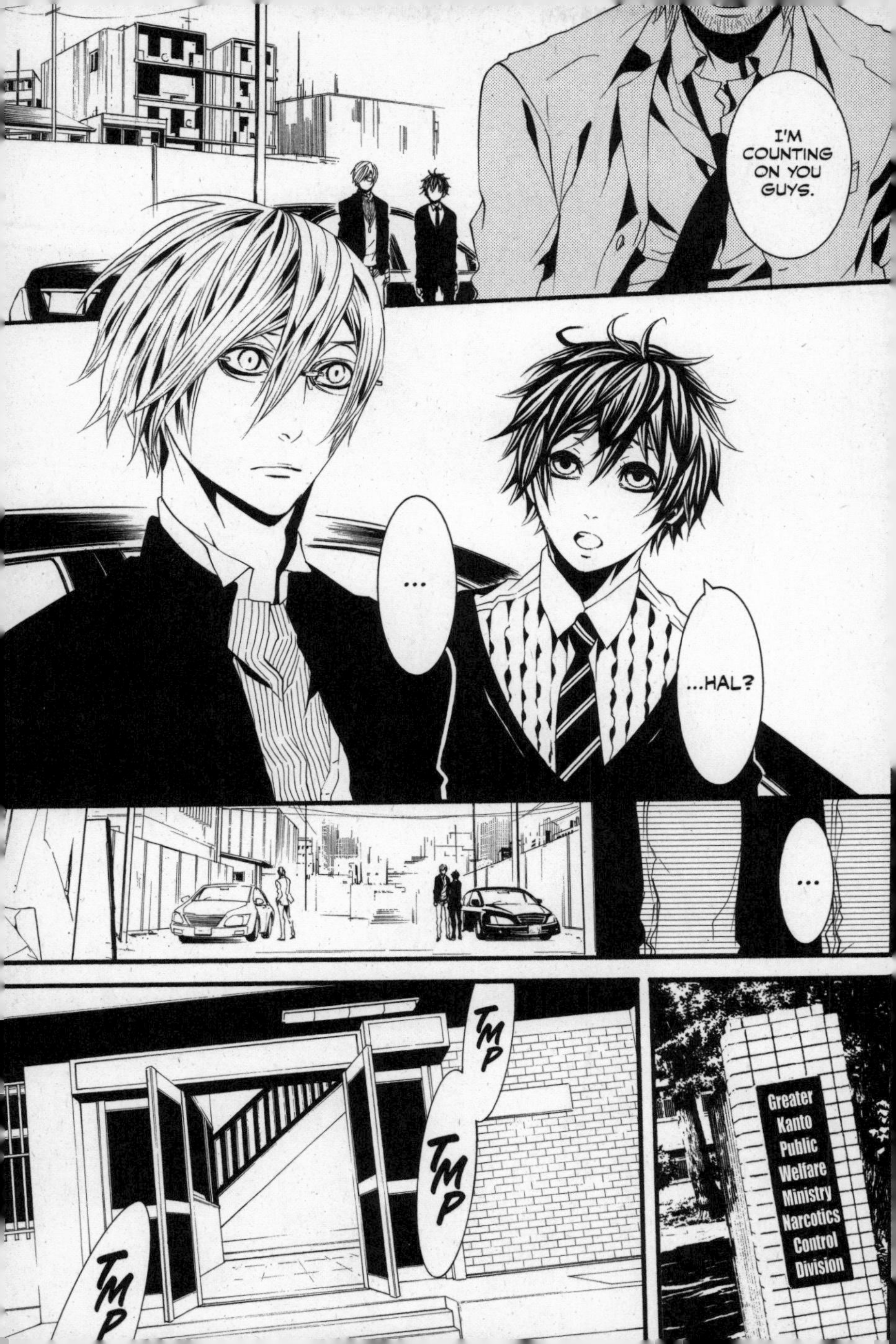
I'M COUNTING ON YOU GUYS.
...HAL?
...
...
Greater Kanto Public Welfare Ministry Narcotics Control Division
TMP
TMP
TMP

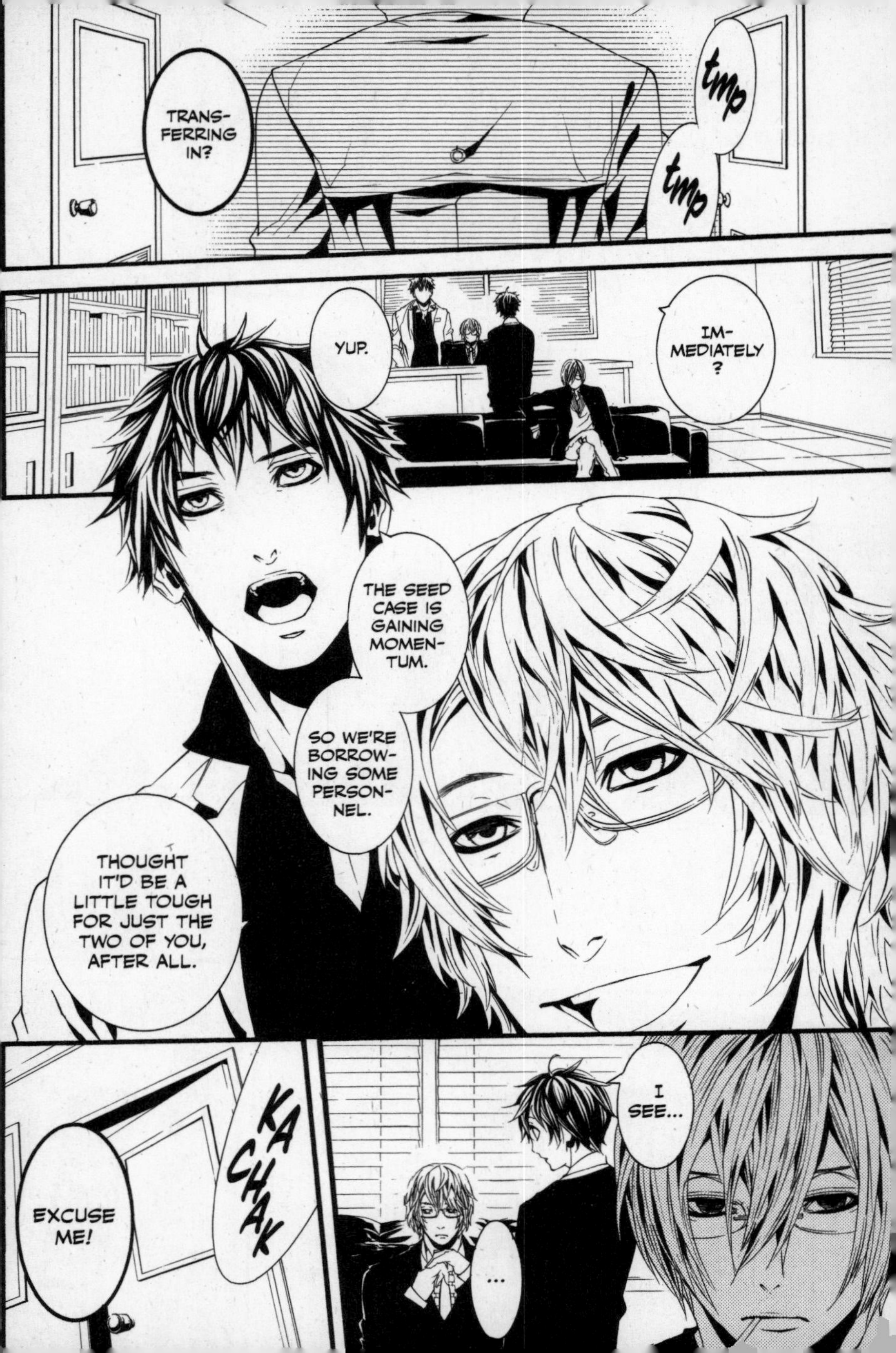
tmp
tmp
TRANS-FERRING IN?
IM-MEDIATELY?
YUP.
THE SEED CASE IS GAINING MOMEN-TUM.
SO WE'RE BORROW-ING SOME PERSON-NEL.
THOUGHT IT'D BE A LITTLE TOUGH FOR JUST THE TWO OF YOU, AFTER ALL.
I SEE...
...
KACHAK
EXCUSE ME!

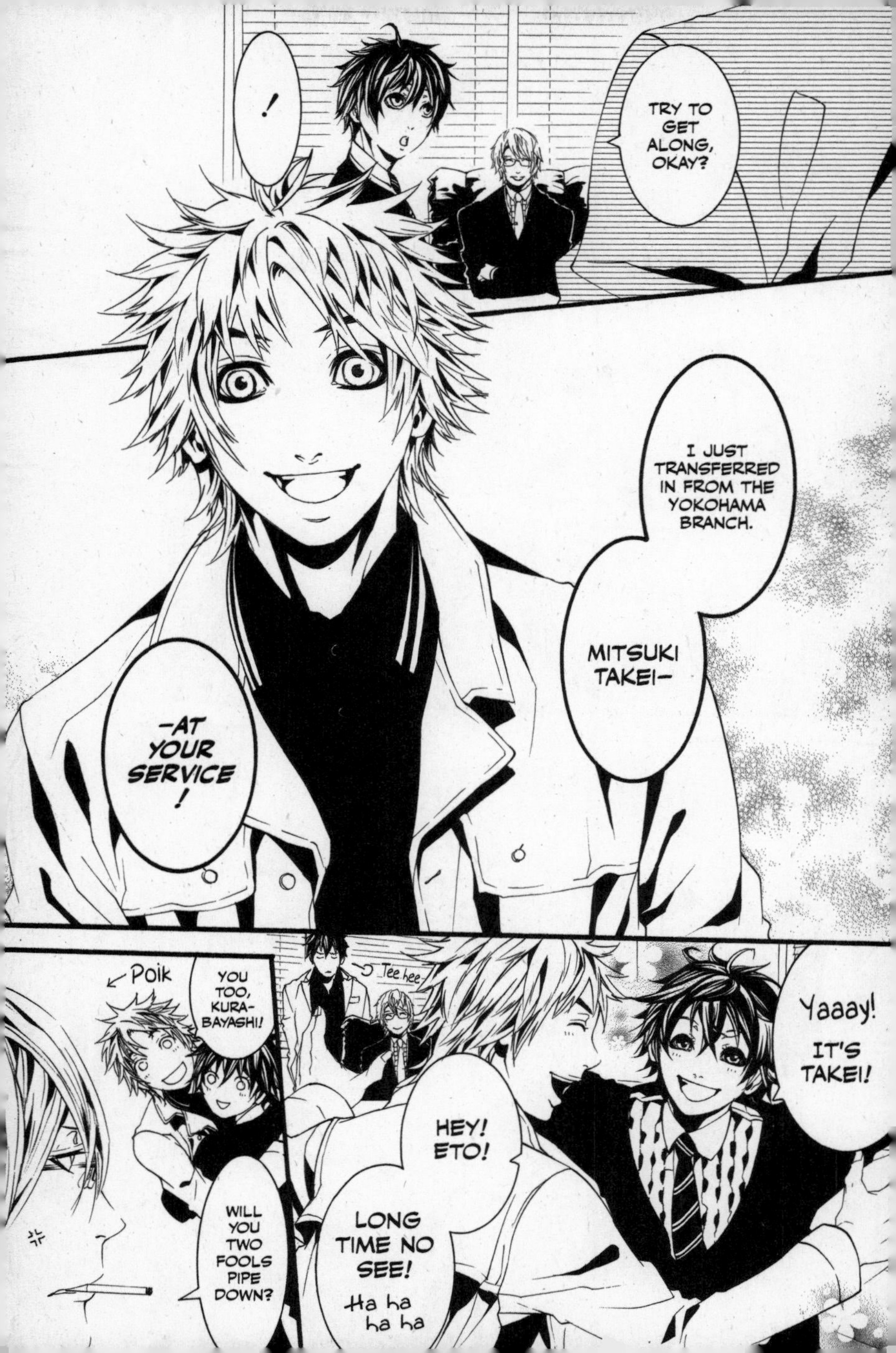

TRY TO GET ALONG, OKAY?
!
I JUST TRANSFERRED IN FROM THE YOKOHAMA BRANCH.
MITSUKI TAKEI—
—AT YOUR SERVICE!
Yaaay! IT'S TAKEI!
HEY! ETO!
LONG TIME NO SEE!
Ha ha ha ha
Tee hee
YOU TOO, KURA-BAYASHI!
Poik
WILL YOU TWO FOOLS PIPE DOWN?

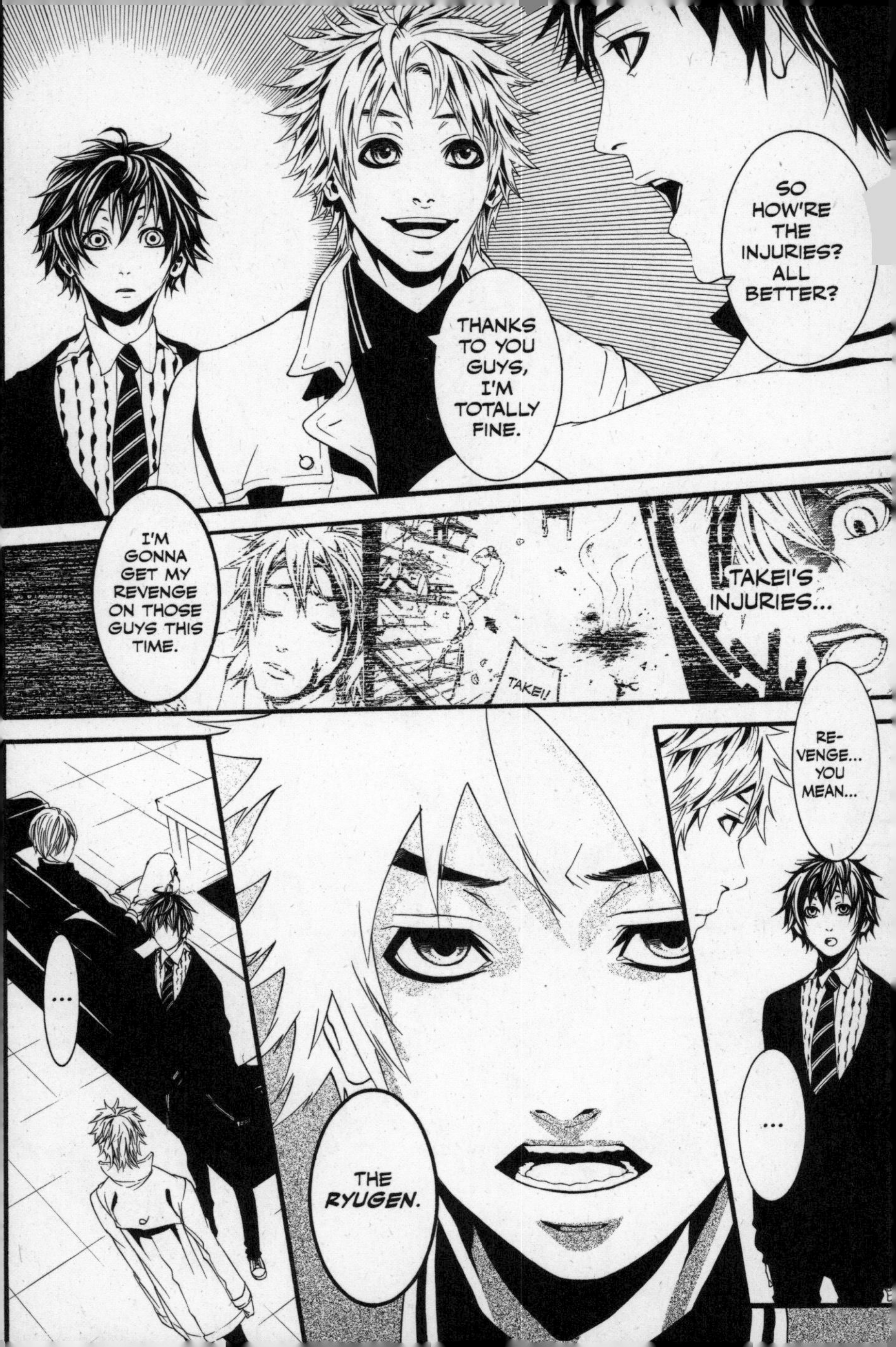
SO HOW'RE THE INJURIES? ALL BETTER?
THANKS TO YOU GUYS, I'M TOTALLY FINE.
TAKEI'S INJURIES...
TAKEI!
I'M GONNA GET MY REVENGE ON THOSE GUYS THIS TIME.
RE-VENGE... YOU MEAN...
...
THE RYUGEN.
...

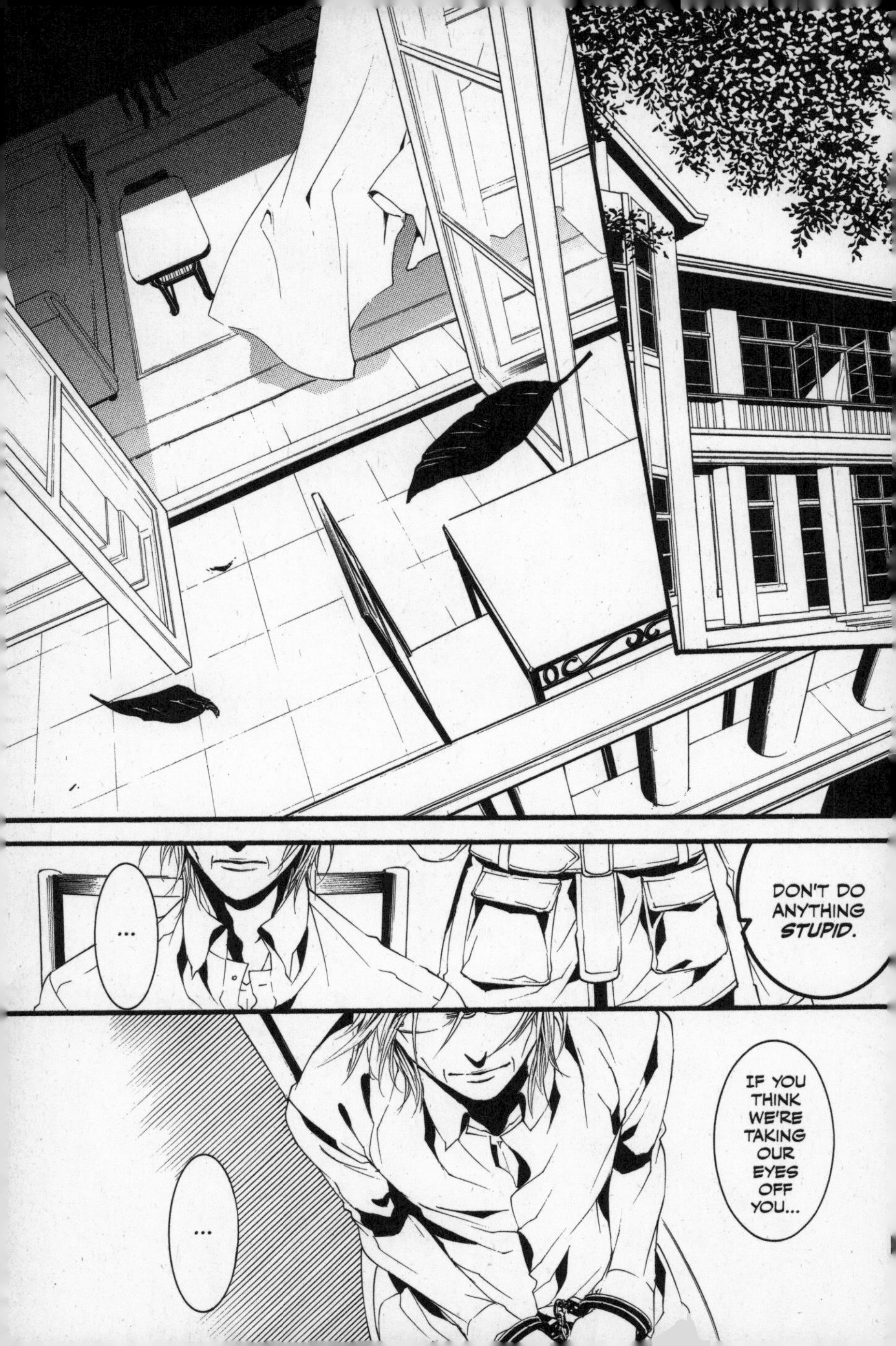
DON'T DO ANYTHING *STUPID*.
...
IF YOU THINK WE'RE TAKING OUR EYES OFF YOU...
...

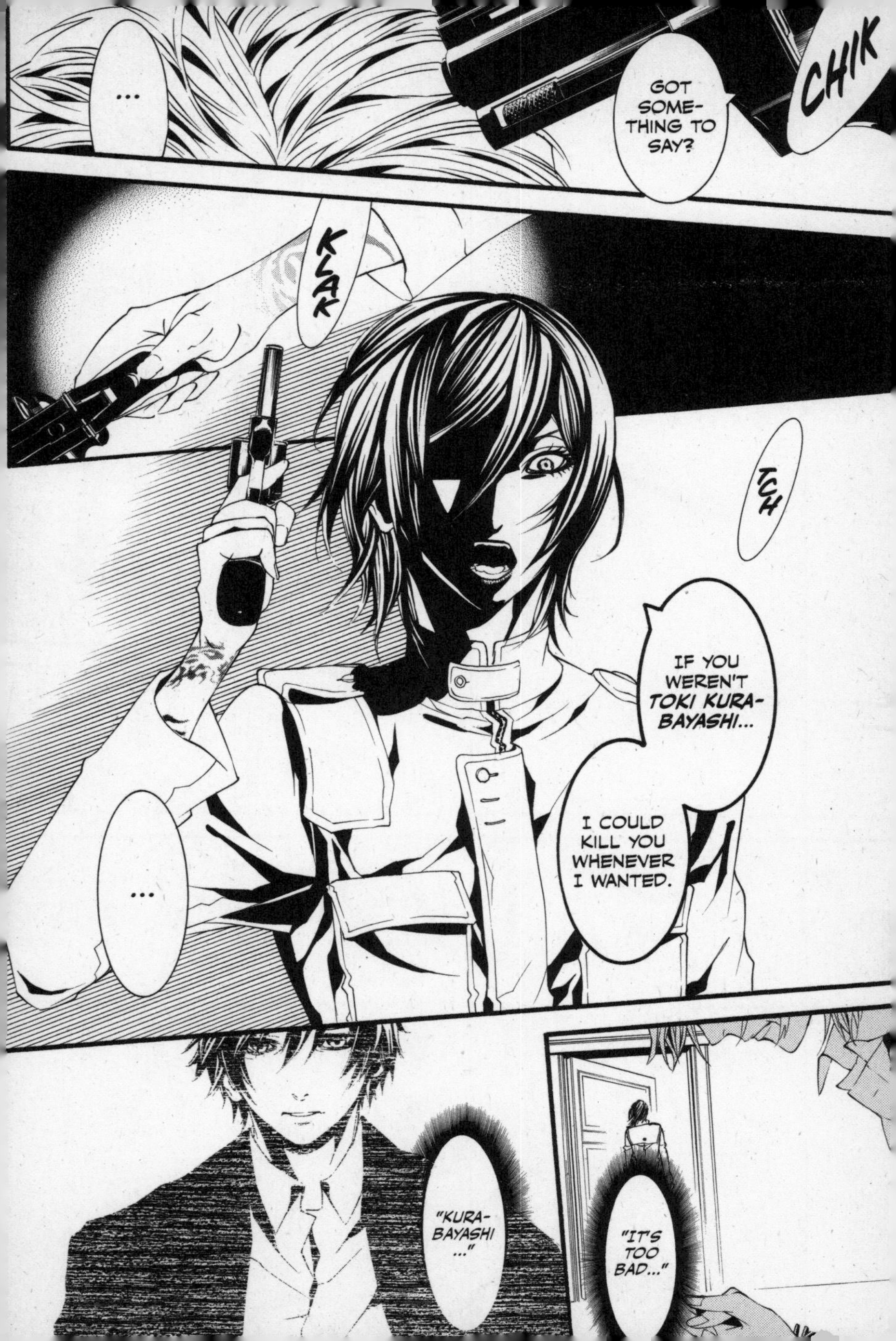
CHIK
GOT SOME-THING TO SAY?
...
KLAK
TCH
IF YOU WEREN'T TOKI KURA-BAYASHI...
I COULD KILL YOU WHENEVER I WANTED.
...
"IT'S TOO BAD..."
"KURA-BAYASHI ..."

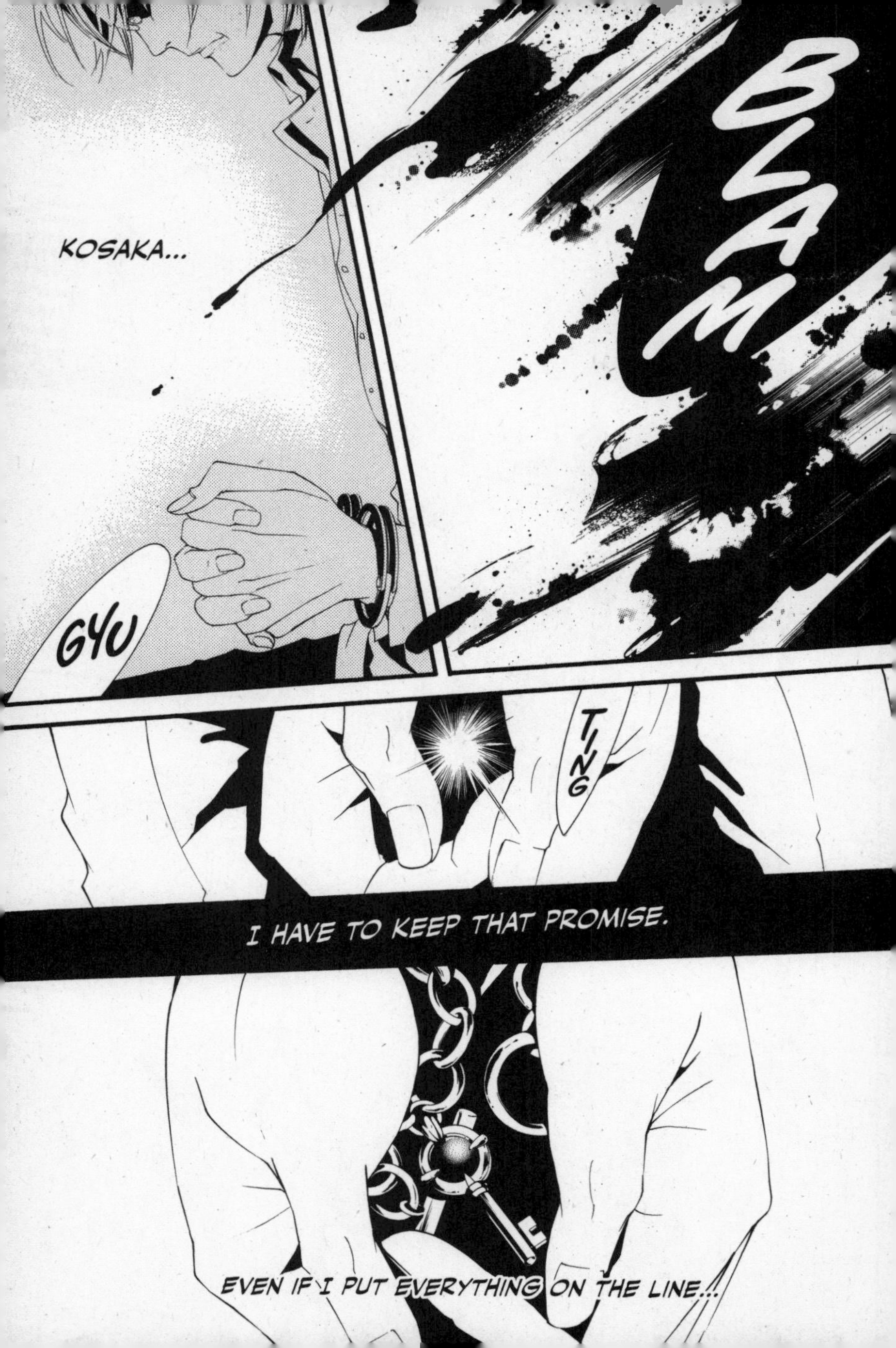
BLAM
KOSAKA...
GYU
TING
I HAVE TO KEEP THAT PROMISE.
EVEN IF I PUT EVERYTHING ON THE LINE...

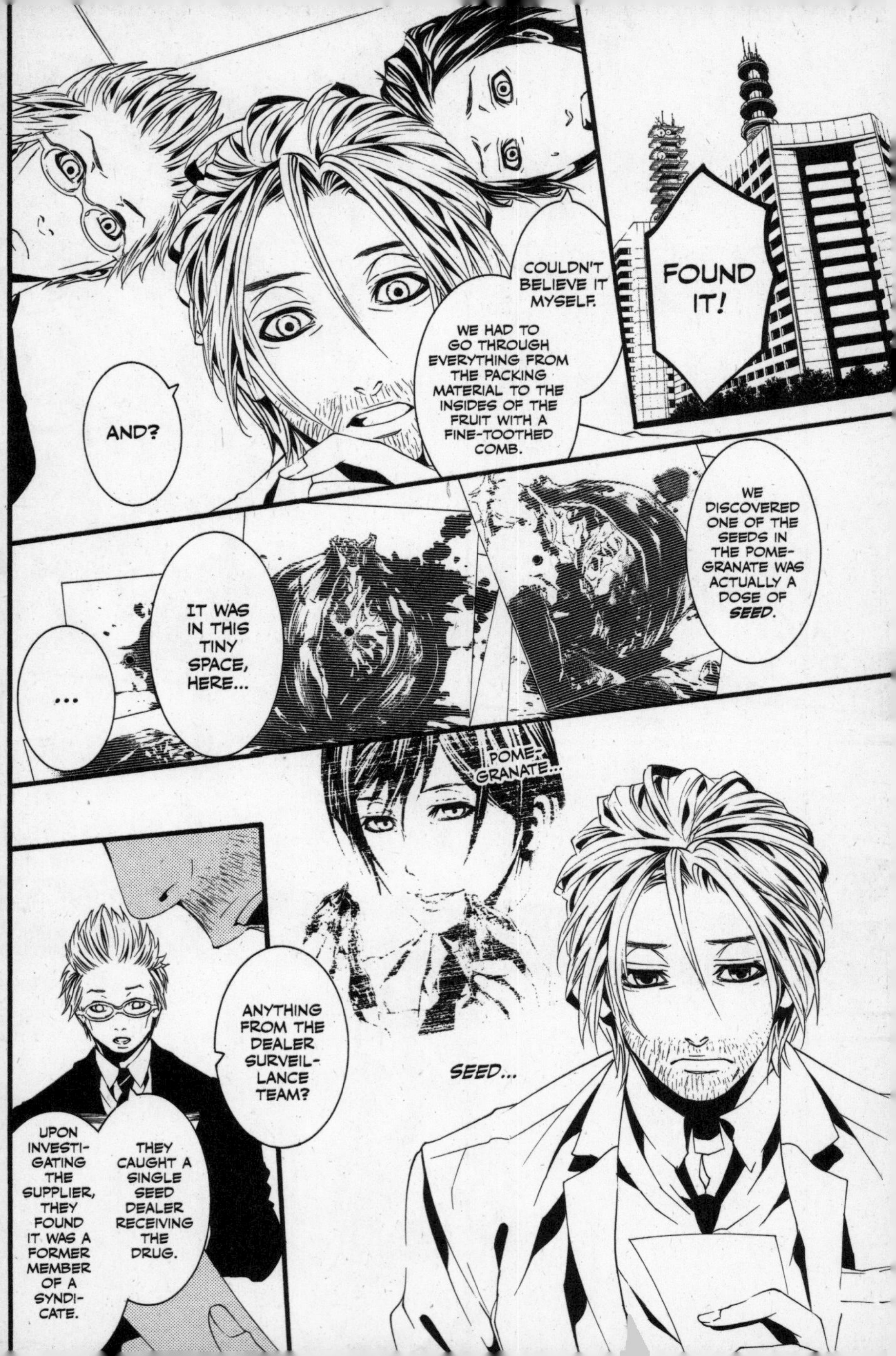
FOUND IT!
COULDN'T BELIEVE IT MYSELF.
WE HAD TO GO THROUGH EVERYTHING FROM THE PACKING MATERIAL TO THE INSIDES OF THE FRUIT WITH A FINE-TOOTHED COMB.
AND?
WE DISCOVERED ONE OF THE SEEDS IN THE POMEGRANATE WAS ACTUALLY A DOSE OF *SEED*.
IT WAS IN THIS TINY SPACE, HERE...
...
POMEGRANATE...
SEED...
ANYTHING FROM THE DEALER SURVEILLANCE TEAM?
THEY CAUGHT A SINGLE SEED DEALER RECEIVING THE DRUG.
UPON INVESTIGATING THE SUPPLIER, THEY FOUND IT WAS A FORMER MEMBER OF A SYNDICATE.

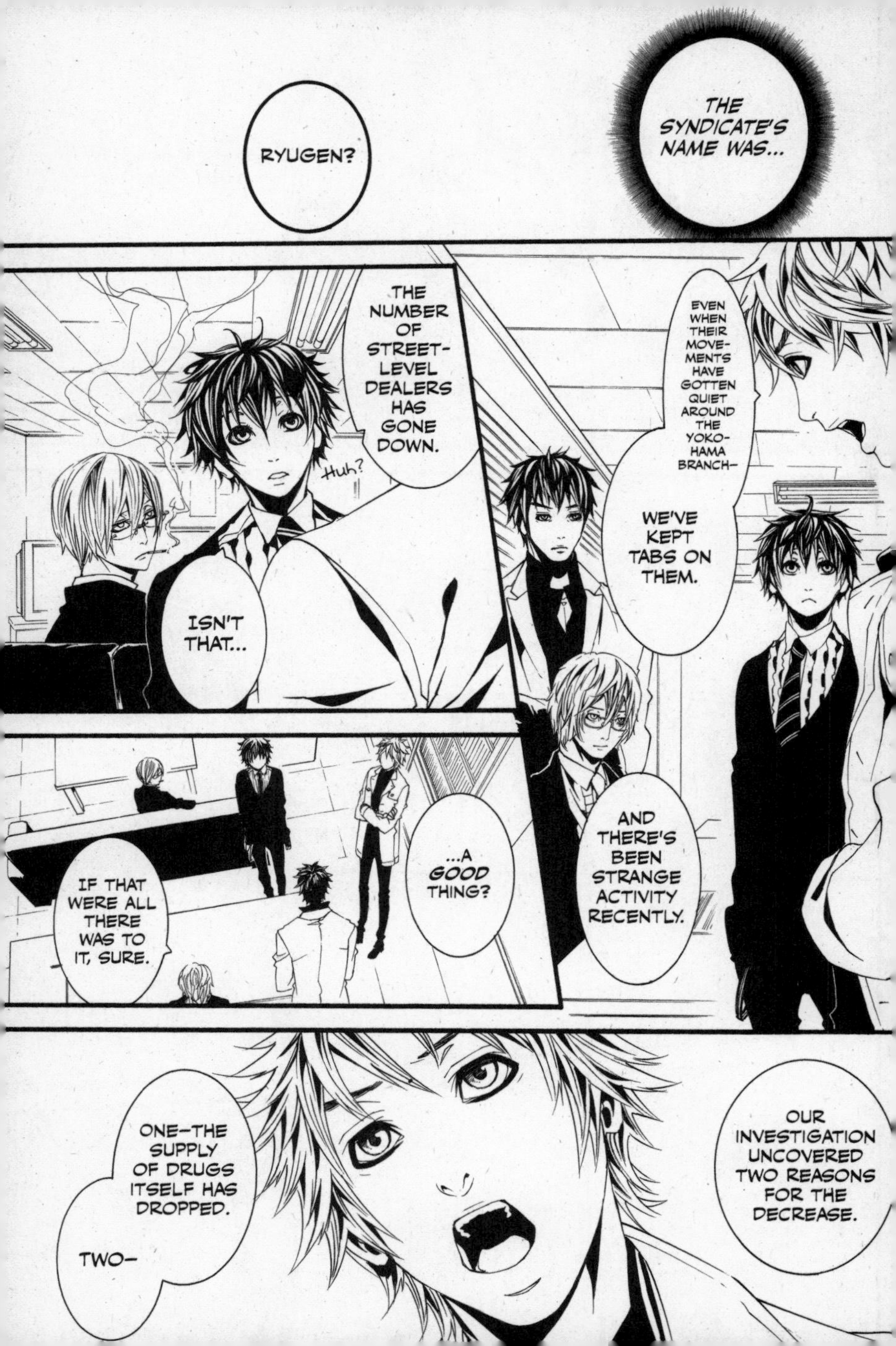
THE SYNDICATE'S NAME WAS...
RYUGEN?
EVEN WHEN THEIR MOVEMENTS HAVE GOTTEN QUIET AROUND THE YOKOHAMA BRANCH—
WE'VE KEPT TABS ON THEM.
AND THERE'S BEEN STRANGE ACTIVITY RECENTLY.
THE NUMBER OF STREET-LEVEL DEALERS HAS GONE DOWN.
Huh?
ISN'T THAT...
...A *GOOD* THING?
IF THAT WERE ALL THERE WAS TO IT, SURE.
OUR INVESTIGATION UNCOVERED TWO REASONS FOR THE DECREASE.
ONE—THE SUPPLY OF DRUGS ITSELF HAS DROPPED.
TWO—

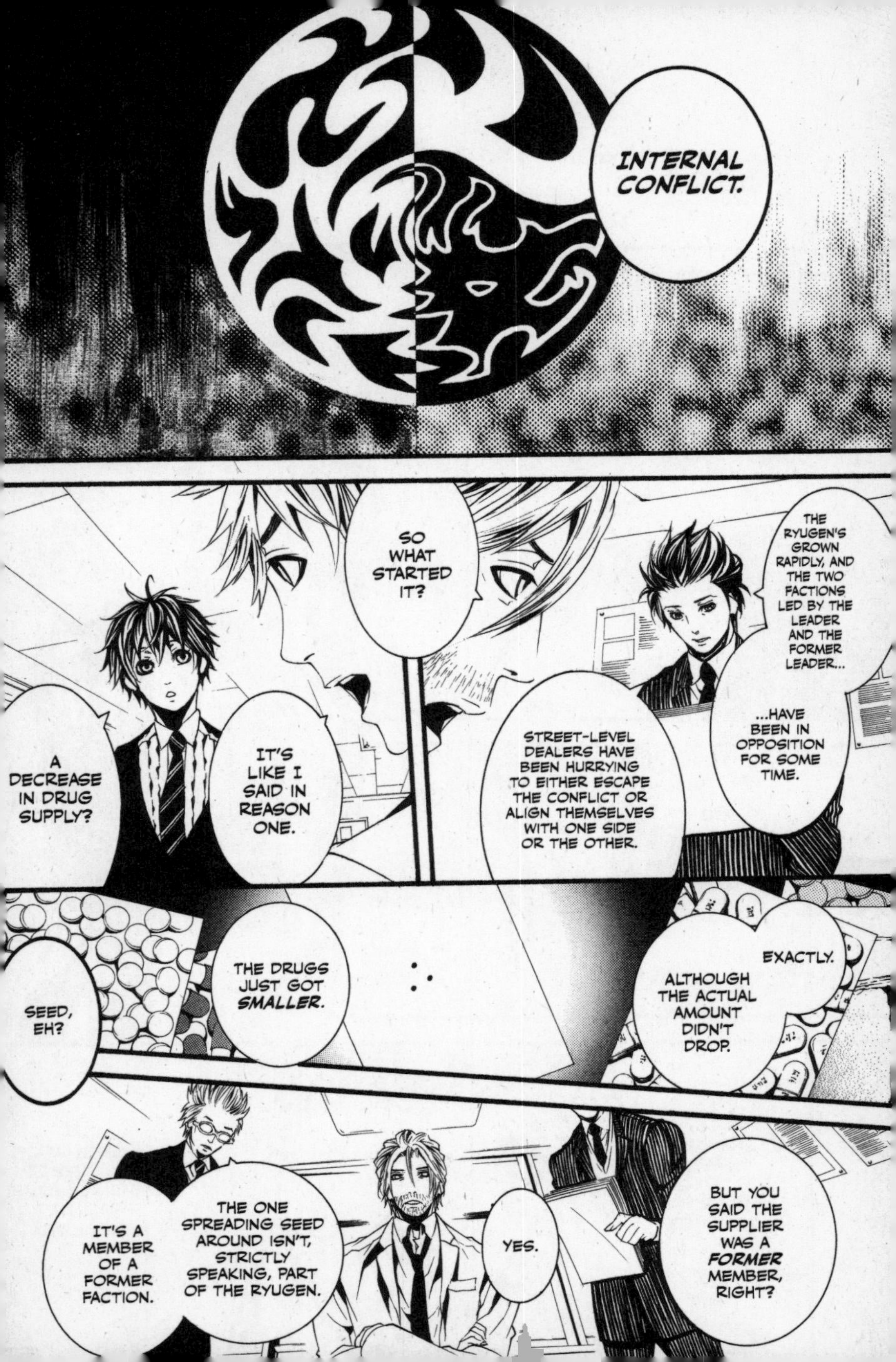
INTERNAL CONFLICT.
THE RYUGEN'S GROWN RAPIDLY, AND THE TWO FACTIONS LED BY THE LEADER AND THE FORMER LEADER...
...HAVE BEEN IN OPPOSITION FOR SOME TIME.
STREET-LEVEL DEALERS HAVE BEEN HURRYING TO EITHER ESCAPE THE CONFLICT OR ALIGN THEMSELVES WITH ONE SIDE OR THE OTHER.
SO WHAT STARTED IT?
IT'S LIKE I SAID IN REASON ONE.
A DECREASE IN DRUG SUPPLY?
EXACTLY.
ALTHOUGH THE ACTUAL AMOUNT DIDN'T DROP.
THE DRUGS JUST GOT *SMALLER*.
SEED, EH?
BUT YOU SAID THE SUPPLIER WAS A *FORMER* MEMBER, RIGHT?
YES.
THE ONE SPREADING SEED AROUND ISN'T, STRICTLY SPEAKING, PART OF THE RYUGEN.
IT'S A MEMBER OF A FORMER FACTION.

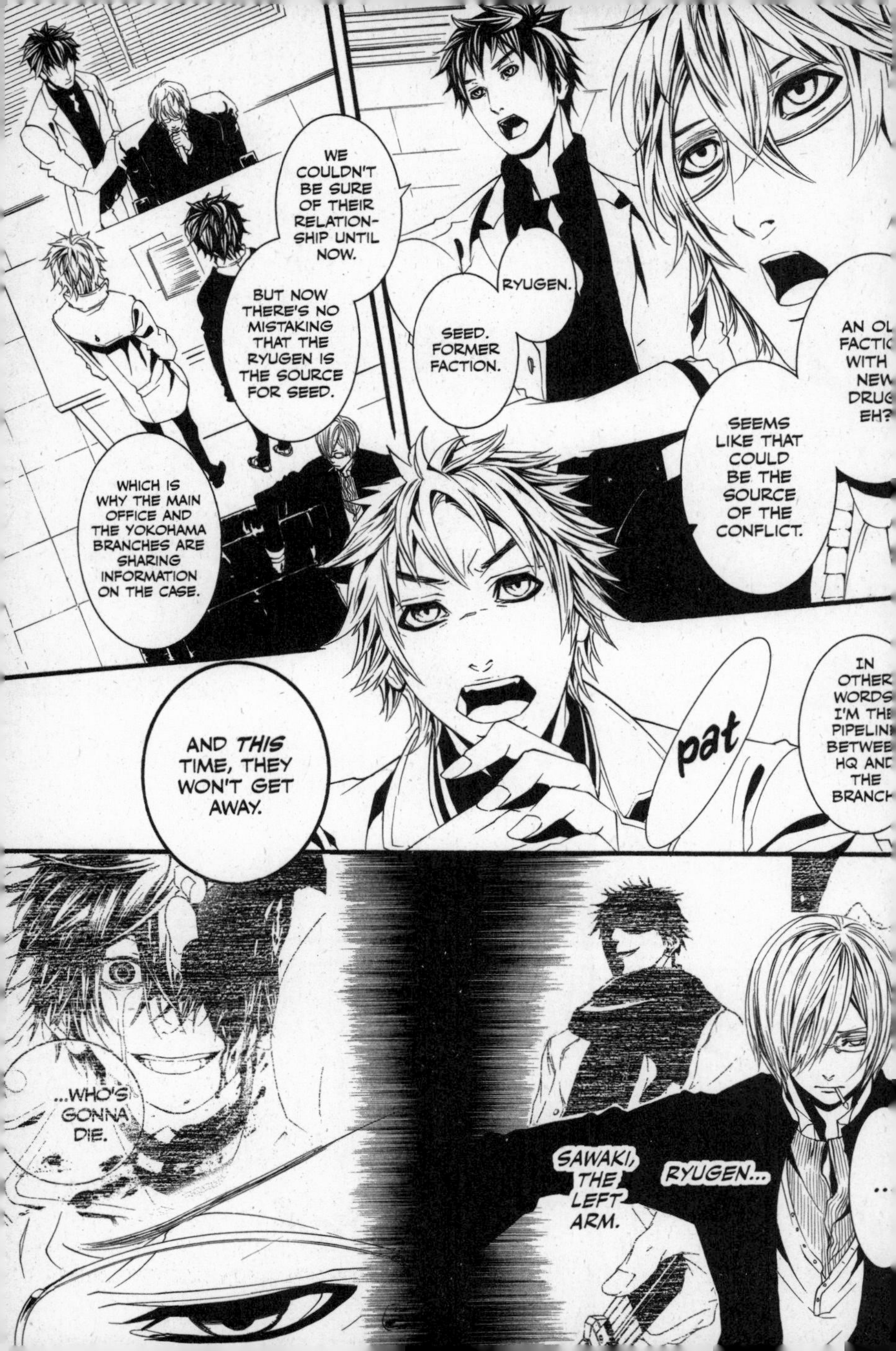
AN OL FACTIC WITH NEW DRUG EH?
SEEMS LIKE THAT COULD BE THE SOURCE OF THE CONFLICT.
RYUGEN.
SEED. FORMER FACTION.
WE COULDN'T BE SURE OF THEIR RELATION-SHIP UNTIL NOW.
BUT NOW THERE'S NO MISTAKING THAT THE RYUGEN IS THE SOURCE FOR SEED.
WHICH IS WHY THE MAIN OFFICE AND THE YOKOHAMA BRANCHES ARE SHARING INFORMATION ON THE CASE.
IN OTHER WORDS I'M THE PIPELIN BETWEE HQ AND THE BRANCH
pat
AND *THIS* TIME, THEY WON'T GET AWAY.
...
RYUGEN...
SAWAKI, THE LEFT ARM.
...WHO'S GONNA DIE.

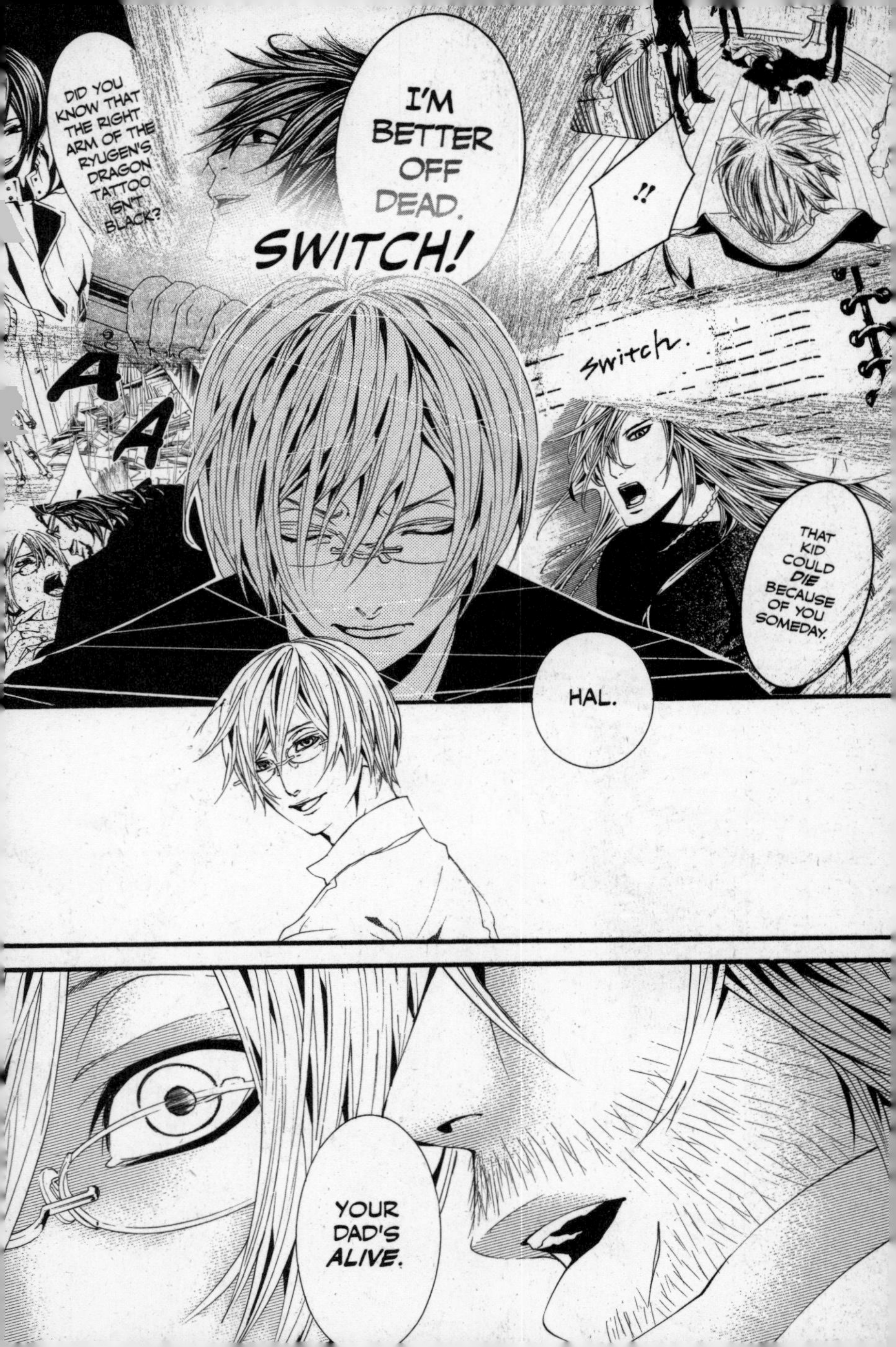
!!
Switch.
THAT KID COULD DIE BECAUSE OF YOU SOMEDAY.
I'M BETTER OFF DEAD.
SWITCH!
DID YOU KNOW THAT THE RIGHT ARM OF THE RYUGEN'S DRAGON TATTOO ISN'T BLACK?
AA
HAL.
YOUR DAD'S ALIVE.

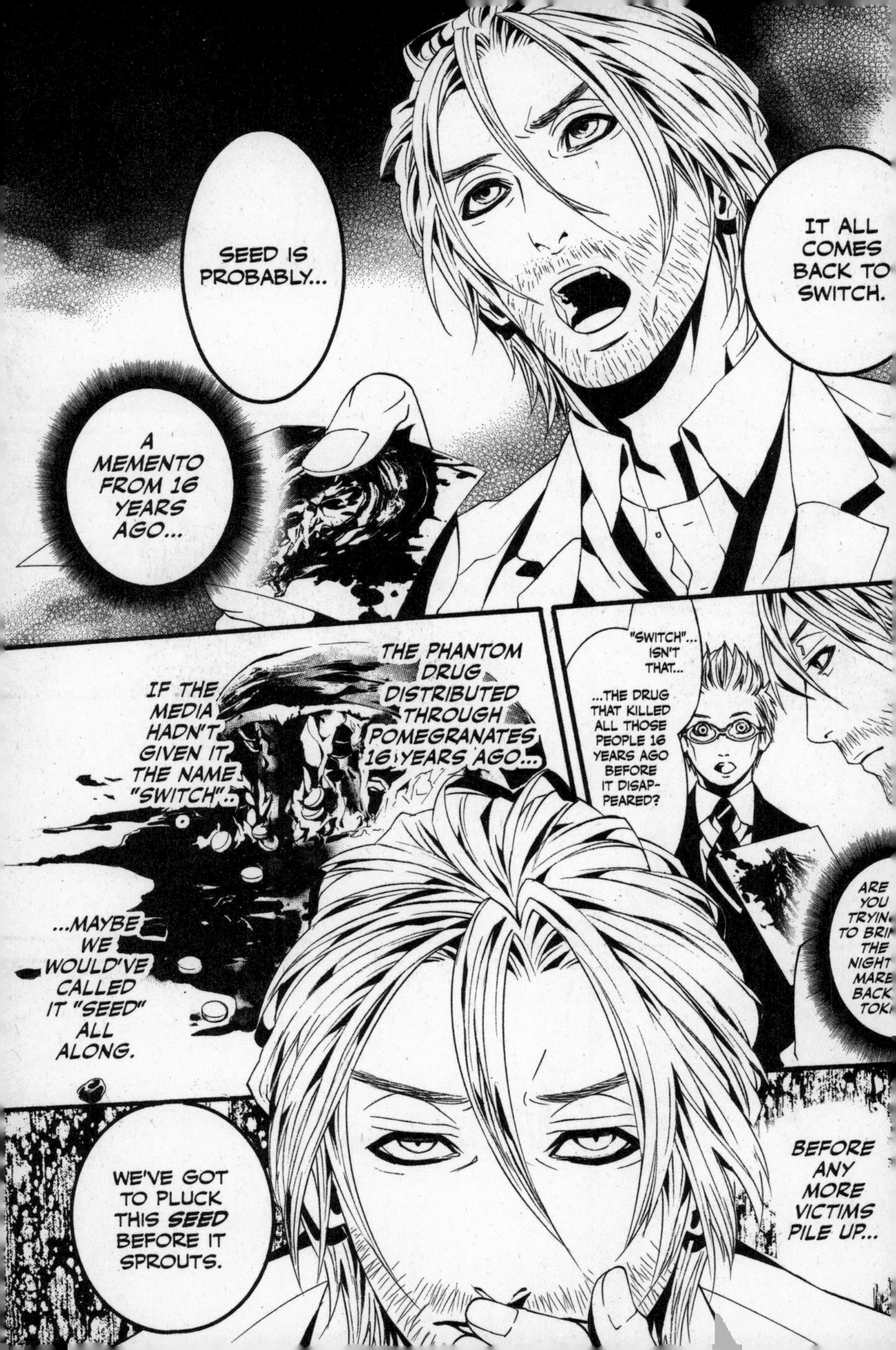
IT ALL COMES BACK TO SWITCH.
SEED IS PROBABLY...
A MEMENTO FROM 16 YEARS AGO...
"SWITCH"... ISN'T THAT...
...THE DRUG THAT KILLED ALL THOSE PEOPLE 16 YEARS AGO BEFORE IT DISAP-PEARED?
ARE YOU TRYIN TO BRI THE NIGHT MARE BACK TOK
THE PHANTOM DRUG DISTRIBUTED THROUGH POMEGRANATES 16 YEARS AGO...
IF THE MEDIA HADN'T GIVEN IT THE NAME "SWITCH"...
...MAYBE WE WOULD'VE CALLED IT "SEED" ALL ALONG.
BEFORE ANY MORE VICTIMS PILE UP...
WE'VE GOT TO PLUCK THIS *SEED* BEFORE IT SPROUTS.

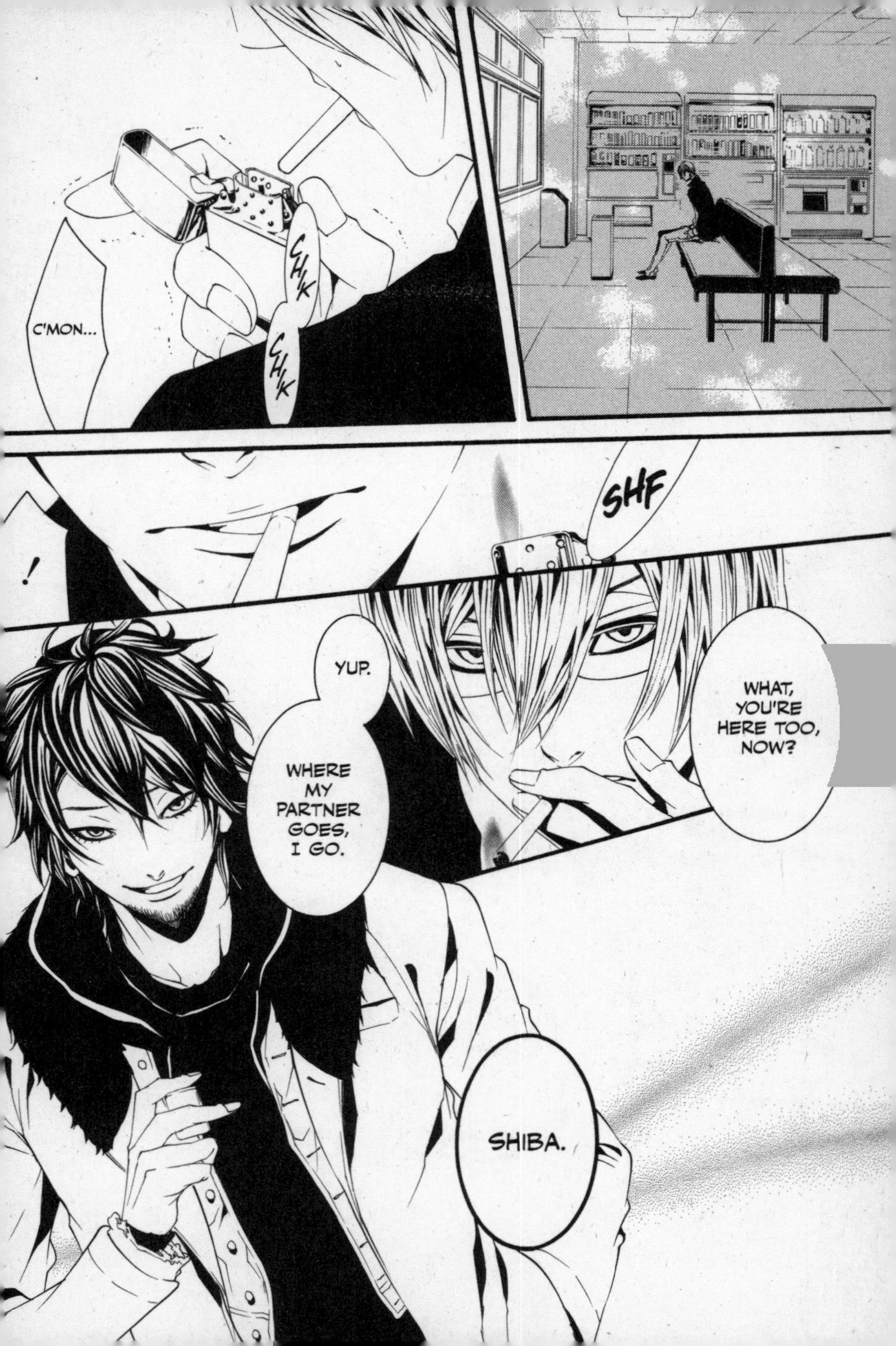
CHIK
CHIK
C'MON...
SHF
!
WHAT, YOU'RE HERE TOO, NOW?
YUP.
WHERE MY PARTNER GOES, I GO.
SHIBA.

switch

naked ape : Saki Otoh & Nakamura Tomomi

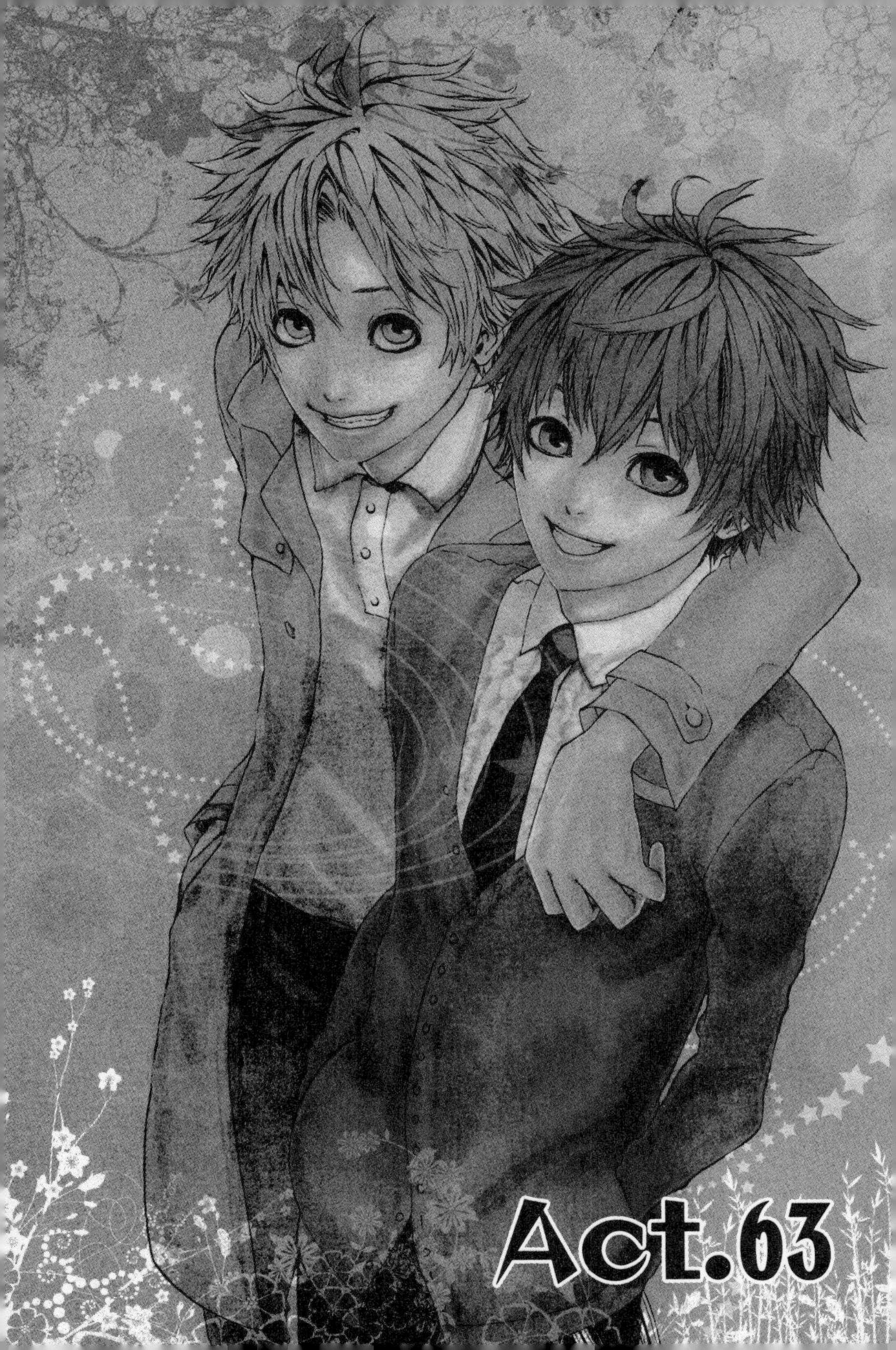
Act.63

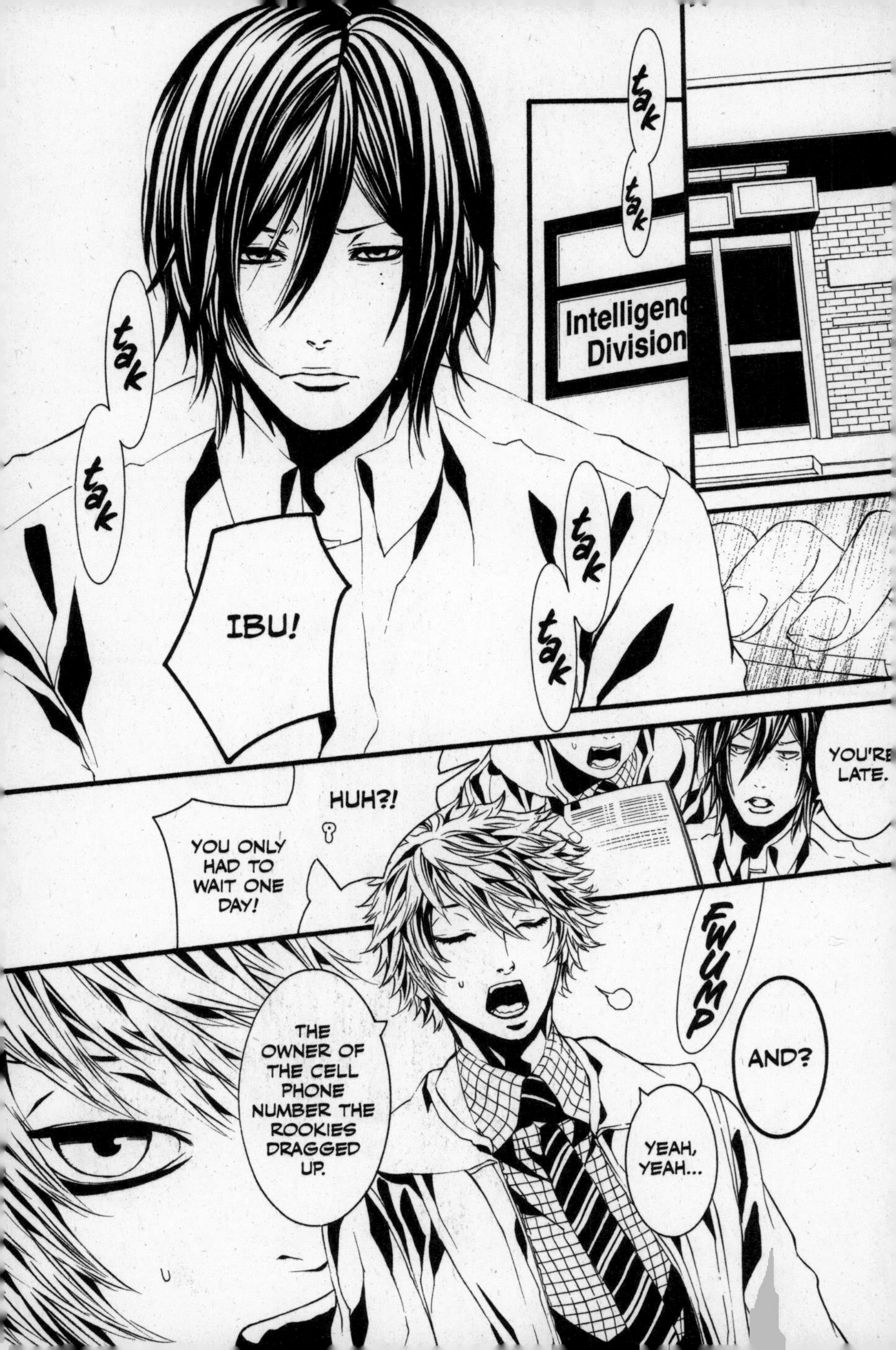
tak tak
Intelligenc
Division
tak tak
tak tak
IBU!
YOU'RE LATE.
HUH?!
YOU ONLY HAD TO WAIT ONE DAY!
FWUMP
AND?
YEAH, YEAH...
THE OWNER OF THE CELL PHONE NUMBER THE ROOKIES DRAGGED UP.

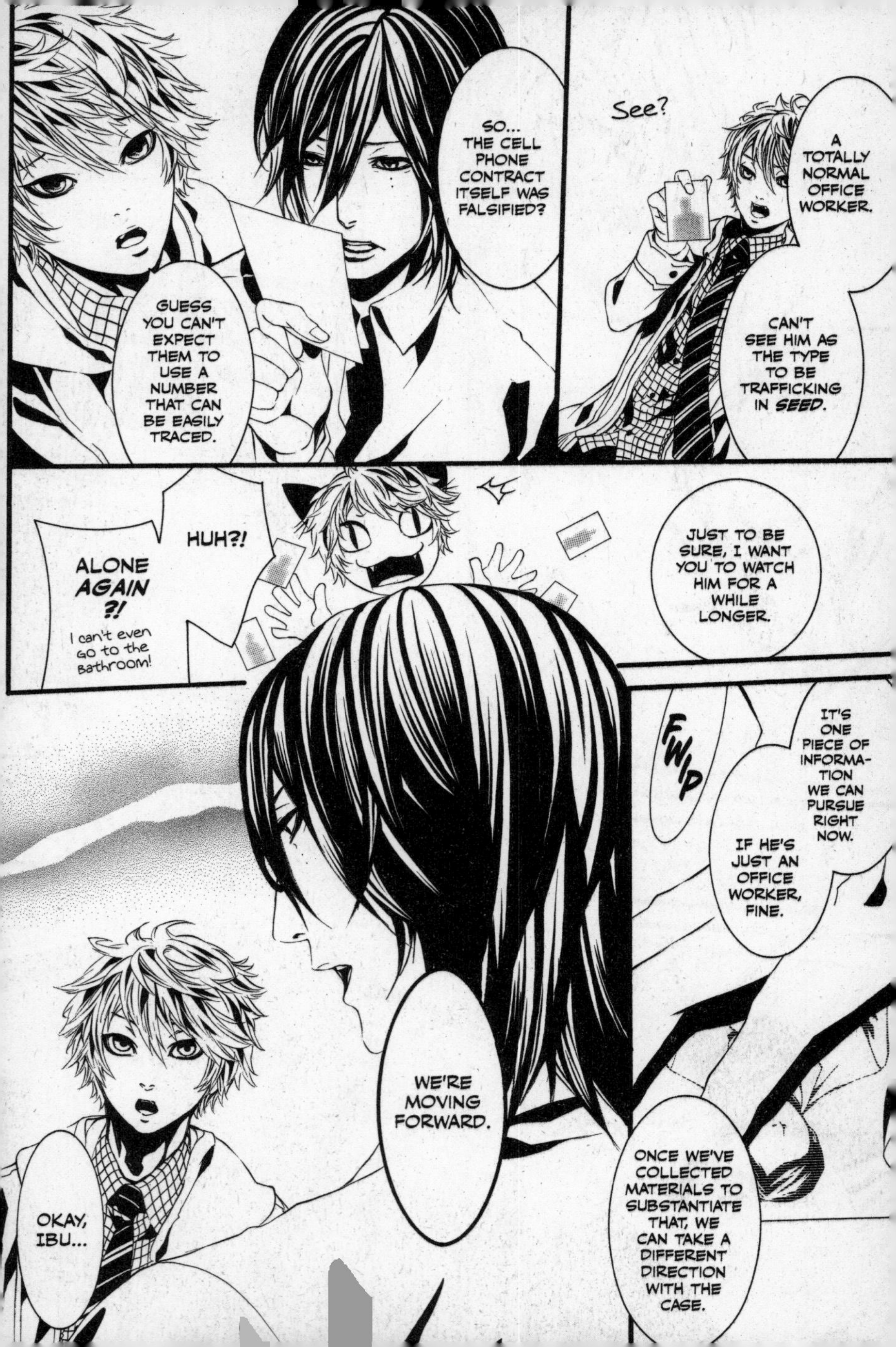

See?
A TOTALLY NORMAL OFFICE WORKER.
CAN'T SEE HIM AS THE TYPE TO BE TRAFFICKING IN SEED.
SO... THE CELL PHONE CONTRACT ITSELF WAS FALSIFIED?
GUESS YOU CAN'T EXPECT THEM TO USE A NUMBER THAT CAN BE EASILY TRACED.
JUST TO BE SURE, I WANT YOU TO WATCH HIM FOR A WHILE LONGER.
HUH?!
ALONE AGAIN?!
I can't even go to the bathroom!
FWIP
IT'S ONE PIECE OF INFORMATION WE CAN PURSUE RIGHT NOW.
IF HE'S JUST AN OFFICE WORKER, FINE.
ONCE WE'VE COLLECTED MATERIALS TO SUBSTANTIATE THAT, WE CAN TAKE A DIFFERENT DIRECTION WITH THE CASE.
WE'RE MOVING FORWARD.
OKAY, IBU...

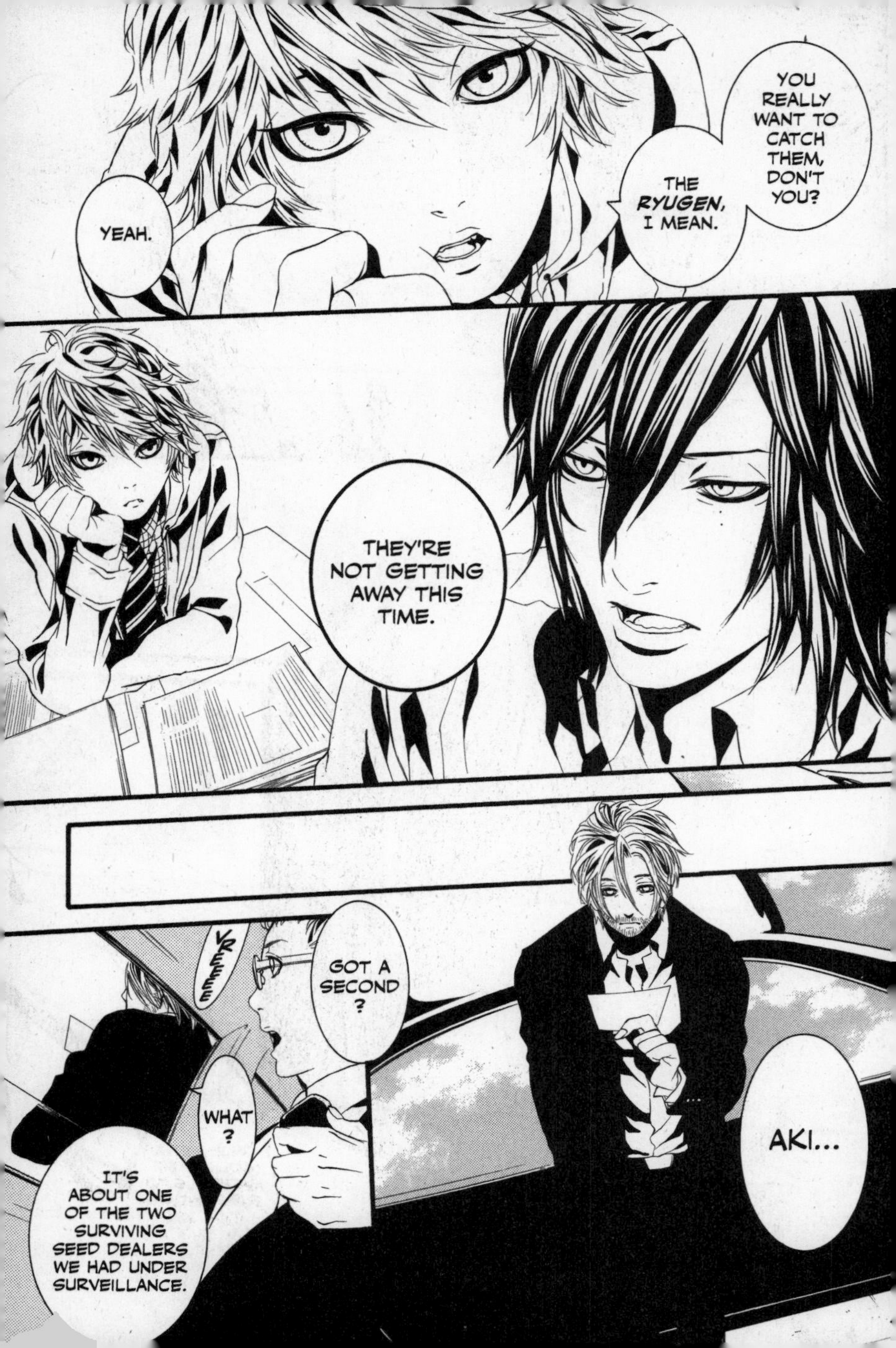
YOU REALLY WANT TO CATCH THEM, DON'T YOU?
THE *RYUGEN*, I MEAN.
YEAH.
THEY'RE NOT GETTING AWAY THIS TIME.
...
AKI...
GOT A SECOND?
VREEEE
WHAT?
IT'S ABOUT ONE OF THE TWO SURVIVING SEED DEALERS WE HAD UNDER SURVEILLANCE.

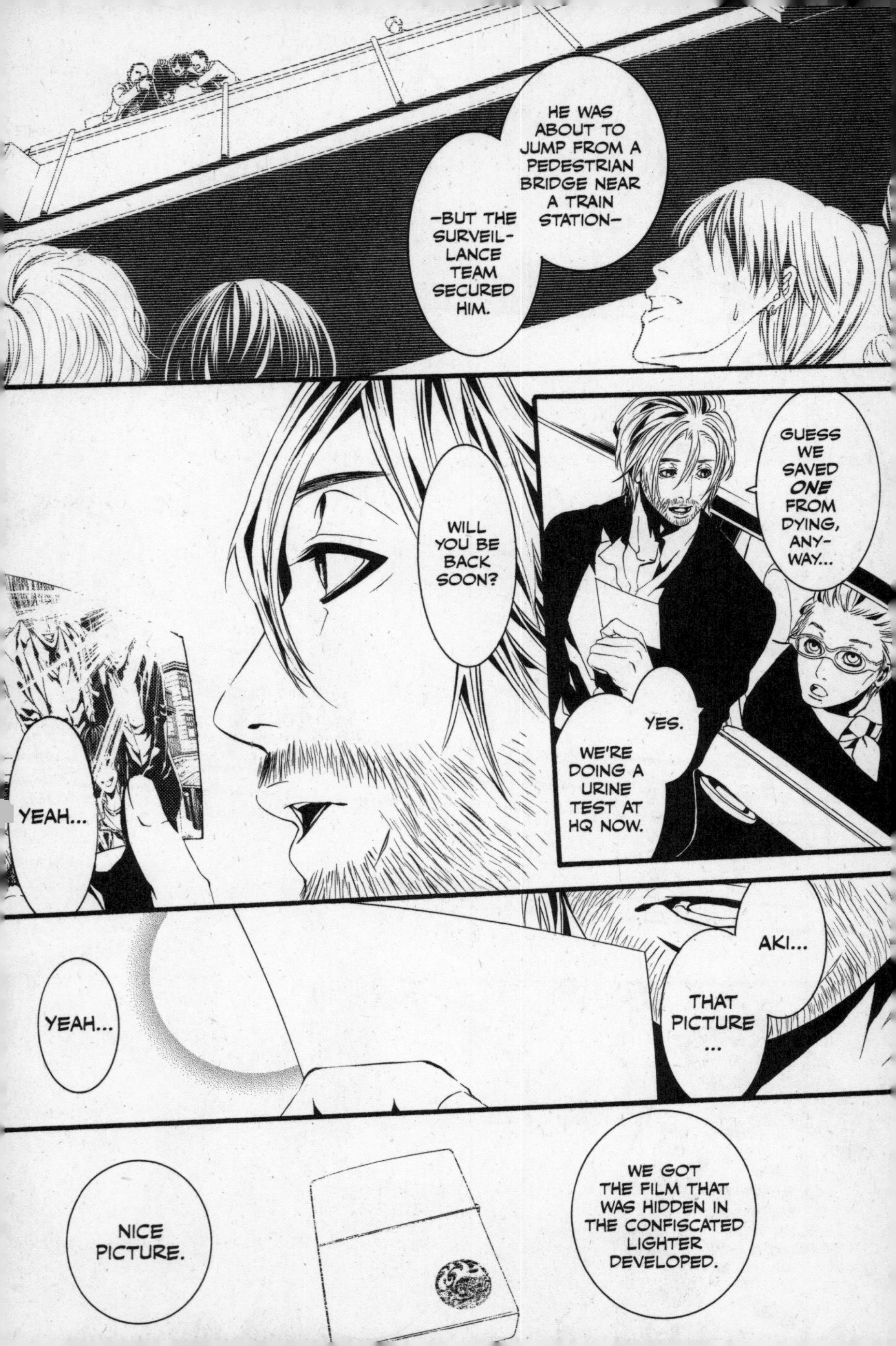
HE WAS ABOUT TO JUMP FROM A PEDESTRIAN BRIDGE NEAR A TRAIN STATION—
—BUT THE SURVEIL-LANCE TEAM SECURED HIM.
GUESS WE SAVED *ONE* FROM DYING, ANY-WAY...
YES.
WE'RE DOING A URINE TEST AT HQ NOW.
WILL YOU BE BACK SOON?
YEAH...
AKI...
THAT PICTURE ...
YEAH...
WE GOT THE FILM THAT WAS HIDDEN IN THE CONFISCATED LIGHTER DEVELOPED.
NICE PICTURE.

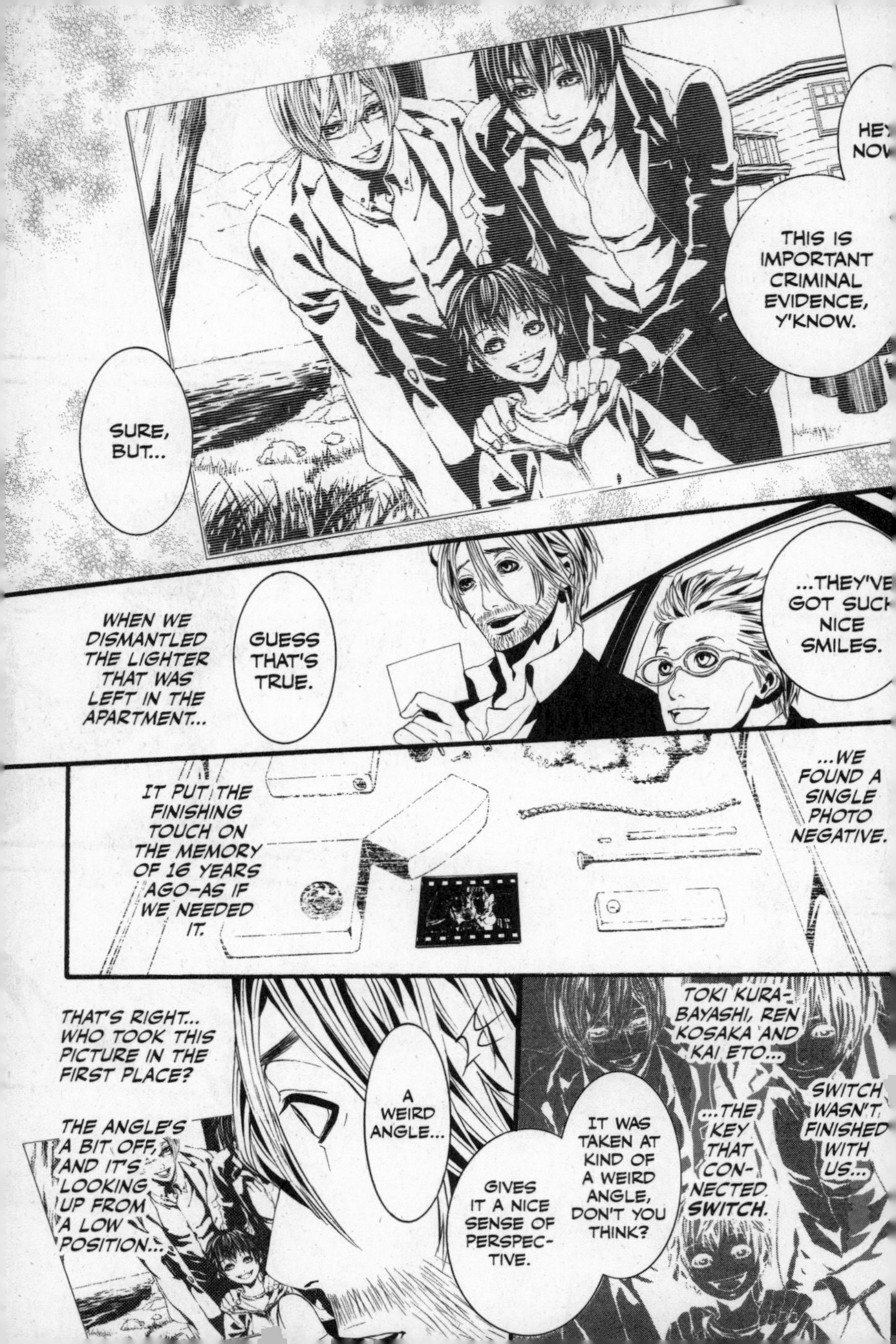
HEY NOW
THIS IS IMPORTANT CRIMINAL EVIDENCE, Y'KNOW.
SURE, BUT...
...THEY'VE GOT SUCH NICE SMILES.
GUESS THAT'S TRUE.
WHEN WE DISMANTLED THE LIGHTER THAT WAS LEFT IN THE APARTMENT...
...WE FOUND A SINGLE PHOTO NEGATIVE.
IT PUT THE FINISHING TOUCH ON THE MEMORY OF 16 YEARS AGO—AS IF WE NEEDED IT.
TOKI KURA-BAYASHI, REN KOSAKA AND KAI ETO...
SWITCH WASN'T FINISHED WITH US...
...THE KEY THAT CON-NECTED SWITCH.
IT WAS TAKEN AT KIND OF A WEIRD ANGLE, DON'T YOU THINK?
GIVES IT A NICE SENSE OF PERSPEC-TIVE.
A WEIRD ANGLE...
THAT'S RIGHT... WHO TOOK THIS PICTURE IN THE FIRST PLACE?
THE ANGLE'S A BIT OFF, AND IT'S LOOKING UP FROM A LOW POSITION...

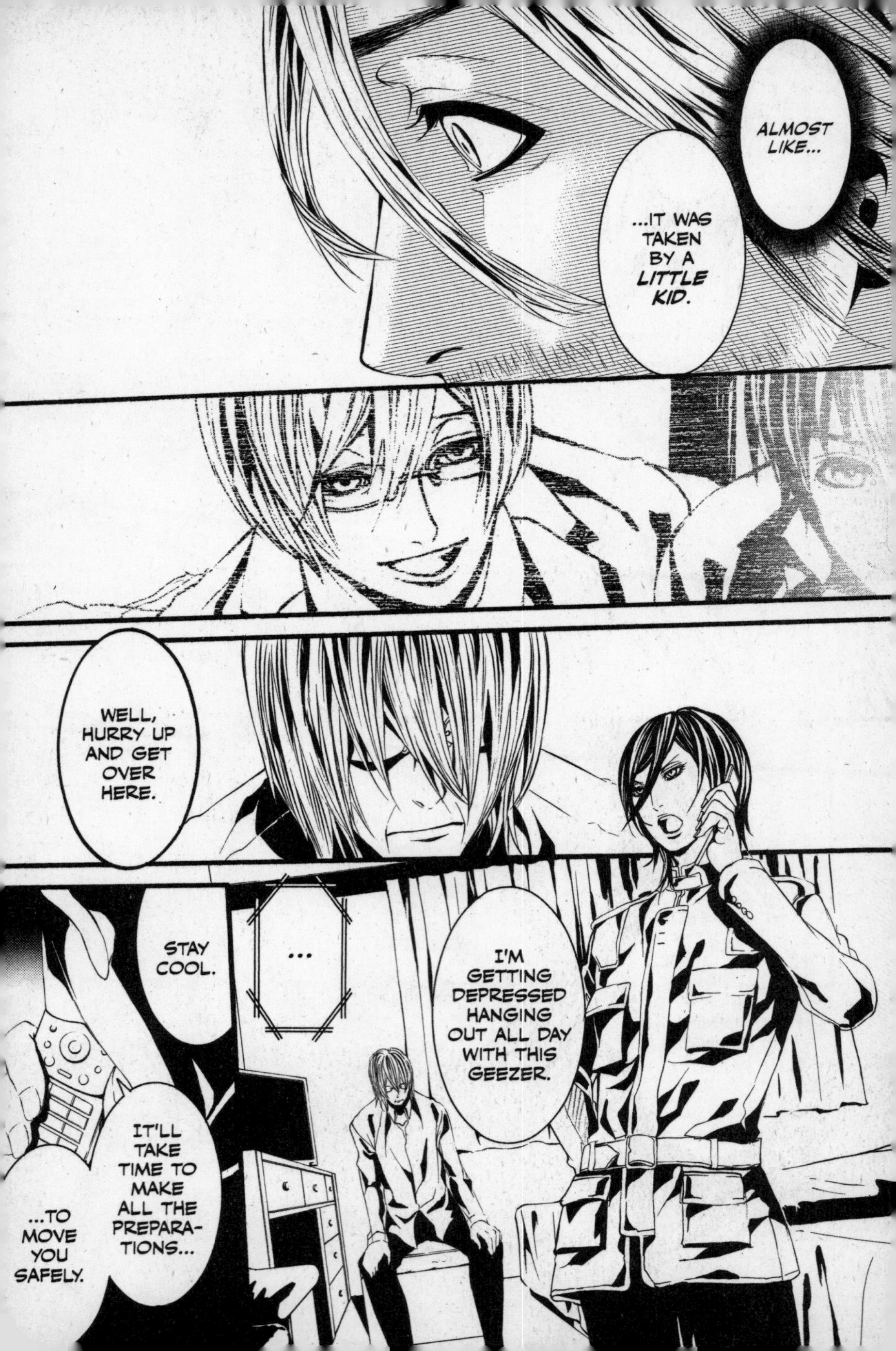
ALMOST LIKE...
...IT WAS TAKEN BY A *LITTLE KID*.
WELL, HURRY UP AND GET OVER HERE.
I'M GETTING DEPRESSED HANGING OUT ALL DAY WITH THIS GEEZER.
...
STAY COOL.
IT'LL TAKE TIME TO MAKE ALL THE PREPARATIONS...
...TO MOVE YOU SAFELY.

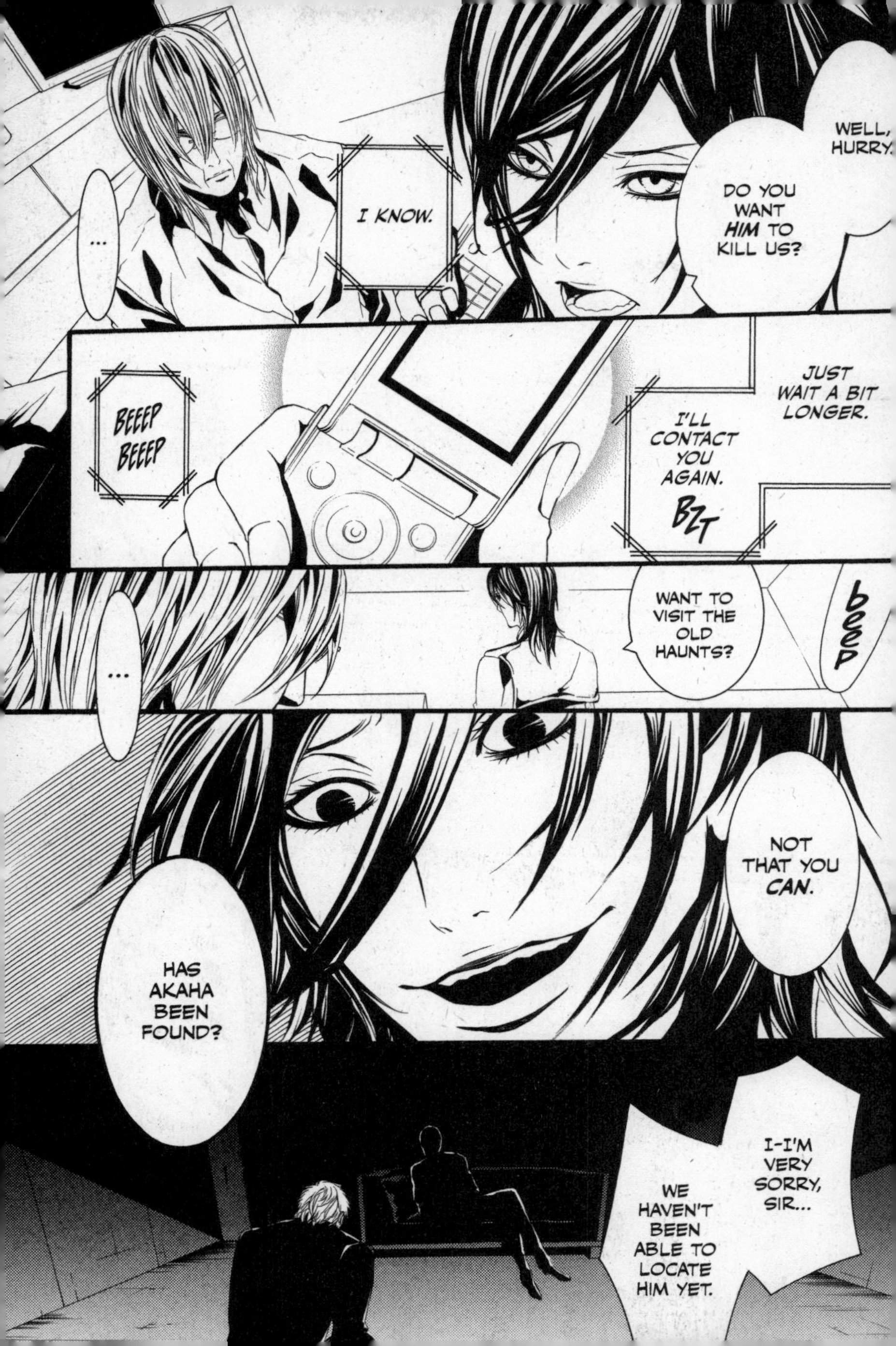
WELL, HURRY.
DO YOU WANT HIM TO KILL US?
I KNOW.
...
JUST WAIT A BIT LONGER.
I'LL CONTACT YOU AGAIN.
BZT
BEEEP BEEEP
beep
WANT TO VISIT THE OLD HAUNTS?
...
NOT THAT YOU CAN.
HAS AKAHA BEEN FOUND?
I-I'M VERY SORRY, SIR...
WE HAVEN'T BEEN ABLE TO LOCATE HIM YET.

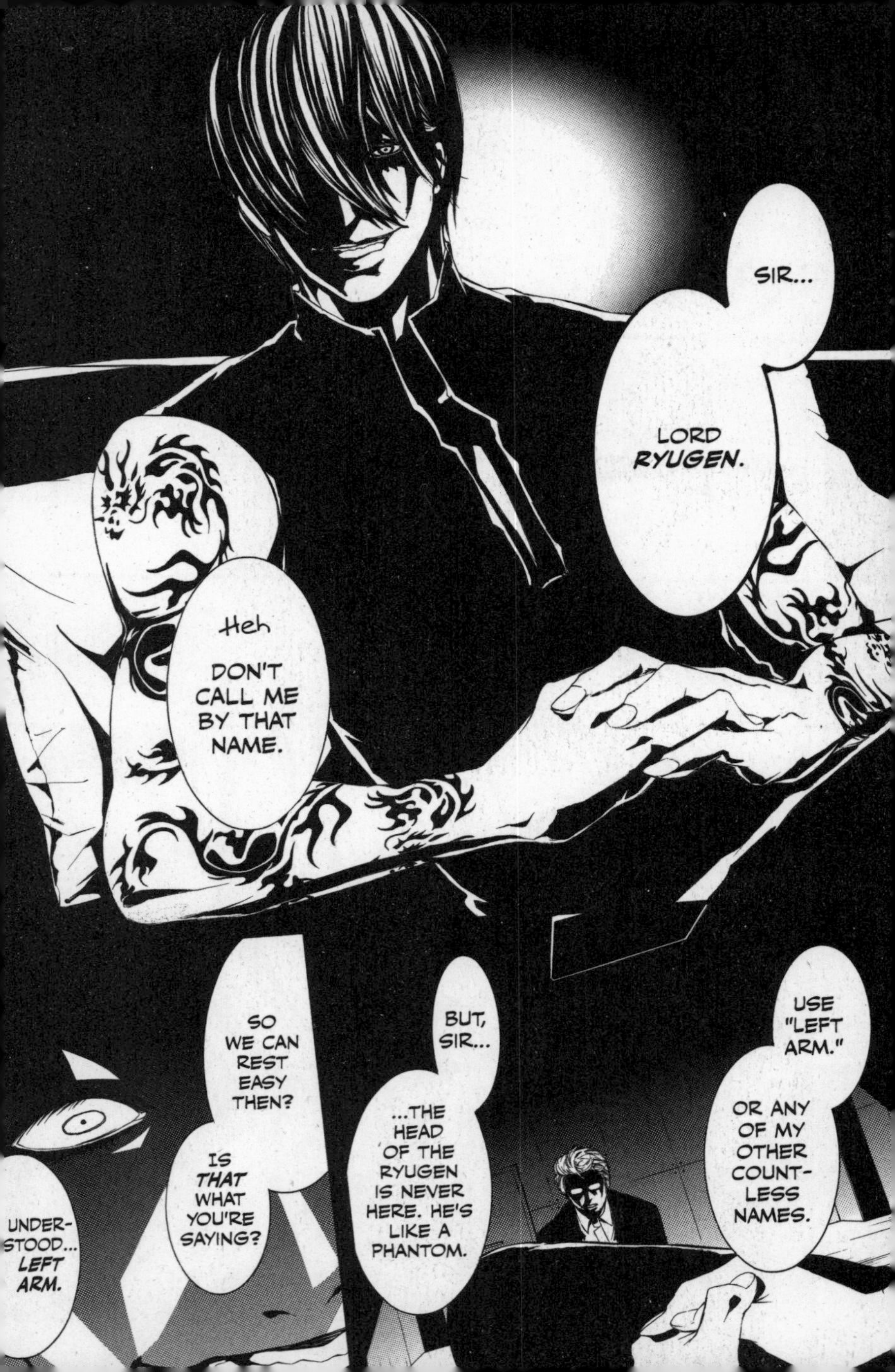
SIR...
LORD *RYUGEN.*
Heh
DON'T CALL ME BY THAT NAME.
USE "LEFT ARM."
OR ANY OF MY OTHER COUNT-LESS NAMES.
BUT, SIR...
...THE HEAD OF THE RYUGEN IS NEVER HERE. HE'S LIKE A PHANTOM.
SO WE CAN REST EASY THEN?
IS *THAT* WHAT YOU'RE SAYING?
UNDER-STOOD... *LEFT ARM.*

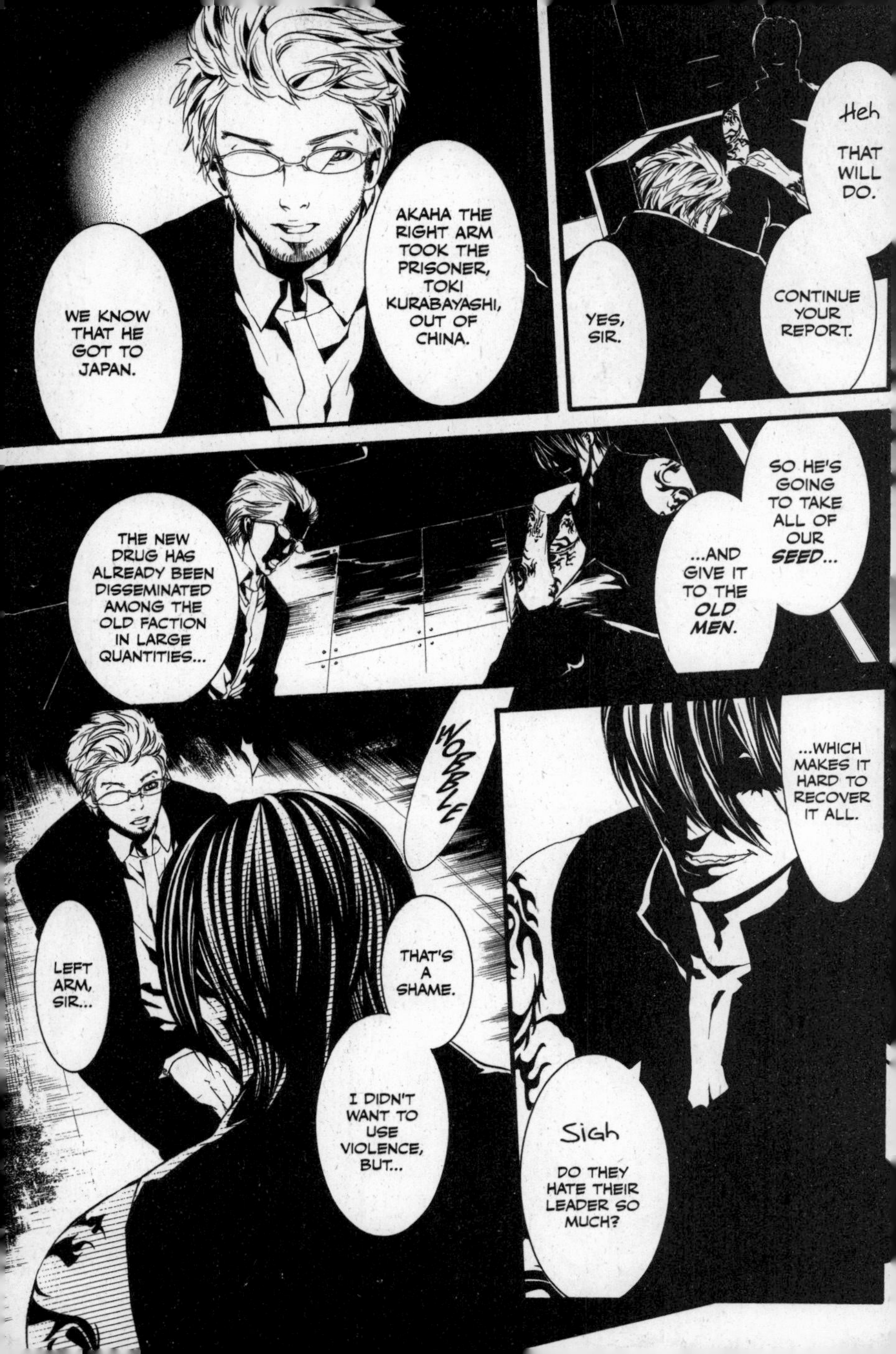
Heh
THAT WILL DO.
CONTINUE YOUR REPORT.
YES, SIR.
AKAHA THE RIGHT ARM TOOK THE PRISONER, TOKI KURABAYASHI, OUT OF CHINA.
WE KNOW THAT HE GOT TO JAPAN.
SO HE'S GOING TO TAKE ALL OF OUR SEED...
...AND GIVE IT TO THE OLD MEN.
THE NEW DRUG HAS ALREADY BEEN DISSEMINATED AMONG THE OLD FACTION IN LARGE QUANTITIES...
...WHICH MAKES IT HARD TO RECOVER IT ALL.
Sigh
DO THEY HATE THEIR LEADER SO MUCH?
WOBBLE
THAT'S A SHAME.
I DIDN'T WANT TO USE VIOLENCE, BUT...
LEFT ARM, SIR...

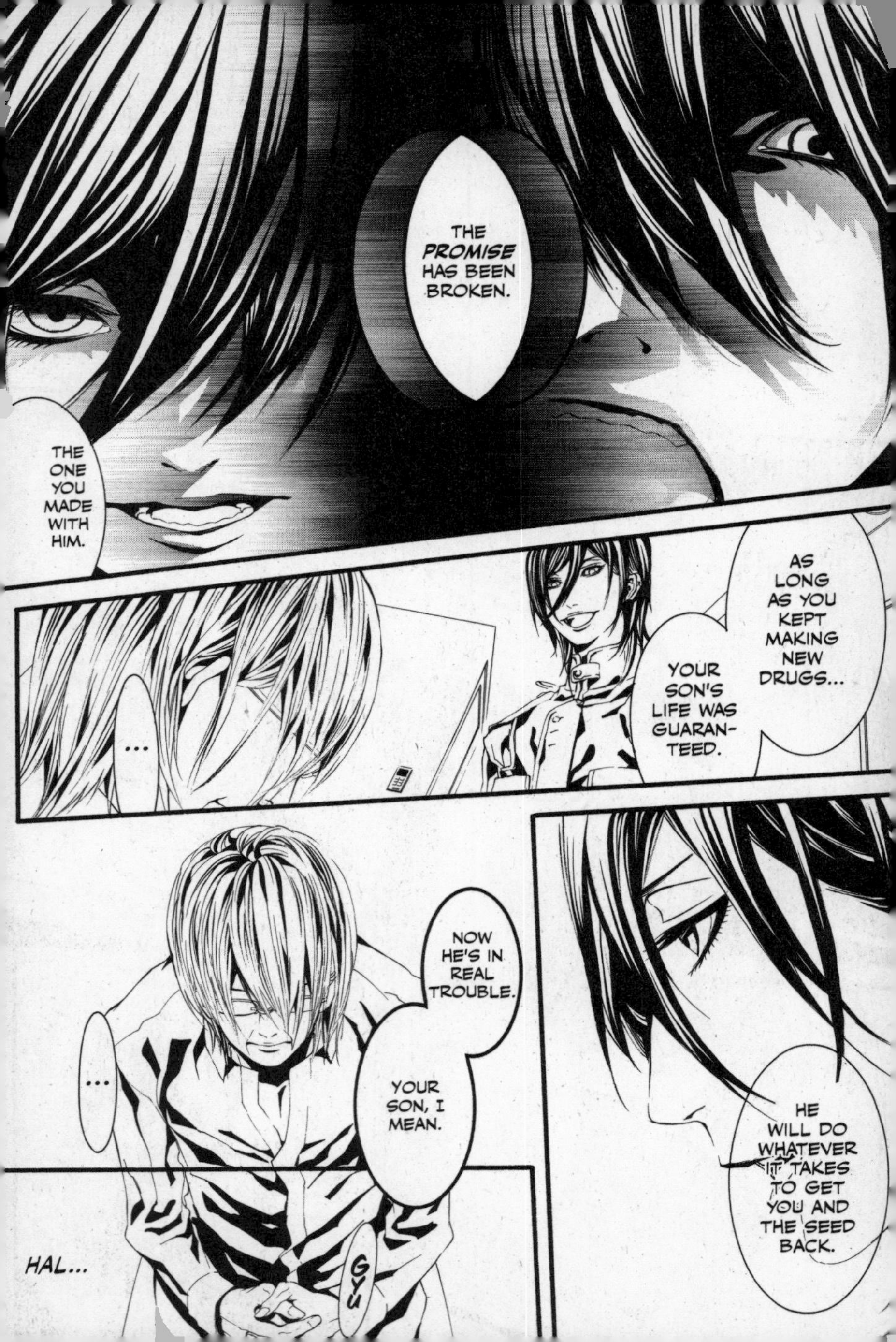
THE PROMISE HAS BEEN BROKEN.
THE ONE YOU MADE WITH HIM.
AS LONG AS YOU KEPT MAKING NEW DRUGS...
YOUR SON'S LIFE WAS GUARANTEED.
...
HE WILL DO WHATEVER IT TAKES TO GET YOU AND THE SEED BACK.
NOW HE'S IN REAL TROUBLE.
YOUR SON, I MEAN.
...
GYU
HAL...

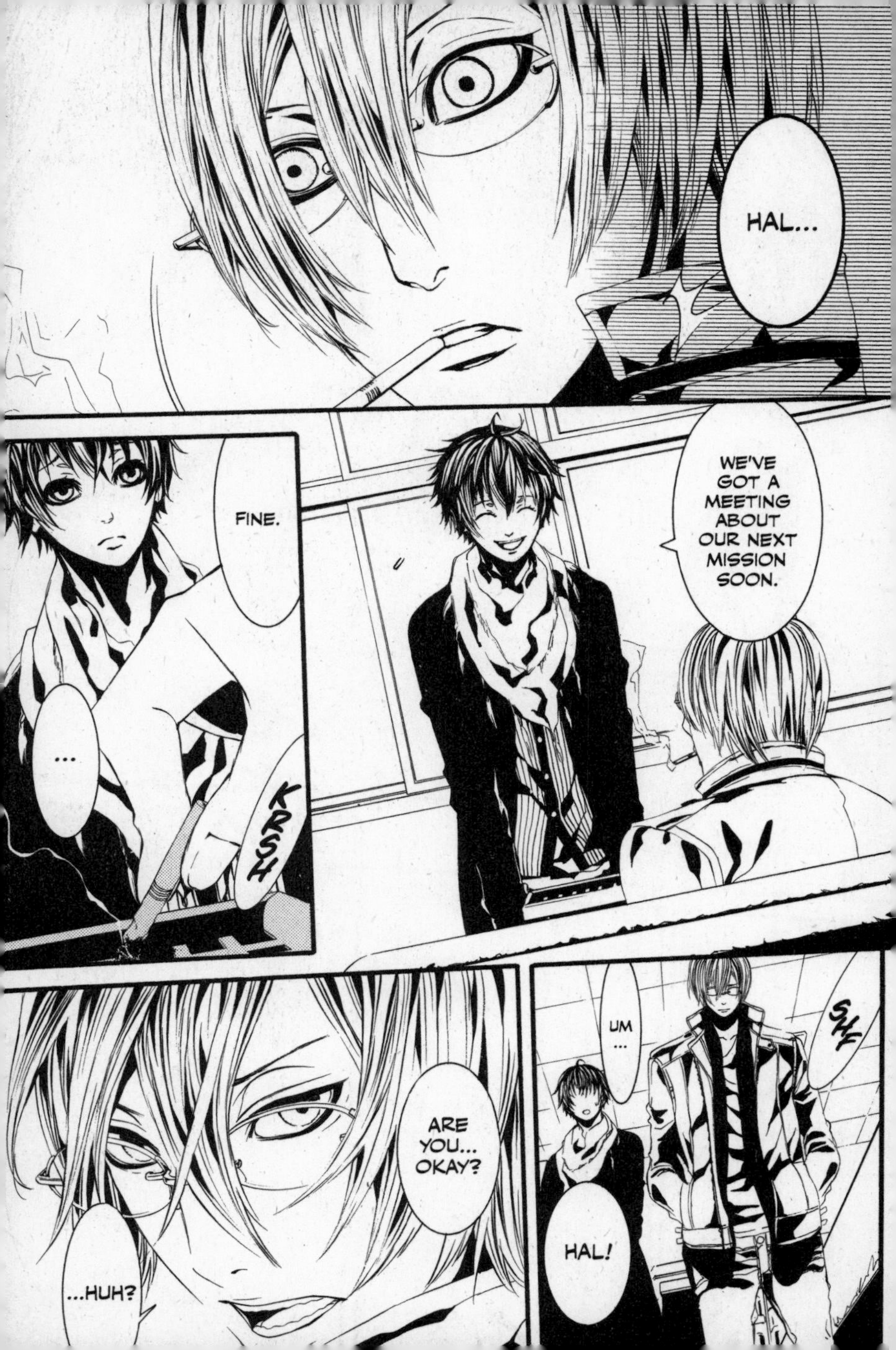
HAL...
WE'VE GOT A MEETING ABOUT OUR NEXT MISSION SOON.
FINE.
KRSH
...
SHF
UM ...
HAL!
ARE YOU... OKAY?
...HUH?

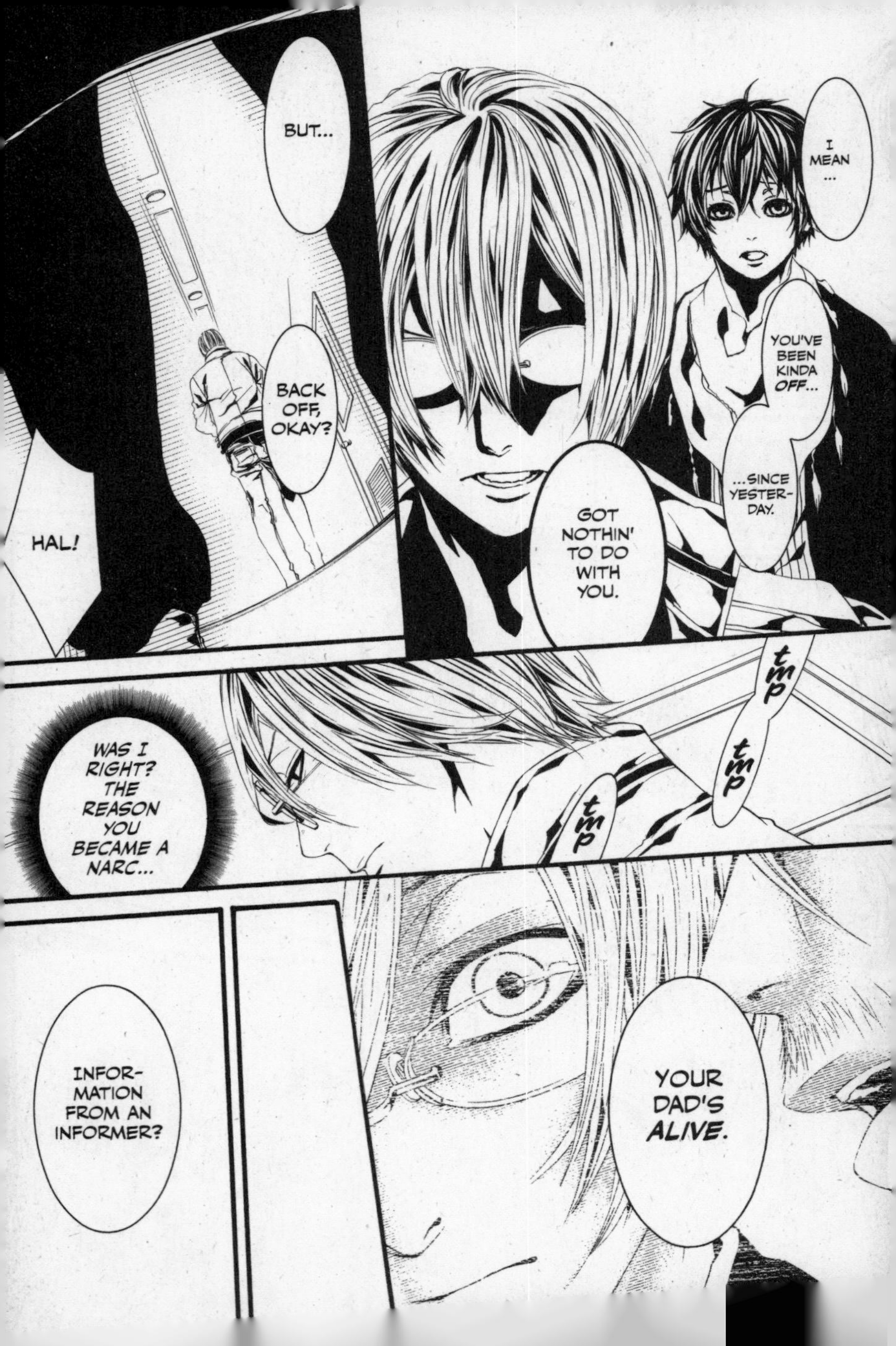

I MEAN ...
YOU'VE BEEN KINDA *OFF*...
...SINCE YESTER-DAY.
GOT NOTHIN' TO DO WITH YOU.
BUT...
BACK OFF, OKAY?
HAL!
tmp
tmp
tmp
WAS I RIGHT? THE REASON YOU BECAME A NARC...
YOUR DAD'S *ALIVE*.
INFOR-MATION FROM AN INFORMER?

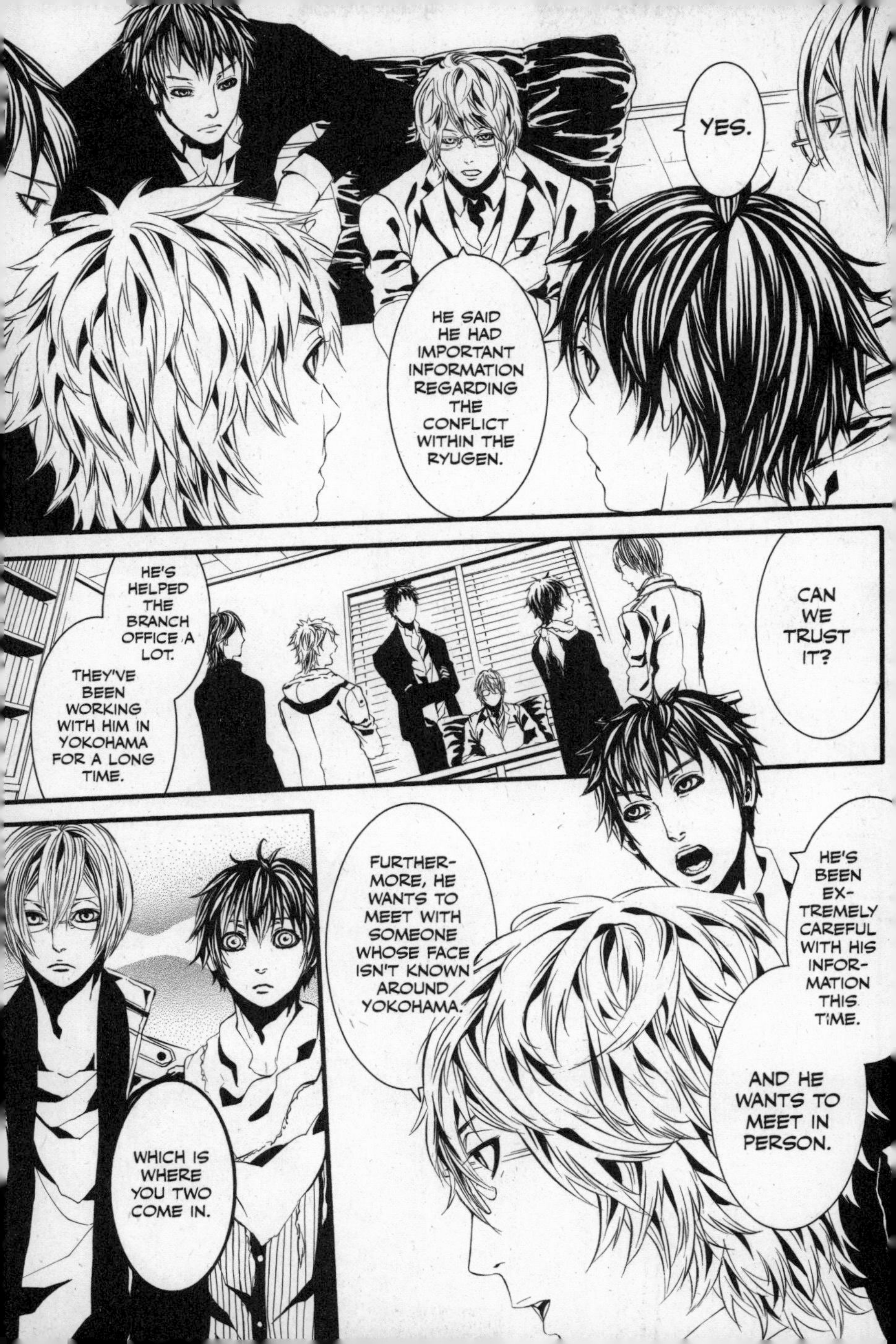
YES.
HE SAID HE HAD IMPORTANT INFORMATION REGARDING THE CONFLICT WITHIN THE RYUGEN.
CAN WE TRUST IT?
HE'S HELPED THE BRANCH OFFICE A LOT.
THEY'VE BEEN WORKING WITH HIM IN YOKOHAMA FOR A LONG TIME.
HE'S BEEN EXTREMELY CAREFUL WITH HIS INFORMATION THIS TIME.
AND HE WANTS TO MEET IN PERSON.
FURTHERMORE, HE WANTS TO MEET WITH SOMEONE WHOSE FACE ISN'T KNOWN AROUND YOKOHAMA.
WHICH IS WHERE YOU TWO COME IN.

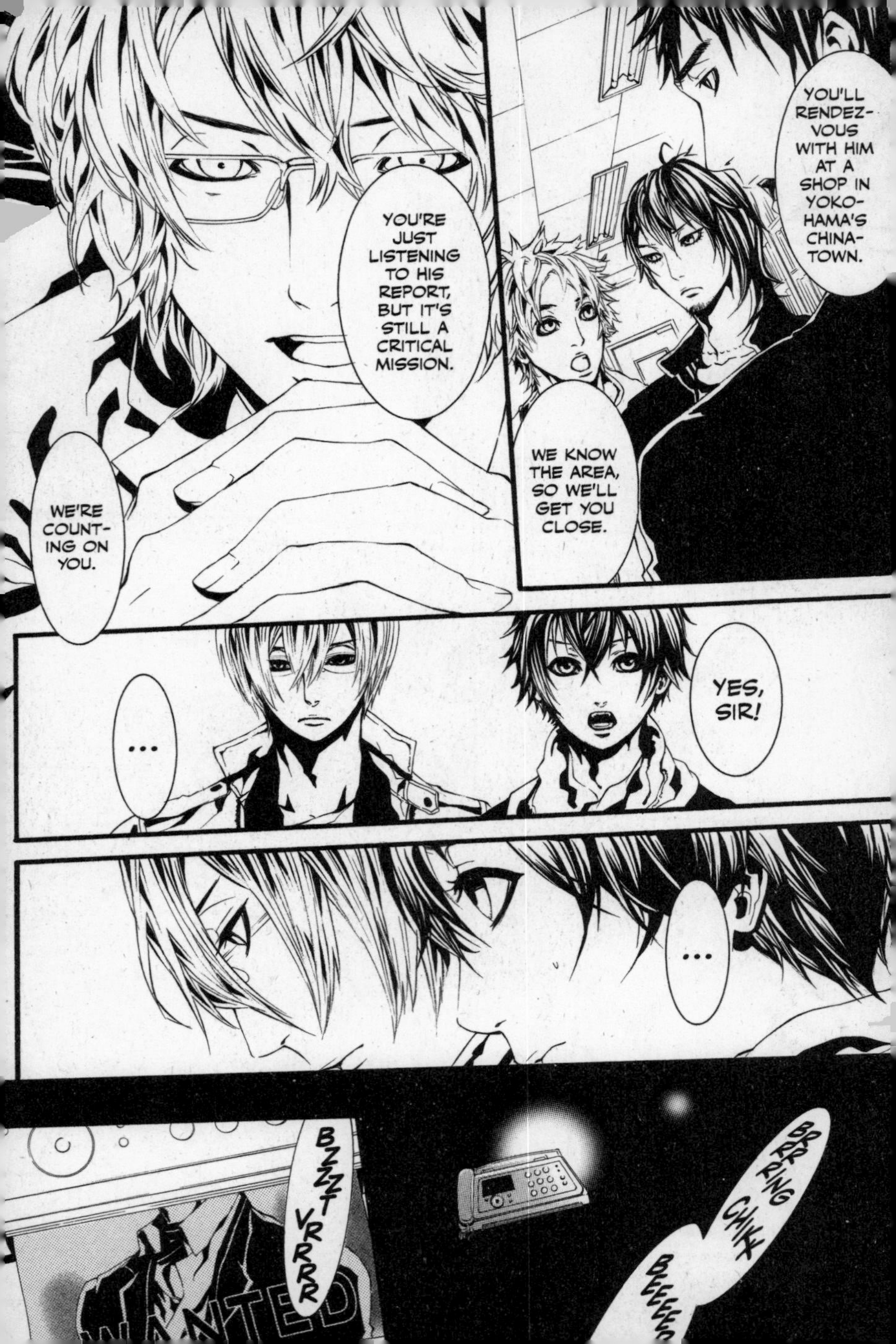

YOU'LL RENDEZVOUS WITH HIM AT A SHOP IN YOKOHAMA'S CHINATOWN.
WE KNOW THE AREA, SO WE'LL GET YOU CLOSE.
YOU'RE JUST LISTENING TO HIS REPORT, BUT IT'S STILL A CRITICAL MISSION.
WE'RE COUNTING ON YOU.
YES, SIR!
...
...
BRRRING CHIKK
BZZZT VRRRR

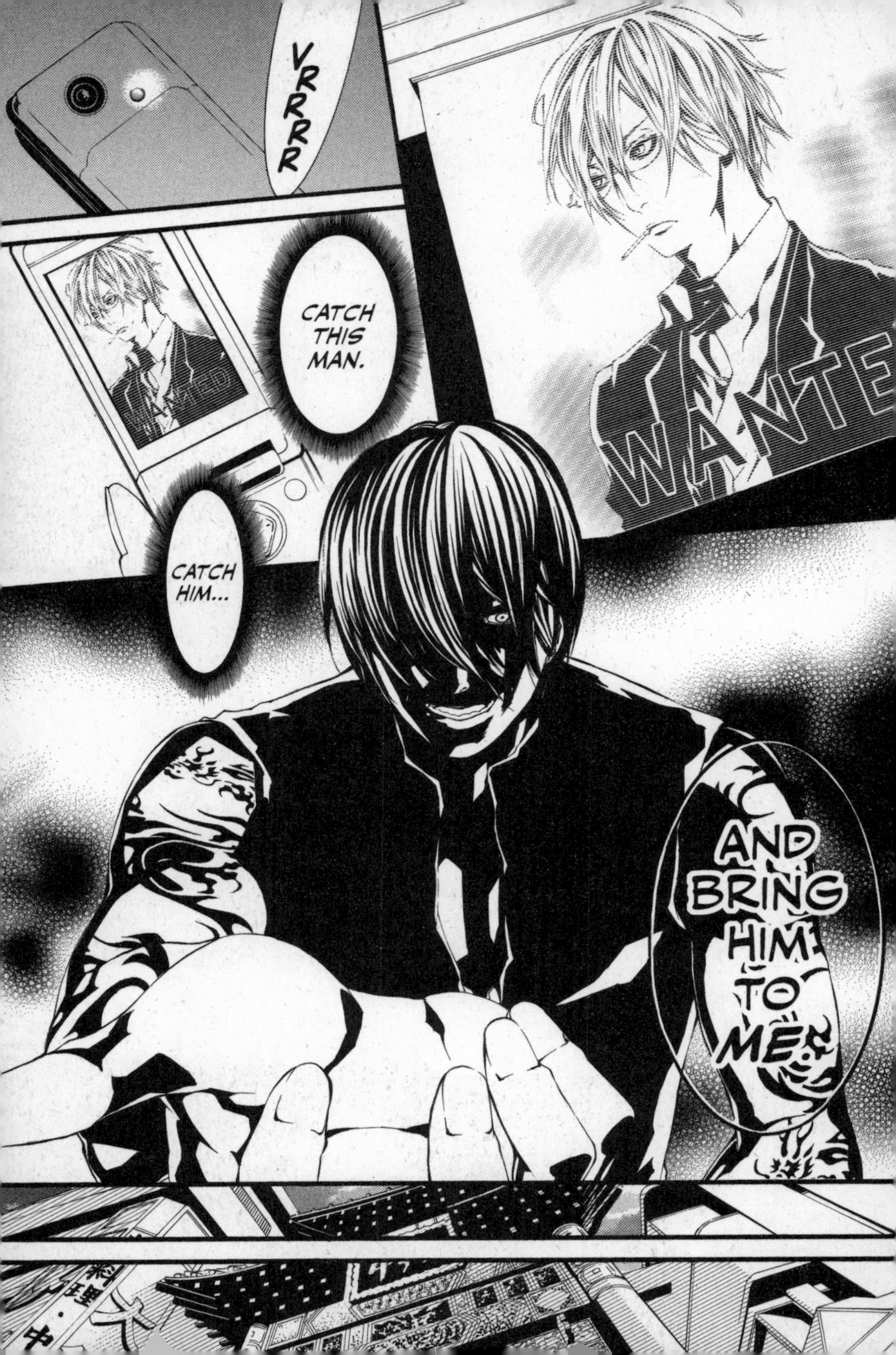
WANTE
VRRRR
CATCH THIS MAN.
CATCH HIM...
AND BRING HIM TO ME.

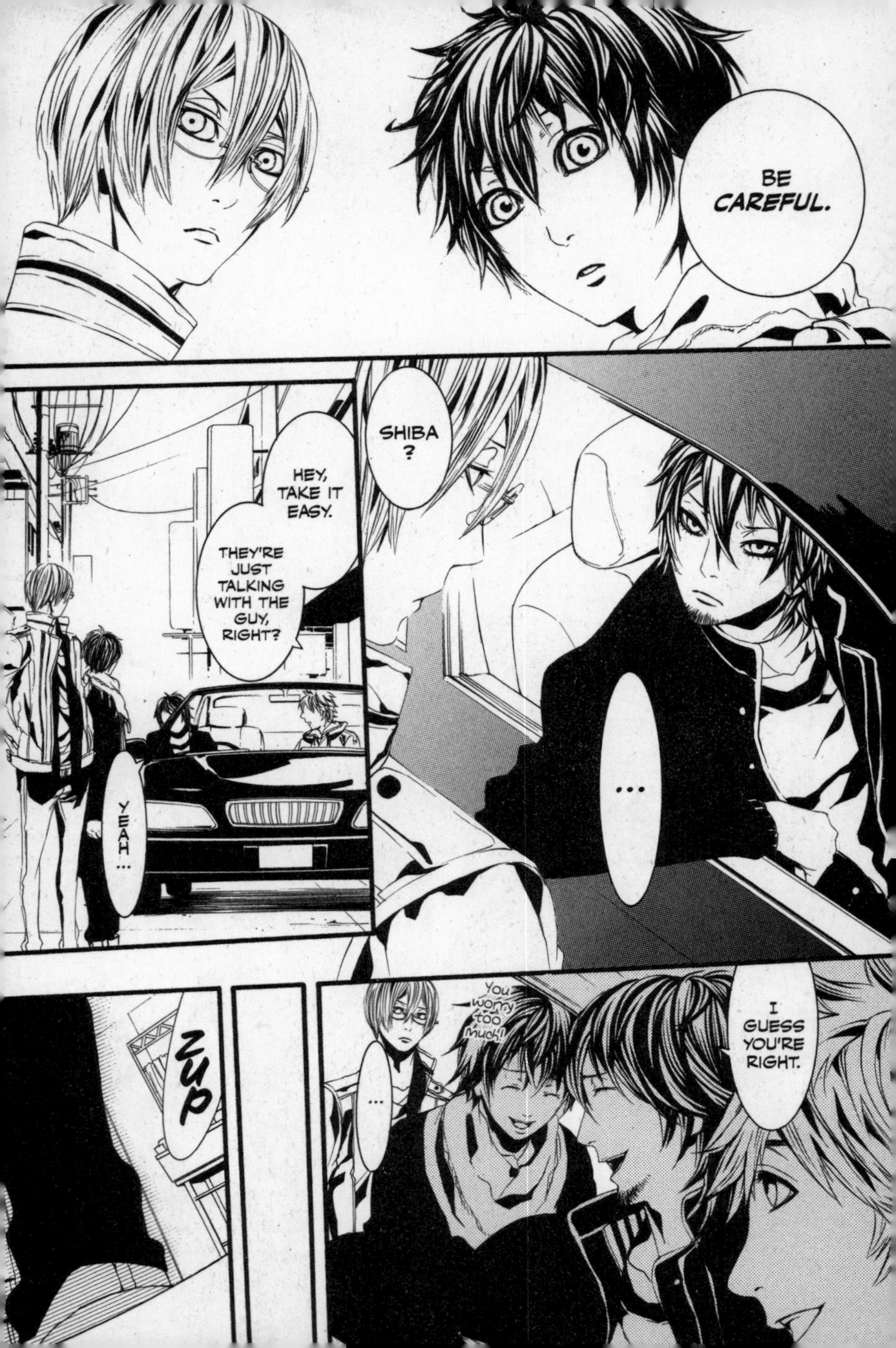
BE CAREFUL.
SHIBA?
...
HEY, TAKE IT EASY.
THEY'RE JUST TALKING WITH THE GUY, RIGHT?
YEAH...
I GUESS YOU'RE RIGHT.
You worry too much!
...
ZUP

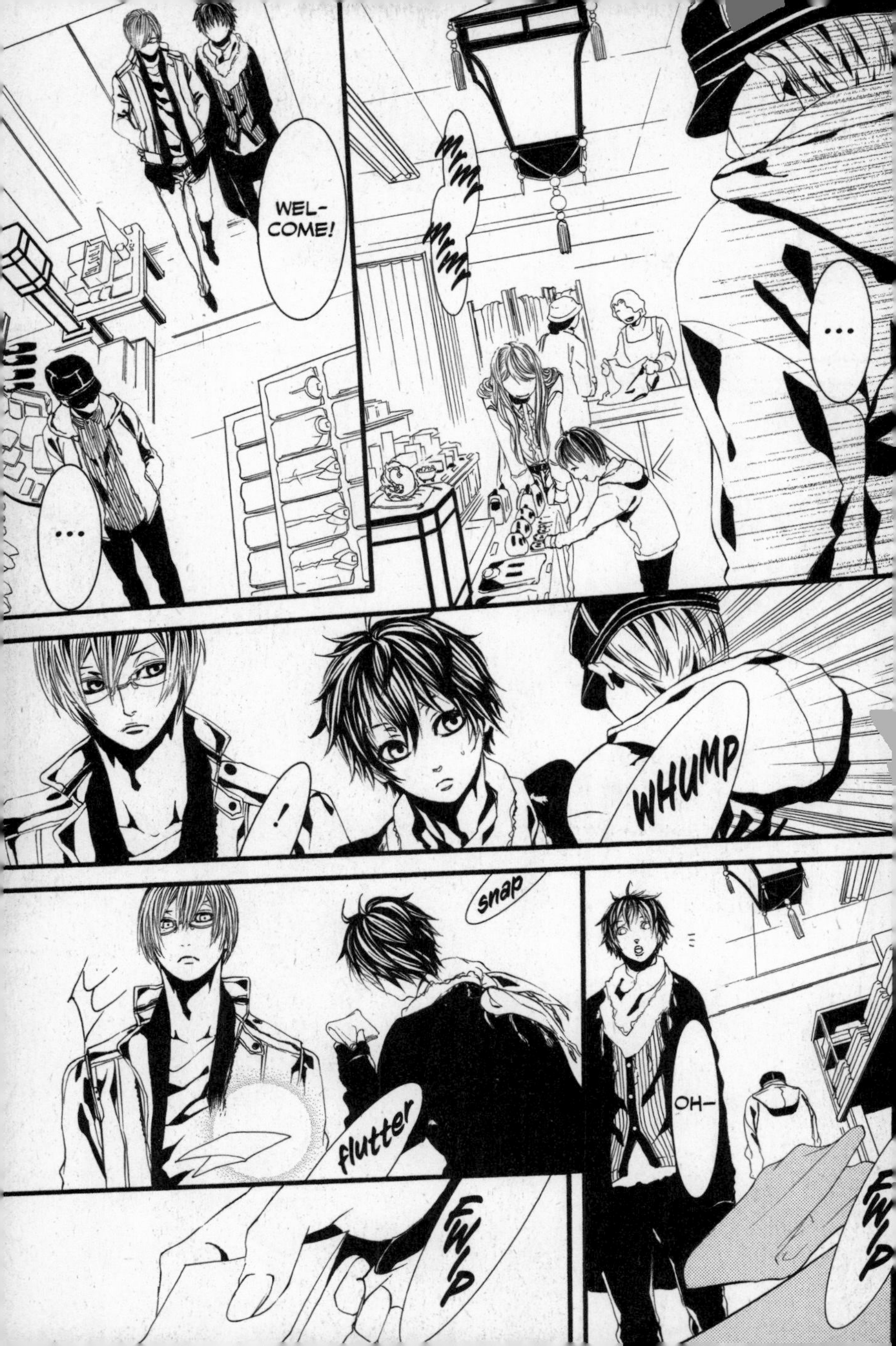
...
WEL-
COME!
...
WHUMP
!
OH-
FWIP
snap
flutter
FWIP

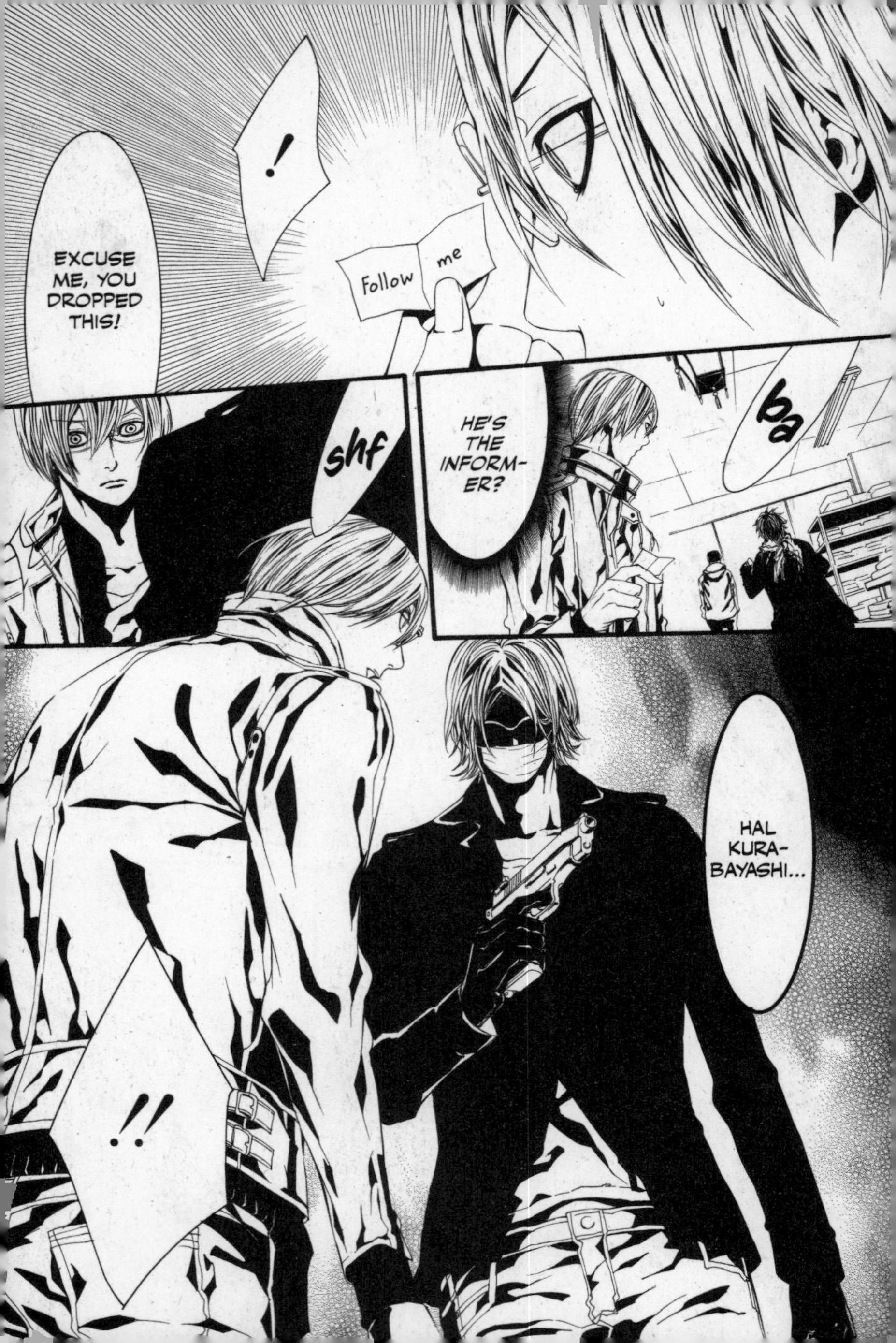
Follow me
!
EXCUSE ME, YOU DROPPED THIS!
ba
HE'S THE INFORMER?
shf
HAL KURA-BAYASHI...
!!

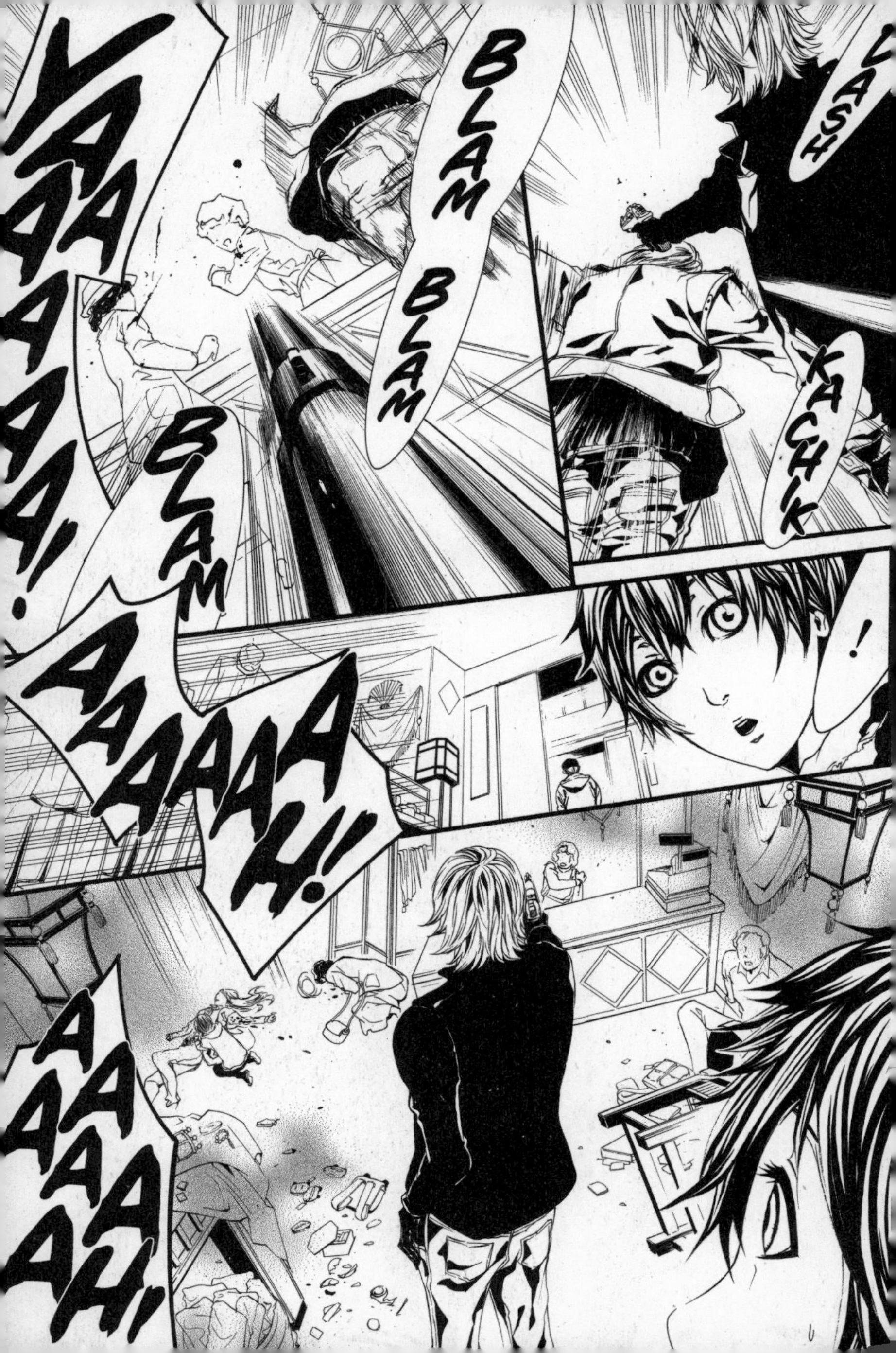
VASH
KACHIK
BLAM BLAM BLAM
BLAM
YAAAAAAA!!
!
AAAAAAH!!
AAAAAAH!!

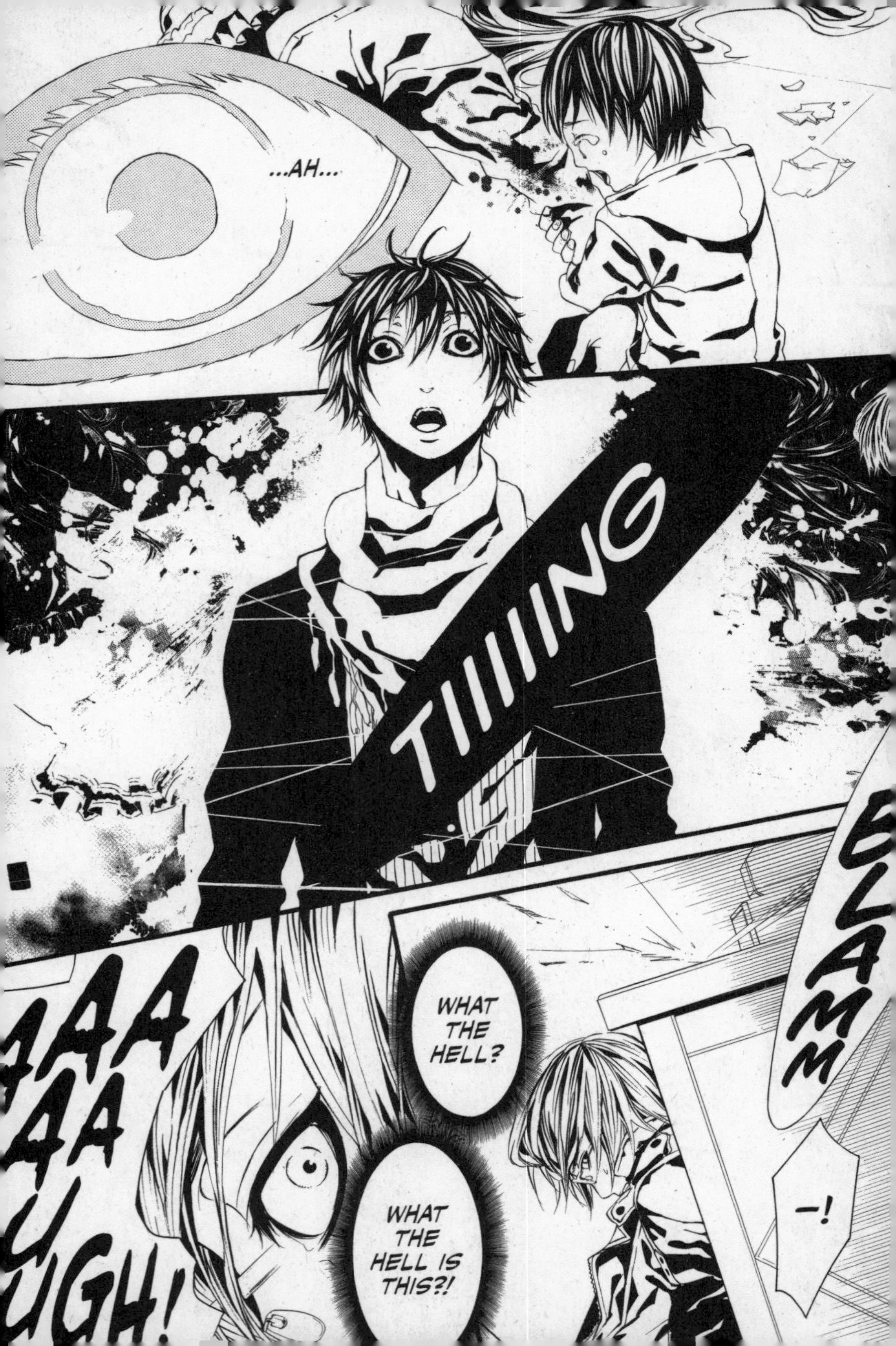
...AH...
TIIIING
BLAMM
—!
WHAT THE HELL?
WHAT THE HELL IS THIS?!
AAAAAUUGH!

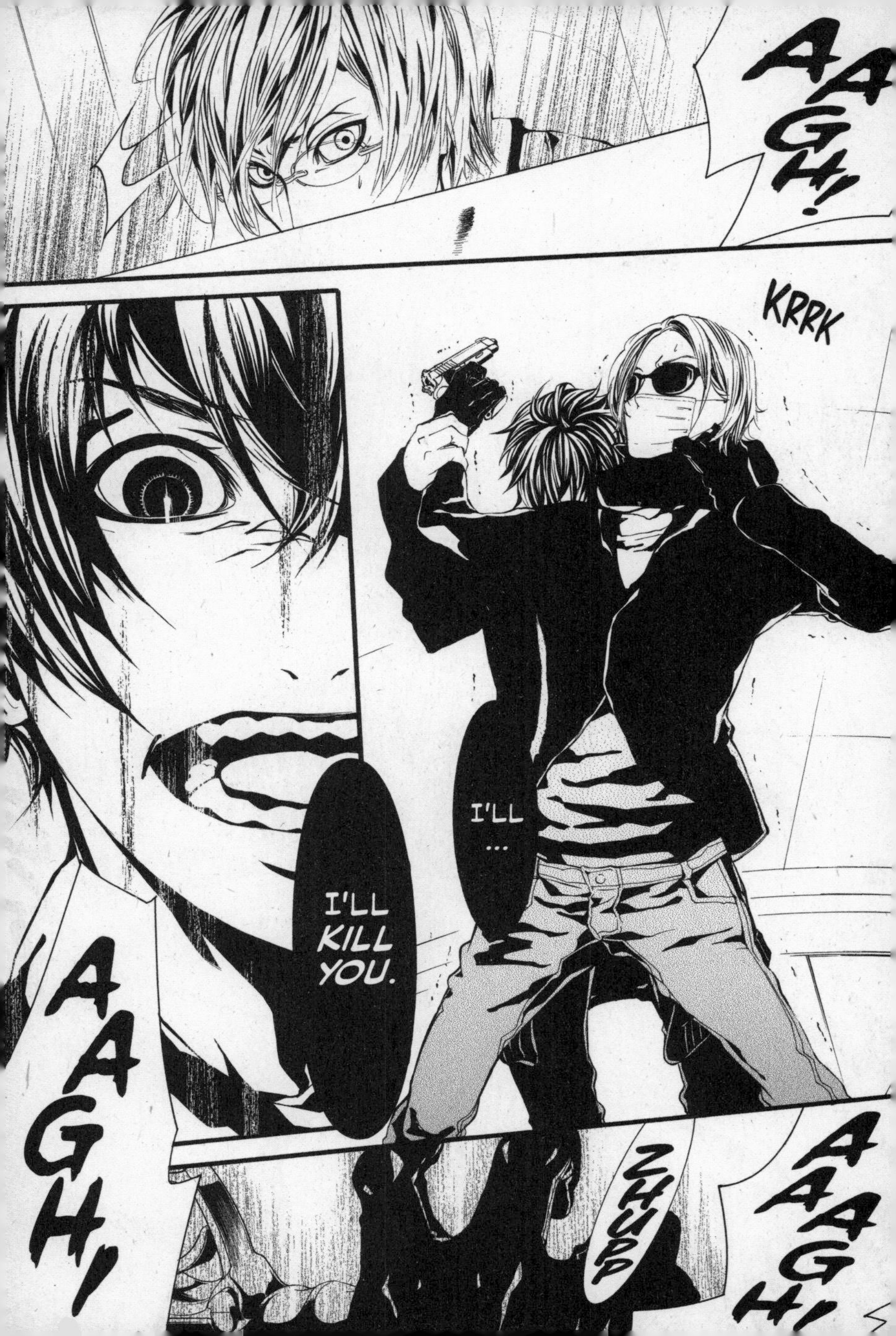
AAGH!
KRRK
I'LL ...
I'LL KILL YOU.
AAGH!
AAAGH!
ZHUPP

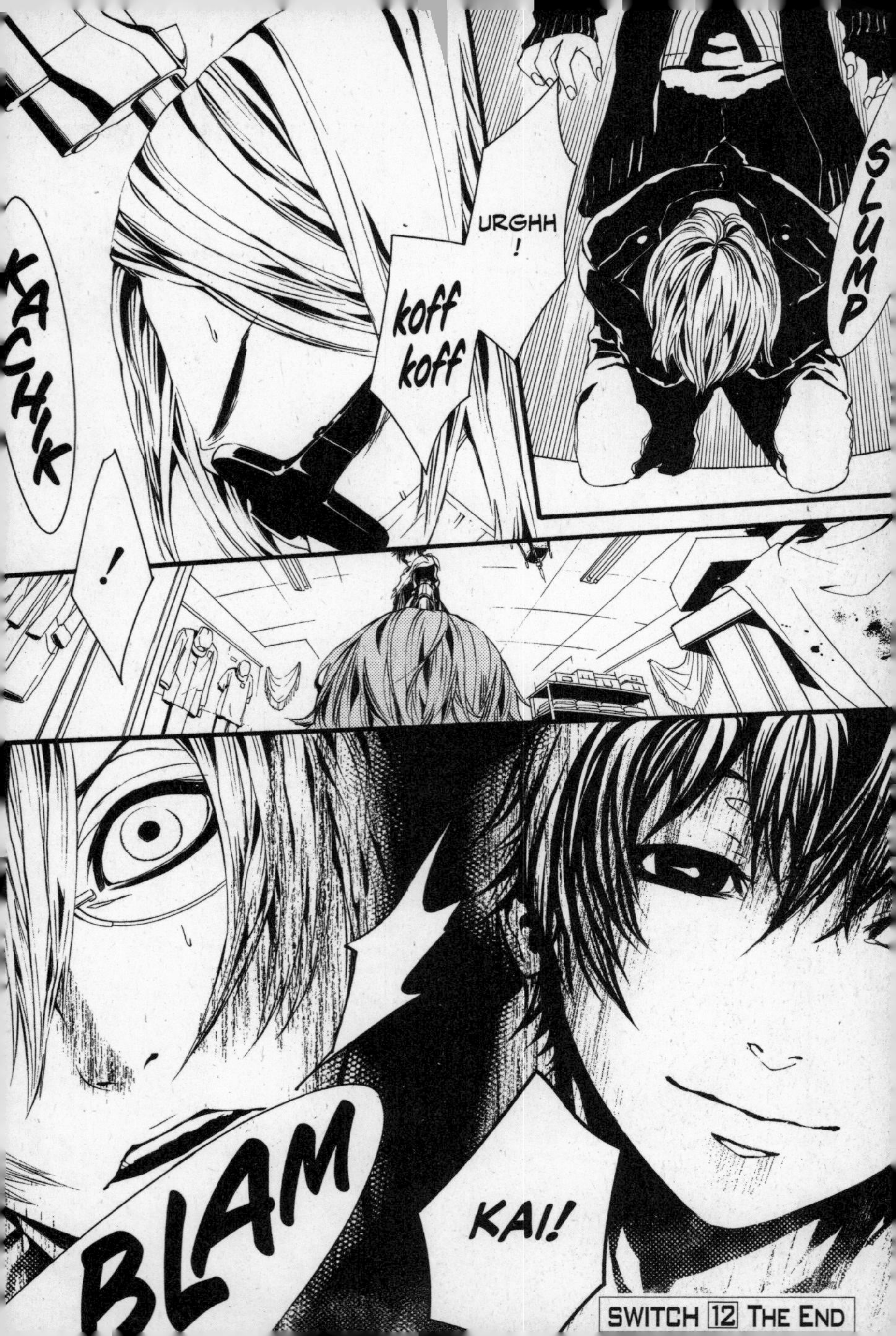
SLUMP
URGHH!
koff koff
KACHIK
!
KAI!
BLAM
SWITCH 12 The End

We took a trip to the capital of the Ryugen, Hong Kong. It was so hot and humid... Neon signs stabbed at our eyes! The scenery was chaotic, beautiful, dirty—it was incredible. We went crazy taking reference pictures. Now all we have to do is write this thing.

naked ape is the collaboration of Tomomi Nakamura and Otoh Saki, who were born just three months apart. Nakamura, the artist, takes things at her own pace and feels no guilt for missing deadlines. Saki, the writer, also does cover design and inking and is called President by the assistants. naked ape's other works include *Black tar* and the ongoing futuristic crime thriller *DOLLS*.

SWITCH
Vol. 12

Story and Art by naked ape

Translation & English Adaptation/Paul Tuttle Starr,
Translation by Design
Touch-up Art & Lettering/Susan Daigle-Leach
Design/Sean Lee
Editor/Jonathan Tarbox

VP, Production/Alvin Lu
VP, Publishing Licensing/Rika Inouye
VP, Sales & Product Marketing/Gonzalo Ferreyra
VP, Creative/Linda Espinosa
Publisher/Hyoe Narita

Printed in the U.S.A.

Published by VIZ Media, LLC
P.O. Box 77010
San Francisco, CA 94107

10 9 8 7 6 5 4 3 2 1
First printing, January 2010

www.viz.com

RATED T+ FOR OLDER TEEN

PARENTAL ADVISORY
SWITCH is rated T+ for Older Teen and is recommended for ages 16 and up. Contains violence, strong language, drug use, and some sexual situations.
ratings.viz.com